PEARSON   ALWAYS LEARNING

Stephen J. Porth

Contributing Authors:
John B. Lord • A.J. Stagliano • Claire A. Simmers
Ravi Kathuria • Alfredo Mauri • Marty Meloche
Edward Balotsky • Tim Swift • Matt Kelly
Richard Sherman • Robert Dean • Patrick Maggitti
Maheshkumar Joshi • Ann Mooney

Strategic Management
A Cross-Functional Approach

Sixth Edition

Taken from:
*Strategic Management: A Cross-Functional
Approach*, Fifth Edition
by Stephen J. Porth

ISBN 10: 1-323-80113-8
ISBN 13: 978-1-323-80113-0

To Mary, Stephen, Molly, Leo, Tom, and Conor

BRIEF CONTENTS

Strategic Management: A Cross-Functional Approach

CONTENTS

PREFACE

Welcome to the fifth edition of *Strategic Management: A Cross-Functional Approach*. We believe this book is unique. It takes a truly cross-functional perspective on strategic management, written by a professor and consultant of strategic management and enhanced by significant contributions from experts in the fields of finance, marketing, accounting, international business, and operations management.

The need for this cross-functional perspective first became apparent to me when a group of faculty at Saint Joseph's University began to work on a revision of our Business Policy course. As we discussed our hopes for the new course, we identified a common challenge we wanted to overcome. We wanted students to see that successful strategic management requires an ability to see the organization as a whole; to step out of the functional mindsets that students tend to acquire through previous work experience and/or prior courses, and to see the organization in a new way. The marketers and HR folks needed to understand the financials and how to use them, and the finance and accounting people needed to see that customer and employee relationships were the lifeblood of the organization. Good strategic managers are capable of seeing the big picture and managing across the organization—they are not stuck in functional silos!

Our revised Business Policy course is cross-functional and integrative, emphasizing strategic concepts and tools from the fields of management, finance/accounting, international business, information systems, and marketing. As we prepared to launch the course, our review of textbooks led us to conclude that there is a gap in the market. Truly cross-functional and integrative texts that also cover the tools and theory of the strategic management field are difficult if not impossible to find. This book is an attempt to fill that gap.

Some of the special features of this book are:

- The fifth edition includes information and resources reflecting the latest research and thinking in the field. It includes an increased focus on environmental sustainability, the Triple Bottom Line, sustainability reporting and the Stakeholder model of management.
- Examples are updated and refreshed to help students understand recent developments in global markets.
- The financial side of managing strategy is emphasized, including tools for analyzing and forecasting the financial results of strategies, and how to determine the worth of a company (i.e., business valuation for mergers and acquisitions).
- We include an emphasis on business ethics and frameworks for analyzing ethical issues in strategic management.

- Key concepts in each chapter are illustrated with reference to real companies.
- Chapters begin with an outline and a set of questions addressed in the chapter, and conclude with a set of key terms and concepts, discussion questions, and an experiential exercise.

ACKNOWLEDGEMENTS

I have many people to thank for their support and cooperation in writing this book, beginning with the contributing authors—John Lord, A.J. Stagliano, Claire Simmers, Ravi Kathuria, Mahesh Joshi, Marty Meloche, Alfredo Mauri, Bob Dean, Ann Mooney, Ed Balotsky, Rick Sherman, Pat Maggitti, Matt Kelly and Tim Swift. I am grateful to my colleagues for their cooperation in writing this book—and for putting up with me throughout the process!

George Lutzow, George Latella, Ann McNally, and George Sillup are faculty colleagues and friends who have supported this project from the beginning. In addition, I have had the privilege of working for an outstanding dean and leader, Joe DiAngelo, who understands the importance of this course and this book to me, my colleagues, and our students.

Kelsey Kostelnik served as the research assistant for the project. Kelsey was outstanding—he is bright and industrious. He met every deadline. I am grateful for his support of and contributions to the project. Mary Porth served as my unofficial copy editor. Mary is a truly gifted writer with an unsurpassed ability to express thoughts clearly and to identify edits needed. I have had administrative assistance for this project from Jacquie Panto who I can always count on for quality work, completed on time and with a smile. Jacquie is a key member of the team and I am fortunate to have her support.

It is a gift to enjoy your life's work. For that joy I thank my students—undergraduate, MBA, and executives. I look forward to my time in the classroom because of you. This book was written with you in mind.

Finally and most importantly, I want to thank my wife and children. Mary and kids—this book is dedicated to you. You're the best. Thanks!

Steve Porth
Saint Joseph's University

Chapter 1

Strategic Management: An Overview

CHAPTER LEARNING OBJECTIVES

After studying this chapter, you should be able to

- Understand the purpose and process of strategic management;
- Define the steps in the strategic management process and how they interrelate;
- Identify the role of value creation in the strategic management process and the key stakeholders for whom value must be created;
- Understand the nature of three types of decisions—financing, investing and operating—that strategic managers make;
- Appreciate the importance of ethics and corporate social responsibility in the strategic management process.

*N*ike, the global sports and fitness company, is known by customers for its high-performance athletic shoes, apparel, and equipment and its brash "just do it" image. Investors know Nike for its reputation of stellar growth and remarkable returns to stockholders. Emerging from the tumultuous 2009 recession seemingly unscathed, like Usain Bolt in the 100 meter dash, Nike has continued to distance itself from the competition. Nike has more than doubled its revenue and nearly tripled its earnings per share since 2005. This success reflects Nike's ability to strategically manage its resources in order to create value for all of its stakeholders.

Through the process of strategic management, every organization needs to determine a course of action that will enable it to achieve its mission and objectives. The course of action must address the interests of many stakeholders, especially customers, stockholders, and employees. Specifically, organizations must create and implement strategies that produce superior products or services for customers, economic value for stockholders, and rewarding employment experiences for managers and associates, and do all of this in a socially responsible way.

Nike has been able to meet its strategic challenges and achieve success by aligning its strategies with its resources to fulfill its mission of bringing "inspiration and innovation to every athlete in the world." This alignment has consisted of (1) implementing a hyperfocused approach to the consumer called the Category Offense, which is a compartmentalization of its business into eight distinct categories to create a more intimate relationship with its consumers, (2) offering striking new products in both old and new brands by infusing them with innovative technologies such as Dri-FIT and Flyknit technology, and (3) continuing to grow its e-commerce business which reached $1 billion in 2015.[1] CEO Mark Parker's annual letter to Nike's stockholders suggests that these strategies were successful in 2015: "We demonstrated that momentum yet again as revenues grew by 10% to $30.6 billion, gross margin expanded 120 basis points, diluted earnings per share grew by 25% to $3.70, and return on invested capital increased by 28.1%."[2]

How has Nike maintained this level of success? That is what strategic management is all about.

WHAT IS STRATEGIC MANAGEMENT?

Strategic management is a process of formulating, implementing and evaluating cross-functional decisions that enable the organization to define and achieve its mission, and ultimately to create value. The process involves three activities—analysis, decision-making, and action. Strategic management focuses on a series of fundamental questions about the organization: *What is our business? What do we want to become and how will we get there? Who are our customers? What do our customers value?*[3] By answering these types of questions the strategic management process helps to establish the future direction of the firm.

In the case of Nike, it was the strategic management process that helped its managers to assess the global economy and make the appropriate and necessary decisions for the company.

The strategic management process is comprised of five interrelated steps:

1. Establish the vision and mission of the organization—to identify the reason for the organization and what it aspires to become.
2. Perform a situation analysis—to understand the strengths and weaknesses of the organization and to scan its external environment for opportunities and threats (also known as SWOT analysis).
3. Set objectives and craft a strategy—to determine the future direction of the organization and to decide how it will achieve its mission and vision.
4. Implement the strategy—to execute the chosen strategy in an efficient and effective manner.
5. Assess the success of the strategy—to determine whether the strategy has created value for key stakeholders and to provide feedback for corrective action if necessary.

Each step of the process focuses on one overriding purpose—to create value. The *Strategic Management Framework*, displayed in Figure 1-1, identifies the major steps in the strategic management process and the relationships between the steps. Let's briefly examine each component of the model as an introduction to the major topics and remaining chapters of the book.

Value Creation

The essence of strategic management is the challenge of rewarding key stakeholders, especially customers, employees, and ultimately, owners. Organizations that *create value* for these stakeholders survive and prosper. Those that do not will inevitably decline. Whether the organization is large or small, privately owned or public, for

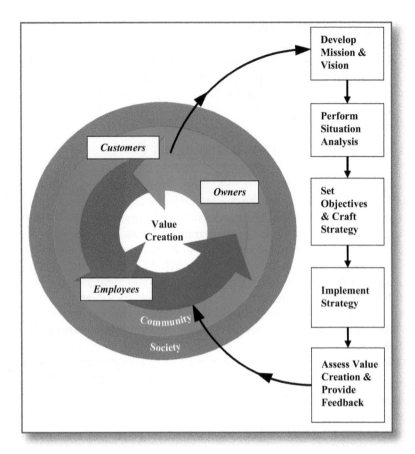

Figure 1-1
The Strategic
Management
Framework

profit or not, the primary focus and the ultimate outcome of successful strategic management is *value creation.*

For example, Nike creates value for *customers* by designing and marketing high-performance athletic shoes, apparel and equipment. Value for *owners* is produced when Nike shoes are sold at a price that generates a profit and contributes to stockholders' interests. And value for *employees* is created through the financial and non-financial rewards and satisfaction received by employees for their efforts. This process of value creation occurs within the context of the communities in which the firm operates and its obligations to society at large. In other words, the firm needs to create value for its customers, employees and owners while simultaneously recognizing its impact on society and honoring its social responsibilities.

Nonprofit organizations face a similar value creation challenge. For example, "seeking to put God's love into action, Habitat for Humanity brings people together to build homes, communities and hope."[4] Habitat creates value by constructing and refurbishing houses for the poor and marginalized (the "*customers*"), by *employees* and *volunteers* who are (intrinsically) rewarded for their contributions to an important and just social cause. Value creation is the engine that drives Habitat for Humanity, just as it drives Nike.

Table 1-1 Examples of Value Creation

Customers	Employees	Owners
• Quality products and services • Perceived value in terms of price paid and costs incurred versus benefits received	• Rewarding jobs … in terms of both financial compensation and social and psychological benefits	• An increasing and acceptable return on financial investment

The Concept of Value

Value creation is an organizational imperative, and the ultimate outcome of a successful strategic management process. But *value* means different things to different stakeholders. These meanings are defined and examined in Chapter 2.

Table 1-1 identifies examples of different types of value created for customers, employees and owners by a successful strategic management process. It is important to stress that these types of value are not incompatible. To the contrary, they are interdependent. Over the long-term, the organization cannot create value for its owners if it does not first create value for customers and employees. Leading companies recognize the vital link between customers, employees, and owners, and are committed to creating value for each group. That's why value creation is depicted as a dynamic cycle of interlocking pieces in Figure 1-1.

Developing a Mission & Vision

The focus of Chapter 3 is the first step in the strategic management process—developing a clear understanding of the mission and vision of the organization. The *mission* statement identifies the enduring purpose of the organization and answers questions such as *Who are we? What is our business? Why do we exist?* The mission statement is grounded in the present; that is, it focuses on the current markets and customers served by the organization.

Not only do managers need to articulate the organization's *current* purpose and sense of identity, but also their aspirations for the *future* of the company. The *vision* of an organization is a statement about its future—where the firm is headed, what it aspires to become, how it hopes to be viewed by the public. The vision statement expresses a view of the future that is realistic, credible, and attractive for the organization,[5] and answers the question "What do we want to become?"

The conceptual distinction between mission and vision is evident in the case of PepsiCo. The PepsiCo mission is: "As one of the largest food and beverage companies in the world, our mission is to provide consumers around the world with delicious, affordable, convenient and complementary foods and beverages from wholesome breakfasts to healthy and fun daytime snacks and beverages to evening treats. We are committed to investing in our people, our company and the communities where we operate to help position the company for long-term, sustainable growth." Its vision is "to deliver top-tier financial performance over the long term by integrating sustainability into our business strategy, leaving a positive imprint on society and the environment."[6] The distinction between mission and vision is relevant for most though certainly not all companies.

Research indicates that most organizations have a mission statement and/or a vision statement, and that these statements are becoming increasingly common. Some companies, such as Johnson & Johnson, have a credo that serves essentially the same purpose as a mission (the J&J Credo is shown in Chapter 3).[7] A *credo* is a statement of the organization's values, or a *philosophy* of business, and may be used instead of, or in addition to, a mission or vision.

Mission and vision statements are meant to be important elements of strategic management. In some organizations, however, they can be nothing more than window dressing—words on a laminated poster hung on the wall. When this is the case, the statement has no power; it does not influence strategic choice in any meaningful way. These types of statements are worth no more than the paper on which they are written. The true test of a mission or vision statement is the degree to which managers and employees understand it, embrace it, and use it to guide the business decisions they make.

Chapter 3 also introduces the concept of "Stakeholder Theory" which is the foundation of the Strategic Management Framework (Figure 1-1). When we discuss creating value for customers, employees and owners, we are discussing Stakeholder Theory. We compare and contrast Stakeholder and Shareholder Theory in this chapter. Stakeholder Theory is an integrative theory that supports sustainability and sustainable development, providing justification for including a social and environmental purpose to the firm, in addition to an economic purpose.

Performing a Situation Analysis

Before managers can define organizational objectives and choose strategies, they must understand the internal condition of the organization and its external environment. This understanding is gained through a *situation analysis*, a careful and ongoing assessment of the organization's external and internal circumstances. The situation analysis is performed in two parts: an *internal audit* to identify the organization's strengths and weaknesses (SW), and an *external audit* to determine opportunities and threats (OT). The external audit is also known as *environmental scanning*. Because of their emphasis on identifying strengths, weaknesses, opportunities and threats, the audits are often collectively referred to as a *SWOT Analysis*.

The Internal Audit

As discussed in Chapter 4, assessing the organization's internal environment for strengths and weaknesses is a key step in the strategic management process. This step requires an evaluation of the organization's financial condition, as well as a survey and assessment of its infrastructure, human resources, technology development, procurement, inbound and outbound logistics, operations, marketing and sales, and support services.[8] Essentially, the task is to critically evaluate all activities performed by the firm to identify sources of strength or weakness. Some of the critical questions to answer in the internal audit include:

- What are the firm's financial strengths and weaknesses?
- Are employees competent and committed to the organization's mission? How well does the organization recruit, retain and reward qualified employees?
- How well does the firm manage customer relationships? What does the firm do or not do that creates or loses value for customers?
- What are the firm's core competencies? That is, what are the firm's special skills, abilities and resources relative to competitors? What core competencies will be needed in the future to compete successfully?

Accomplishing the internal audit is a matter of extensive research and analysis, and includes examining financial statements, staffing and productivity standards, information resources, organization charts, customer and employee surveys, and interviewing internal stakeholders (e.g., managers and staff) and external stakeholders (suppliers, distributors, customers).[9]

Returning to this chapter's focus company, Nike uses the internal audit process to monitor ongoing operations and to manage its resources for the future. In 2009, Nike needed to identify areas for improvement to survive the recession. Financial statements revealed that expenses were higher than anticipated, and a reduction in costs was necessary. This is an example of an internal audit that focused on current operations in order to produce improved future financial results. By 2015, Nike's financial condition had improved considerably. Their internationally recognized brands, high customer satisfaction numbers, and financial results were all internal strengths. Still, Nike's internal assessment found room for improvement in managing global customer relationships. In response, Nike implemented the Category Offense to organize all of its product offerings and brands to learn more about its customers and provide a more personal touch with each interaction.[10]

The External Audit

With technological advancements occurring at a break-neck speed, companies must have the most innovative technology to gain a competitive advantage or just to remain relevant. Due to this rapidly changing external environment, Nike has leveraged its NIKE + digital platforms to create more entry points for the consumer to participate in Nike's e-commerce. In his 2015 letter to Nike shareholders, Mark Parker highlighted these advancements, such as broadening access to the NIKE + Running application through strategic partnerships, introducing NIKE+ Run Clubs now available in more than twenty cities around the world, and increasing the global reach of NIKE+ Training Club to 17 languages.[11] Nike has addressed an external threat, the ever-evolving tech landscape, by deploying one of its emerging strengths, its e-commerce resources and NIKE+ applications.

External forces create *opportunities* and/or *threats* for organizations. During the situation analysis, the external environment is monitored and emerging or potential strategic opportunities and threats are identified. This process is described in Chapter 5.

The external environment of any organization includes both a *macro environment* made up of broad forces such as technology, economic and social conditions, demographic trends, and political and international forces, and a *task environment* consisting of customers, competitors, suppliers, creditors, government agencies and regulators, and perhaps unions and other groups. Each component of the external environment may have a critical influence, either positive (opportunity) or negative (threat), on the organization and its ability to create value. Thus, each needs to be monitored and evaluated for its impact on the organization. The external audit not only informs strategic choice, but through a feedback mechanism, may also suggest the need to revise the firm's vision and mission.

In the case of Nike, technology has created new opportunities for the apparel giant—as well as its competitors. These new opportunities require companies to be vigilant, and to reconsider and manage their strategies. The same environmental change may create opportunities for some organizations and threats for others. For example, technology has transformed the media subscription industry by allowing consumers to download, store, and access the latest editions of their favorite newspapers, magazines, and periodicals whenever and wherever they prefer. The impact on print media subscriptions has been dramatic as online/electronic magazine and newspaper subscriptions have skyrocketed while print media subscriptions have plummeted.

Setting Objectives and Crafting Strategy

In Chapter 6, we turn our attention to the process of setting objectives and making strategic choices. Objectives are set during the strategic management process so that the organization can specify its intended results and track its progress toward achieving its mission and vision. Objectives are specific, measurable standards of performance that the organization seeks to achieve. At this stage of the process, the objectives that are set are *long-term*, meaning that they extend beyond the current year. Annual, short-term objectives are set as part of the implementation phase of the process. Examples of long-term objectives are shown in Table 1-2.

Strategy is the organization's means to achieve its vision, mission, and objectives. While the mission addresses "*who* we are," and the objectives indicate "*what* we want to achieve," the strategy states "*how* we will achieve our mission and objectives."

Choosing or crafting a strategy involves generating feasible alternative strategies, evaluating the alternatives, and selecting a strategy that will create value. Strategies are *crafted* and not merely *selected* in the sense that strategic choice is a mixture of both intuition and analysis, art and science. Strategies are subjective decisions based on both *objective* information and *behavioral* considerations. Objectively, the strategy is based on the firm's vision, mission, and situation analysis, and how well

Table 1-2 Examples of Long-Term Objectives

- Increase sales volume by at least 10% per year for the next three years.
- Build market share in Mexico by 5% within 18 months.
- Maintain Return on Equity (ROE) at 15% over the next 5 years.
- Establish a joint venture in China before any of our direct competitors.

the strategy is expected to contribute to achieving long-term goals. Strategic choice is influenced by the firm's SWOT analysis, as well as other analytical tools described later in the book. But strategic choice is not strictly the result of analytical thinking. The behavioral aspects of strategic choice are the result of human nature and our inability to obtain and process all relevant information. Strategies are also influenced by factors such as the firm's culture, the characteristics of the senior management team, politics within the company, ethical considerations, and social responsibility. In addition, corporate Boards of Directors are exercising more control over strategic choice in today's organizations.

Levels of Strategy

Strategic choices are made and implemented at different levels of the organization. Specifically, strategic decisions are made at three levels, although for smaller and very focused companies with only one "business" the first two levels are the same. The three levels of strategy are (1) corporate or organizational, (2) business unit, and (3) functional.

Corporate Level Strategy

Corporate or organizational level strategy focuses on two major issues—(1) determining the organization's *business scope*, that is, in what businesses the organization will compete, and (2) deciding how organizational resources are allocated to these businesses. For example, in the 1960s Nike started as a running shoe company. Since then, Nike has evolved and expanded its business scope. Nike's brand portfolio now includes NIKE, Jordan, Converse Inc., and Hurley International LLC, which designs and distributes apparel and accessories for action sports. Nike's business scope has grown from running shoes to all types of athletic footwear, athletic apparel, athletic equipment such as golf clubs and footballs, and more. These forays into new businesses are examples of changes in corporate strategy.

PepsiCo is best known as a leading manufacturer and marketer of carbonated soft drinks. As shown in Figure 1-2, however, PepsiCo is much more than a beverage company, and includes iconic brands such as Pepsi, Tropicana, Gatorade, Doritos,

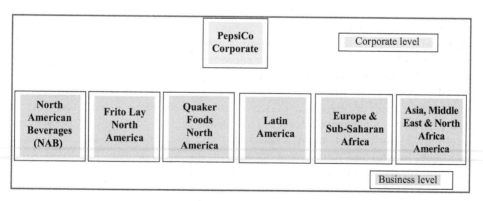

Figure 1-2
PepsiCo and Levels of Strategy

and Quaker. The company is organized into six global divisions, with each business unit serving different markets and customers. All of these brands support the mission of PepsiCo.

Until the late 1990s, PepsiCo also competed in the fast food industry through its ownership of Pizza Hut, Taco Bell and KFC. PepsiCo's decision to spin off or divest these units and thereby alter its business scope represented a change in corporate level strategy. Similarly, when Hershey Foods sold its pasta division and then acquired Leaf, Inc., another candy company, Hershey was making a corporate strategy decision to focus on its core business—confections—and at the same time expand its position in that business. Nike also pursued a corporate strategy of divestiture in 2012 when it sold off Cole Haan, a luxury footwear and handbag retailer, and Umbro, a U.K. based soccer brand.

Portfolio analysis and other tools for corporate strategy decisions are discussed in Chapter 6. Portfolio theory suggests that the most attractive business units with the greatest growth potential and the most significant business strengths are candidates for aggressive investment designed to grow the business. Alternatively, weaker business units receive that level of investment necessary to maintain position, harvest revenues or, in extreme cases, exit the industry.

Business Level Strategy

At the business unit level, strategic decisions are made about how to compete within the industry and how to gain a competitive advantage. At PepsiCo, for example, NAB division managers must decide how to compete with Coca-Cola, Snapple, energy drinks, vitamin water, and others. Can PepsiCo build and sustain an advantage by creating a unique and valuable position in these markets?[12] In addition, managers need to decide how to allocate the resources of the business unit across product lines and functional areas.

For example, Amazon has made the decision to allocate resources to a new business venture, physical brick-and-mortar stores. Amazon opened its first physical bookstore in Seattle in November 2015 and plans to roll out 300 to 400 new stores in 2016 and 2017. Analysts attribute this to the success that other online retailers, like Warby Parker (sunglasses), Blue Nile (diamonds), and Bonobos (clothing), have had with physical store locations. Apple was the early model for how a successful online brand could replicate its appeal with physical stores. Analysts believe another reason why Amazon is allocating a large portion of its resources to rolling out brick-and-mortar stores is the legitimacy that is associated with having a physical retail presence. Not only will these locations serve as brand boosters, Amazon hopes these stores will attract customers that do not ordinarily shop online.

Amazon's Seattle bookstore is the marriage of the traditional retail experience and the new analytics-driven experience that aims to create an intimately personalized experience for every customer. This means offering customized book sections, sorted by highest-rated, most wished for, and most popular, etc., and allowing customers to scan and price-check books with the Amazon app. This gives Amazon the opportunity to build a more comprehensive customer profile, which then allows them to provide personalized recommendations and pricing. The physical retail presence enables Amazon to deliver a more highly focused customer experience to loyal Amazon customers and to new physical retail customers alike.[13]

PS4, Internet connected TVs, iPhones, iPads, iPod Touches, and Nintendo Wiis. This made Netflix a much more accessible service to customers as they could now watch their favorite movies and shows wherever they preferred. Although domestic subscribers of Netflix's streaming content rose in 2012 and the company expanded into Canada, Latin America, and Europe in the same year, Netflix was still facing stiff competition for subscribers from other streaming services like Hulu and Amazon Prime. Wanting to increase subscriber count, Netflix released its first original content in 2013, with critically acclaimed shows such as "House of Cards," "Marvel's Jessica Jones," and "Orange is the New Black." These original series started a trend in the streaming business where the streamers are no longer at the mercy of traditional content providers. By 2016 Netflix had over 120 originals and produced its first feature length movie, "Beasts of No Nation."[20]

This example illustrates strategy that is both deliberate and emergent. Netflix's long-term strategy is to be a pioneer in the Internet TV era. Originally, this meant that Netflix would provide streaming content to subscribers through a nonlinear TV watching experience. If someone wanted to watch their favorite episode of "The X-Files" and decided halfway through that they wanted to watch a romantic comedy instead, Netflix gave them that option by virtue of its strategic partnerships. However, Netflix realized that its success in the streaming industry placed it in a prime position to produce its own content to complement its wide array of licensed movies and shows. After the success of its first wave of original content, Netflix no longer viewed its original productions as side projects, but viable and key aspects of its emerging strategy. What started in 1997 as an online movie rental service has blossomed into a billion dollar, Emmy winning streaming content provider due to both intended and emergent strategies.

Thus, strategy is based on research and analysis as well as on ingenuity and opportunism. It is both proactive and reactive. As we have already stated, it is based on both analysis and intuition , science and art. It includes both a rational, logical, left-brain orientation and creative and spontaneous right-brain thinking.

Henry Mintzberg has developed a model to capture these dynamics of the strategic process.[21] The model, shown in Figure 1-4, reflects both sides of the strategic process. The process begins with a clearly defined *intended strategy*, the result of a formal and structured planning process. In response to changing conditions inside and outside of the organization, some of the original intended strategy is discarded and some of it is retained. The retained or *deliberate strategy* combines with a new emergent strategy to produce the *realized strategy*. Realized strategy is a combination of both deliberate, rational planning and more spontaneous, opportunistic thinking. This is precisely the type of thinking that Netflix used when producing its own content.

The concept of realized strategy harks back to the discussion of financing, investing and operating (FIO) decisions. FIO decisions are the means by which strategy is realized. FIO decisions are made in light of intended strategies and, at the same time, are the true test of realized strategy. An organization may espouse any strategy it wishes, but its true or realized strategy is the result of the financing, investing and operating decisions it actually makes. This is shown in Figure 1-4.

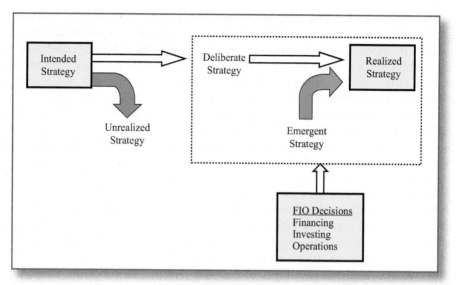

Figure 1-4
Intended and Realized Strategies and FIO
Source: Adapted from "Strategy Formation in an Adhocracy," by Henry Mintzberg and Alexandra McGugh, published in *Administrative Science Quarterly*, Vol. 30, No. 2, June 1985.

The focus of this book is strategy at the business and corporate levels. These types of strategic decisions have the following characteristics:

1. **Directive.** Strategic decisions set or influence the future direction of the organization.
2. **Cross-functional.** Strategic decisions require the cooperation and coordination of multiple functions and activities across the organization.
3. **Resource-dependent.** Strategic decisions require resource commitments by the organization. Strategies must be financed (internally or externally), investments are made and operations are changed in some way.

Who are the Players in the Strategic Process?

The senior management team (SMT) and especially the Chief Executive Officer (CEO) or senior manager of the organization are ultimately responsible for the strategy and performance of the organization. But that does not necessarily mean that they are the only ones responsible for strategy. As we have seen, there are different levels of strategy and different managers and employees involved in making those strategic decisions.

No universal approach to the strategy process exists. In most large corporations though, the CEO and senior corporate executives have primary responsibility for corporate strategy decisions. Senior managers in the business units develop and implement business level strategies. Functional strategies are typically the domain of the Vice Presidents of the functional areas (manufacturing, marketing, R&D, human resources, etc.) in cooperation with operating managers who report to the Vice Presidents.

In addition to ultimate responsibility for strategy, another important issue is *participation* in the process. The *traditional approach* to planning is top-down and suggests that strategy formulation is the sole and exclusive domain of the senior management team. The SMT makes the strategic choices, and then relies on other managers and employees to implement strategy. As organizations grow and become more diverse in the products or services they provide and the global markets they serve, the traditional approach becomes increasingly more complex and difficult to manage. Senior executives may be too isolated from customers and operations to be adequately informed. A more inclusive approach to strategic management becomes important.

One such practice is *high-involvement strategic planning*, also known as the *direct participation* (DP) approach.[22] This more inclusive planning approach is discussed in Chapter 9. It is achieved by moving away from the top-down, control-oriented traditional model of planning to a process that invites and nurtures the innovative ideas of managers at all levels, as well as front-line employees such as sales representatives, engineers, and operating employees. As we shall discuss later in the book, broad participation has important advantages for managing strategic change.

Corporate Governance

Another group that plays a critical role in the strategic management process is the organization's *board of directors*, the corporate governors of the organization. The board is usually comprised of the organization's CEO and other senior executives and a larger number of *outside directors* (people who are not employed by the firm). Boards will typically meet at least on a quarterly basis to review, discuss and evaluate the organization's plans and performance.

A common practice is for the board to form committees which are responsible for getting the work done between the quarterly meetings. Regular committees, often called *standing committees*, are permanent committees with duties and responsibilities outlined in the organization's charter or by-laws. Temporary or *ad hoc committees* can also be formed to oversee special tasks as needed. Typical standing committees are the executive, compensation, audit, nominating, and finance committees. The executive committee acts for the entire board between meetings. The audit committee reviews the financial operations of the organization. The nominating committee recruits new board members and the compensation committee evaluates compensation packages, especially of senior executives. More organizations are also forming a "corporate governance" or "board" committee to manage board processes like training, evaluation, and compensation.

The board of directors has a fiduciary obligation to represent the owners in the affairs of the organization. In the case of nonprofit organizations, each board member has a legal responsibility to the organization's donors (corporate, foundation, individual, and government) and the public interest/public trust. Directors also have the responsibility to ensure that the organization operates within the parameters of the law. The summary term for these duties is *corporate governance*.

Laws and standards defining the responsibilities and obligations of corporate governance are different from country to country. For example, in the United States, corporations disclose much more information, especially financial, than in other countries, so board actions are open to more scrutiny. Corporate governance in France focuses more on workers and the environment than it does in the U.S.[23]

Even within the United States, specific requirements of directors vary, depending on the state in which the corporate charter is issued. There is, however, general agreement on the following common responsibilities of corporate governance:

- Monitoring the overall direction of the organization.
- Hiring, firing, and compensating the CEO
- Controlling, monitoring, or supervising top management
- Reviewing and approving the use of resources; and
- Caring for shareholder or public interests[24]

Thus, the role of the board in the strategic management process is primarily oversight and approval of strategies and major resource commitments, as well as supervision of the CEO rather than direct participation in developing strategies.

Several trends are influencing corporate governance. One of the most far-reaching changes in a long time in corporate governance and federal securities laws is the increased accountability of CEOs, senior managers, board members and auditors brought about by the passage of the *Sarbanes-Oxley Act of 2002*. Sponsored by U.S. Senator Paul Sarbanes and Representative Michael Oxley, the law was enacted in the aftermath of the large corporate financial scandals involving Enron, WorldCom, Global Crossing and Arthur Andersen. It requires all publicly-traded companies to submit an annual report of the effectiveness of their internal accounting controls to the Securities and Exchange Commission (SEC). In short, Sarbanes-Oxley holds CEOs and directors accountable for their internal accounting controls and the accuracy of their financial statements. Violations of Sarbanes-Oxley can result in punishments to CEOs and directors of up to $5 million and 20 years in prison for the crimes of the company, even if they had no knowledge of those crimes.[25] Key provisions of the Sarbanes-Oxley Act are shown in Table 1-4.

The increasing power of *institutional investors*, those shareholders representing large institutions like pension funds or mutual funds, is another trend in corporate governance. Institutional investors hold over half of all listed corporate stock in the U.S. and are at the forefront of efforts to increase board accountability, especially in the area of corporate financial performance.[26]

Shareholder social activism is expanding the range of issues that boards consider. Beginning in the 1970s, peace and social justice issues were put forward as shareholder proposals, requiring action at the annual shareholders' meetings. Today, shareholder resolutions have increased and cover a range of social justice issues. For the better part of two decades, Nike was the target of public protest and shareholder social activism for its overseas operations, particularly on issues such as sweatshops, child labor, and wages.[27]

Improving board structures and processes is another trend in corporate governance. Increasingly, boards are seen as active partners in the strategic management process and as such, are exercising tighter oversight and control on the organization. Good boardroom practices include having a majority of outside directors, formal evaluations of director performance, responsiveness to investors, open communications

Table 1-4   Key Provisions of Sarbanes-Oxley Act

1. **PCAOB** Established the Public Company Accounting Oversight Board (PCAOB)
2. **Financial records** Companies are required to maintain detailed financial records.
3. **Certification of financial statements and reports by CEOs and CFOs** Section 906 of the Act requires each public company's Chief Executive Officer (CEO) and Chief Financial Officer (CFO) to certify, on threat of severe criminal penalties, that periodic reports containing financial statements fully comply with securities laws. CEOs and CFOs found to have knowingly violated Section 906 will be punished with a fine of up to $1 million and imprisonment of up to 10 years. Willful false certification will be punishable by fines of up to $5 million and imprisonment of up to 20 years.
4. **Work papers** It is now a felony with penalties of up to 10 years to willfully fail to maintain "all audit or review work papers" for at least five years. The U.S. Securities and Exchange Commission will establish a rule covering the retention of audit records, and the U.S. Public Accounting Oversight Board will issue standards that compel auditors to keep other documentation for seven years.
5. **Document destruction** Destroying documents in a federal or bankruptcy investigation is considered a felony and can carry penalties of up to 20 years.
6. **Fraud discovery** The statute of limitations for the discovery of fraud is extended to two years from the date of discovery and five years after the act. Previously it was one year from discovery and three years from the act.
7. **Internal auditing** U.S. companies are required to have an internal audit function. This function must be certified by external auditors.
8. **Unrelated services** External audit firms cannot provide non-audit services to their clients.
9. **Protection for whistleblowers** New provisions protect corporate whistleblowers.
10. **Disclosure** CEO and CFO compensation and profits must be made public.

Sources: 15 Key Provisions of Sarbanes-Oxley, by J. Carlton Collins, CPA. www.microsoft.com/dynamics/nav/product/navision_15_major_sox_provisions.mspx, accessed February 24, 2006.

with the CEO and other board members, and attention to details, including asking tough questions about the future direction of the organization as well as its past performance[28].

SOCIAL RESPONSIBILITY AND ETHICS

Firms are under increasing scrutiny by the media, regulators, environmental groups, and the general public. The pressure to operate based on sound ethical principles and a concern for social responsibility has never been stronger. CEOs and senior executives who breach their ethical obligations are being held accountable and are now subject to stiffer criminal penalties under Sarbanes-Oxley. For example, Bernard Ebbers of WorldCom was convicted and sentenced to 25 years in prison in an $11 billion accounting fraud case. Dennis Kozlowski was convicted of stealing hundreds of millions of dollars from Tyco International and was sentenced to 8 to 25 years in prison, and John Rigas of Adelphia Communications was convicted and sentenced to 15 years in prison for looting and fraud.[29] Public confidence in business and especially in the accuracy of corporate financial statements has been badly damaged by these corporate scandals and others involving Volkswagen (fraudulent emissions tests) and Takata (defective airbags). Rebuilding that confidence is essential.

Good business ethics are an absolute requirement for good strategic management. Business strategies have ethical consequences and managers must identify and carefully consider what those consequences are. Managers who choose to bury their heads in the sand and ignore the social implications of their strategic choices are no less culpable than those who knowingly and willingly make unethical decisions. Ignorance is no excuse when it comes to business ethics and corporate social responsibility. In Chapter 6, we discuss a process for evaluating the ethical dimensions of strategic choices and a framework for making ethical strategic decisions.

Cases of unethical business conduct are reported in the press on a daily basis. In response, organizations are increasingly developing a *code of ethics*, a formal and official document that describes the standards that all employees of an organization are expected to know and follow.

A code of ethics is an important and necessary step but most firms find that it is not sufficient. Workshops, training sessions, simulations and even board games are other ways that firms try to instill an understanding of and commitment to ethical principles. Perhaps the most important issue, however, is the behavior and decisions of the senior management team. Managers at the top set the tone in the organization and others learn from their example. To create an organizational culture based on sound ethics, senior managers must lead the way.

The Natural Environment

As emphasized in Chapter 3, one of the most pressing issues of corporate social responsibility in the 21st century will be sustainability and the natural environment. Firms will be increasingly scrutinized for their treatment of the environment. More stringent environmental regulations are likely to be enacted, especially if businesses are not willing or able to regulate themselves.

Proactive businesses have taken the initiative to go beyond the minimum regulatory requirements to address environmental issues by setting environmental goals and tracking progress toward those goals. For example, Johnson & Johnson's aim is to improve the health and well-being of families, and they believe this includes protecting the environment in which we live and work. Therefore, the company sets high standards for environmental responsibility in the areas of emissions, waste, and water reduction. Johnson & Johnson has also invested in alternative energy, installing solar power at several of their facilities. Each year they publish a sustainability report that highlights their goals, progress, and new targets.[30] These environmental "report cards" will become more common in the future. Some firms are already using their proactive stance toward the environment as a way to position themselves as environmentally friendly companies.

Let's return to our example of Nike, a company that has been criticized in the past for its environmental performance and its foreign labor practices. In response to the former, Nike initiated new environmental standards and policies for its foreign manufacturing partners. Nike's 2014 corporate responsibility report detailed the development of a series of sustainability-related aims, targets and commitments to help ensure Nike remains on track and continues to make progress. One of its main points of emphasis was its *Make Today Better* initiative, which covers the company's progress in six key areas: cutting energy, empowering workers, rejecting toxics, reducing wastes, slashing water use, and supporting local communities.[31]

Allegations against Nike and/or Nike's foreign manufacturing partners included unsafe working conditions, low wages, and child labor. Nike took these criticisms seriously and responded, in part, by disclosing information about its foreign partners in a detailed 108-page report,[32] publicizing its labor policies, and creating a program with its partners to promote best labor practices and to achieve continuous improvement.

According to Nike founder and former CEO Phil Knight, "Nike has zero tolerance for under-age labor." The company increased the minimum age of footwear factory workers to 18 years old, and the minimum age for all other light-manufacturing workers (apparel, accessories, and equipment) to 16 years old. These new minimum age requirements exceed those mandated by most governments.

THE BENEFITS OF STRATEGIC MANAGEMENT

Research has shown that organizations that use a strategic planning process tend to perform better than similar organizations that do not. That is not to suggest that all successful firms follow a highly formal, structured, and detail-oriented strategic process nor that unsuccessful firms do not plan. Studies indicate that the formality of the process tends to increase as the size of the organization increases, and as the turbulence and complexity of the firm's external environment increase. In any case, strategic thinking is important for the success of all organizations for both financial and non-financial reasons. Some of the most important benefits of a strategic management process include:

1. More forward-looking, future-oriented thinking results in more effective strategies and better financial performance. Value creation is enhanced.
2. Better internal communication is fostered when managers from different functional areas listen and discuss their views in strategic management meetings. This interaction yields learning and understanding among managers who otherwise may not interact on a frequent basis.[33]
3. Firms become more proactive and less reactive and are better able to anticipate, influence or initiate changes in the external environment.

CONCLUSION

Value creation is ultimately what the strategic management process is all about. Successful organizations are adept at rewarding their customers, employees and owners. But to create value, organizations must adapt to change. As markets become more globally competitive and technology more advanced, the need for strategic flexibility and responsiveness grows. Strategies, both intended and realized, are the engines that produce value and allow the organization to adapt to its changing circumstances. A firm's realized strategy is largely the result of the financing, investing, and operating decisions it makes.

The chapters that follow describe each aspect of the strategic management process in more detail. The essential need to create value for customers, employees, and owners is emphasized throughout the book. By viewing strategy through the lens of value creation, the cross-functional nature of strategic management is emphasized. These themes are critical for strategic management in the 21st century.

KEY TERMS AND CONCEPTS

After reading this chapter you should understand each of the following terms.

- Strategic management
- Mission
- Strategic Management Framework
- Cross-functional
- Intended strategy
- Corporate Governance
- Value creation
- Objectives
- External audit

- Implementation
- Realized strategy
- Senior Management Team
- Vision
- Environmental Reports
- Internal audit
- Outside directors
- Code of ethics
- Sarbanes-Oxley Act

DISCUSSION QUESTIONS

1. What are the five major steps of the strategic management process?
2. What is *value creation*? Review Johnson & Johnson's credo (see Chapter 3, Table 3-1). For whom does J&J attempt to create value? How?
3. How are the concepts of vision, mission, long-term objectives and strategy related? How are they different?
4. What role do financing, investing and operating decisions (FIO) play in the strategic management process?
5. In what way is the fundamental purpose of a business organization the same as a not-for-profit social agency such as Habitat for Humanity?
6. Use the Internet to learn more about the current condition of Nike. How well is Nike creating value for customers, employees, and owners?

EXPERIENTIAL EXERCISE

Social Responsibility. Nike's track record in the area of social responsibility is controversial. Research Nike and its manufacturing partners. In what ways has Nike been a good corporate citizen? How has Nike not met its social obligations? Do you agree or disagree with the following statement: Nike strives to be a socially responsible organization. Explain.

ENDNOTES

1. Symington, Steve. "5 Things Nike's management wants you to know" *The Motley Fool.* 25 March 2015. Web. 1 April 2016. http://www.fool.com/investing/general/2014/09/03/5-things-nike-incs-management-wants-you-to-know.aspx

2. "2015 Nike Letter to Shareholders" Nike, Inc. Accessed 10 April 2016.

3. Magretta, J., and N. Stone, "The Original Management Guru," The *Wall Street Journal*, November 11, 1999, A20.

4. "Habitat for Humanity International mission statement and principles" Habitat for Humanity. Accessed 28 March 2016. http://www.habitat.org/how/mission_statement.aspx

5. Bennis,W., and B. Nanus. *Leaders: The Strategies for Taking Charge.* New York: Harper & Row Publishers, 1985, 89.

6. "Our Mission & Values" *Pepsico.* Accessed 1 April 2016. http://www.pepsico.com/Purpose/Our-Mission-and-Values

7. Johnson & Johnson, Our Credo, www.jnj.com, accessed February 11, 2006.

8. Duncan, W. J., P. M. Ginter, and L. E. Swayne, "Competitive Advantage and Internal Organizational Assessment," *Academy of Management Executive* 12, no. 3 (1998): 6–16.

9. Ibid, 7.

10. Symington, Steve, op cit

11. "2015 Nike Letter to Shareholders" *Nike, Inc.* Accessed 10 April 2016.

12. Porter, M. E., "What is Strategy?" *Harvard Business Review* (November–December 1996): 61–77.

13. Peyre, Florent. "What Amazon understands about offline retail" *MarketingLand.com.* 30 March 2016. Web. 11 April 2016, and Bensinger, Greg; Kapner, Suzanne. "Amazon Rips Page from Rivals' Playbook." WSJ. The Wall Street Journal. 5 February 2016. Web. 15 March 2016.

14. Porth, S. J., R. Kathuria, and M.P. Joshi, "Performance Impact of The Fit Between Manufacturing Priorities of General Managers and Manufacturing Managers," *Journal of Business and Economic Studies* 4, no. 1 (1998): 13–35.

15. Hagerty, James R. "Harley Davidson Tries to Rejuvenate Motorcycle Sales." *WSJ.* The Wall Street Journal. 11 January 2016. Web. 9 March 2016.

16. Garvin, D. A., "Building A Learning Organization," *Harvard Business Review* (July–August 1993): 89.

17. Kaplan, Robert S., and D. P. Norton, "The Balanced Scorecard - Measures That Drive Performance," *Harvard Business Review* (January-February 1992): 71–79.

18. Ibid, 71.

19. Op cit "2015 Nike Letter to Shareholders" *Nike, Inc.* Accessed 10 April 2016.

20. "About Netflix." https://media.netflix.com/en/about-netflix Accessed 6 April 2016.

21. Mintzberg, H., and A. McGugh, "Strategy Formulation in an Adhocracy," *Administrative Science Quarterly* 30, no. 2 (June 1985), 160–197.

22. Ellis, C. M., and E. M. Norman, "Real Change in Real Time," *Management Review* (February 1999): 33–38.

23. "Foreign Companies Lag U.S. Model," *Investor Relations Business* 5, no. 16 (August 14, 2000): 14.

24. Demb, A., and F.F. Neubauer, "The Corporate Board: Confronting the Paradoxes," *Long Range Planning* 25, no. 3 (1992): 9–20.

25. Collins, C. J., "15 Key Provisions of Sarbanes-Oxley," www.microsoft.com/dynamics/nav/product/navision_15_major_sox_provisions.mspx, accessed February 24, 2006.

26. McRitchie, J., ed. Corporate Governance, www.corpgov.net/, 2000, accessed February 11, 2001.

27. Nisen, Max "How Nike Solved Its Sweatshop Problem." *Business Insider.* 8 May 2013. Web. 12 April 2016.

28. Coombes, P., and M. Watson, "Three Surveys on Corporate Governance," *The McKinsey Quarterly* 2000, no. 4 (2000): 74-77; Steinberg, R.M., "A Roadmap to Board Effectiveness," Corporate Board 21, no. 125 (2000): 9–16.

29. Kanaley, R., "Pushing Ethics in Management," *Philadelphia Inquirer*, December 16, 2005, C1.

30. Johnson and Johnson, "Sustainability Report," http://www.investor.jnj.com/2009sustainabilityreport/chairman/index.html, accessed February 14, 2011.

31. "Nike, Inc. Social Responsibility Report" Accessed 12 April 2016.

http://www.nikeresponsibility.com/report/content/chapter/targets-and-performance#infographic458

32. op cit Nisen, Max "How Nike Solved Its Sweatshop Problem." *Business Insider*. 8 May 2013. Web. 12 April 2016.

33. David, F. *Strategic Management Concepts*. 7th ed., Upper Saddle River, NJ: Prentice Hall (1999): 18.

Chapter 2

Creating Value: A Strategic Imperative

CHAPTER LEARNING OBJECTIVES

After studying this chapter, you should be able to

- Explain the role of value creation in the strategic management process;
- Define the concepts of value for customers, employees, and owners;
- Identify the interrelationships between the types of value;
- Understand the strategic management challenge.

THE IMPORTANCE OF VALUE CREATION

Organizations and senior managers in particular are under relentless pressure to satisfy stockholders' demands for profit and growth. The pressure is especially strong in the United States because of a financial system that expects results on a short-term, often quarterly, basis.

The implications of not meeting financial goals can be dire. Since the financial collapse of 2008, many notable companies like General Motors and Radio Shack, have faced those harsh implications. The Great Atlantic & Pacific Tea Company, better known as A&P supermarkets, is another case in point. Founded in 1859, A&P was the preeminent supermarket chain in the United States with 15,418 stores across the country by 1929. Over time though, A&P failed to adapt to the modern supermarket model predicated on branded products, heavy advertising, and suburban store locations. After decades of declining sales and missed financial targets due to increasing pressures from high-end grocers, like Whole Foods, and discounters, like Wal-Mart, Target Corp., and Aldi, A&P filed for Chapter 11 bankruptcy protection in 2010 as a move to restructure its debt and to renegotiate its labor and vendor relations.[1] Less than five years later, A&P once again filed for Chapter 11 bankruptcy after posting revenue declines of 6% in 2015 and 7.6% in 2014. Unlike its first filing, A&P had no plans for restructuring and in November 2015, its remaining 28,000 employees were either rehired by the companies that bought their stores or terminated and A&P's remaining assets were liquidated.[2] The bankruptcies were devastating for both employees and owners.

This example illustrates the consequences of not meeting financial objectives. After A&P's first bankruptcy filing, the embattled grocery retailer gave a significant equity portion to private investors in exchange for $490 million. At the time of its second bankruptcy, A&P's assets totaled $1.6 billion and its debts totaled $2.3 billion.[3] For the quintessential 20th century American supermarket operator, it was a deadly combination of high operating costs and declining profitability during a time when major overhaul was needed. Failing to create value for owners was the ultimate reason for the demise of once iconic A&P.

This example highlights the importance of creating *financial or economic* value for stockholders. But a successful strategic management process focuses not just on satisfying stockholders or owners. Effective organizations understand that the financial performance of the company is an outcome that depends on pleasing customers, and that employees play a pivotal role in doing so. Satisfied employees create delighted and loyal customers which in turn, create economic value in the form of cash flow for owners and stockholders. A short-term and exclusive focus on value for stockholders can be counterproductive.

The Strategic Management Framework shown in Figure 2-1 emphasizes the preeminent role of value creation, and identifies key questions addressed in this chapter. The figure shows that value creation is both the beginning and end of strategic management—it is the goal of the process and the standard by which it is ultimately judged. The purpose of this chapter is to examine the concept of value creation, and to discuss its role in strategic management. As we will see, the success of the organization and its strategic planning process in particular, are judged with respect to its ability to satisfy key stakeholders, especially customers, employees and owners.

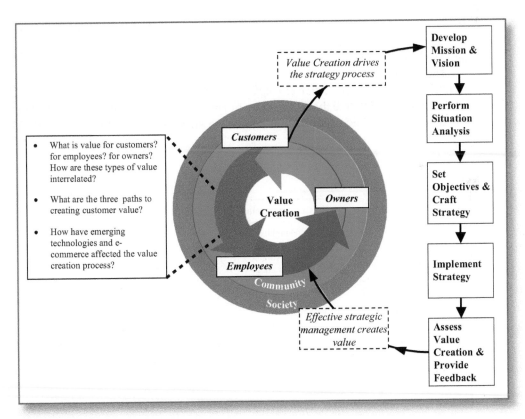

Figure 2-1
The Strategic Management Framework

Customer-Employee-Owner Linkages

Chevron is an example of a company that understands that value creation is the key to strategic management, and that customers, employees, and owners are closely linked in the value creation process. The company strives "to be *the* global energy company most admired for its people, partnership and performance."[4] Chevron recognizes that its ability to create value for stockholders depends upon first developing loyal and productive employees who, in turn, create satisfied customers.

Chevron developed an enterprise-wide model for value creation that depicts these key relationships in the strategic management process (see Figure 2-2). The model begins with a committed team of skilled employees. Chevron places a great deal of emphasis on investing in quality employees to strengthen organizational capability and to develop a talented workforce.[5] The employee team is responsible for creating customer satisfaction and productive and efficient operations. Delighted customers and efficient operations contribute to superior financial performance and favorable stockholder returns. Satisfying both customers and stockholders by means of socially responsible operations, which is a Chevron cornerstone, will contribute to a favorable public image. Chevron believes that these are the necessary ingredients for its continued success: "Energy is at the heart of everything we do. Our success is driven by our people and their commitment to get results the right way—by operating responsibly, executing with excellence, applying innovative technologies and capturing new opportunities for profitable growth."[6]

This series of interdependent relationships between customers, employees, and owners is known as the *customer-employee-owner cycle,* or the *C-E-O Cycle.* The C-E-O Cycle is a dynamic force that drives any business. Each component of the cycle is like a link in a chain. The organization can be no stronger than its weakest link. Value

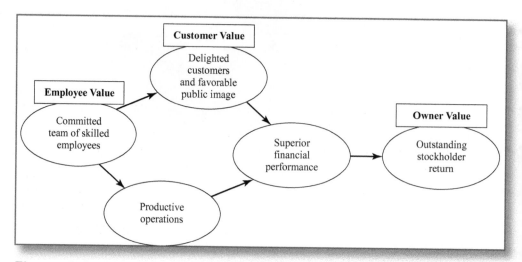

Figure 2-2
Chevron and Value Creation
Source: Adapted from www.chevron.com

creation depends on cultivating and strengthening these links in the Customer-Employee-Owner Cycle. A mismanaged and disgruntled work force doesn't serve customers well, poorly served customers translate into declining sales, and sagging sales don't create shareholder value. And as we have seen above, failure to create financial value often leads to employee layoffs. As Figure 2-1 shows, this focus on value creation takes place within the context of the organization's responsibilities to society and to the natural environment. As discussed in Chapter 3, businesses must be mindful of their impact on the communities in which they operate and the need to operate in a sustainable and responsible way.

Like Chevron, many organizations formalize and codify their commitment to customers, employees, shareholders and sustainability in statements to the public. As shown in Table 2-1, for example, JPMorgan Chase is "committed to creating an open, entrepreneurial and dynamic workplace that encourages each employee to contribute to the best of his or her ability in order to reach our goal of being the best financial services firm in the world."[7] Table 2-1 also shows that PepsiCo,[8] Pfizer,[9] and Microsoft[10] explicitly identify the need in their corporate statements to create value for customers, employees, and shareholders in an ethical and sustainable way. For example, PepsiCo is committed to "investing in our people (employees), our company (stockholders) and the communities where we operate (customers) to help position the company for long-term, sustainable growth." This in turn will position PepsiCo to become a dynamic place to work and an attractive investment choice for shareholders.

Businesses search for ways to solidify and strengthen relationships with customers, employees and owners by aligning the interests of these key stakeholders. One example is the trend toward introducing employee incentive programs. Stock options and employee stock ownership programs have always been important forms

Table 2-1 Examples of Corporate Statements of Value Creation

JPMorgan Chase:
"To reach our goal of being the best financial services firm in the world, JPMorgan Chase is committed to creating an open, entrepreneurial and dynamic workplace that encourages each employee to contribute to the best of his or her ability."

PepsiCo:
"Our mission is to provide consumers around the world with delicious, affordable, convenient and complementary foods and beverages from wholesome breakfasts to healthy and fun daytime snacks and beverages to evening treats. We are committed to investing in our people, our company and the communities where we operate to help position the company for long-term, sustainable growth."

Pfizer:
"To ensure we can continue to deliver on our commitments to the *patients, customers and shareholders* who rely on us, we are focused on improving the way we do business; on operating with transparency in everything we do; and on listening to the views of all of the people involved in health care decisions."

Microsoft:
"Our mission is to empower every person and every organization on the planet to achieve more. We value innovative research, trustworthy computing, corporate social responsibility, empowering philanthropic efforts, the inclusion of all our employees, and preserving the global environment."

of compensation for senior executives. The trend now is to make all employees, regardless of level, eligible for these stock programs. The effect is to directly link the interests of employees and owners. Value created for owners becomes value shared by employees.

VALUE FOR CUSTOMERS

To understand the concept of customer value we have to understand economic exchange. In its simplest form an exchange is giving up something to get something in return. A child may trade her slice of pizza for her friend's turkey sandwich, or her dessert for a candy bar. In each case she felt better off with the turkey sandwich or the candy bar which is why she made the exchange. A firm's customers act in the same manner. They give up money to get the products or services that the firm is selling and they do this because they feel they are better off having the product than the money. Of course this is not always that simple. We may not feel better off when we pay the utility bill, but try turning off the heat on a cold winter night and see if that does not change.

So value is created for customers of the firm through the exchanges they make with the firm. That is, through the services and/or products they purchase. Creating the products and/or services requires the cooperation and input of every functional area within the firm. Facilitating the exchange process requires the coordination of the marketing area. Thus, marketing may be defined as an organizational function and a set of processes for contemplating, communicating, and delivering value to customers and consumers as well as for managing customer and consumer relationships in ways that benefit the organization, its shareholders, and stakeholders.

Stated more simply, *marketing* is the facilitation of exchange. Marketing aims to make it easier for people to buy your products or services. But just making it easier is not enough. We want to maximize the value they gain from that purchase. We want to maximize how much better they feel after the purchase than they did before. In this sense, we could define *customer value* as the satisfaction customers receive relative to what they have to give up to receive that satisfaction.

Essentially, customer value is a cost/benefit relationship as shown in Figure 2-3. To be more precise, *customer value* is the degree of satisfaction derived by the customer relative to the all costs associated with acquiring and using the product or service. *Satisfaction* is defined in terms of benefits received by the customer from possession and use of the product, including how well the product solves specific customer problems relative to customer expectations. The *total cost* includes the price paid for the product plus everything else the customer must do (search activities, travel, activities such as carrying and setting up) to accomplish the acquisition and use of the product.

A company that does a better job than its competitors of maximizing customer value has created a competitive advantage and has positioned itself as the preferred exchange partner. Since customers make exchanges to satisfy a need or solve a problem, marketing is ultimately about creating customer value by becoming the preferred solution or satisfaction provider.

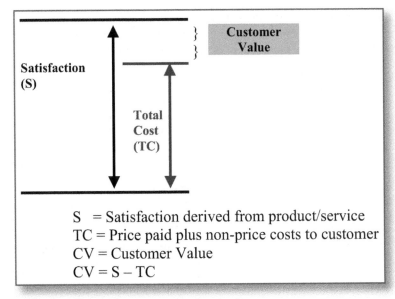

Figure 2-3
The Concept of Customer Value

To accomplish this goal, marketing must first provide the conditions necessary for an exchange (you have to make something possible before you can make it easy) and then seek to continuously improve the way in which you satisfy these conditions.

The four conditions necessary for an exchange are:

1. Two or more parties have to be able to make the exchange (ability).
2. They each have to have a desire to exchange (need or desire).
3. They have to know about what is to be exchanged (awareness).
4. They have to be willing to make the exchange (willingness).

These four conditions are satisfied through the four elements of the marketing mix often referred to as the four Ps: Product, Place, Promotion, and Price. Table 2-2 provides examples of how the elements of the marketing mix facilitate exchange.

A firm's marketing strategy is supported by the four elements of the marketing mix. To be efficient and effective, this strategy has to aim at a specific group of customers who have similar needs. This group of customers is referred to as a *target market*. The greater the similarity of customer needs within the target market, the better the match and the more likely the firm is to be the preferred solution/satisfaction provider.

Whole Foods Markets understands the concept of focusing on a target market. Whole Foods' customers tend to be individuals who are concerned with the environment and their health. Whole Foods products are largely organic and locally sourced, have minimal artificial preservatives or additives, and are environmentally

Table 2-2 Facilitating Exchange Through the Marketing Mix

MARKETING MIX	ROLE IN FACILITATING EXCHANGE	EXAMPLE
Product	The parties have to have something of value to exchange	Hybrid automobiles at first appealed mainly to individuals who were environmentally conscious. The volatility of gas prices and the increased mileage of hybrids have made them a more attractive option to a much broader market.
Place	Two or more parties have to be able to make the exchange	E-Bay makes it possible for sellers to interact and physically exchange with buyers all over the world.
Promotion	The parties have to know about what is to be exchanged	Until the mid-1990s disability insurance was not purchased by most (some individuals received it as an employer-paid benefit). When a little duck waddled onto the scene and quacked "*AFLAC*," disability insurance became a mainstream product and AFLAC was the leading brand.
Price	The parties have to be willing to give up what they have for the exchange	Wal-Mart understands that to be the price leader you need to drive costs out of the system. Their tactics are often questioned but Wal-Mart has historically offered everyday low prices because it has the lowest cost structure among retailers.

friendly. Their stores tend to be located in higher income suburban areas to coincide with their target market. They rely heavily on word-of-mouth promotion, and because their customers want unique products of high quality, prices are higher than traditional supermarkets. Whole Foods has been mockingly referred to as "Whole Paycheck" due to their prices, but people who value fresh, environmentally friendly, locally produced products have been willing to pay more.

Whole Foods' tight focus on a clear target market has been one of the keys to its success. Managing and nurturing that relationship with the target market is critical and an ongoing effort. In 2015 Whole Foods learned that the hard way when New York officials accused Whole Foods of mislabeling the weights of some containers of prepared foods and an activist group, Direct Action Everywhere, revealed footage of the harsh conditions inside a northern California chicken farm that supplies eggs to Whole Foods.[11]

Of course, the same individual may be a member of different targets given the usage situation. For example, hotel chains follow a premium pricing strategy during the week when business travelers keep the hotels rooms occupied. The same business traveler may come to the same hotel for a weekend with his or her family and expect value pricing, including free lodging for children, a complimentary breakfast, and bonus coupons for use at area attractions. The hotel chain uses these additional incentives for weekend guests to attract a different target market.

For a time, the airlines followed a similar multi-level pricing strategy requiring passengers to stay over a Saturday night to get the lowest fares. This worked because business travelers did not want to stay the extra night and therefore would pay the higher fare. Vacation and casual travelers wanted the lower fare and were willing to stay the extra night to get it. This strategy worked until airlines like Southwest and AirTran stopped multi-level pricing and gave the discounted fare to all of their passengers. Although they would restrict the number of seats sold at the lowest fares, even their highest fares were less than half of the regular fares on the traditional airlines. This attracted a much broader target market and is one of the reasons the traditional airlines got into financial trouble.

Providing Customer Value

Goods and services provide value in a number of ways. Delivering a product with a radical new technology that significantly improves product performance creates value plus makes all other products in the category seem outdated. Apple experiences this each time it releases a new generation of the iPhone, iPad, or other Apple devices. Providing add-ons, such as frequent shopper points, helps airlines, online retailers, hotels, food retailers and many other firms create added value for the customer. Branding can add value through both physical and psychological attributes. In fact, branding a category that has historically been a commodity, for example, what Frank Perdue did with chicken "raised the right way,"[12] is a path to creating added perceived value for customers. Along with added value comes the ability to charge higher prices and generate higher margins, provided that consumers associate added value with the branded item.

Campbell Soup Company launched a website called Campbell's Kitchen to provide value for both customers and consumers. Campbell's Kitchen allows you to share recipes, create shopping lists, find dinner ideas, and print coupons. Recipes and dinner ideas are searchable by product (e.g., Swanson broth or Prego sauce) and category (e.g., entertaining or healthy eating). To make access to Campbell's Kitchen even easier, Campbell introduced a free mobile application that you can download from iTunes. Campbell's Kitchen also has a program whereby a consumer can subscribe to a service called *Campbell's Meal-mail*.[13] Every day, subscribers receive an e-mail with a recipe that gives not only suggestions regarding what to have for dinner, but the instructions for making a quick and easy meal, using Campbell's products. Campbell's Kitchen most recently became one of the first consumer brands to feature an app for Amazon's Echo, a voice activated assistant that allows the user to ask questions, create tasks, order something online, or in this case, find and relay recipes from Campbell's Kitchen to the user.[14] By helping to solve the consumer's "what's for dinner?" dilemma, Campbell is providing value for consumers.

Customers' value judgments are influenced by the usage situation. At McDonald's, you expect food that is filling and tasty, not a gourmet meal. There is also the expectation that the order will be filled accurately and very quickly. You might pay $5 for a value meal, including specialty hamburger, French fries and soft drink. If expectations for a quick, satisfying meal are met, the customer will be satisfied, and given the relatively low cost in money, time and effort, this transaction may generate high-perceived value. At Shake Shack, Chipotle, and Panera Bread, the customer perceives fast food but of a higher quality than McDonald's. These three restaurants represent the fast casual category that have a cool, contemporary atmosphere with healthier food options. Therefore, customers are willing to pay slightly more than they would at McDonald's. The same person on a different occasion might pay $100 or substantially more for a dinner for two in a fine restaurant with food and service that is of significantly higher quality than McDonald's or Shake Shack. However, if that meal does not meet the substantially higher expectations in terms of quality, service, ambience and other elements unique to a fine dining experience, the customer may be left less-than satisfied and perceive a low level of value.

Who is Responsible for Creating Customer Value?

Since it is so closely tied to the customer, the marketing function plays a particularly important role in creating customer value. But creating value for customers is a cross-functional responsibility shared by all areas of the company. This notion, that everyone within an organization has responsibility for creating value for customers, is often called the *marketing concept*. The marketing concept states that the role of the firm is to create and satisfy customers at a profit, through an organization-wide effort and in a socially responsible way.

Facebook follows this concept. Every person within the organization is a source of new ideas and values. Facebook sponsors what they call all night "Hackathons" to inspire the rapid creation and testing of new ideas. Not only are engineers invited to participate, but also marketing and legal employees. These events facilitate creative discussion, offer employees the chance to share their ideas with coworkers, and open the door for innovation. Some of the ideas that have emerged from Facebook's fifty plus Hackathons are the friend suggester tool, Facebook Chat, and video messaging.[15] At Facebook, employees are playing a direct role in adding value for customers.

Advances in technology can change who creates value and how it is created. Consider the example of car buying. For some, buying a new car is seen as a real hassle. Sparring with salespeople, spending countless hours in dealerships and never feeling confident about being treated fairly and getting the best deal have been characteristic of automobile shopping. The Internet and the rise of mobile devices have created a completely different approach to new car shopping. Internet sites, such as www.kbb.com sponsored by Kelley Blue Book, have allowed consumers to efficiently search for the best car deals, providing buyers with more information about alternatives and prices, and allowing them to cut better deals. Internet sites for auto shopping act as referral services. They provide shoppers with detailed information about prices, models, and options. Revenues come from member auto dealers who do the actual car selling. By serving as the matchmaker between dealer and shopper, these Internet auto-buying services have enhanced customer value by both facilitating the shopping experience and by lowering the prices consumers must pay. This buying experience has become even more technological and user friendly with sites like Vehix.com, carfax.com, and car manufacturers' web sites now providing you the opportunity to build and price your car and select delivery options.

VALUE DISCIPLINES AS PATHS TO MARKET LEADERSHIP

Companies like Dell Computer, Home Depot and Nike redefined value for their customers, created business systems that could deliver more of that value than competitors, and ultimately raised the expectations of customers beyond the reach of competition. Each of these companies, and many other successful organizations, took leadership positions in their respective industries by narrowing their business focus to delivering superior customer value via one of three "value disciplines." These *value disciplines*, or paths to market leadership, are: (1) operational excellence, (2) customer intimacy, and (3) product leadership.[16] Each discipline creates a different kind of value for customers by relying on superior performance in different functional areas. The value disciplines and their functional requirements are shown in Table 2-3.

Table 2-3 Value Disciplines

TYPE OF VALUE EMPHASIS	DESCRIPTION	FUNCTIONAL EXCELLENCE REQUIRED
Operational Excellence	Providing customers with reliable products or services at competitive prices and delivered with minimal difficulty or inconvenience	Efficiency of Operations, Distribution/Logistics
Customer Intimacy	Segmenting and targeting markets precisely and then tailoring offerings to match exactly the demands of those niches	Marketing, Sales, Flexibility of Operations
Product Leadership	Offering customers leading-edge products and services that consistently enhance the customer's use or application in the market, thereby making rivals' goods obsolete	Research & Development

Operational Excellence

Operational excellence means "providing customers with reliable products or services at competitive prices and delivered with minimal difficulty or inconvenience."[17] Due to the steep decline in the commodity price of oil in 2015, Chevron was forced to reduce its workforce by 5% to streamline operations and reduce operating costs to compensate for the decline in profitability. Despite workforce reductions, Chevron also set new record lows in employees' days away from work and its motor vehicle crash rate, while their total recordable incident rate and petroleum spill volume matched the previous year's record lows.[18] Chevron is an example of a company that seeks operational excellence based on five objectives: (1) achieve an injury-free workplace; (2) promote a healthy workplace and mitigate significant health risks; (3) eliminate spills and environmental incidents and mitigate environmental risks; (4) operate incident-free with industry-leading asset reliability; (5) maximize the efficient use of resources and assets.[19] All of these objectives help to ensure the health and safety of its community of employees, but also keep Chevron's operating expenses low.

Rapid response to customer demands has become more and more necessary as the speed of change accelerates. Developments in communications technology and greater emphasis on supply chain partnering have lowered mean response times for almost all competitors. Firms that want to compete on the basis of operational excellence are challenged to stay on the leading edge both in terms of technology and processes.

Firms competing on the basis of operational excellence often strive for flat and flexible organizations. They must design tightly focused organizations to maintain the simple and efficient structure necessary to be truly "lean and mean." Thus, operationally excellent firms define core operations fairly narrowly and may rely on outsourcing and partnering to perform non-core functions. Finally, operationally excellent firms must have a culture that "abhors waste and rewards efficiency."[20]

Companies such as Dell Computer, UPS and Wal-Mart have invested in supply chain, production and distribution technologies, and processes and systems that generate reliable delivery at low cost. For the better part of two decades, Wal-Mart was so successful in driving down costs and prices, it gained a significant market share in both mass merchandise and food retailing, forcing traditional supermarkets to respond. Supermarkets did so in the early 1990's with the Efficient Consumer Response (ECR) initiative, designed to drive non-value added activities out of the food supply chain so that traditional food retailers could compete with Wal-Mart. By 2016 though, Wal-Mart's market position and its profitability were being threatened by the success of online retailers such as Amazon. To reduce costs and gain efficiencies, Wal-Mart closed down all of its underperforming Wal-Mart Express stores and planned to do the same with its Wal-Mart Neighborhood Market stores in 2016.[21] These cost reduction efforts by Wal-Mart are designed to lower operating costs, improve operational excellence and allow Wal-Mart to defend and sustain its low price strategy.

Customer Intimacy

Customer intimacy means "segmenting and targeting markets precisely and then tailoring these offerings to match exactly the demands of those niches."[22] Companies such as Home Depot, Nordstrom's, Ritz-Carlton Hotels and Amazon.com combine detailed knowledge about customers with operational flexibility to enable them to respond rapidly to emerging and changing customer demands, to customize offerings for specific customers, and to fulfill special requests. In turn, this creates tremendous customer loyalty.

One important aspect of customer intimacy as a path to market leadership is the recognition that customers have a lifetime value to the supplier and that emphasis must be placed on a long-term relationship, not short-term individual transactions. Another important aspect of customer intimacy as a value discipline is that not all customers are equally important to a company in terms of profitability, or value creation for owners. Successful companies pick and choose the customers they want to cultivate. Finally, computer technology has enabled true customization, both of goods and services, meaning that successful companies cannot rest on their laurels; there must be a constant push to become more and more responsive to customers.

Barnes & Noble, the nation's largest bookstore chain, is an example of a company that has competed on customer intimacy through the flexibility of its operations. Barnes & Noble has had to adapt its business model to the digital age. Unlike its now defunct rival, Borders, which was slow to respond to changes in technology, Barnes & Noble invested in its online bookselling business, barnesandnoble.com, to better compete with Amazon. In addition, Barnes & Noble responded to customer demand for portable e-reading devices in the late 2000s with the Nook reader. By 2016, with stagnant financial results, Barnes & Noble looked to redefine itself once again, striving to be *more* than just a bookstore. Its sales of goods like children's toys and games, and trendier items, such as vinyl records and adult coloring books, have provided a much needed boost.[23]

McDonald's is the world's leading fast food restaurant chain, but business has not always been as golden as its iconic arches. Due to changing consumer taste preferences in the 2010s, McDonald's saw many customers flee to trendier fast casual restaurants while McDonald's remained in a rut. From 2010 to 2013, revenue growth gradually declined, and in 2014, McDonald's posted a 2.4% decline in total revenue.[24] In early 2015, McDonald's appointed Steve Easterbrook as the new CEO to address the fast food titan's major challenges. Easterbrook has since lifted McDonald's out of its slump by transforming McDonald's into "a customer led organization." Under Easterbrook's reign, McDonald's is focused on delivering outstanding customer service by making comprehensive simplification efforts, enhancing its core menu offerings, and providing a compelling everyday value platform.[25] These customer-led principles were on display when McDonald's offered its All-Day Breakfast menu and introduced the McPick 2, which allows customers to choose any two items from its Extra-Value Menu for $5.[26] These initiatives, along with using cage-free eggs, have produced a significant financial turnaround for McDonald's.

Netflix is another company with a strong sense of customer intimacy. While its less popular DVD service is convenient for those who value a DVD copy of their movie delivered right to their front door, Netflix is most known for its customer-intimate streaming service that is accessible on all major devices. The subscriber pays one flat fee per month and has unlimited access to thousands of movie titles and television shows for as long as they want. There are no hidden fees for usage or account termination. Customer intimacy also resonates with Netflix because of the company's customization features. Netflix provides recommendations for movies and television shows based on the subscriber's past watches/rentals, making it much easier for the user to find a movie that suits their interests.

Product Leadership

Product leadership means "offering customers leading-edge products and services that consistently enhance the customer's use or application in the market, thereby making rivals' goods obsolete"[27] Firms such as Nike, Intel, Merck and 3M have demonstrated product leadership through significant investment in research and development plus corporate cultures designed to encourage and reward innovation and creativity. Product leaders provide customer value via innovative solutions to important customer problems. These companies are successful at discovering and nurturing new ideas that not only solve customer problems but do so in ways much different, and more effective, than those solutions currently available. They do a great job of monitoring the external environment and reacting quickly as windows of opportunity open, albeit for a brief time.

Product leaders are also willing to compete with themselves. Samsung Electronics is constantly on the leading edge in the television market, with their new models cutting into sales for existing models, eventually rendering them obsolete. For example, Samsung's new interactive home appliances, like its Family Hub™ refrigerator, which has built-in cameras for food management and a full entertainment and information center on the exterior of the door, may replace existing Samsung refrigerators. But Samsung is willing to do this in order to preempt competition. Like most companies, Samsung prefers that Samsung products, not other manufacturer's products, are Samsung's chief competition.

Technological advancements have also permeated the sportswear industry as product leader, Nike, is constantly looking to create the most innovative tech-driven athletic products possible. In 2016, Nike unveiled the HyperAdapt Trainer 1.0 with self-lacing technology. The battery-powered sneakers have sensors in the heel to adjust the sneakers to conform to the wearer's foot; the laces can be tightened or loosened by pressing side buttons.[28] The HyperAdapts are just another reminder of Nike's position in the sportswear industry as a product leader.

Achieving a Customer Value Discipline

To gain an advantage over competitors, a firm must "push the boundaries of one value discipline while meeting industry standards in the other two."[29] This entails a clear focus and a strong commitment to one specific value discipline. This sharp focus starts with a lucid description and a vivid understanding of the firm's mission and vision. As shown in the Strategic Management Framework (see Figure 2-1), value creation rests on this clarity of focus. Only then does a value discipline become a path to market leadership.

The value discipline chosen as a company's strategic focus must be supported by its culture, competencies and competitive situation. And once a value discipline is chosen and a path to market leadership has been achieved, the firm must continue to invest heavily in the technology, processes and people necessary to sustain that leadership.

Faced with the realities of strong and dynamic competitive conditions—market changes, technological advances, regulatory changes and economic policy decisions—maintaining this focus on a single value discipline is a challenge. This is especially difficult for publicly held companies beholden to shareholders, and subject to the vagaries and instability of financial markets. The temptation to generate revenues or cost efficiencies quickly, to meet the quarterly (or monthly or even weekly) numbers can lead a company away from its value discipline.

EMPLOYEES AND VALUE CREATION

Before the mid-1800s, when farming and agriculture were the driving forces behind national economies, land was the key to creating value. With the advent of the Industrial Revolution in the late 1800s, when productive capacity surged as a result of new inventions, machinery and equipment, access to capital became perhaps the most critical factor for value creation. In the Information Age of today, however, the key to creating value for customers and owners and gaining a competitive advantage, is no longer land or capital but employees and innovation. According to Pfeffer and Veiga, authors of *The Human Equation: Building Profits by Putting People First*, "An irrefutable business case can be made that the culture and capabilities of an organization—derived from the way it manages its people—are the real and enduring sources of competitive advantage. Managers today must begin to take seriously the often heard, yet frequently ignored, adage that 'people are our most important asset.'"[30]

An organization's ability to create financial value is linked to its capacity to build a committed team of employees,[31] unified by a shared vision of the future,[32] and adept at innovation and organizational learning.[33] This combination of factors—commitment, vision and innovation—helps organizations to adapt, change and grow in a dynamic and competitive era. Building high-performance teams, creating shared vision and achieving innovation require a fundamentally different approach to managing employees than the centralized, control-oriented approach espoused by Frederick Taylor during the era of the industrial revolution.[34] They require *human resource (HR) practices* that view employees not as costs to be minimized, but as strategic assets whose energy, initiative, and creativity shape the future of the organization.

Creating Value by Putting People First

A substantial and growing body of research speaks to the strong connection between how firms manage their people and the financial success they achieve. This evidence is drawn from a variety of samples and industries, and "shows that substantial gains, on the order of 40 percent, can be obtained by implementing *high performance management practices*"[35], such as self-managed teams, information sharing, extensive training, and pay tied to organizational performance.

One compelling study looked at the survival rates of a sample of 136 companies that all went public in the same year. Five years later only 60% of those companies were still in existence. Analyses of the sample showed that the value firms placed on employees and how they rewarded their people were strongly related to survival. Specifically, firms that placed a higher emphasis on employees were 20% more likely to survive than those that placed a low emphasis on employees.[36] Furthermore, the difference in survival rates was even more pronounced depending on how firms scored on rewarding employees. Those that used rewards effectively were 42% more likely to survive. Another study based on a sample of 702 firms found that high performance HR practices were associated with an increase in shareholder wealth of $41,000 per employee.[37]

Valuing employees is a common sense principle not only because it contributes to better organizational performance, but because it is the right thing to do. Unfortunately, common sense is not necessarily common practice. In the end, the key to managing people in ways that lead to profits and innovation, according to Pfeffer and Veiga, is the manager's perspective. When managers look at their people do they see costs to be reduced or assets to be nurtured? Do they see recalcitrant employees who can't be trusted and who need to be closely controlled or do they see intelligent, motivated, trustworthy individuals?*

The Chevron model of value creation (Figure 2-2) emphasizes the importance of employees in the value creation process. Chevron executives state that their success is driven by the ingenuity and commitment of their employees. Leadership is the single most important factor for their success in Operational Excellence (OE) as well. "Leaders (at Chevron) are focused not only on getting results but getting results the right way and behaving in accordance with our values...By their actions, leaders cascade, manage and drive execution; reinforce the Operational Excellence culture; instill operational discipline and work to ensure that they and the entire workforce comply with OE requirements."[38]

At Chevron, just as with all organizations, value creation begins with employees. It is their commitment, energy and creative spirit that fuels the Customer-Employee-Owner Cycle. Employees are responsible for creating enthusiastic and loyal customers, customers who are willing to pay prices for the company's products and services which in turn creates value for the owners. But the Customer-Employee-Owner Cycle is not linear; it does not stop with the owners. Value must be returned to employees in exchange for their contributions to the process. To sustain the success of the organization, value is created and shared throughout the Customer-Employee-Owner Cycle.

What is Value for Employees?

Employees expect to receive rewards, or value, for their contributions to the firm. In general, employee value is derived from two sources. Depending upon the organization and the individuals involved, *value for employees* may be largely *financial*, or it might be dominated by *psychological and social* considerations. Examples of the former include money and benefits, and examples of the latter might be a sense of accomplishment, feelings of pride and commitment to the work being done, status, self-esteem, a meaningful existence, or contributions to a larger social cause.

---

*These opposing views about employees are known as Theory X and Theory Y, developed by Douglas McGregor. Theory X assumes employees dislike work, have little ambition, and need to be directed and controlled. Theory Y assumes employees can be highly committed to the organization and can exercise a high degree of creativity and initiative. According to the theory, the proper management style is contingent upon the employees. In today's Information Age when firms rely on employees to adapt, innovate, and grow, the Theory Y approach works well. This is implied in the discussion above.

Financial Value

Employees expect to receive financial rewards for their contribution to the organization. This includes a competitive salary and fringe benefits package, but it means more than that. Indeed, one component of a high performance management system is *contingent compensation*, that is, compensation that is tied to organizational performance.

Contingent compensation can take a number of different forms, including gain sharing, profit sharing, and stock options and ownership. Each of these compensation schemes shares a common thread: employees receive financial rewards when the organization meets or exceeds performance standards. *Gain sharing* is a program whereby employees are rewarded for new programs or initiatives that result in measurable improvements in productivity. For example, produce department employees in a supermarket are rewarded for finding ways to cut the percentage of waste associated with fruits and vegetables that have to be tossed out because they exceed their shelf life. *Profit sharing* differs from gain sharing in that it focuses on bottom line profits. When the organization exceeds a predetermined profit goal, some portion of the excess profit is shared among employees.

Stock options and stock ownership plans are one way to reward employees by aligning employees' interests with those of the company and shareholders. A stock option gives an employee the right to purchase a certain number of shares at their company for a fixed price and within a set amount of time. As of 2014, the National Center for Employee Ownership (NCEO) concluded that 7.2 million employees held stock options with an additional 700,000 employees having other forms of individual equity. That statistic is down from its peak in 2001.[39] The economic recession of 2009 forced companies to readjust the price at which employees could use their stock options to buy shares in the company. This was in response to declining stock prices. Companies like Starbucks, Google, and Intel lowered prices with the hopes of motivating employees. Google gave its employees the option to swap their underwater stock options for new ones. Underwater stock options are those with an exercise price that is higher than the market price.[40]

The wages and salaries received by employees are an obvious component of employee value, even for minimum wage jobs. In 2016, the big-box retailer, Costco Wholesale Corp., raised its minimum wage for store workers by $1.50 to $13 per hour, its first such increase in nine years.[41] Increased social and political commentary about the quality of life of minimum wage employees has increased public scrutiny of minimum wage employers. McDonald's, Wal-Mart, and Starbucks have all increased their starting pay recently.

Psychological and Social Value

Employees also seek social and psychological rewards from their work. For instance, there can be great psychological value in work that the employee finds meaningful or important to a larger cause. Employees also find value in a stimulating work environment that affords them opportunities for personal growth and development on the job. Perceptions of value may be influenced by the amount of training received by employees, feedback and recognition given for their performance, and in general, the respect they are accorded.

A great deal of research has been conducted over the years on employee motivation, and on what employees value in an organization. One long-standing project attempts to identify the 100 best companies to work for in the United States based on a variety of factors.[42] The research indicates that *value for employees* means much more than good pay. In fact, the social and psychological aspects of work are often more powerful motivators than money.

Examples of non-financial programs and practices that create value for employees include the following:[43]

- **Team-building**—Organizations that help make people feel part of a team are valued. This includes open communication and the sharing of information on things such as financial results and strategy. Shared accountability for results and the reduction of status differences between managers and employees is also part of team-building.
- **Extensive training**—Training is an essential component of high performance work systems and an opportunity for employees to develop new skills and knowledge. It also should prepare employees to identify and resolve problems, to initiate changes in work methods, and to take responsibility for quality.
- **A pleasant work environment**—Attention and resources devoted to maintaining a clean, safe, positive work environment are valued by employees.
- **Employment security**—The idea of providing employment security in today's competitive world seems outdated and at odds with what most companies are doing. But employees are not likely to be innovative or embrace change if they fear that this will jeopardize their own job security. Avoiding layoffs by making an effort to place employees in other jobs either within the company or elsewhere supports employee confidence.
- **Recognition for a job well done**—Employees appreciate constructive feedback on their performance and acknowledgment for good work.

These non-financial ways of creating value for employees are as important as, and often more important than, stock ownership programs and other financial approaches. According to the research by Pfeffer and Veiga, creating a corporate culture that values employees is a key to superior organizational performance: "When employees are owners, they act and think like owners. However, little evidence suggests that employee ownership, by itself, affects organizational performance. Rather, employee ownership works best as part of a broader philosophy or culture that incorporates other practices" such as team-building, training, information sharing, and delegation of responsibility.[44] Thus, providing opportunities for employees to develop skills and be a part of a team has its own rewards.

OWNERS AND VALUE CREATION

There has long been a vigorous debate on the importance of shareholder value relative to other measures of corporate performance such as those related to employment, social responsibility, and the firm's environmental impact. Although we have argued against an exclusive, narrow focus on owners, the centrality of creating value for owners is not to be taken lightly. Managers of public corporations have a fiduciary responsibility, a legal obligation, to create value for stockholders. Failure to do

Chapter 2 **Creating Value: A Strategic Imperative**

DISCUSSION QUESTIONS

1. What is the Customer-Employee-Owner Cycle and how is it related to the strategic management process?
2. Discuss why both Nordstrom's (high price, high service) and Wal-Mart (low price, low service) can provide value to their customers.
3. How have advances in information and communications technology enhanced the ability of organizations to create value for their customers?
4. What is the relationship between how firms manage their employees and value creation?
5. What is value for owners? How is it assessed?
6. Learn more about the current condition of Chevron at www.chevron.com. How well is Chevron currently creating value in the Customer-Employee-Owner Cycle? How do you know?

EXPERIENTIAL EXERCISE

Value Creation: E-Commerce Versus Brick and Mortar. Evaluate an e-commerce web site and a brick and mortar web site for two companies in the same or a closely related industry. How do they compare on attention to value creation for customers, employees and owners? What specific examples of value creation are evident?

Case Study: A Slick Problem

On April 20, 2010 the BP Horizon well exploded. The blast killed 11 workers and the resulting leak spewed 206 million gallons of oil into the Gulf. While the BP Horizon well was declared sealed and no further threat on September 25, 2010, the impact of the disaster is still felt today. Submersibles found a 10 cm film of oil sludge, dispersants, and dead organisms on the gulf floor as late as February 10, 2011. Fishermen in the gulf are still uncertain of the total economic impact on them. While many areas have been reopened to fishing many more are still closed, so the fishermen's losses continue to mount. Those dependent on oysters are particularly affected as the oyster beds for the near-term are closed to harvesting.

BP reports that the oil spill has been a disaster for the company as well. Their stock price initially fell by 50% from $60 to $30. Its market cap fell from about $190 billion to about $98 billion. Furthermore, the downturn has negatively impacted BP's institutional investors, the largest of which are British pension funds. Most of these funds have about 8% of their UK equity holdings in BP. These pension funds had lost over $1.7 billion due to the BP disaster. In 2015, due to the rock bottom commodity prices of oil and the remaining legal costs of the oil spill, BP cut approximately 4,000 jobs and plans to make significant cuts in the future.[54]

Case Discussion Questions

1. Free enterprise is based on the profit motive. Did the profit motive contribute to the BP oil disaster?
2. What could BP do in the future to discourage the kinds of behavior that led to the disaster?

ENDNOTES

1. Gasparro, Annie; Checkler, Joseph. "A&P Bankruptcy Filing Indicates Likely Demise." *WSJ*. The Wall Street Journal. 21 July 2015. Web 20 April 2016.
2. Ramey, Corinne. "A&P's Imprint on New York Region Fades as Stores Close" *WSJ*. The Wall Street Journal. 19 November 2015. Web. 21 April 2016.
3. Ibid
4. Chevron Corporation, Vision, www.chevron.com, accessed March 7, 2006.
5. "The Chevron Way." *Chevron*. Accessed 21 April 2016. https://www.chevron.com/about/the-chevron-way
6. Ibid
7. "JP Morgan & Chase Work Environment" Accessed 8 April 2016. https://www.jpmorganchase.com/corporate/About-JPMC/company-culture.htm
8. "Our Mission & Values" *Pepsico*. Accessed 1 April 2016. http://www.pepsico.com/Purpose/Our-Mission-and-Values
9. Pfizer, About Pfizer, www.pfizer.com, accessed January 21, 2011.
10. "About Microsoft." Accessed 23 April 2016. https://www.microsoft.com/en-us/about/default.aspx
11. Brat, Ilan. "Whole Foods Boss Calls Himself a 'Pusher Leader'." *WSJ*. The Wall Street Journal. 9 Feb 2016. Web. 19 Feb 2016.
12. "Perdue Farms Homepage." Accessed 24 April 2016. https://www.perdue.com/
13. Campbell's Kitchen, www.campbellskitchen.com, accessed January 22, 2011.
14. Wohl, Jessica. "Campbells Ready to Serve Recipe Ideas Through Amazon Echo." *AdvertisingAge*. Crain Communications. 8 October 2015. Web. 14 April 2016.
15. Zax, David. "Secrets of Facebook's Legendary Hackathons Revealed." *Fastcompany*. Mansueto Ventures. 9 November 2012. Web. 22 April 2016.
16. Treacy, M., and F. Wiersema, "Customer Intimacy and Other Value Disciplines," *Harvard Business Review* (January–February 1993): 84–93.
17. Ibid, 84.
18. "2015 Letter to the Shareholders." *Chevron*. Accessed 17 April 2016.
19. Chevron, Operational Excellence, www.chevron.com, accessed January 22, 2011.
20. Treacy, M., and F. Wiersema, "How Market Leaders Keep Their Edge," *Fortune* (February 6, 1995): 88–98.
21. Nassauer, Sarah; Davidson, Kate. "Wal-Mart Makes Rare Retreat on Home Turf." *WSJ*. The Wall Street Journal. 16 January 2016. Web. 9 March 2016.
22. Treacy, M., and F. Wiersema, op. cit., 84.
23. Alter, Alexandra. "Why Barnes & Noble Isn't Going Away Yet." New York Times. The New York Times Company. 3 March 2016. Web. 12 April 2016.
24. "2014 Annual Report." *McDonald's*. Accessed 17 April 2016.
25. Jargon, Julie. "All-Day Breakfast is a Pick-Me-Up for McDonald's." *WSJ*. The Wall Street Journal. 23 January 2016. Web. 28 February 2016.

26. Strom, Stephanie. "All-Day Breakfast Helps Lift McDonald's Out of Its Slump." *New York Times*. The New York Times Company. 23 April 2016. Web. 24 April 2016.

27. Treacy, M., and F. Wiersema, op. cit.

28. Germano, Sarah. "Nike Adds Self-Lacing Shoes to Sneaker Arms Race." *WSJ*. The Wall Street Journal. 17 March 2016. Web. 25 March 2016.

29. Treacy, M., and F. Wiersema, op. cit., 84.

30. Pfeffer, J., and J. F. Veiga, "Putting People First for Organizational Success," *Academy of Management Executive* 13, no. 2 (1999): 37.

31. Ibid.

32. Collins, J.C., and Porras, J. *Built To Last: Successful Habits of Visionary Companies*. New York: HarperCollins, 1994.

33. Senge, P. M., C. Roberts, R. Ross, B. Smith, and A. Kleiner. *The Fifth Discipline Fieldbook: Strategies and Tools for Building a Learning Organization*. New York: Doubleday/Currency, 1994, 299.

34. Taylor, F. *Principles of Scientific Management*. New York: Harper and Row, 1911.

35. Pfeffer, J., and J. F. Veiga, "Putting People First for Organizational Success," *Academy of Management Executive* 13, no. 2 (1999): 37.

36. Ibid, 39.

37. Huselid, M. A., and B. E. Becker. "The Impact of High Performance Work Systems, Implementation Effectiveness, and Alignment with Strategy on Shareholder Wealth." Unpublished paper, Rutgers University, New Brunswick, NJ, 1997.

38. "Chevron Operational Excellence Management System—An Overview of OEMS." Accessed 19 April 2016. https://www.chevron.com/-/media/chevron/shared/documents/OEMS_Overview.pdf

39. "Stock Options, Fact Sheet." *National Center for Employee Ownership*. Web. Accessed 24 April 2016. http://www.nceo.org/articles/employee-stock-options-factsheet.

40. Glater, Jonathon D., "Stock Options are Adjusted After Many Share Prices Fall," *The Wall Street Journal*, March 26, 2009.

41. Nassauer, Sarah. "Costco to Raise Minimum Wage." *WSJ*. The Wall Street Journal. 4 March 2016. Web. 22 April 2016.

42. Levering, R., M. Moskowitz, and M. Katz. *The 100 Best Companies to Work for in the United States*, New York: Addison-Wesley, 1984, ix.

43. This list of value-creating programs and practices comes primarily from two sources: Pfeffer, J., and J. F. Veiga, "Putting People First for Organizational Success," *Academy of Management Executive* 13, no. 2 (1999); and Levering, R. M., R. M. Moskowitz, and M. Katz. *The 100 Best Companies to Work for in the United States*. New York: Addison-Wesley, 1984.

44. Pfeffer, J., and J. F. Veiga, "Putting People First for Organizational Success," *Academy of Management Executive* 13, no. 2 (1999): 37.

45. "2015 Chairman's Letter." *Chevron*. Accessed 21 April 2016. https://www.chevron.com/annual-report/2015/chairmans-letter

46. George, B. *Authentic Leadership: Rediscovering the Secrets to Creating Lasting Value*, Somerset, NJ: Josey-Bass Publishing, *2004. Value*, 103.

47. Ibid, 153.

48. Kennedy, A. A. *The End of Shareholder Value: Corporations at the Crossroads*. Cambridge, MA: Perseus Publishing, 2000.

49. George, B., op cit., 153.

50. Chu, K. and E. Emmerentze Jervell "At Western Firms Like Adidas, Rise of the Machines Is Fueled by Higher Asia Wages," *Wall Street Journal*, June 9, 2016, accessed September 13, 2016.

51. Meyer, D. "Why Adidas is Turning to Robots in Germany and the U.S." *Fortune*, May 25, 2016, accessed September 13, 2016.

52. Swedberg, Claire. "Avis Uses RFID for Remote Location Rentals." *RFID Journal*. RFID Journal LLC. 30 August 2011. Web. 24 April 2016.

53. "2015 Nike Letter to Shareholders" *Nike, Inc.* Accessed 10 April 2016.

54. Sheck, Justin. "BP to Cut Approximately 4,000 Exploration and Production Jobs." *WSJ*. The Wall Street Journal. 12 January 2016. Web. 9 March 2016.

Chapter 3

Developing a Mission & Understanding Strategy

CHAPTER LEARNING OBJECTIVES

After studying this chapter, you should be able to

- Define the concepts of mission, vision, and core values;
- Distinguish between mission, vision, values and strategy;
- Understand the five elements of strategy and how they are interrelated;
- Identify different types of strategic initiatives.

Johnson & Johnson

Johnson & Johnson

Johnson & Johnson., Inc. (J&J) is a leading health-care products company with worldwide sales of $70 billion. J&J has more than 127,000 employees who discover, develop, manufacture, and market a broad range of products from first aid, prescription pharmaceuticals, and diagnostics to shampoo and baby care products.[1] To learn more about J&J click on www.jnj.com

*C*onstancy and change; stability and transformation—these terms capture the essence of the paradox faced by strategic managers, the challenge of finding ways to manage the tension between constancy and change. Specifically, this challenge entails being able to stay true to an enduring organizational mission (stability) while operating in an evolving and dynamic world (change).

How can this paradox be reconciled? Can change and stability co-exist within organizations? Johnson & Johnson (J&J), a leader in pharmaceuticals and health care products, has found a way to do just that by remaining committed to an unchanging set of core values and its enduring organizational purpose while adapting to a constantly changing world. The mission and values of J&J carry on while new strategies are developed to adapt to an ever-changing competitive landscape.

Mission, vision, values and strategy. These are the means to manage the dynamic tension between constancy and change, and are the focus of this chapter. The purpose of this chapter is to explain the concepts of mission, vision and core values, and to discuss how they are developed. These concepts are the bedrock, enduring elements of strategic management. In addition, the role of stakeholders, including stakeholder theory and values, highlighted by examples of sustainable management practices, are discussed. Finally, we provide an overview of the elements of strategy along with a description of various types of strategies that organizations use to adapt to and become transformed by change. An understanding of these strategy types is necessary before we can proceed to explore the remaining steps in the Strategic Management Framework. After reading this chapter, you should be able to answer each of the questions shown in Figure 3-1.

CORE VALUES, MISSION, AND VISION

The aim of strategic management, as we have discussed, is to create value, so that the organization can survive and prosper over the long term. Studies of *visionary*

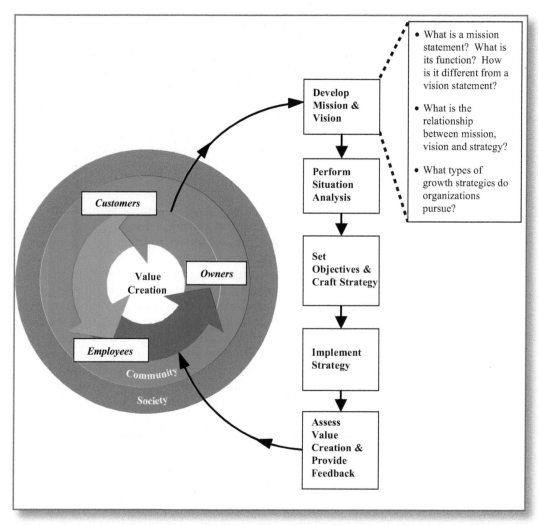

Figure 3-1
The Strategic Management Framework

companies, that is, companies that have achieved enduring, long-term success, have found that these companies are characterized by a purpose and core values "that remain fixed while their business strategies and practices endlessly adapt to a changing world."[2] *Core values* are the fundamental beliefs and ideals of an organization.

In other words, visionary companies know how to manage constancy and change. Employees understand why the organization exists and where it is going. A sense of enduring and shared purpose pervades the organization, along with a vividly clear understanding of what the organization aspires to become. The ability to manage this constancy and change leads to superior organizational performance. According to the research, over a 64-year period, one dollar invested in the visionary companies would have grown to $6,356 compared to $955 in non-visionary comparison companies.

How is this commitment to an enduring and shared purpose fostered? Visionary companies attain their stature by finding ways to express their values, priorities, and sense of identity throughout the organization. Among the most prominent and important ways this is done is with their list of core values, and their mission and vision statements. As we can see in Figure 3-1, developing the mission statement (and vision and values) is the beginning step in the strategic management process.

Johnson & Johnson is a company that has achieved enduring success with a corporate philosophy and set of values that have stood the test of time. Consistently ranked among *Fortune's* "Most Admired Companies" list, it is one of the world's most respected companies (J&J was ranked #1 in 2016 among biopharmaceutical companies and 15th overall).[3] J&J is admired not only for its financial success but also for its crystal clear and unwavering sense of mission and identity.

What is Johnson & Johnson's secret? The answer is simple: an enduring commitment to a core set of values and a philosophy of business that was written decades ago by the patriarch of the company, Robert Wood Johnson, and continues to guide the company today. The philosophy statement is known as the *Johnson & Johnson Credo* and is shown in Table 3-1. The Credo, written more than 70 years ago, identifies the responsibilities of the company and the priority of those responsibilities. The first responsibility of J&J is to their customers—the mothers, fathers, doctors and health care professionals who depend on J&J for safe and effective products. Robert Wood Johnson believed that by putting the customer first and the stockholder last, the business would be well served and profits would follow.

The tragic case of the Tylenol® poisonings, when seven people died in the Chicago area, reveals the extent of J&J's commitment to its Credo. Johnson & Johnson "has drawn heavily on the strength of the Credo for guidance through the years, and at no time was this more evident than during the Tylenol® crises of 1982 and 1986, when the McNeil Consumer & Specialty Pharmaceuticals product was adulterated with cyanide and used as a murder weapon. With Johnson & Johnson's good name and reputation at stake, company managers and employees made countless decisions that were inspired by the philosophy embodied in the Credo. The company's reputation was preserved and the TYLENOL® acetaminophen business was regained."[4]

More recent incidents have critics questioning J&J's commitment to the credo. In 2010 J&J recalled 43 million units because of inadequate equipment-cleaning procedures at the company's Fort Washington, PA plant.[5] Staying true to its credo and putting customers first, J&J chose to pull the bottles off the shelf to ensure the health of all those who use their products. In 2016, J&J was ordered to pay $72 million in damages to the family of a woman who died of ovarian cancer reportedly due to her lifelong usage of J&J's baby powder.[6] Critics and supporters alike will keep watch as J&J moves forward in light of its credo and its standing as one of the most admirable companies in the world.

Robert Wood Johnson's words have become the bedrock foundation for generations of employees, helping the company to understand, preserve and model its core values and corporate philosophy: "Over the years, some of the language of the Credo has been updated and new areas recognizing the environment and the balance between work and family have been added. But the spirit of the document remains the same today as when it was first written."[7]

Table 3-1   Johnson & Johnson Credo

We believe our first responsibility is to the doctors, nurses and patients
to mothers and fathers and all others who use our products and services.
In meeting their needs everything we do must be of high quality.
We must constantly strive to reduce our costs
in order to maintain reasonable prices.
Customers' orders must be serviced promptly and accurately.
Our suppliers and distributors must have an opportunity to make a fair profit.

We are responsible to our employees,
the men and women who work with us throughout the world.
Everyone must be considered as an individual.
We must respect their dignity and recognize their merit.
They must have a sense of security in their jobs.
Compensation must be fair and adequate,
and working conditions clean, orderly and safe.
We must be mindful of ways to help our employees fulfill
their family responsibilities.
Employees must feel free to make suggestions and complaints.
There must be equal opportunity for employment, development
and advancement for those qualified.
We must provide competent management, and their actions must be just and ethical.

We are responsible to the communities in which we live and work
and to the world community as well.
We must be good citizens—support good works and charities
and bear our fair share of taxes.
We must encourage civic improvements and better health and education.
We must maintain in good order the
property we are privileged to use,
protecting the environment and natural resources.

Our final responsibility is to our stockholders.
Business must make a sound profit.
We must experiment with new ideas.
Research must be carried on, innovative programs developed and mistakes paid for.
New equipment must be purchased, new facilities provided and new products launched.
Reserves must be created to provide for adverse times.
When we operate according to these principles,
the stockholders should realize a fair return.

Source: Johnson & Johnson, Johnson & Johnson Credo, www.jnj.com, accessed April 19, 2016.

Being a truly visionary company requires more than writing a list of core values and a mission statement. After all, if these pronouncements are not understood by employees or infused into the culture of the organization, they can become nothing more than fluff—nifty public relations statements but irrelevant to the life of the firm. They are powerless to influence the behavior of employees and the direction of the organization.

But developing and communicating a set of values, mission, and vision can be a helpful step in the process of building a visionary company. In fact, research shows that the visionary companies "wrote such statements more frequently than the comparison companies and decades before it became fashionable."[8]

Some organizations develop both a mission and vision statement. From Chapter 1 we know that the mission statement answers the question "What is our business?" and the vision statement addresses the question "What do we want to become?" The goal of value creation for customers, employees and owners begins to become more concrete with the development of a mission and vision statement, helping to foster a unified focus or 'commonality of interests'[9] among employees.

The Mission Statement

The mission statement of Microsoft Corporation under then CEO Bill Gates in the late 1980s and early 1990s was:

to have a computer (PC) on every desk and in every home.[10]

This clear and concise mission statement revealed Microsoft's core business focus: to be the premier and most recognizable computer company. It stated what products Microsoft sold: computers (PCs). This mission statement implied a global geographic target market and it conveyed to employees and external stakeholders how Microsoft was going to allocate its resources. All business decisions were going to be made with the expressed intent of putting a Microsoft computer on every desk and in every home. Furthermore, this mission statement was a straightforward signal to the computer and software companies of the time, such as IBM, Compaq, Dell, and Apple, of Microsoft's intentions for moving forward.

During the late 1980s and early 1990s, Microsoft pursued this mission through a series of financing, investing, and operating decisions. After less than successful releases of Windows 1.0 and 2.0 in the late 1980s, Microsoft unveiled its incredibly successful Windows 3.0 in 1990. This model, which featured iconic computing functions like Copy & Paste, introduced the graphical interface to the PC and sold more than 10 million copies in the next two years. Also at this time, Microsoft began to back away from its software partnership with IBM to work together on the OS/2 platform. Microsoft decided to focus on its own software, which consisted of the successful Windows 3.0 and Windows NT, instead of working with an industry competitor. To further distance itself from its competitors, Microsoft signed exclusive licensing contracts with computer hardware manufacturers, like HP, IBM, and Dell, which allowed only those hardware companies to sell Windows in their computers. If someone bought a non-licensed Windows computer, they would have to buy the software separately. Then in 1995, Microsoft released its highly anticipated Windows 95 with a $300 million marketing blitz including the Rolling Stones' classic song, "Start Me Up." This new version of Windows introduced the now standard graphical desktop which featured the "Start" button.[11] Microsoft's operating, financing, and investing decisions in the late '80s and early '90s can be traced back to its early mission statement of putting a PC on every desk and in every home.

By the mid to late '90s, however, Microsoft began to focus its efforts more on the Internet. In a now famous company memo titled, "The Internet Tidal Wave," Bill Gates informed his employees of Microsoft's new mission.

> Now I assign the Internet the highest level of importance. In this memo, I want to make clear that our focus on the Internet is crucial to every part of our business. The Internet is the most important single development to come along since the IBM PC was introduced in 1981.[12]

With these words, Microsoft shifted the allocation of its resources from its PC business to its Internet business, and in 1995, Microsoft launched its flagship browser, Internet Explorer (IE). At the time, Netscape was the clear-cut leader in the Internet browser market. However, Microsoft began to bundle its IE with Windows and by 1998, IE was the leader in Internet browsing. In a now defunct agreement, Microsoft agreed to buy some of Apple's nonvoting stock in 1997 to keep the company out of bankruptcy. A part of the agreement stated that Apple would bundle Internet Explorer with its Mac Operating System. In remaining true to its new mission, Microsoft also went on to develop its Windows and Office services as web-based offerings in 2006. This was a part of Microsoft's strategy of offering its services over the web, which was titled "Software + Services." In 2002, Microsoft developed an online gaming platform, XBOX Live, for its XBOX gaming console which allowed gamers to play co-op missions and challenges with other XBOX users from around the world. This feature was made available for its later XBOX iterations: the XBOX 360 released in 2005 and the XBOX One released in 2013. In the ten plus years after Bill Gates changed Microsoft's mission statement to one more focused on the Internet, Microsoft evolved from a strictly PC focused company to one that recognized the power and profitability of the Internet.

Microsoft changed its mission statement again in 2013 under then CEO Steve Ballmer:

> to create a family of devices and services for individuals and businesses that empower people around the globe at home, at work and on the go, for the activities they value most.

In 2015 Microsoft revised its mission again under new CEO Satya Nadella:

> to empower every person and every organization on the planet to achieve more.

Both of these statements are far different from Microsoft's mission statement under Bill Gates in the early 1990s. These statements are more abstract and state that Microsoft's mission is not simply to sell PCs or capitalize on the Internet, but to offer products and services that will allow its customers to create their own intrinsic value. Specifically, Microsoft's current mission statement conveys to internal and external stakeholders that Microsoft wishes to become a more ubiquitous company that is not limited to computers, tablets, video games, and cellphones. In his letter to employees, Nadella states that Microsoft is going to achieve this mission through three key steps: (1) reinventing business processes and productivity, (2) building the intelligent cloud platform, and (3) creating more personal computing. It is uncertain what Microsoft will develop in the future or how it will adapt to the constantly changing software industry, but what is clear is that Microsoft is willing to adapt and redefine its mission to evolve with market changes.

The Role of a Mission Statement

The example of Microsoft Corporation reveals quite a bit about the nature of a mission statement. An effective mission statement may serve several purposes, both within the firm and to external stakeholders. Table 3-2 identifies some of the common functions of a mission statement. Among the most critical of these is to help build a sense of *shared purpose* in the organization, to establish direction, and to communicate that direction and purpose internally and to the public. A clear mission statement is needed to guide and set parameters for the strategic management process; it helps managers set objectives, make strategic choices, resolve their differences, and is a basis for allocating resources. A clear mission can set the tone within the organization and communicate a positive and compelling image to the outside world.

Table 3-2 Functions of a Mission Statement

- To establish a sense of direction within the firm and to guide the strategic management process by providing a basis for objectives and strategies
- To influence decisions about resource allocation
- To help build and communicate among employees a sense of shared purpose
- To communicate an attractive and compelling image to external stakeholders
- To support the core values of the organization

The Microsoft example also shows that a mission, while enduring, is not stagnant. It may need to evolve over time. On the other hand, a mission that changes frequently may be the sign of a company that does not know where it wants to go or what it wants to become. With each new mission statement at Microsoft, new strategies were formulated and implemented. This iterative process involves the evaluation of current strategies in relation to internal capabilities and external challenges, and if need be, a revision of the mission statement.

The Components of a Mission Statement

Mission statements vary in length, content, format and specificity (see Table 3-3 for several examples). If mission statements are too general, they provide no direction and are worthless as decision making and communication tools. While some debate the usefulness of mission statements altogether,[13] ample evidence suggests that they are viable tools and are critical in a strategic management process that builds value. In a survey of executives, Bain and Company found that mission statements were ranked as the number one tool of strategic management every year since the study began in 1989[14]. While there is no single formula for the content of a mission statement, some common components are:[15]

> *Value Creation.* How and for whom will the organization create value?
> *Principal products and services.* What are the firm's major products and services?

Table 3-3 Examples of Mission Statements

McDonald's

Our purpose goes beyond what we sell. We're using our reach to be a positive force. For our customers. Our people. Our communities. Our world.

Target

Our mission is to fulfill the needs and fuel the potential of our guests. That means making Target your preferred shopping destination in all channels by delivering outstanding value, continuous innovation and exceptional experiences—consistently fulfilling our Expect More. Pay Less.® brand promise.

Kellogg Company

To nourish families so they can flourish and thrive.

Starbucks

Our mission: to inspire and nurture the human spirit—one person, one cup and one neighborhood at a time.

Patagonia

To build the best product, cause no unnecessary harm, use business to inspire and implement solutions to the environmental crisis.

Warby Parker

To offer designer eyewear at a revolutionary price, while leading the way for socially conscious businesses.

sweetgreen

Founded in 2007, sweetgreen is a destination for delicious food that's both healthy for you and aligned with your values. We source local and organic ingredients from farmers we know and partners we trust, supporting our communities and creating meaningful relationships with those around us. We exist to create experiences where passion and purpose come together.

Geographical area. Where does the firm compete?

Philosophies. What are the basic beliefs, values, and ethical priorities of the firm?

Self-image. What are the firm's distinctive competencies or how is it unique?

Public image. Is the firm responsive to social, community, and environmental concerns?

Evaluating and Building a Mission Statement

An examination of the mission statement is part of the strategic management process. The components discussed above can be used to either break down the current mission statement for evaluation, or to build a new one. Since this statement helps all employees focus their efforts on the critical priorities, it is important to involve as many as possible in the process of evaluating or building the mission statement. To stimulate thinking and discussion, each person could be asked to consider the

Table 3-4 Evaluating and Building the Mission Statement

COMPONENT	DESCRIPTIONS (KEY WORDS) OF OUR MISSION
Value Creation	
Principal products and services	
Geographical area	
Philosophies	
Self-image	
Public image	

Adapted from: Ginter, P.M., Swayne, L.M., and Duncan, W.J. *Strategic Management of Health Care Organizations.* 3rd ed. Blackwell Publishers, Inc.Malden, MA, 1998.

points listed in Table 3-4. This initiates discussion, but also gives some structure to the process.

Raising the question of "What is our business?" can trigger debate and reveal differences among those evaluating or building the mission statements. Negotiation, compromise, and eventual agreement on this important issue are critical to give focus to the rest of the strategic management process. This is especially important as more and more companies merge and develop alliances across national boundaries.

The Vision Statement

Vision statements are less common than mission statements. Microsoft does not have a vision statement and Johnson & Johnson relies exclusively on its corporate credo (Table 3-1). Pfizer, Inc. has what they call a "mission statement" that reads more like a vision statement: "to be the premier, innovative biopharmaceutical company."[16] Under Armour's vision is to: "Empower athletes everywhere."[17]

A clearly articulated vision of the future is at once simple, easily understood, clearly desirable, and energizing.[18] A vision statement should address four key attributes: *idealism, uniqueness, future orientation,* and *imagery*.[19] As in the case of Under Armour, vision statements tend to be very brief, forward-looking and inspirational. They attempt to evoke the emotions. A vision articulates a view of a credible but very attractive future for the organization. Like the mission statement, there is no single formula for crafting a vision statement. An effective vision statement, however, passes the *three C test*—it is *clear, concise* and *compelling*.[20]

Evaluating and Building a Vision Statement

Table 3-5 may be used as a tool in the process for evaluating or building a vision statement. As with the mission statement process described above, each person involved could be asked to think about the points listed in Table 3-5. The table provides a list of vision statement components, with space provided for participants

Table 3-5 Evaluating and Building the Vision Statement

COMPONENT	DESCRIPTIONS (KEY WORDS) OF OUR VISION
Clear hope for future	
Challenging; inspires excellence	
Energizing to employees and customers/clients	
Memorable	

Adapted from: Ginter, P.M., Swayne, L.M., and Duncan, W.J. *Strategic Management of Health Care Organizations.* 3rd ed. Blackwell Publishers, Inc.Malden, MA, 1998.

to brainstorm and articulate key words to address each component. This initiates discussion and provides some structure for the process.

The Vision Framework

The superior financial performance of visionary companies has been partly attributed to a well-conceived *vision framework*. The concept of a vision framework includes the vision statement but goes further. It consists of two major components: core ideology and envisioned future. The *core ideology* or *core purpose* defines the enduring character of the organization and is the glue that holds the organization together over time. Merck's core reason for being, for example, is "to improve health and well-being around the world." Walt Disney wants "to make people happy," and Nike's core purpose is "to experience the emotion of competition, winning, and crushing opponents."[21] Core ideology is a constant over time.

For many companies, core ideology is expressed not in a vision statement but in a set of core values (see, for example, Pfizer's core values listed in Table 3-6) or a credo (see the J&J Credo in Table 3-1). Merck's values are Improving Life, Ethics & Integrity, Innovation, Access to Health, and Diversity & Teamwork.[22]

The second component of the vision framework—*envisioned future*—includes two parts: a 10-to-30 year "audacious goal" plus vivid descriptions of what it will be like to achieve the goal. These vivid descriptions may be analogous to a vision statement as described above. The audacious goal is a very aggressive long-term goal that looks far into the future and requires thinking beyond the current capabilities of the organization. It "serves as a unifying focal point of effort, and acts as a catalyst for team spirit. It has a clear finish line, so the organization can know when it has achieved the goal … (the goal) engages people—it reaches out and grabs them."[23]

On May 25, 1961 U.S. President John F. Kennedy delivered a message before a joint session of Congress. In that message he established one of the great examples of an envisioned future:

"I believe that this nation should commit itself to achieving the goal, before this decade is out, of landing a man on the moon and returning him safely to the earth."

Table 3-6 Pfizer Core Values

1. **Collaboration:** We know that to be a successful company we must work together, frequently transcending organizational and geographic boundaries to meet the changing needs of our customers. We want all of our colleagues to contribute to the best of their ability, individually and in teams. Teamwork improves the quality of decisions and increases the likelihood that good decisions will be acted upon. Teamwork sustains a spirit of excitement, fulfilment, pride and passion for our business, enabling us to succeed in all of our endeavors and continually learn as individuals and as a corporation.

2. **Community:** Pfizer plays an active role in making every country and community in which it operates a better place to live and work, knowing that the ongoing vitality of our host nation and local communities has a direct impact on the long term health of our business.

3. **Customer Focus:** We are deeply committed to meeting the needs of our customers and constantly focus on customer satisfaction. We take genuine interest in the welfare of our customers, whether internal or external. We recognize that we can prosper only if we anticipate and meet customer needs, respond quickly to changing conditions and fulfil customer expectations better than our competitors. We seek long-term relationships based on our comprehensive understanding of all our customers' needs and on the value we provide through superior products and services.

4. **Innovation:** Innovation is the key to improving health and sustaining Pfizer's growth and profitability. The quest for innovative solutions should invigorate all of our core businesses and pervade the Pfizer community worldwide. In our drive to innovate, we support well-conceived risk-taking and understand that it will not always lead to success. We embrace creativity and consistently pursue new opportunities. We look for ways to make our research and development capabilities, products and services more useful to our customers, and our business practices, processes and systems more efficient and effective. We listen to and collaborate with our customers to identify potential new products and make them widely available.

5. **Integrity:** We demand of ourselves and others the highest ethical standards, and our products and processes will be of the highest quality. Our conduct as a company, and as individuals within it, will always reflect the highest standards of integrity. We will demonstrate open, honest and ethical behavior in all dealings with customers, clients, colleagues, suppliers, partners, the public and governments. The Pfizer name is a source of pride to us and should inspire trust in all with whom we come in contact. We must do more than simply do things right, we must also do the right thing.

6. **Leadership:** Leaders advance teamwork by imparting a clarity of purpose, a shared sense of goals and a joint commitment to excellence. Leaders empower those around them by sharing knowledge and authority and by recognizing and rewarding outstanding individual effort. We are dedicated to providing opportunities for leadership at all levels in our organization. Leaders are those who step forward to achieve difficult goals, envisioning what needs to happen and motivating others. They utilize the particular talents of every individual and resolve conflict by helping others to focus on common goals. Leaders build relationships with others throughout the company to share ideas, provide support, and help assure that the best practices prevail throughout Pfizer.

7. **Performance:** We strive for continuous improvement in our performance. When we commit to doing something, we will do it in the best, most complete, most efficient and timeliest way possible. Then we will try to think of ways to do it better the next time. We will measure our performance carefully, ensuring that integrity and respect for people are never compromised. We will compete aggressively, establishing challenging but achievable targets and rewarding performance measured against those targets. We wish to attract the highest-caliber employees, providing them with opportunities to develop to their full potential and to share in the success that comes from winning in the marketplace.

(continued)

Table 3-6 Continued

8. **Quality:** Since 1849, the Pfizer name has been synonymous with the trust and reliability inherent in the word quality. Quality is ingrained in the work of our colleagues and all our Values. We are dedicated to the delivery of quality healthcare around the world. Our business practices and processes are designed to achieve quality results that exceed the expectations of patients, customers, colleagues, investors, business partners and regulators. We have a relentless passion for quality in everything we do.

9. **Respect for People:** We recognize that people are the cornerstone of Pfizer's success. We come from many different countries and cultures, and we speak many languages. We value our diversity as a source of strength. We are proud of Pfizer's history of treating employees with respect and dignity and are committed to building upon this tradition. We listen to the ideas of our colleagues and respond appropriately. We seek a business environment that fosters personal and professional growth and achievement. We recognize that communication must be frequent and candid and that we must support others with the tools, training and authority they need to succeed in achieving their responsibilities, goals and objectives.

Reprinted by permission from Pfizer.

In 1961, the United States lagged behind the Soviet Union in space exploration and was far from capable of realizing the goal of landing on the moon. Kennedy's bold pronouncement, however, made in full view of the world, was a commitment and a powerful catalyst for focusing the nation's and NASA's resources and energy.

Developing a Vision Framework

Synthesizing and crafting a vision framework is a challenging task. Intuition, perhaps even a spark of genius, are necessary "to assemble - out of all the variety of images, signals, forecasts, and alternatives - a clearly articulated vision of the future that is at once simple, easily understood, clearly desirable, and energizing".[24] This synthesis requires:

- *Foresight*, to ensure that the vision will be appropriate for the future environment;
- *Hindsight*, so that organizational tradition and culture are not violated;
- *A worldview*, to capitalize on the impact of new developments and trends;
- *Depth perception*, to see the whole picture in perspective;
- *Peripheral vision*, to foresee possible responses from competitors;
- *A process of revision*, so that the vision is reviewed in light of changes in the environment.[25]

This discussion of core values, mission and vision emphasizes that successful organizations have a clear sense of identity and purpose. Putting these pieces together and creating a vision framework allows the organization to send a strong and clear message to its employees and external stakeholders: "This is who we are and what we stand for. Anything less is not acceptable."

Arthur Andersen LLP was once one of the Big Five accounting firms and a worldwide leader in auditing, tax, and management consulting services. The company

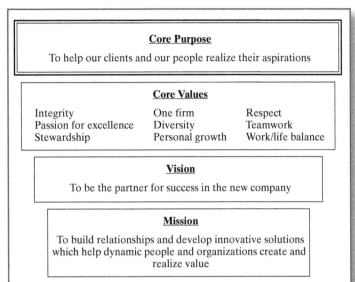

Figure 3-2
Before the Fall: Arthur
Andersen's Vision
Framework

Core Purpose

To help our clients and our people realize their aspirations

Core Values

Integrity	One firm	Respect
Passion for excellence	Diversity	Teamwork
Stewardship	Personal growth	Work/life balance

Vision

To be the partner for success in the new company

Mission

To build relationships and develop innovative solutions which help dynamic people and organizations create and realize value

enjoyed an impeccable reputation in the field, characterized by honesty, integrity and professionalism. This reputation was built and nurtured over many years by the founder of the firm, Arthur Andersen, who at the age of 28 was confronted by a client, a very lucrative client, who demanded that Andersen revise his audit of the client's company. Andersen's reply was legendary and became a part of the culture of the firm. He said, "There is not enough money in Chicago to induce me to change that report."[26] This commitment to integrity became known as "The Andersen Way." It eventually led to and is reflected in the Andersen vision framework shown in Figure 3-2.

Unfortunately, there is no happy ending to the Arthur Andersen story. Despite its honorable past, a small number of Andersen employees ruined the entire company by ignoring the values espoused in the firm's vision framework and compromising the Andersen Way. In 2002, the firm surrendered its license to practice as Certified Public Accountants in the United States after being prosecuted by the U.S. Department of Justice in connection with the Enron scandal.[27] This scandal and others like it in the early 2000s paved the way for the passing of the Sarbanes-Oxley Act of 2002. As discussed in Chapter 1, this made both publicly traded company executives and their independent auditing agencies more accountable for their actions. These are examples of the direct and indirect costs of compromising a firm's ethical principles and core values.

STAKEHOLDER THEORY

When we discuss creating value for customers, employees and owners, as well as the role of mission and vision statements in articulating value creation, we are discussing stakeholder theory. For many years, the primary purpose of business was expressed in terms of maximizing shareholder value. This view, known as the Shareholder Theory of the firm focuses on creating value only for the owners or stockholders through profit generation[28] reflected in either dividends or when the worth of investment increases beyond the cost of capital invested. Today we know that many other groups do and should benefit from a business's operations in addition to its owners. This more inclusive view of the purpose of the firm is known as the Stakeholder Theory of Business. A stakeholder is defined as "any group or individual who can affect or is affected by the achievement of the organization's objectives."[29]

Many top CEOs embrace the stakeholder view of the firm and denounce an exclusive focus on shareholders as the sole purpose of the business (value creation only for owners).[30]

Jack Welch, former General Electric CEO, states that maximizing shareholder value is "the dumbest idea in the world."

Paul Polman, CEO of Unilever [UN], has denounced "the cult of shareholder value."

John Mackey of Whole Foods [WFM] has condemned businesses that "view their purpose as profit maximization and treat all participants in the system as means to that end."

Marc Benioff, Chairman and CEO of Salesforce [CRM], joined these CEOs and declared that this still-pervasive business theory is wrong. "The business of business isn't just about creating profits for shareholders—it's also about improving the state of the world and driving stakeholder value."

Alibaba CEO Jack Ma has said that "customers are number one; employees are number two and shareholders are number three."

Stakeholder Analysis

Stakeholder analysis should be a collaborative, multi-step process that begins with the identification of relevant stakeholders. Stakeholders can be identified for all types of organizations—publically traded, private, non-profit and government agencies as well as for all levels within the organization. The second step is to draw a map illustrating the relationships between stakeholders and the firm; this map can be general or detailed. For example, a stakeholder map for a publically traded business at the corporate level may appear like this:

Note the general categories of partners, vendors, competitors, communities, and of special note is the inclusion of the environment as a stakeholder.

A stakeholder map for a University's Advising Department (Figure 3-4) provides more specific details and classification of stakeholders as "core," "internal but indirect" and "external and indirect."

Decision makers within the business identify stakeholders based on the perceived influence, power, and legitimacy of each stakeholder group. This means

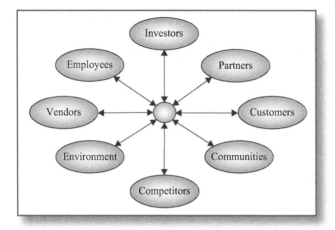

Figure 3-3
Stakeholder Map
Source: http://www.ethinact.
com/what-we-do/stakeholder-
strategy-development/

doing research, having a process and periodically updating your Stakeholder Analysis. BSR Stakeholder Engagement Consulting Services offers these recommendations for prioritizing stakeholders and identifying issues:[31]

- It is not practical and usually not necessary to engage with all stakeholder groups with the same level of intensity all of the time. Being strategic and clear about whom you are engaging with and why, before jumping in, can help save both time and money.
- Look closely at stakeholder issues and decide whether they are material, asking the following questions:
  – What are the issues for these priority stakeholders?
  – Which issues do all stakeholders most frequently express?
  – Are the real issues apparent and relevant to our business?
- Rank your stakeholders into a prioritized list and map.

Stakeholder Analysis

What is the purpose of analyzing stakeholders? The reasons for analyzing stakeholders can be grouped into two main categories: to communicate and to make decisions. You can communicate to your stakeholders about your activities, resources, and needs and you can receive information from your stakeholders about their activities, resources and needs. This information helps in making decisions at the strategic and operational levels, for example, in setting objectives and choosing and implementing strategies. A Stakeholder analysis provides information useful for creating a Balanced Scorecard, a concept discussed in Chapter 11.

Criticisms of Stakeholder Theory

While there is much support for Stakeholder Theory, there are some common criticisms. The first is how does a business know what each stakeholder wants and

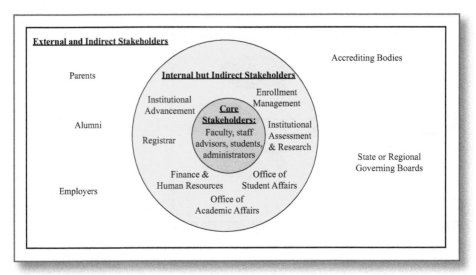

Figure 3-4
External and Indirect Stakeholders
Source: http://www.nacada.ksu.edu/Resources/Clearinghouse/View-Articles/Defining-Advising-Stakeholder-Groups.aspx

at what level of decision making within the business should that stakeholder be included? In the face of competing and often mutually exclusive demands among stakeholders, how does a business choose which to consider in its decision-making? What is the limit to the scope of stakeholders?

The key to addressing these criticisms is to develop a process for stakeholder analysis. To stay relevant, recognize that your stakeholder analysis and map will change over time and you will need to monitor and revise your thinking based on new information. Answering the following questions will strengthen your confidence in your analysis.[32]

- Is our list focused on relevant stakeholders who are important to our current and future efforts?
- Do we have a good understanding of where stakeholders are coming from, what they may want, whether they would be interested in engaging with our organization, and why?
- How can we further understand and qualify these stakeholders? Through discussions with internal colleagues? Reading reference reports? Finding specific blogs or Twitter accounts to follow?
- Will this list inform tactics, strategies, and investment considerations?
- Have we given thought to what type of resources (expertise, people, information and budget) we need to support our communications, decision-making and follow-up activities?

Thus, Stakeholder Theory is an integrative theory supporting sustainability and sustainable development and providing justification for including a social and environmental purpose to the firm, in addition to an economic purpose.

Sustainability/Sustainable Development

The concept of sustainable development originated in The World Commission on Environment and Development and is defined as: "Humanity has the ability to make development sustainable—to ensure that it meets the needs of the present without compromising the ability of future generations to meet their own needs."[33] While there is not complete consensus about the domain of sustainable development,[34,35] there is agreement that it includes economic, social and environmental dimensions.[36] Just as the creation of shareholder value requires performance on multiple dimensions, the global challenges associated with sustainable development are also multifaceted.[37]

Triple Bottom Line (TBL)

A sustainable enterprise contributes to sustainable development by delivering economic (profit), environmental (planet) and social (people) benefits.[38] The TBL encourages businesses to give closer attention to the impact of all of their commercial activities, not just their financial performance.[39] This framework emphasizes economic, social and environmental values and results. It is intended to capture the whole set of values, issues, and processes that companies *should* address in order to minimize harm that results from their activities and to ensure the creation of positive economic, social and environmental value.[40, 41]

Organizations of all sizes are embracing sustainable practices. The world's largest corporations are fast finding a place for TBL,[42] motivated in part by political visibility, public scrutiny, and the need for reputation management.[43] Sustainable entrepreneurship (SE) in Small-Medium Enterprises (SMEs) consists of demonstrating "responsible creativity while achieving viable, livable, and equitable development through the integration of management of natural and human resources in business."[44] Even small firms are able to influence communities and individuals toward more sustainable practices (e.g., plastic-free towns).[45]

Commitment to sustainable development is motivated by both "push" and "pull" forces. Various stakeholders such as governments (through laws, regulations and enforcement), professional societies (through standards and norms), NGOs (through public pressure), and customers (through loyalty) push organizations to adopt sustainable practices.[46] In addition, some businesses are pulled to sustainable development by internal advocates who accept a higher level of obligation and moral responsibility than that demanded by mere compliance with the law.[47] Both "push" and "pull" sustainable developments are necessary. "Push" forces provide an external impetus for change but deep-rooted change in organizations only occurs when there are internal champions that advocate for sustainable development in strategic decisions and tactical operations.

The Origins of Sustainability Reporting

Climate change has emerged as a major topic of debate and concern. While environmentalists and social activists concerned with sustainability have argued the point for decades, the range of interested parties has broadened recently because of significant new legislation and government regulation.

Responding to mounting pressure from public and private forces, the U.S. Securities and Exchange Commission (SEC) approved guidelines for publicly traded companies regarding disclosures related to climate change. The guidelines have four main components: 1) impacts from existing regulation and legislation, 2) effects generated by international climate change accords, 3) expected indirect consequences of new environmental protection rules, and 4) risk consequences derived from the physical effects of climate change on business activities. The somewhat vague nature of the SEC guidance in these four areas fostered many questions and uncertainties concerning the materiality of climate change financial risks as they apply to publicly held businesses.

Evolution of the Sustainability Accounting Standards Board (SASB)

The Sustainability Accounting Standards Boards (SASB) developed as an outgrowth of a Harvard University research project called the Initiative for Responsible Investment (IRI). The IRI, founded in 2004, focused on responsible public-sector investment, particularly the best means for investors to recognize mergers and acquisitions that create long-term sustainable value.[48, 49] The project identified industry-specific sustainability metrics as well as key performance indicators for six industries. Based upon a very positive response from various groups associated with these industries, the need for a recognized central clearinghouse for generating sustainability metrics was identified. The Sustainability Accounting Standards Boards grew from this initiative.[50]

SASB has evolved as the organization that provides sustainability accounting standards over a range of 79 industries in ten industry sectors (see Table 3-7). Incorporated in July 2011, SASB is a 501(c)3 non-profit organization based in San Francisco California. The SASB mission is:

> to develop and disseminate sustainability accounting standards that help our corporations disclose material, decision-useful information to investors in a cost-effective manner, in mandatory filings such as the SEC Form 10-K and 20-F. That mission is accomplished across 79 industries through a rigorous process that includes evidence-based research and broad, balanced stakeholder participation.[51]

Presently, compliance with SASB standards is a voluntary process and recognition of these standards is rarely highlighted in SEC reports. An enhanced usage of SASB standards is promising, however, because SASB research demonstrates that firms with good reporting performance on sustainability issues enjoy strong financial returns. Additionally, 75% of the disclosure issues and metrics in the SASB standards are already acknowledged as material and disclosed by companies in their

Table 3-7   SASB's Sustainable Industry Classification System By Sector and Associated Industries

Consumption:
- Agricultural Products
- Meat, Poultry, & Dairy
- Non-Alcoholic Beverages
- Alcoholic Beverages
- Tobacco
- Household & Personal Products
- Multiline and Specialty Retailers & Distributors
- Food Retailers & Distributors
- Drug Retailers & Convenience Stores
- E-Commerce
- Apparel, Accessories & Footwear
- Building Products & Furnishings
- Appliance Manufacturing
- Toys & Sporting Goods

Financials
- Commercial Banks
- Investment Banking & Brokerage
- Asset Management & Custody Activities
- Consumer Finance
- Mortgage Finance
- Security & Commodity Exchanges
- Insurance

Health Care
- Biotechnology
- Pharmaceuticals
- Medical Equipment & Supplies
- Health Care Delivery
- Health Care Distributors
- Managed Care

Infrastructure
- Electric Utilities
- Gas Utilities
- Water Utilities
- Waste Management
- Engineering & Construction Services
- Home Builders
- Real Estate Owners, Developers & Investment Trusts
- Real Estate Services

Non-Renewal Resources
- Oil & Gas Exploration & Production
- Oil & Gas Midstream
- Oil & Gas Refining & Marketing
- Oil & Gas Services
- Coal Operations
- Iron & Steel Producers
- Metals & Mining
- Construction Materials

Renewable Resources & Alternative Energy
- Biofuels
- Solar Energy
- Wind Energy
- Fuel Cells & Industrial Batteries
- Forestry & Logging
- Pulp & Paper Products

Resource Transformation
- Chemicals
- Aerospace & Defense
- Electrical & Electronic Equipment
- Industrial Machinery & Goods
- Containers & Packaging

Services
- Education
- Professional Services
- Hotels & Lodging
- Casinos & Gaming
- Restaurants
- Leisure Facilities
- Cruise Lines
- Advertising & Marketing
- Media Production & Distribution
- Cable & Satellite

Technology & Communications
- Electronic Manufacturing Services & Original Design Manufacturing
- Software & IT Services
- Hardware
- Semiconductors
- Telecommunications
- Internet Media & Services

Transportation
- Automobiles
- Auto Parts
- Car Rental & Leasing
- Airlines
- Air Freight & Logistics
- Marine Transportation
- Rail Transportation
- Road Transportation

Reprinted from *SASB Annual Report*, 2015, by permission of Sustainability Accounting Standards Board.

Table 3-8 Restaurant Industry Metrics

Sustainability Issue	Metrics	Measure
Energy and Water Management	1. Total Energy Consumed, Percentage Grid Electricity, Percentage Renewable	Gigajoules Percentage
	2. Total Water Withdrawn, Percentage in Regions with High or Extremely High Baseline Water Stress	Cubic Meters Percentage
Food and Packaging Waste Management	1. Amount of Waste, Percentage Food Waste, Percentage Diverted	Metric Tons Percentage
	2. Weight of Packaging, Percent Made from Recycled or Renewable Materials, Percentage that is Recyclable or Compostable	Metric Tons Percentage
Food Safety	1. Percentage of Restaurants Inspected by a Food Safety Oversight Body, Percentage Receiving Critical Violation	Percentage
	2. Number of Recalls, Total Amount of Food Product Recalled	Number, Metric Tons
	3. Number of Confirmed Foodborne Illness Outbreaks, Percentage Resulting in CDC Investigation	Number, Percentage
Nutritional Content	1. Percentage of Meal Options Consistent with the Dietary Guidelines for U.S. or Foreign Equivalent, Sales from these Options	Percentage, U.S. Dollars
	2. Percentage of Children's Meal Options Consistent with the National Dietary Guidelines for Children or Foreign Equivalent, Sales from these Options	Percentage, U.S. Dollars
	3. Number of Children Advertising Impressions Made, Percentage Promoting Products that Meet National Dietary Guidelines for Children or Foreign Equivalent	Number, Percentage
Fair Labor Practices	1. Voluntary and Involuntary Employee Turnover Rate for Restaurant Employees	Percentage
	2. Average Hourly Wage for Restaurant Employees by Region, Percentage of Employees Earning Minimum Wage	U.S. Dollars, Percentage
	3. Amount of Legal and Regulatory Fines and Settlements Associated with Labor Law Violations	U.S. Dollars
	4. Amount of Tax Credit Received for Hiring through Enterprise Zone Programs	U.S. Dollars
Supply Chain Management and Food Sourcing	1. Percentage of Food Purchased Meeting Environmental & Social Sourcing Standards, Percentage Third-Party Certified	Percentage by COGS Percentage, Percentage by weight
	2. Percentage of Eggs Purchased from Cage-Free Sources	Percentage, Percentage by weight
	3. Percentage of Pork Purchased from Gestation Crate-Free Sources	
	4. Discussion of Strategy to Manage Environmental and Social Risks within the Supply Chain	N/A

Form 10-K, although the actual reporting mechanisms are not clearly defined and certainly not standardized across industry sectors.[52]

To bring greater consistency and clarity to the process of sustainability disclosure and reporting, the SASB designed a methodology for measuring sustainability by industry. SASB standards average five sustainability issues and thirteen associated metrics for each industry, thereby simplifying the analysis process. These measures have been codified by using input from industry focus groups as well as extended public comment periods. As a result, over 80% of metrics in the SASB standards are consistent with metrics already in use and disclosed by firms. [53]

Example of Industry Sector Sustainability Metrics: The Restaurant Industry

The restaurant industry is one of ten industries housed in SASB's Services Sector. Table 3-8 lists the sustainability issues identified for this sector along with the metrics used to measure these issues.

At the present time sustainability accounting is still in its infancy and the business world does not yet fully understand its economic and social value to the individual organization.[54] In the long run, SASB has lofty goals, however. Quoting from its conceptual framework manual:

> Ultimately, the goal of sustainability accounting and disclosure is to form development of an integrated business strategy for corporate management and assess sustainability risks and opportunities inherent to investment decisions. Sustainability accounting and disclosure is intended as a compliment to financial accounting, such that financial and sustainability information can be evaluated side-by-side and provide a complete view of a corporation's performance and value creation, both financial and nonfinancial, and across all forms of capital.[55]

STAKEHOLDER RAMIFICATIONS

As previously noted, both the individual and institutional investment communities have indicated a willingness to support organizations that demonstrate that their operations do not harm the environment. Traditionally, it has been difficult to truly understand the impact that many industries have on the environment. One intention of SASB standards is to provide information that enables investors to select firms in which environmental concerns are part of daily operations. In this light, SASB standards are designed to give investors a holistic view of a company's financial and nonfinancial performance. A second intention is to give investors the opportunity to compare companies within the same industry along accepted sustainability standards.[56]

Examples of "Pull" Sustainable Development

Very few industries generate the interest and have the external visibility of professional sports, particularly at the major league level. The major professional leagues have grown significantly in the 21st Century. For example, in 2016 the NFL generated approximately $13 billion in revenue as compared to 4.3 billion in 2001. As the business of professional sports has grown, the leagues and their local franchises have expanded outreach in their communities as a way of shedding positive light on ownership, increasing fan engagement, and giving back something tangible and important to the fans and taxpayers who support them. In addition, many teams that play in large outdoor facilities have made a commitment to "going green" via sustainability initiatives, extending from recycling of waste from food and beverage concessions to generating their own "clean" electricity by installing wind turbines and solar panels.

The Philadelphia market supports franchises in all five major leagues, MLB, MLS, NBA, NFL and NHL. Each of these clubs participates in league wide charitable and community-based activities and each sponsors its own initiatives and programs. In addition, the Philadelphia Eagles (NFL) and the Philadelphia Phillies (MLB) have established sustainability programs for their facilities, Lincoln Financial Field and Citizens Bank Park, respectively.

The Eagles have one of the most visible and extensive "green" energy programs in sports, which they call Go Green, a great play on words since green is the primary team color. The Eagles use corn-based food and beverage containers, LED lighting, a water system infused with electrolytes and salt—better than chemicals—for cleaning, waterless urinals, and water filtration systems in the stadium to reduce the use of plastic water bottles, which they have cut by 46,000 by giving refillable water bottles to all staff members. One writer noted that the Eagles are "thinking from head to toe when it comes to going green."[57]

Through a partnership with Princeton-based NRG, the Eagles installed 14 wind turbines and 11,108 solar panels in the stadium and atop an adjacent parking lot, generating four megawatts of energy per year. Through continuous efforts in the areas of recycling and composting, the club is able to divert 99%—some 850 tons—of all of their waste from landfills. The Eagles were awarded LEED certification from the US Green Building Council for Lincoln Financial Field in 2013, only the second such NFL team to receive this designation. Additionally, the Eagles offset the carbon footprint of all team travel through reforestation, participating in yearly tree planting events at the "Eagles Forest" in Neshaminy, PA.[58]

The Philadelphia Phillies have put together some programs designed to make Citizens Bank Park more energy efficient and to reduce the impact of the tons of waste generated by fans. The Phillies sponsor a program called "Red Goes Green" which involves such activities as recycling waste in the ballpark, cleanup programs at city parks and recreation centers, and "Home Runs for Trees" (in partnership with the Philadelphia Gas Works and the Philadelphia Horticultural Society) in an effort to plant one million trees. The Phillies also participate in the Green Sports Alliance, whose mission is "Leveraging the cultural and market influence of sports to promote healthy, sustainable communities where we live & play."[59]

Diageo, PLC is an example from the corporate world of a company that is focused on pull sustainable development. Headquartered in London, Diageo is the leading premium spirits business in the world by volume, net sales, and operating profit. It produces and distributes eight of the world's top 20 spirits brands. Diageo is also one of the few international drinks companies that spans the entire beverage alcohol market, offering beer, wine, and spirits. Its well-known brands include Smirnoff vodka, Baileys cream liqueur, Johnnie Walker Scotch whisky, José Cuervo tequila, Tanqueray gin, Captain Morgan rum, Guinness beer, and wines from Mey Icki, Chalone, and the Acacia Winery. The company divides its operations along geographic lines with North America accounting for nearly a third of sales, followed by Europe (22%), Asia Pacific (18%), Africa (12%), and Latin America and the Caribbean (8%). Diageo owns 200-plus production facilities, including malting, distilleries, breweries, packaging, maturation, vineyards, wineries, and distribution, spread across 30 countries.

In its 2016 Annual Report, Diageo reported strong progress against its 2020 sustainability and responsibility targets especially water efficiency, carbon emissions and waste materials. They also took new steps to promote responsible drinking.

Key performance highlights include:[60]

- Decreasing GHG emissions in direct operations by 7.7%
- Improving water efficiency by 12.5% compared with 2015 and by 38% compared with the baseline
- Replenishing 21% of total water used in final product in water-stressed areas through reforestation, desilting of dams, water storage and safe water and sanitation projects
- Reaching 380,622 people this year with responsible drinking messages through training programs such as DrinkIQ and increasing underage education initiatives by 50% which are now available in 86 countries
- Empowering 260,000 women to date through the Plan W program, aiming to reach 2 million women by the end of 2016
- Providing access to safe water and sanitation to 351,700 more people through the Water of Life program which has helped more than 10 million people since 2006

Ivan Menezes, Chief Executive, Diageo plc commented, "Our sustainable development strategy reflects how the elements of our value chain are interdependent and how contributing to society, to communities, and to the environment strengthens our business. This year, we have made good progress towards our environmental goals, with some substantial gains in the management of our water, carbon and waste. We have also introduced a new target of procuring 100% of our electricity from renewable sources by 2030. We have also made significant progress in our aim to improve the role of alcohol in society and in our work to tackle misuse. We do this through our implementation of the Global Producers' Commitments to Reduce the Harmful Use of Alcohol, an unprecedented partnership of the world's largest alcohol companies coming together to tackle harmful drinking. As an industry, we are seeing good progress against the targets we set ourselves for 2017." [61]

THE ELEMENTS OF STRATEGY

We began this chapter by discussing the paradox of constancy and change in strategic management. The company's core values and ideology anchor the company to an enduring purpose and provide a secure foundation for managing the turbulence of the business world. This is the constancy. But if organizations don't adapt with the times, they go the way of the dinosaurs. So how can firms remain true to their core ideology but also transform themselves to fit the changing world? That is where *strategy* comes into the picture. Strategy is the bridge that spans the gap from the organization's present to its future. While changing their strategies but remaining true to their mission and values, organizations are able to adapt and grow.

Before we move to Chapter 4 and the second step of the strategic management process—the situation analysis—we need to understand this concept of strategy. In the next sections we introduce and define the five elements of strategy and the types of strategies that organizations can use to adapt and change with the times.

Donald Hambrick and James Fredrickson have written an influential article presenting a framework for understanding the concept of strategy. The problem, as they argue, is that strategy is an overused word and "has become a catchall term used to mean whatever one wants it to mean. Executives now talk about their service strategy, their branding strategy, their acquisition strategy, or whatever kind of strategy that is on their mind at a particular moment."[62] What the executives are calling *strategy* is really a collection of strategic threads, or pieces of a larger and, one hopes, more integrated and coherent strategy.

As Hambrick and Fredrickson state, a strategy consists of an integrated set of choices but it does not include all the important choices an executive must make. The Microsoft example of striving to "have a PC on every desk and in every household" is an important choice but it is not a strategy. Rather it is part of the company's mission. This aspiration comes before and informs the choice of a strategy. Likewise, if Microsoft were to decide to change its supply chain systems, organization structure, or its employee training programs these would be important decisions but most likely would reinforce and support a strategy rather than be the strategy itself.

Strategy has five coordinated elements, providing answers to a series of corresponding questions:[63]

- Arenas—Where will we be active? Which product categories, market segments, geographic areas, core technologies will be our focus?
- Vehicles—How will we get there? Will we grow through internal development, joint ventures, acquisitions, partnerships, franchising, licensing, etc?
- Differentiators—How will we compete? Will we differentiate based on price, customization, styling, image, reliability, safety, etc?
- Staging or timing—What will be our speed and sequence of moves? Will we rollout our strategy over time or go full steam ahead? Will we be a "prospector" who is first to the market or an "analyzer" who moves more slowly but learns from the first-mover, etc?
- Economic logic—How will we obtain our profit? What is our business model— low cost and high scale, premium prices and unmatched service or quality, premium price due to proprietary product features, etc?

A strategy, according to Hambrick and Fredrickson, needs to encompass all five elements and the elements should align and support each other. Consider the example of IKEA, the $32 billion home furnishing retailer headquartered in Sweden.

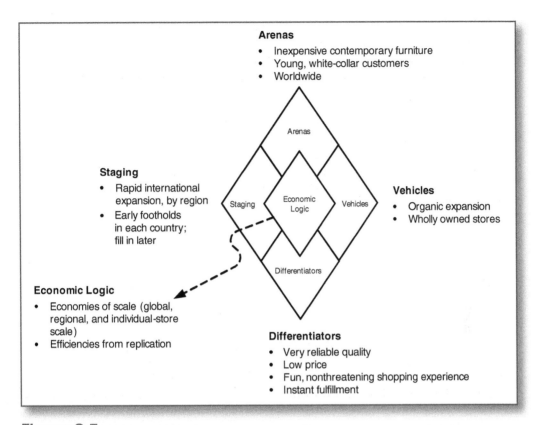

Arenas
- Inexpensive contemporary furniture
- Young, white-collar customers
- Worldwide

Staging
- Rapid international expansion, by region
- Early footholds in each country; fill in later

Vehicles
- Organic expansion
- Wholly owned stores

Economic Logic
- Economies of scale (global, regional, and individual-store scale)
- Efficiencies from replication

Differentiators
- Very reliable quality
- Low price
- Fun, nonthreatening shopping experience
- Instant fulfillment

Figure 3-5
The Five Elements of IKEA's Strategy
Reprinted from *Academy of Management Executive*, Vol. 19, No. 4, by permission of Oxford University Press.

IKEA sells relatively inexpensive Scandinavian-style furniture, much of it requiring self-assembly. Figure 3-5 defines each of the five elements of IKEA's strategy and shows how they tie together into an integrated whole.

Types of Strategic Initiatives: Arenas

An integrated strategy is comprised of five building blocks or elements as we have described above. Let's examine and define different strategic initiatives used by firms in light of the elements of strategy, beginning with arenas. As we know, a firm's arena refers to its products, market segments, geographic areas, and core technologies. Firms can pursue several strategic initiatives to achieve top-line revenue growth, many of which involve the basic strategic elements of products and markets. For example, new product development is a growth strategy aimed at achieving sales increases, and is one of the strategic alternatives in the growth model shown in Figure 3-6. This model posits that a firm's arenas, and more specifically its products and markets, can be divided into two categories, that is, those that are current and

Markets		
	Present	New
Products Present	Market Penetration	Market Extension
New	Product Development	Diversification

Figure 3-6
The Growth Matrix
Adapted from: David A.
Aaker, *Strategic Market
Management* (5th edition).
New York: John Wiley &
Sons, Inc., 1998, page 31.

those that are new.[64] Using a two by two matrix with four cells we can identify four different growth strategies:

1. *Market Penetration*—achieving growth by selling more of our existing products in existing markets
2. *Market Development* (or *market extension*)—achieving growth by taking existing products into new markets or market segments
3. *Product Development*—the creation of new products for markets we currently serve
4. *Diversification*—branching out into a new industry; diversification suggests an expansion outside the firm's current core business(es) into a new product/ market sector.

These growth strategies are not mutually exclusive. Several options are pursuable simultaneously and the categories sometimes overlap. For example, Bayer Aspirin is primarily positioned and marketed as a pain-reliever. Attempting to increase sales within that market segment is classified as market penetration. If Bayer is promoted to a new target market as a therapy for heart attack and stroke victims, however, it would be classified as a market extension (or market development). A similar example is Tums, an antacid product that relieves indigestion. Tums began losing its base of customers with the introduction of once-a-day therapies to eliminate chronic indigestion. Tums was repositioned in the market to take advantage of a clinical study that identified the need for women to increase their daily calcium intake. Since the acid reducer in Tums was primarily calcium, the product was marketed to women as an easy and inexpensive calcium supplement. This is an example of both market penetration and market development. In the end you may be relieved to know (even without taking a Tums) that how the strategic initiative is classified is not as important as understanding the way in which the initiative contributes to revenue growth.

Market Penetration

Businesses can grow using current products in current markets through a strategy of *market penetration*. Penetration strategies typically include changing and/or increasing advertising and promotion, temporary price reductions, and promoting new uses. Returning to a previous example, Microsoft spent $300 million to promote the launch of Windows 95 in 1995. The $300 million was spent on a massive advertising blitz that included global print, radio, and television ads, a Windows 95 banner draped over the CN Tower in Toronto, and even securing the rights for the Rolling Stones' song, "Start Me Up" to serve as the campaign's theme song.[65] Samsung employed a market penetration strategy in 2016 when it slashed prices in emerging markets such as China, Indonesia, and India to regain lost market share in regions where they had previously been the undisputed leader.[66]

Market Extension

Alternatively, companies can grow by taking an existing product to new markets using a *market development* or *market extension* strategy. Wawa, the privately owned convenience store and food service operation, is pursuing a market extension strategy in Florida as it builds and opens dozens of new stores each year in that state. In 2010, Ford gained ground in new markets in Asia, specifically India,[67] with its global strategy of designing smaller, more fuel-efficient cars while exiting luxury markets. Starbucks pursued a market extension strategy in South Africa beginning in 2016 when the coffee giant opened its first store in Johannesburg with plans to open 12 to 15 more within the year. Starbucks is looking to tap into a nascent consumer economy in sub-Saharan Africa and believes it can be profitable in a new market with its well-known coffee brews.[68] Other big brands targeting Africa as their next market extension include Wal-Mart, Zara, Krispy Kreme, H&M, and Domino's.[69] Yum Brands Inc., operator of KFC, Taco Bell, and Pizza Hut, has had a presence in Africa since 2010.[70]

Product Development

Firms can grow by creating new products for existing or related markets, an initiative called *new product development*. Microsoft, J&J, and Merck all rely heavily on product development strategies to drive growth. Tesla Motors pursues an ongoing strategy of developing the most innovative electric automobiles, electric powertrain components, and battery products. Tesla, which *Forbes* listed as the most innovative company in the world for 2015, invests millions of dollars each year in research for new product development.[71] It has become a pioneer in the emerging electric car market, launching its electric plug-in Model S luxury sedan in June 2012, and selling its 100,000[th] model in December 2015.[72]

Another example of a product development strategy is MasterCard's facial recognition feature for online shopping or "Selfie Pay," launched in 2015. This strategy was developed to decrease the probability of online shopping fraud. Users of this feature must download the MasterCard app and enter their credit card information per usual. Then when completing an online purchase, the user must hold the device up to their face and blink to thwart any thief from holding up photographs in attempt to trick the sensor. The face scans are translated into binary (0's and 1's) and transmitted to MasterCard's central servers for detection. Insiders believe that MasterCard is moving away from online security passwords and may offer heartbeat identification as the amount of wearable tech devices increases.[73]

Diversification

When organizations expand beyond the existing scope of their core business, they are pursuing *diversification*. In other words, diversification entails entering a new industry. One justification for adopting a diversification initiative is to reduce risk, based on the logic that diversification allows the organization to spread its assets over a larger cross-section of industries. When one industry is down, another may compensate by being up. Ironically, many firms have found just the opposite to be true. Diversification may actually increase risk since the firm is expanding into a new and unfamiliar industry or because it has to manage the added complexity of disparate businesses.

Diversification may either be *related*, in terms of the type of customer, technology employed, production process, distribution channels and so on, or *unrelated or conglomerate*, meaning expansion into a business which is entirely new and very different to the company. Diversification, as mentioned above, is most often achieved through mergers, acquisitions, partnerships or alliances, but is also possible via internal development.

An example of *related diversification* is Nike's expansion from athletic *shoes* for track, then basketball and other sports, into athletic *apparel* and sports *equipment*, including its latest foray into golf. Another example of related diversification is Comcast Corporation. In 2011 Comcast, the nation's largest cable operator, acquired NBCUniversal, the television network. Then in 2016 Comcast acquired DreamWorks SKG, the animation company with popular franchises such as *Shrek, Kung Fu Panda,* and *How to Train Your Dragon*. The franchises are not only lucrative options at the box office, but can also be valuable assets for potential merchandising and amusement park attractions. Comcast's related diversification strategy shows that it is hedging its bets on the future of its cable business. Comcast cable is reaching 4 million fewer people than in 2013 as consumers can get their entertainment from various other mobile outlets and have decided to pick and choose which channels they truly want.[74]

An example of *unrelated diversification* is DuPont's acquisition of Danisco. DuPont is best known as the biggest U.S. chemical maker. However, it is also active in energy, construction, transportation and manufacturing. In 2011, DuPont acquired Danisco in order to enter the food and biofuels business. Danisco is not only a maker of food ingredients, but also an emerging biofuels company. The two are long-time partners, which should make for an easy merger.[75]

General Electric (GE) is a good example of a firm that has found a way to successfully manage unrelated diversification. GE competes in a wide spectrum of different industries from lighting, to transportation, data management, aircraft engines, and financial services. The Minnesota Mining and Manufacturing Company, more commonly known as 3M, which operates in office products, health care, industrial products, and other major markets, is another example of a successful firm with an unrelated diversification strategy.

Types of Strategic Initiatives: Vehicles

Another of the five elements of strategy discussed above is *vehicles*, which refers to how organizations choose to grow. Organizations can pursue two vehicles or modes of growth—internal or external. *External growth* is achieved through mergers, acquisitions or strategic alliances involving more than one organization. By contrast, firms that grow on their own by introducing new products or expanding into new markets are pursuing *internal growth,* also known as *organic growth*. Internal growth occurs without partnering with another organization.

Diversification is typically an external growth initiative achieved via a merger or acquisition, whereas market penetration, market extension and new product development are often accomplished through internal expansion. Like diversification, alliances and integration initiatives are typically achieved via external growth in partnership with other organizations.

Vertical Integration

Integration strategies may be either *vertical* or *horizontal*. Firms can integrate vertically by acquiring or developing their own sources of supply (known as *backward integration*) or by acquiring or developing their own distributors or retailers (known as *forward integration*). The two major motives driving vertical integration are the desire for (1) increased control over the channel of distribution, and (2) operational efficiencies.

Coca-Cola altered its vertically integrated business strategy of producing, bottling, and distributing its beverages in-house in 2016. Coke divested its asset-heavy operations like manufacturing and distribution by means of franchising to long-time business partners such as both North Carolina and Alabama based Coca-Cola Bottling Cos. to focus its efforts on satisfying changing consumer tastes. Prior to the divestment, Coca Cola was a completely vertically integrated firm, manufacturing, bottling and distributing its own beverages.[76]

Archer Daniels Midland is an integrated producer and processor of grain products, owning production at the farm level, intermediate processing into ingredients, and final processing into finished goods for sale at retail and foodservice establishments. Another example of a vertically integrated firm is Chevron. We know from the last chapter that Chevron is involved in every aspect of the petroleum industry, from exploration and production to transportation, refining and retailing to the final consumer.

Horizontal Integration

When a firm acquires one of its competitors, it is pursuing *horizontal integration*. This initiative has been very common in certain industries such as publishing, banking, accounting, telecommunications, and food. Industries that are experiencing a great deal of horizontal integration are going through what is known as *industry consolidation*. The aftermath of industry consolidation is fewer and much larger competitors. Because of their impact on competition and antitrust laws, horizontal mergers in the United States are subject to close levels of scrutiny and require approval by the FTC (Federal Trade Commission).

An example of a horizontal merger is the Charter Communications acquisition of Time Warner Cable in 2016 for $65.5 billion. After the FTC denied the merger of Comcast and Time Warner in 2015, Charter Communications swooped in to acquire the cable provider. With this merger, Charter becomes the second-largest broadband provider with 19.4 million users and the third largest cable television provider with 17.4 million customers. Charter agreed to many government imposed regulations as contingencies to the FTC approving the deal, including imposing no data caps on broadband users, who can run up big bills when watching online videos, and not charging companies, like Netflix, extra to connect to Charter customers for the next seven years.[77]

An illustration of the integration strategies is shown in Figure 3-7.

Strategic Alliances, Joint Ventures

A *strategic alliance* is a broad term encompassing many forms of cooperative agreement between two or more organizations. *Joint ventures* are a specific kind of strategic alliance with equity contributions (if appropriate) from partners to form a third, separate entity that stands alone for a specified time period. The two or more sponsoring firms establishing the joint venture share ownership rights in the new entity.

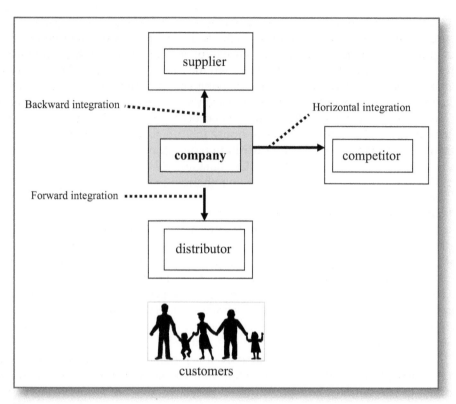

Figure 3-7
Integration Strategies

Strategic alliances and joint ventures are increasingly common and important ways to achieve growth. Many companies have relied on joint ventures to enter new countries and markets. In 2015, Macy's formed a joint venture with Chinese e-commerce retailer, Alibaba, to operate in China. The venture has allowed for Macy's to sell in China through Chinese retailer Fung Retailing Ltd. Alibaba launched an exclusive online flagship store for Macy's in Tmall Global in late 2015 making Macy's the first American department store to join Alibaba's Tmall Global. This partnership has enabled Macy's brands to reach millions of Chinese consumers by leveraging Alibaba's data-driven infrastructure. Alibaba Group CEO Daniel Zhang stated: "Macy's exclusive Tmall Global flagship store is a major win for consumers across China. It reinforces Tmall Global's status as the premiere solution for brands and retailers in their strategic online presence and direct engagement with customers in China."[78]

Strategic alliances are especially attractive in certain industries such as pharmaceuticals, automobiles, and computers. The alliances are driven by increasing cost pressures, shorter product life cycles, and the forces of global competition. The cost-sharing of a partnership may improve the cost structures of the cooperating businesses and/or allow a business to gain access to new geographic markets or introduce new products. Another key advantage is speed. Alliances typically allow a company to achieve growth much faster than the alternative of internal development.

Alliances tend to work well for firms whose products or geographic markets are *complementary* rather than *overlapping*. For example, professional networking website, LinkedIn, recently formed an alliance with the global business consulting firm, Ernst & Young (EY), to help companies around the world fully realize and utilize their technology, networks, and sales techniques. This strategic alliance will be a blending of EY's professional expertise and LinkedIn's technology with social media as the main driver for building relationships with buyers. EY will also integrate LinkedIn's Sales Navigator feature into its own day-to-day operations that provide tens of thousands of EY employees with the product.[79]

Types of Strategic Initiatives: Differentiators

Another element of strategy is *differentiators*, or how the firm distinguishes itself from competitors in a positive and attractive way. An insightful model for understanding different ways to differentiate was developed by Michael Porter, professor and author of several important strategy books.[80] According to Porter, organizations need to pursue a competitive advantage in essentially one of two ways: by establishing a position of either *cost leadership* or *differentiation*. *Competitive advantage* comes from creating customer value and we know that customer value comes from offering a product with equivalent benefits at a lower price or unique benefits that more than offset a higher price.

The scope of competitive advantage may be realized either on a broad, mass-market basis or by focusing on a narrow market niche. These two dimensions—scope of advantage and type of advantage—are used to identify what Porter calls *generic strategies* for differentiating and competing in any business. Figure 3-8 shows the generic strategies.

The ability to establish a *cost leadership* position rests on the organization's ability to be more efficient than competitors and serve customers at a lower per-unit cost. Having this low-cost position allows the firm to charge a lower price (if it chooses to do so) and still generate a healthy profit margin. Southwest Airlines is a good example

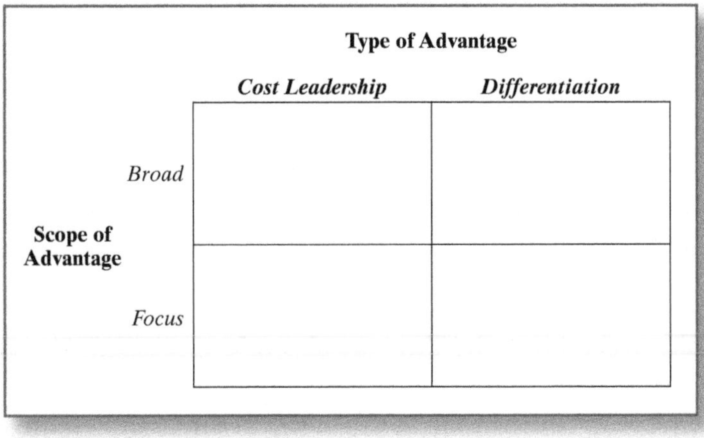

Figure 3-8
Porter's Generic Strategies

of a company that has established a very tight cost structure and passed that on to consumers in the form of lower airfares. Southwest has succeeded with a focused cost leadership strategy. Similarly, as noted in Figure 3-3, IKEA prides itself on offering inexpensive but stylish and innovative furniture. IKEA's low cost structure allows it to offer quality furniture and a unique shopping experience at a lower price to consumers.

A *differentiation* strategy pursues competitive advantage in a different way, by producing products and services perceived to be unique in some way. Uniqueness is typically thought of in terms of product features but can actually be derived from any number of sources, including product or service benefits, quality, convenience, reliability, safety, a special warranty, after-sale service, or a trendy image from successful marketing. When a product attains a position of uniqueness, customers are often willing to pay more for it. Customers perceive the extra value to be worth the extra price. For example, a Mercedes has a much higher price tag than a Honda. But the perceived superior performance of Mercedes makes the added price worthwhile to some customers. Ritz Carlton is a hotel chain that has successfully differentiated itself from other chains, and as a result is able to charge more for its rooms. Despite higher room rates, customer value remains high because of the perceived added benefits of staying at Ritz Carlton.

Stuck in the Middle

While advances in technology and changes in competition have created opportunities for firms to compete on both a low cost basis and on differentiation, one must still heed Porter's warnings about winding up "stuck in the middle." Failure to achieve one of the generic strategies leaves a company stuck in the middle—with no competitive advantage and below average performance. As mentioned in Chapter 2, A&P was once the nation's oldest and largest supermarket chain, owner of both Pathmark and Super Fresh. After years of decline and being stuck in the middle, A&P went out of business in 2015. Competition from high-end supermarkets like Wegmans and mass merchants like Wal-Mart and Target eroded A&P's market share.

So far our discussion of strategic initiatives and the elements of strategy has focused on ways to grow the business. This is not surprising since most organizations have a strong bias to continually grow and improve performance—to achieve greater productivity, more sales, a larger share of the market, and higher profits, and for publicly-held companies to constantly strive to enhance shareholder value. Strategy is the means to achieve these growth goals. It is important to note, however, that not all performance improvement strategies necessarily involve growth.

Retrenchment

Firms can attempt to improve performance not only through growth, but also by reducing their expenses and controlling their asset base. Efforts to cut expenses and/or reduce assets are known as *retrenchment* or *consolidation* strategies. These strategies were a common way that firms tried to build shareholder value and please the investment community in the 1990s. But there are also risks associated with these strategies. Let's examine different types of retrenchment.

Cost-Cutting

With oil prices at historically low levels in 2016, many large oil companies initiated job cuts for 2016 and 2017. British Petroleum (BP) proposed 4,000 job cuts in addition to the 4,000 jobs it cut after its massive oil spill in the Gulf of Mexico in 2010. Chevron proposed cuts of 6,000 to 7,000 jobs, as did Royal Dutch Shell (6,500 proposed job cuts by 2016), French oil producer, Total S.A. (2,000 proposed cuts by 2017), and Norwegian oil producer, Statoil A.S.A. (5,000 total cuts by 2016).[81]

Cost-cutting strategies are often reactive, that is, in response to declining organizational performance or companywide scandal. For example, in 2016 the EPA found that Volkswagen installed computer software in 11 million vehicles to cheat diesel-emissions tests. Stock prices for Volkswagen plummeted along with the company's public image. VW's Chief U.S. Executive, Michael Horn, resigned. Facing heavy fines and lawsuits, VW will likely need to implement retrenchment strategies to withstand the consequences of its own unethical behaviors.[82] These types of reactive cost-cutting strategies raise ethical concerns about employee rights and are not conducive to a healthy and productive corporate climate.

On the other hand, cost-cutting strategies need not be reactive nor involve employee layoffs. Johnson & Johnson, for example, continually seeks ways to reduce expenses through optimizing plant utilization, improving technology transfer between research and manufacturing, and redesigning or "reengineering" core and administrative processes.

The Risks of Downsizing

Researchers who have studied the relationship between layoffs and corporate performance have found mixed results. Downsizing may reduce costs and improve cash flow in the short-term but may also damage customer relationships and the morale of surviving employees. One study found companies that announced mass layoffs or repeated layoffs underperformed the market over a three-year period. A similar study found that 68% of firms using cost-cutting strategies did not achieve their profit goals for five years.[83] These studies suggest that layoffs cannot be a knee-jerk reaction during downturns. The firm's ability to create value depends not on short-term fixes but on serving customers, employees and owners over the long-term. Employee commitment to a shared purpose is not engendered when a company resorts to layoffs as its first line of defense.

Divestment and Liquidation

While cost-cutting focuses on the efficiency of operations, asset reduction focuses on eliminating assets. Two types of asset reduction are divestiture and liquidation. In a *divestiture* the firm reduces its asset base by selling off or divesting divisions and other parts of the organization. The divested division may continue as an ongoing concern but under different corporate ownership. *Liquidation* involves dissolving the business or a portion of it, and selling it for its tangible worth. It ceases to exist as an ongoing concern.

The U.S. white goods (i.e., major appliances) market has been dominated by three players—Whirlpool, GE, and Sweden's Electrolux—but a divestiture by one of the big three has upset the status quo. In Spring 2016, GE sold its white good appliance division to Chinese appliance manufacturer, Haier, for $5.4 billion. Haier, the global leader in appliances (in terms of unit sales), is known for its niche products such as compact refrigerators and air conditioning window units. Haier does not have a strong market presence in the United States, but this recent acquisition is a foot in the door. For GE, this divestiture is another indication of the conglomerate's intention to shed its non-core assets to focus on becoming a digital industrial company, one that is allocating resources to be able to write complex software codes to efficiently run its jet engine, power turbine and medical equipment divisions.[84]

Dean Foods divested its vegetable company, generating cash to invest in its core dairy business while at the same time exiting from a category affected by the volatility of the vegetable commodities markets. Another example of a divestment strategy involves PepsiCo, which spun off its foodservice unit (KFC, Taco Bell and Pizza Hut) in order to concentrate on the beverage and snack food industries with Pepsi and Frito Lay products. The foodservice businesses continue to operate under new ownership and a new name, Yum!Brands.

Blockbuster, once worth $5 billion with 60,000 locations worldwide and 9,000 employees in 2004, filed for bankruptcy in September 2010. After being bought by DISH Network in a 2011 stock auction, Dish could not use the former video rental titan and liquidated all remaining Blockbusters in 2013.[85]

In some industries, the opportunity to improve performance through cutting expenses or reducing the firm's asset base is increasingly difficult. Many companies have already "cut to the bone" so that further reductions can only undermine the business's ability to serve its customers. Even in an economy characterized by slow population growth, mature markets and cutthroat competition, the emphasis ultimately is on generating more revenue. This leads to the need to follow a growth strategy.

Stability

A final category of strategic initiatives seeks to neither grow nor cut but to stabilize operations. A successful company in a mature industry may seek to do no more than hold its competitive position. The goal of a stability strategy is to maintain the status quo. A harvest strategy is a type of stability strategy used in portfolio planning, which is described in Chapter 6. A *harvest* strategy attempts to hold a competitive position with minimal reinvestment in the business.

Table 3-9 identifies the different types of strategic initiatives and provides examples of each.

Table 3-9 Types of Strategic Initiatives

TYPE	STRATEGY	EXAMPLE
Expansion	Market Penetration	Samsung aggressively slashing its premium cellphone prices to regain market share in emerging markets.
	Market Development	The expansion of Ford Motor Company into Asia and Starbucks into Africa.
	Product Development	Tesla Motors predicts that all Tesla cars will be fully autonomous by 2018.
Diversification	Related Diversification	Nike's expansion from athletic *shoes* for track, then basketball and other sports, into athletic *apparel* and sports *equipment*.
	Unrelated Diversification	3M operates in office products, health care, industrial products, and other major markets

(continued)

Table 3-9 Continued

TYPE	STRATEGY	EXAMPLE
Alliances and Integration	Vertical Integration	Chevron's involvement in every aspect of the petroleum industry, from exploration and production to transportation, refining and retailing to the final consumer.
	Horizontal Integration	The merger of Charter Communications and Time Warner Cable.
	Strategic Alliance	The alliance formed between Ernst & Young and LinkedIn to integrate LinkedIn's Sales Navigator into EY's day-to-day operations. .
	Joint Venture	Macy's joint venture with Alibaba Group to enter China.
Retrenchment	Cost-Cutting	Oil companies cut jobs in response to historically low oil prices.
	Divestment	GE selling its white goods division to Haier to focus more on becoming a digital industrial company.
	Liquidation	Blockbuster being liquidated in 2013 by parent company, DISH Network.

CONCLUSION

Through an unwavering commitment to serve customers first and a steadfast focus on its corporate Credo, Johnson & Johnson is able to manage change from a base of stability. This is the paradox of change and constancy discussed throughout the chapter.

The organization's core values, mission, and vision help to establish an unambiguous and enduring focus. The process used to develop the mission, vision, and values, including the inclusion of stakeholder demands and needs, are as important as the ways that the issues are communicated. When the process is open and includes employees and other key stakeholders, understanding and commitment are enhanced.

Organizations pursue various types of strategies as a way to adapt to their changing circumstances. Most firms have a bias for growth, but other strategic initiatives are also important depending on the circumstances. Growth, retrenchment, integration and strategic alliances are explained in this chapter. A company's strategy needs to be a coordinated approach to the market, building on the elements of strategy discussed in this chapter—arenas, vehicles, differentiators, staging and economic logic.

After reading this chapter you should understand each of the following terms.

- Mission
- Credo
- Differentiators
- Vision Framework
- Market expansion or extension
- Strategic alliances
- Forward integration
- Divestiture
- Differentiation
- Stakeholders
- Sustainability
- Core Values
- Arenas
- Staging
- Market penetration

- Related diversification
- Horizontal acquisitions
- Retrenchment strategy
- Joint Venture
- Focus
- SASB
- Vision
- Vehicles
- Economic Logic
- Product development
- Unrelated or conglomerate diversification
- Backward integration
- Liquidation
- Cost Leadership
- Triple Bottom Line

DISCUSSION QUESTIONS

1. How are the concepts of vision, mission, core values and strategy related? How are they different?
2. Critique the following mission statement of the Harley Davidson company.

   "Fulfilling dreams of personal freedom is more than a phrase. It's our purpose and our passion. We bring a commitment of exceptional customer experiences to everything we do—from the innovation of our products to the precision of our manufacturing—culminating with our strong supplier and dealer networks."

3. Compare and contrast the core values of three leading pharmaceutical firms: Merck, Pfizer, and Johnson & Johnson. Use Johnson & Johnson's Credo, Merck's core values, and Pfizer's values, all found in this chapter.
4. Identify the key stakeholders that Johnson & Johnson must consider when considering strategic activities.
5. Select a company and evaluate its strategy using the five elements of strategy.
6. What are the advantages and disadvantages of strategic alliances compared to internal expansion strategies?
7. Check Merck's website to see if its vision and mission statements have changed. If so, what might account for the changes?

EXPERIENTIAL EXERCISE

Building and Evaluating a Mission Statement. Select a company or organization that you know well (e.g., your university or your place of employment). Use the table below as a guide to write your own mission statement for the organization. Then obtain a copy of the organization's actual mission. How does your mission compare to the actual? Which do you think is better? Why?

COMPONENT	DESCRIPTIONS (KEY WORDS) OF MISSION
Value Creation	
Principal products and services	
Geographical area	
Philosophies	
Self-image	
Public image	

ENDNOTES

1. "Johnson & Johnson 2015 Annual Report." March 2016. Web Accessed 22 April 2016.
2. Collins, J. C., and J. L. Porras, "Building Your Company's Vision," *Harvard Business Review* (September-October 1996): 65.
3. "World's Most Admired Companies: 2016" *Fortune*. Accessed 21 April 2016. http://fortune.com/worlds-most-admired-companies/
4. Johnson & Johnson, "Credo History," www.jnj.com, accessed March 7, 2006.
5. Johnson & Johnson, "Another J&J Recall," http://www.fiercepharma.com/story/another-jj-recall-another-hit-jjs-image/2011-01-18, accessed February 1, 2011.
6. Susan Berfield, Jef Feeley, Margaret Cronin Fisk "Johnson & Johnson Has a Baby Powder Problem." *Bloomberg*. 30 March 2016. Web. 27 April 2016.
7. Johnson & Johnson, "Credo History," www.jnj.com, accessed March 7, 2006.
8. Collins, J.C., and J. L. Porras, op cit., 65.
9. Quigley, J., "Vision: How Leaders Develop It, Share It, and Sustain It," *Business Horizons* (September-October 1994): 39.
10. Peter Bright "Microsoft has a new mission statement, and it's basically the same as its old one" *arstechnica*. 25 June 2015. Web. 25 April 2016. http://arstechnica.com/information-technology/2015/06/microsoft-has-a-new-mission-statement-and-its-basically-the-same-as-its-old-one/

11. Mike Barton, Craig Stedman Timeline: The Gates era at Microsoft *ComputerWorld*. 24 June 2008. Web. 28 April 2016. http://www.computerworld.com/article/2534379/microsoft-windows/timeline--the-gates-era-at-microsoft.html
12. Gates, Bill. "Internal Memo: The Internet Tidal Wave." *United States Justice Department*. 26 May 1995. Web. 28 April 2016. https://www.justice.gov/sites/default/files/atr/legacy/2006/03/03/20.pdf
13. Ackoff, R.L., "Mission Statements," *Planning Review* 15, no. 4 (July–August 1987): 30–31.
14. Mosner, D., "Mission Improbable," *Across the Board* (January 1995) : 1.
15. Pearce, J.A., III, and F. David, "Corporate Mission Statements and the Bottom Line," *Academy of Management Executive* 1, no. 2 (1987): 109–116.
16. "Mission, Vision, and Purpose." Pfizer, Inc. Accessed 18 April 2016. http://pfizercareers.com/career-types/mission-purpose-values
17. Under Armour Mission & Values, http://www.underarmour.jobs/why-choose-us/mission-values/, accessed September 8, 2016.
18. Bennis, W., and B. Nanus. *Leaders: The Strategies for Taking Charge*. New York: Harper & Row Publishers, 1985, 103.
19. J. Kouzes and B. Z. Posner, "Envisioning Your Future: Imagining Ideal Scenarios," *The Futurist*, 1996, Vol. 30.

20. Truskie, S. D. *Leadership in High-Performance Organizational Cultures.* Westport, CT: Quorum Books, 1999, 66

21. Collins, J. C., and J. I. Porras, "Building Your Company's Vision," *Harvard Business Review* (September–October 1996): 69.

22. Merck & Co. Inc., "Our Values", www.merck.com, Accessed April 18, 2016.

23. Ibid, 73.

24. Bennis, W., and B. Nanus. *Leaders: The Strategies for Taking Charge.* New York: Harper & Row Publishers, 1985, 103.

25. Ibid, 102–103.

26. Toffler, B. *Final Accounting: Ambition, Greed, and the Fall of Arthur Andersen.* New York: Broadway Books, 2003.

27. Wikipedia, The Free Encyclopedia, "Arthur Andersen," www.en.wikipedia.org, accessed March 9, 2006.

28. Friedman, M. 1970. The social responsibility of business is to increase its profits. New York Times Magazine, 13(1970), 32–33.

29. Freeman, R. Edward (1984). Strategic Management: A stakeholder approach. Boston: Pitman.

30. Denning, S. (2015, February 05). Salesforce CEO Slams 'The World's Dumbest Idea': Maximizing Shareholder Value. http://www.forbes.com/sites/stevedenning/2015/02/05/salesforce-ceo-slams-the-worlds-dumbest-idea-maximizing-shareholder-value/#70f3a9e35255. Retrieved August 09, 2016.

31. BSR Stakeholder Engagement Consulting Services (2014). http://gsvc.org/wp-content/uploads/2014/11/Stakeholders-Identification-and-Mapping.pdf. Accessed June 20, 2016.

32. Ibid.

33. The World Commission on Environment and Development. 1987. Our Common Future. Oxford, UK: Oxford University Press.

34. Esquer, J., Velazquez, L. & Munguia, N. 2008. "Perceptions of core elements for sustainability management systems." Management Decision, 46(7): 1027–1038.

35. Velazquez, L.E., Esquer, J., & Munguia, N.E. 2011. Sustainable learning organizations. The Learning Organization, 18(1): 36–44.

36. Byrch, C., Kearins, K., Milne, M. & Morgan, R., 2007. "Sustainable what? A cognitive approach to understanding sustainable development." Qualitative Research in Accounting & Management, 4(1): 26–52.

37. Hart, S.L. & Milstein, M.B. 2003. "Creating sustainable value." Academy of Management Executive, 17(2): 56–67.

38. Ibid.

39. Robins, F. 2006. "The challenge of TBL: A responsibility to whom?" Business and Society Review, 111 (1): 1–14.

40. Elkington, J. 1994. "Towards the sustainable corporation: Win-win-win business strategies for sustainable development." California Management Review 36(2): 90–100.

41. Elkington, J. 1997. Cannibals with Forks: The Triple Bottom Line of 21st Century Business. Oxford UK: Capstone Publishing.

42. Desjardins, J. 2010. "Will the future be sustainable?" Business Ethics Quarterly, 20(4): 723–725.

43. Rice, M. 2004. Bottoming out. CPA Australia, November 16, http://www.capaustralia.com.au/cps/rde/xchg/, accessed September 20, 2010.

44. Spence, M., Gherib, J.B.B., & Bivolé, V.O. 2011. "Sustainable entrepreneurship: Is entrepreneurial will enough? A north-south comparison."Journal of Business Ethics, 99: 335–367.

45. Carrigan, M., Moraes, C., & Leek, S. 2011. "Fostering responsible communities: A community social marketing approach on sustainable living." Journal of Business Ethics, 100: 515–534.

46. Escobar, L., & Vredenburg, H. 2011. "Multinational Oil Companies and the Adoption of Sustainable Development: A Resource-Based and Institutional Theory Interpretation of Adoption Heterogeneity." Journal of Business Ethics, 98(1), 39–65.

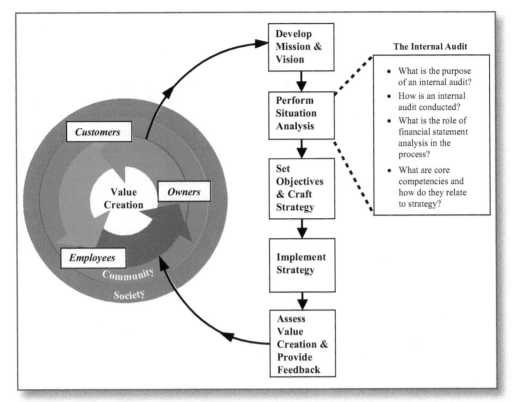

Figure 4-1
The Strategic Management Framework

may also be used to alter or redefine the organization's mission, vision, and objectives. The external audit is discussed in Chapter 5. It focuses on monitoring and evaluating the forces and factors outside the organization, in the firm's external environment. The purpose of this chapter is to describe a four-step process for performing an internal audit. By applying this process to 3M and other companies, we will demonstrate the internal audit process and answer each of the questions listed in Figure 4-1.

THE INTERNAL AUDIT PROCESS

As shown in Figure 4-1, an organization bases its strategic choices on a variety of considerations, one of the most important of which is its understanding of its own strengths and weaknesses. This understanding is a result of the organization's internal audit process. Using this information, the organization can leverage its strengths to take advantage of emerging growth opportunities, to counteract the effects of external threats, or to attempt to overcome or improve upon its weaknesses.

Identifying a list of strengths and weaknesses for a firm is a relatively easy task but also a relatively useless one from a strategic management perspective. This type of information tends to be too superficial and unfocused for decision-making purposes. The real challenge is to determine a workable number of *competitively relevant strengths and weaknesses*. This is not always an easy or obvious task. In fact, it is generally agreed in the strategic management field that the development of tools for analyzing the external environment has proceeded more rapidly than the development of tools for the internal audit.[2] By following a systematic process of internal assessment, however, these strengths and weaknesses can be determined.

Figure 4-2 provides an overview of a four-stage process for identifying an organization's competitively relevant strengths and weaknesses. The process requires managers to assess the organization's current and past performance at creating value, analyze the organization's value chain activities, understand its distinctive competencies, and using this information, determine its strengths and weaknesses. Each step in the process is explained in the following sections. 3M is used as an example to illustrate applications of the process.

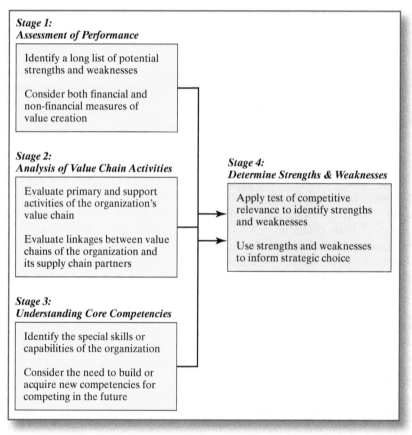

Figure 4-2
The Internal Audit Process

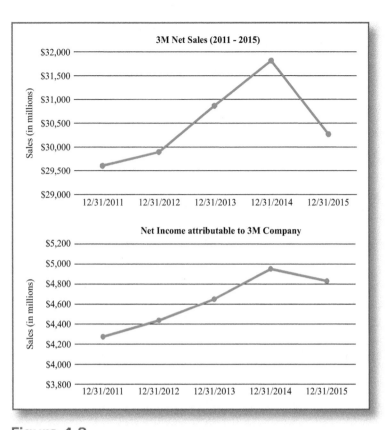

Figure 4-3
Trend Analysis of 3M Sales and Net Income from 2011 to 2015
Source: 3M Annual Report 2015. http://s2.q4cdn.com/974527301/files/doc_financials/2015/ar/2015_3M_Annual_Report.pdf. Accessed 25 April 2016.

REVENUE BY GEOGRAPHIC SEGMENT

These revenue figures for product segments and geographic markets could be compared to prior years (a trend analysis) to determine changes over time. We could conduct a similar analysis of operating income for 3M. These comparisons would help us to discover any potential strengths or weaknesses in its underlying business segments. Similarly, using the three-part ROE analysis we can evaluate more precisely the profitability of 3M.

Year	Efficiency	Effectiveness	Leverage	= ROE
2011	14.46%	0.96	1.99	27.6%
2012	14.86%	0.91	1.99	26.9%
2013	15.09%	0.92	1.92	26.6%
2014	15.57%	0.98	2.12	32.4%
2015	15.96%	0.95	2.58	39.1%

Product Segment	Net Sales (millions)	% of Worldwide Sales
Industrial	$ 10,328	34.1%
Safety and Graphics	$ 5,515	18.2%
Health Care	$ 5,420	17.9%
Electronics and Energy	$ 5,220	17.2%
Consumer	$ 4,422	14.6%
Corporate and Unallocated	$ 1	0.0%
Elimination of Dual Credit	$ (632)	−2.1%
Total	$ 30,274	100%

3M Revenue by Geographic Segment (2015)

Geographic Area	Net Sales (millions)	% of Worldwide Sales
United States	$ 12,049	39.8%
Asia Pacific	$ 9,041	29.9%
Europe, Middle East & Africa	$ 6,228	20.6%
Latin America/ Canada	$ 2,982	9.9%
Other Unallocated	$ (26)	−0.1%
Worldwide	$ 30,274	100%

Figure 4-4
3M Revenue by Product Segment (2015)
Source: 3M Annual Report 2015. http://s2.q4cdn.com/974527301/files/doc_financials/2015/ar/
2015_3M_Annual_Report.pdf. Accessed 25 April 2016.

3M's ROE has been trending up since it bottomed out at about 24% in 2009, after the recession. Efficiency has improved each year for the last five years, a good sign for 3M, indicating that the company is retaining a higher percentage of its total sales at the end of each year. Even in 2015 when 3M sales declined, the company's efficiency indicator (net profit margin) continued to increase. Effectiveness has held stable for the past five years. For every dollar of assets, 3M is generating an average of $0.94 of revenue for the past five years. Finally, 3M increased its leverage from 2011 to 2015. A larger leverage indicator signals that a company is relying more on debt to finance its assets.[4] In summary, 3M has increased its ROE over the five year period. It is interesting to note, however, that the overall increase in ROE is driven more by a leverage effect than by the improvement in efficiency. 3M should continue to seek operating efficiency, increase its effectiveness indicator, and keep an eye on its dependence on external debt.

In addition to these financial analyses, we would want to analyze market share trends, market research studies, customer and employee satisfaction studies, and other meaningful indicators of the heath of the company. In 2015, 3M cut 354 jobs after averaging roughly 1,800 new hires each year for the previous four years. Especially given the job cuts, data on employee morale would be valuable information for 3M to track when conducting its internal audit.

Thus, a Stage 1 assessment of 3M in 2016 would reveal financial strengths, such as strong operational margins and an improving return on equity, and financial weaknesses, including a steep decline in sales and an increased amount of debt financing. Non-financial information, like changes in market share and changes in employee rates of satisfaction will be critical indicators for 3M.

STAGE 2: ANALYSIS OF VALUE CHAIN ACTIVITIES AND LINKAGES

The *value chain*, a concept developed by Michael Porter, is an important tool for strategic planning purposes. It identifies the activities performed internally by a firm, and the relationships between those activities. Because no two firms are exactly alike (firms configure themselves differently), each firm's value chain is unique. In Stage 2 of the internal audit process a value chain analysis is performed in two parts: (1) an internal evaluation of the firm's value chain activities, costs, and profit margins, and (2) an evaluation of the relationships between the value chains of the firm and its supply chain partners. Before we discuss this two-part analysis, let's further examine the concept of the value chain.

The Value Chain

The *value chain* is a tool to help managers visualize and analyze an organization's value creating activities. A general example is shown in Figure 4-5. The value chain emphasizes the fact that multiple and varied activities, performed in a coordinated and efficient manner, are necessary to create value for the firm's customers.[5] According to Porter, *competitive advantage* is a result of the value a firm is able to create for its customers that exceeds the firm's cost of creating it. Superior customer value stems from value chain activities that allow the firm to offer lower prices than competitors for equivalent benefits or provide unique or differentiated benefits that more than offset a higher price.[6] These generic strategies—low cost or differentiation (discussed in Chapter 3)—are a direct result of the activities performed by the firm in its value chain.

Primary Activities
Value chain activities can be divided broadly into primary and support activities, as shown in Figure 4-5. The *primary activities* relate directly to the production, distribution and sale of the product or service. Typical examples include inbound logistics,

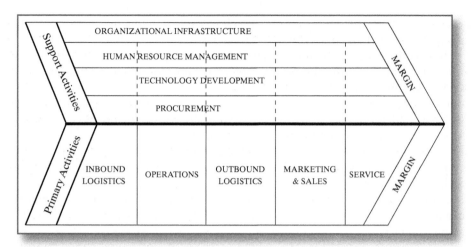

Figure 4-5
The Value Chain
Reprinted from *The Competitive Advantage of Nations* (1990), by Michael Porter,
by permission of Simon and Schuster Inc.

operations or manufacturing, outbound logistics, marketing and sales. A strict time sequencing of these activities does not necessarily apply. For example, note in Figure 4-5 that marketing occurs after production. In reality, market-focused organizations base decisions about product design, production and distribution on market information to achieve efficient and effective production of products that will satisfy customer needs.

Support Activities

Support activities are required to perform the primary activities. Examples of support activities include financing (raising the capital needed for operations), human resource management, technology development, and procurement of materials and supplies.

Let's consider an example of value chain activities using Starbucks. The world's largest coffee house with over 23,000 locations worldwide, Starbucks has a massive value chain to ensure that its customers enjoy a superior coffee experience.[7] Starbucks sources its unroasted coffee beans from coffee plantations in Africa, Asia, and Latin America and has them delivered to six regional Starbucks roasting plants and smaller co-manufacturers around the world.[8] Inbound logistics, the first step in Starbuck's value chain, is critical as fresh beans must be shipped thousands of miles and arrive on time and according to quality specifications. For Starbucks, inbound logistics set the tone for rest of the value chain.

After the "green" or unroasted coffee beans are received, they must be roasted, processed, packaged and transported to distribution centers across the globe. Each of these activities is part of the value chain of Starbucks. Starbucks owns the majority of its massive 300,000 square foot regional distribution centers, with third-party logistics companies managing the rest. Starbucks owns two large warehouses for inventory and supplies, and employs smaller warehouses or central distribution centers (CDCs) in its value chain. As well as carrying and distributing coffee beans,

CDCs carry dairy products, baked goods and paper items, and frequently make deliveries via truck fleets to Starbucks retail stores, retail outlets (e.g., GIANT Food Stores, Bed Bath & Beyond, and Staples), and wholesale buyers, like BJ's Wholesale Club. Starbucks' outbound logistics team made over 70,000 deliveries per week to all Starbucks outlets across the world in 2014.[9]

Different retail vendors require different delivery methods and protocols. Specific time periods are provided by each individual vendor to Starbucks during which time deliveries must be made in order to minimize their handling and inventory accumulation. These vendors also demand orders that are correct, complete and in proper condition, so that their retail customers may be served. Outbound logistics is another critical component of the Starbucks value chain.

Starbucks relies on supply chain data management metrics to determine what provides the most added value to its supply chain partners and customers. Starbucks has identified four high-level criteria that will create a balanced supply chain: (1) safety in operations, (2) service measured by on-time delivery and order fill rates, (3) total end-to-end supply chain costs, and (4) enterprise savings. The final criterion refers to cost savings originating from activities not directly associated with logistics, like marketing and R&D.[10]

Cross-Functional Linkages

The Starbucks example shows that value chain activities are intertwined and highly interdependent, characterized by a network of activities, connected by linkages. These cross-functional linkages occur when the performance of one activity affects the cost or effectiveness of the other activities.

Cross-functional linkages create tradeoffs between activities, underscoring the need to focus on the efficiency and effectiveness of *the whole set of activities*, not just one activity, a concept long-recognized in the field of logistics. For instance, higher design and materials costs may allow creation of a more reliable product that breaks down less frequently, not only lowering costs of after-the-sale service but also enhancing overall customer value by minimizing customer downtime.

Starbucks has invested in supply chain technologies in order to respond in real-time to changing consumer tastes and preferences. Starbucks purchased Oracle's automated manufacturing information system, GEMMS, to monitor real-time demand, allowing production plans and schedules to be developed and modified as needed. This is a behind-the-scenes investment for Starbucks but has a direct impact on the customer's experience.[11] In Fall 2015, Starbucks also introduced delivery for consumers who need their coffee fix but cannot get to their local Starbucks. This business venture takes their value chain one step further—to the consumer's doorstep. Starbucks CEO Howard Schultz touted this new venture in his keynote address at the 2015 Council of Supply Chain Management Professionals (CSCMP) Annual Conference. Schultz emphasized the importance of speed and innovation in today's fast-paced, technology-driven supply chains.[12]

Linkages also mean that activities need to be coordinated. In order to provide on-time delivery of products to customers, all aspects of the value chain must function together smoothly. A production slowdown at one plant, created by an inbound logistics or other supply problem, has a ripple effect on inventory and service levels throughout the system. Coordinated activities improve overall quality, reduce cycle time and create potential competitive advantage.

The value chain also recognizes the interdependence, not only of activities performed by one firm, but also of the value chains of multiple firms. An individual company's value chain for competing in a particular industry is embedded in a larger stream of activities that can be termed the value system. The *value system* includes suppliers to the firm's value chain (also known as *upstream* activities) and may also include distributors who handle the product on the way to the ultimate buyer (known as *downstream* activities). One firm's value chain often represents a supplier to another firm's value chain, who use the products marketed by the first firm to perform value-creating activities of its own, as we have seen in the Starbucks example presented above. Competitive advantage is therefore not only a function of how well a firm integrates and coordinates its own activities, but also how well systems of firms integrate and coordinate activities. This philosophy is the foundation of what we now term *supply chain management*.

Internal Evaluation of Value Chain

As stated above, Stage 2 of the internal audit entails a two-part value chain analysis. In part one, the firm focuses internally on each discrete activity, function or business process it performs and attempts to determine the costs of performing the activity/ process versus the value it creates. The purpose of this step is for the firm to understand its *cost structure*, that is, the costs associated with each activity, and its profit engines, that is, where in the value chain profit margins are realized. A firm must especially understand its central costs, or *cost drivers*, as Porter calls them,[13] and monitor changes over time in these areas. A firm can lose its competitive advantage and ability to create value when even just one key value chain activity is not functioning properly.

An example of this is the big box retailer, Target. The third largest retailer in the U.S. in 2015 has lost sales due to problems with inventory management. Industry analysts believe that Target's issues originate from its over-reliance on external distributors,[14] making Target vulnerable to supply short-falls. Target's foray into e-commerce to compete with mega-online retailer, Amazon, has further complicated its problems. This move has been disruptive to its traditional supply chains and has exacerbated Target's problems with stock-outs. Target, however, has started to take steps in the right direction. The retailer reported 40% fewer stock-outs during the 2015 holiday season and in 2016, it hired a former Amazon executive, Arthur Valdez, to serve as a chief supply chain expert to modernize its logistics by blending a customized e-commerce approach to its inventory distribution system.[15]

The internal value chain analysis includes not only a focus on discrete activities and processes but also on the *cross-functional linkages* between those activities and processes within the firm. Understanding these linkages is critical because the performance of one activity has spillover effects for other activities, and may directly relate to the costs of later activities in the value chain. For instance, Skil Corporation, a maker of power tools, was able to cut its cost structure by streamlining the number of power drills in its product line, and redesigning the tools to reduce the number

Table 4-3 A Comparison of Airlines (2015 Fiscal Year)

COMPANY NAME	REVENUES (IN MILLIONS)	GROSS MARGIN	NET INCOME	PROFIT MARGIN	EBITDA	EBITDA (% OF REVENUES)
American Airlines Group Inc	$40,990	88.12%	$7,610	18.57%	$6,944	16.94%
Delta Air Lines, Inc. (DE)	$40,704	58.00%	$4,526	11.12%	$9,438	23.19%
United Continental Holdings Inc	$37,864	57.11%	$7,340	19.39%	$4,907	12.96%
Southwest Airlines Co	$19,820	69.60%	$2,181	11.00%	$4,575	23.08%

of parts in each drill and to maximize the interchangeability of parts. In this case, a change in one value chain activity (product design) directly affected the costs of later activities (manufacturing and service).

The Case of Southwest Airlines

Southwest Airlines is an example of a company that knows its cost drivers and effectively manages its value chain to create value and a competitive advantage. Table 4-3 shows that Southwest is a relatively small player in the airline industry—its revenues are less than half of most of the larger carriers. Despite its size, or perhaps in part because of it, Southwest is consistently one of the top financial performers in the industry. The table shows that Southwest's EBITDA as a percentage of revenues is one of the highest in industry, which means that the low cost carrier is efficiently managing its operations.

As we will see in Chapter 10, one of the most important factors accounting for the success of Southwest is its *cost leadership* strategy. Southwest has been able to control its cost structure by building a value chain expressly designed to eliminate what it considers to be unnecessary value chain activities and to minimize the costs associated with those activities considered essential. Its strategy is based on short haul, high frequency, point-to-point flights. To cut costs, it relies on a single type of aircraft (Boeing 737), serves no in-flight meals, uses reusable plastic boarding passes, offers no baggage transfers, and turns its flights around faster than other competitors.[16] Southwest creates value by virtue of its ability to manage the cost drivers in its value chain.

Evaluation of Supply Chain Management

The second part of the value chain analysis conducted in Stage 2 is an evaluation of the relationships among firms in the supply chain. As we described above, a firm's value chain is embedded in a larger system of activities that includes the value chains of the firm's suppliers and "downstream" customers or partners.[17] The firm's

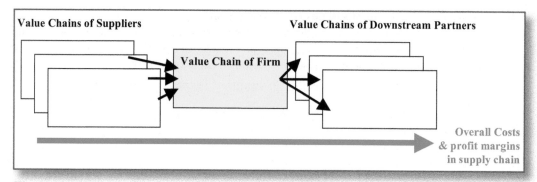

Figure 4-6
Relationships in the Supply Chain
Reprinted from *The Competitive Advantage of Nations* (1990), by permission of Simon & Schuster Inc.

cost competitiveness depends not only on the costs of internally performed activities (its own value chain) but also on the costs passed on to the firm by its suppliers, distributors, buyers, and other partners (the value chains of supply chain partners). These relationships are shown in Figure 4-6.

Value creation and competitive advantage are enhanced or undermined, therefore, not only by how well a firm integrates and coordinates its own activities, but also how well systems of firms integrate and coordinate activities. That is, value creation also depends on *supply chain management*. Amazon is a leader in supply chain management. The online retailer has an enormous national network of order fulfilment centers and sortation centers. In 2014, Amazon implemented a policy of sorting packages on each pallet by the destination zip code and then using the United States Postal Service rather than more expensive carriers like FedEx or UPS for delivery. This is just one way Amazon has taken greater control of its outbound shipping costs.[18]

The outcome of Stage 2 of the internal audit process is a thorough understanding of the firm's internal cost structure and the cost structure of the entire supply chain. This information is critical for achieving the purpose of an internal audit—to determine the firm's competitively relevant strengths and weaknesses.

STAGE 3: UNDERSTANDING CORE COMPETENCIES

In Stage 1 of the internal audit process we evaluate the recent performance of the firm in both financial and non-financial terms to determine potential strengths and weaknesses. In Stage 2 we analyze value chain activities to determine and manage the cost structure and the cost drivers of the entire supply chain. These steps are necessary but not sufficient for a complete internal audit. In fact, if we were to stop here we may miss the real underlying strength of the firm.

To complete the audit, we must understand the special skills, knowledge, and capabilities of the firm, in other words, its *core competencies*. A firm's core competencies cannot be understood by analyzing its financial statements and they may be missed in a value chain analysis. Core competencies are not assets on a balance sheet or activities in a value chain. Core competencies tend to reside in people and processes. In their seminal work on the topic, Hamel and Prahalad define *core competencies* as the collective learning, skills and capabilities of the firm, especially relating to the coordination of diverse skills and the integration of multiple streams of technology.[19] Some authors distinguish between core competencies and *distinctive competencies*.[20] This distinction seems unnecessary and for our purposes the two terms are used interchangeably.* A competence must be something that the firm knows and does well relative to competitors. If it cannot be the basis of a competitive advantage in value creation, it is not considered a competence.

Consider a few examples. American Express is the world's largest credit card issuer and it operates the world's largest travel network. If you are an American Express cardholder, it may come as no surprise that AmEx's core competency is its service. AmEx's direct relationship with millions of customers, businesses, and merchants worldwide allows them to offer unique rewards and benefits that no competitor can match. What makes American Express different from its competitors is the ability to issue cards directly. Unlike AmEx, Visa and MasterCard need financial institutions and banks to issue their credit cards. Similarly, McDonald's invented the fast food industry. It was also the first to introduce innovations such as the drive-though window, a breakfast menu, and kids' meals. The core competence is not the kids' meal but the bundle of skills and knowledge that underlie McDonald's ability to develop successful new products and services over many years.

Companies exhibit many different types of core competencies and world class companies build and exploit several competencies. Examples include expertise in product design, an ability to identify and exploit opportunities for innovation, skills in developing and nurturing customer relationships, or the capability to provide superior after-sale service. In a particular industry, different firms often build reputations for competencies in different areas. For example, in financial services, special knowledge and skill bases have been developed by different companies in investment management, foreign exchange, risk management, and consumer banking.

To be considered a core competence, a skill must pass three tests according to Hamel and Prahalad:[21]

- The first test is *customer value*. A core competence must make a significant contribution to perceived customer benefits of the end product. It is part of the reason the customer chooses the product or service. For example, Honda's competence in engines provides customers with benefits such as superior fuel economy, fast acceleration, and less noise and vibration.
- Second, to qualify as a core competence, a capacity must provide *competitor differentiation*. This means that the skills are not held equally by competitors in the industry. By extension, this also means that the core competence is not easily replicated by other firms.

---

*The distinction made by some authors is that a core competence is something that a firm does well relative to other internal activities while a distinctive competence is something the firm does well relative to competitors. It is argued here that unless the competence is competitively relevant, it is not something on which to build strategy. A competence must have at least the potential for a competitive advantage to be considered important for strategic management purposes.

- The third test is *extendability*. This means that the competence provides potential access to a wide variety of markets. A competence may be used to leverage new opportunities in other markets. For example, Honda has used its competence in motors to enter the automobile, truck, and lawnmower markets.

The importance of core competencies for strategic management is a function of the potential competitive advantage they may provide for the firm. Core competencies are the roots of competitiveness, according to Hamel and Prahalad. Think of a tree as an analogy for a firm. "The trunk and major limbs are core products, the smaller branches are business units; the leaves, flowers, and fruit are the end products. The root system that provides nourishment, sustenance, and stability is the core competence. You can miss the strength of a firm by looking only at its end products, in the same way you miss the strength of the tree if you look only at its leaves."[22]

Thus, core competencies are important because they are key strengths that allow the firm to grow new products and expand into new markets. In turn, strategies may be used to build or acquire new core competencies.

There are two ways to think of any business according to Hamel and Prahalad—the core competence perspective and the strategic business unit (SBU) perspective. Most companies adopt the SBU perspective, though not necessarily by conscious choice. These firms build their corporate identity around market-focused entities, often called "strategic business units," rather than around core competencies. Hamel and Prahalad argue that it is "entirely appropriate to have a strong end-product focus in an organization, (but) this needs to be supplemented by an equally explicit core competence focus. A company must be viewed not only as a portfolio of products or services, but a portfolio of competencies as well."[23]

Firms are vulnerable to at least three risks when they ignore core competencies and focus exclusively on end products.[24] First is the danger of underinvestment in developing core competencies. A company focused only on end products tends to focus on competing today, and may fail to invest in developing new core competencies, the root system for competing in the future.

A second danger is imprisoned resources. A common problem with the SBU mentality of management is that SBU managers, accustomed to working independently of other SBUs, develop a proprietary attitude toward their resources and competencies. "The people who embody these competencies are seen as the sole property of the SBU in which they grew up… SBU managers are not only unwilling to lend their competence carriers but they may actually hide talent to prevent its redeployment in the pursuit of new opportunities."[25] In contrast the core competence perspective is built on resource-sharing and cross-functional teamwork.

A third risk of ignoring core competencies is bounded innovation. SBUs tend to pursue innovation opportunities within their predefined industry domains. This scope often limits innovation to marginal product line extensions, "new and improved" products, or geographic expansions. In contrast, the core competence approach seeks unbounded innovation that allows the firm to create entirely new industries or to rewrite the rules of industry success. Firms are encouraged to find ways to redeploy existing competencies and develop new ones in order to "create products customers need but have not yet even imagined."[26] Examples would include electric cars, mobile devices, and the Post-it Note. This type of innovation

	New	What new competencies will we need to protect and extend our position in current markets?	What new competencies would we need to participate in the most promising markets of the future?
Core Competence			
	Existing	How can we improve our current position by better leveraging our existing competencies?	What new products or services could we develop by creatively redeploying our current competencies?
		Existing	*New*

Product -Markets

Figure 4-7
The Core Competence Agenda

Reprinted from *Competing for the Future* (1994), by G. Hamel and C.K. Prahalad, by permission of Harvard Business Publishing.

emerges only when managers "take off their SBU blinders" and think beyond the confines of their immediate business.

Figure 4-7 is a framework for establishing a core competence agenda. The framework distinguishes between existing and new core competencies, and between existing and new product markets. Each cell in the matrix raises questions about growth opportunities relying on core competencies. The message inherent in the framework is to find new ways to exploit current competencies and to seek new competencies for competing in the future. New competencies may be developed internally over time, acquired via an acquisition or alliance with another company, or outsourced to suppliers or other strategic partners.

In Chaper 3, we mentioned a strategic alliance between LinkedIn and Ernst & Young, which combines their respective competencies. The partnership brings together the online platform of 400 million LinkedIn users with the professional expertise and data analytics of EY. The two organizations will help companies around the world develop deeper and more trusted customer relationships through the use of social media and data analytics. Also, EY will integrate the LinkedIn Sales Navigator tool into its business operations allowing for 10,000 EY employees to interact with the product every day.

Core Competencies and 3M

3M is a world class company and, as such, it has several core competencies. One of its competencies is its special ability to innovate based on its history of turning apparent failures into success and its corporate culture that nurtures entrepreneurial behavior. 3M has succeeded in part because of its ability to "turn lemons into lemonade". One of the company's first true successes came from a mistake. The company was founded in 1902 when five businessmen agreed to mine a mineral deposit for abrasives.[27] The deposits turned out to be hopelessly low-grade. Instead of panicking, 3M developed a new and improved sandpaper for automobile manufacturers in Detroit. Sandpaper, in its many varieties, has turned out to be a core product for 3M.

A similar example is the story of 3M's Post-it® Note.[28] Scientists at 3M were working on a new adhesive compound, which at first glance, seemed to be a total failure. The adhesive failed to pass any of the conventional 3M tests for tackiness and aggressive adhesion. Instead of dismissing the new compound as a mistake, the scientists began to consider its properties and potential market uses. One of its most interesting properties was that the adhesive was strong enough to hold papers together, but weak enough to not tear paper fibers when it was removed. One day while singing in his church choir, the answer came to 3M scientist Art Fry. The new compound could be used as a bookmark for his hymnal. The advantage was that the bookmark was "permanently temporary." It would never fall out on the floor and lose its place yet it could be easily removed and reused when necessary. From this initial insight the Post-it Note was born. Over the last two decades, the Post-it Product line has grown to include Post-it Flags, Post-it Memoboard, Post-it Notes and Cubes, Post-it Fax Notes, Post-it Easel Pads and Rolls, Post-it Notes in Business Card Size, Post-it Correction and Cover-up Tape, Post-it Dispensers and Organizers and more.[29]

Reflecting its emphasis on innovation, one of 3M's strategic goals is to generate 30 percent of total revenues each year from products that have been on the market for less than 4 years. This ability to innovate has differentiated 3M from its competitors and has been used to launch the company into a wide variety of new markets. In order to enter new markets and stay on the forefront of technological innovation, 3M invests heavily in research and development. From 2010 to 2015, 3M invested $16 billion to fund new projects, including the world's largest aperture trough (solar power collector) in 2012. 3M's dedication to R&D earned the company its 100,000th patent in 2014.[30]

3M's ability to innovate operates on a simple principle that no market or product is too small to be ignored. 3M believes that "nothing should be allowed to stand between our people and a brilliant idea that could make life easier, healthier, safer, and more productive for people everywhere." Using the analogy of the tree discussed earlier, "3M has adopted a policy of allowing people to sprout tiny twigs in response to problems and ideas. Most twigs won't grow into anything. But anytime a twig showed promise, 3M would allow it to grow into a full branch—or perhaps into a full-fledged tree. This branching approach became so conscious at 3M that it sometimes explicitly depicted its product families in branching tree form."[31] See Figure 4-8 as an example.

The ability to innovate is not 3M's only core competence. Consider the following list of 3M products: Sandpaper, Scotch Tape, Magic Tape, Post-it Notes, window tinting, Scotchgard, and insulation for apparel. What do these seemingly diverse products have in common? The first four share an adhesive base as a key product element, and indeed 3M has a knowledge of adhesives that is perhaps unsurpassed by any company. The last three products, on the other hand, relate to coverings applied to the surface of an object. What the entire list of products has in common is a shared core competence of coating and bonding. 3M likes to think of itself as a company that specializes in two-dimensional (flat) products. This is because of its special knowledge and ability to attach things to flat surfaces. Many of its core products are a direct result of this core competence. While these 3M products may appear diverse and unrelated, that appearance belies a fundamental commonality—their core competence in coating and bonding.

The branching tree concept reinforces the common core competencies that underlie a related group of products. It also helps product developers to envision new products that fill in the branches of the tree, contributing to the spirit of innovation that permeates 3M.

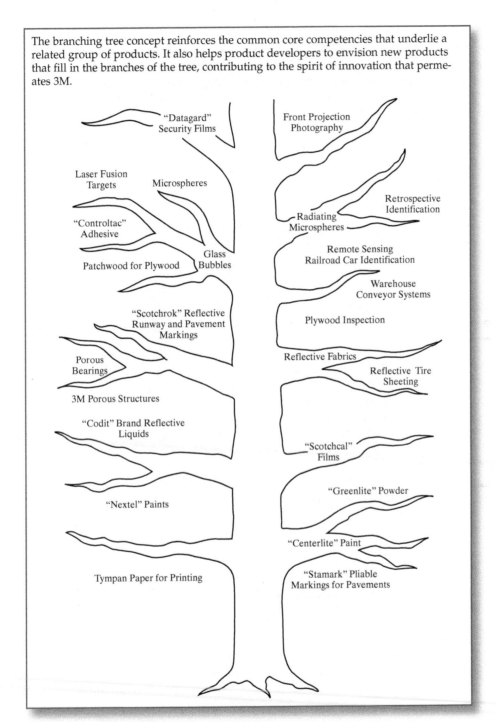

Figure 4-8
A Branching Tree at 3M
Source: Collins & Porras, *Built To Last*, p. 154.

Figure 4-9
A 3M Billboard and a 3M Advertisement for Security Glass

STAGE 4: IDENTIFYING STRENGTHS AND WEAKNESSES

The final stage of the internal audit process is to take the information generated by the first three stages and identify the firm's internal strengths and weaknesses. These strengths and weaknesses are critical factors in making strategic choices. The final list of strengths and weaknesses should be manageable in size. Eight to twelve factors are typical but it is important to emphasize that there is no rigid formula to follow. The appropriate number will depend on the unique situation that is faced.

The list will include both financial and non-financial strengths and weaknesses from Stage 1, key success factors from the value chain analysis of Stage 2, and a set of core competencies from Stage 3. Each factor should address issues that affect the firm's ability to create value for customers, employees, and owners.

Another important characteristic of the final list of strengths and weaknesses, as we have emphasized, is they must be competitively relevant. A weakness is competitively relevant if it places the organization in a competitive disadvantage (or makes it vulnerable to a potential disadvantage) and/or undermines the organization's ability to create value for customers, employees, and owners. To determine whether a potential strength is real and competitively relevant, managers must address four important questions: (1) the question of *value*, (2) the question of *rareness*, (3), the question of *imitability*, and (4) the question of *organization*.[32]

The question of value focuses on whether the firm's "resources and capabilities add value by enabling it to exploit opportunities and/or neutralize threats … 3M has used its skills and experience in substrates, coatings and adhesives, along with an organizational culture that rewards risk taking and creativity, to exploit numerous market opportunities in office products, including invisible tape and Post-it® Notes."[33] A real strength offers something of worth to customers.

The question of rareness asks how many competitors already possess the resources and capabilities in question. If a particular resource or capability is widespread in the industry, it may be a minimum threshold for competing but it does not offer the potential for a competitive advantage. Similarly, the potential strength must pass the third test of competitive relevance by being difficult to imitate. A firm may develop a rare capability but if it is easily learned and copied by competitors it may be important in the short-term, but it does not offer the prospect of *sustainable* competitive advantage.

The final test of relevance focuses on whether the firm is organized to exploit the competitive potential of the resource or capability in question. "Numerous components of a firm's organization are relevant when answering the question of organization, including its formal reporting structure, its explicit management control systems, and its compensation policies."[34] Unless these aspects of the organization are aligned to support the potential strength, its potential cannot be realized. 3M's competence in innovation is fostered by a corporate culture that expects scientists to "bootleg" a portion of their time, or work independently on their own pet projects, and by a reward system that encourages and supports new product champions.

These four questions may be used to screen the long list of potential strengths and weaknesses generated in Stages 1 through 3, and to identify those that are important for value creation and competitive advantage. Those that pass the test of competitive relevance are used in later steps of the strategic management process.

CONCLUSION

Assessing the organization's internal environment for strengths and weaknesses is part of the second step in the strategic management process. This is accomplished by an internal audit based on a four-stage process. The audit requires an evaluation of the current performance of the firm, a value chain analysis, an understanding of the firm's core competencies, and a determination of which strengths and weaknesses are competitively relevant. Essentially, the audit attempts to find internal factors that either enhance or undermine the firm's ability to create value for employees, customers and owners. Some of the critical questions to be answered in the internal audit include:

- What are the firm's financial strengths and weaknesses?
- How well does the firm manage customer relationships? What does the firm do or not do that creates or loses value for customers?
- What are the cost and profit drivers in the firm's value chain and in the supply chain?
- What are the firm's core competencies? What core competencies will be needed in the future to compete successfully?
- Are employees competent, committed to the organization's mission, and satisfied with their association with the firm?

Accomplishing the internal audit is a matter of extensive research and analysis, and includes examining financial statements, staffing and productivity standards, information resources, organization charts, customer and employee surveys, and interviewing both internal stakeholders (e.g., managers and staff) and external stakeholders (suppliers, distributors, customers).[35] The information generated by the internal audit is combined with the opportunities and threats identified during the external audit to complete the situation analysis. The external audit is the focus of the next chapter.

KEY TERMS AND CONCEPTS

After reading this chapter you should understand each of the following terms.

- Internal Audit
- Trend analysis
- Efficiency, Effectiveness & Leverage
- Competitively relevant strengths and weaknesses
- Benchmark

- Core competencies
- DuPont Return on Equity (ROE)
- Financial ratio analysis: Liquidity, Leverage, Activity, Profitability
- Industry norms

DISCUSSION QUESTIONS

1. What is the purpose of an internal audit?
2. Describe how to perform an internal audit. What are the four stages for conducting the audit?
3. Discuss the benefits and limitations of financial ratio analysis and explain the following statement: "For ratio analysis to be meaningful, there must be a basis of comparison."
4. Choose a company and identify its supply chain partners. Which company or companies in your example seem to capture the most value? How do you know?
5. Select two different companies from the same industry (e.g., Ford versus Honda, Wal-Mart versus Target). What core competencies do the two companies have? Does one set of competencies provide more of an advantage than the other? Explain.
6. Check the textbook's website to determine 3M's current financial performance. Has it changed? If so, what might account for the changes?

EXPERIENTIAL EXERCISE

Analysis of Financial Strengths and Weaknesses. Either in teams or on your own, select a company and conduct a complete analysis of the company's current financial condition. Identify financial strengths and weaknesses.

In addition to absolute indicators of the firm's financial performance, consider trend analyses, industry norms, competitive benchmarks, and the firm's mission and stated goals. For guidance on the types of indicators that may be examined, see Table 4-1 (Common Assessment Tools for Stage 1) and Table 4-2 (Selected Financial Ratios). You may also wish to consult financial reporting services (e.g., Standard and Poor's, Value Line, Bloomberg, Moody's, Compustat, D & B) for data on financial operations, results, trends, and future prospects.

ENDNOTES

1. 3M 2015 Annual Report. http://s2.q4cdn. com/974527301/files/doc_financials/ 2015/ar/2015_3M_Annual_Report.pdf. Accessed 25 April 2016.
2. Peters T. J. and R. H. Waterman, In Search of Excellence, New York, Harper and Row, 1982.
3. Op cit, 3M 2015 Annual Report
4. Ibid
5. Porter, M.E. *The Competitive Advantage of Nations.* New York: The Free Press, 1990, 40.
6. Ibid, 41.
7. Starbucks 2015 Annual Report. Accessed 26 April 2016.
8. Cooke, James A. "From bean to cup: How Starbucks transformed its supply chain." *CSCMP's Supply Chain Quarterly.* Quarter 4 2010. Web. 25 April 2016.
9. Ibid
10. Ibid
11. University Alliance. "Starbucks Supply Chain Balances Efficiency with Sustainability." *University of San Francisco.* Web. 26 April 2016.

12. Berman, Jeff. "Starbucks' Schultz stresses the need for supply chain to have a seat at the table." *LogisticsManagement.com*. 2 October 2015. Web. 27 April 2016. http://www.logisticsmgmt.com/article/starbucks_schultz_stresses_the_need_for_supply_chain_to_have_a_seat_at_the

13. Porter, M. E. *Competitive Advantage*. New York: The Free Press, 1985, 37–43.

14. Bose, Nandita. "Target's big problem is clear." *Business Insider*. 20 August 2015. Web. 22 March 2016. http://www.businessinsider.com/r-new-target-coos-headache-too-few-goods-to-keep-shelves-filled-2015-8

15. Ziobro, Paul. "Target Hires Executive to Lead Supply Revamping." *WSJ*. 29 February 2016. Web. 22 March 2016. and Wahba, Phil. "This Is How Target Is Solving Its Out-of-Stock Problems." *Fortune*. 2 March 2016. Web. 22 March 2016.

16. Hartley, R. F. *Management Mistakes and Successes*. 6th ed. New York: John Wiley & Sons, Inc., 2000.

17. Porter, M. E., op cit, 84.

18. "2014 Amazon.com Annual Report" Accessed 20 May 2016.

19. Prahalad, C. K., and G. Hamel, "The Core Competence of the Corporation," *Harvard Business Review* (May-June 1990): 82.

20. See for example, A. A. Thompson and A. J. Strickland. *Strategic Management*. 10th ed. Boston, MA: Irwin/McGraw Hill, 1998, 108.

21. Hamel, G., and C.K. Prahalad. *Competing for the Future*. Boston, MA: Harvard Business School Press, 1994, 204–206.

22. Ibid, 82.

23. Ibid, 221.

24. Ibid, 86–88.

25. Ibid, 87.

26. Ibid, 80.

27. Minnesota Mining and Manufacturing Co. (3M), "3M History: A Quick Glance," www.3m.com/profile/looking/history.html, accessed August 12, 2000

28. Minnesota Mining and Manufacturing Co. (3M), "Art Fry and the Invention of Post-it Notes," www.3m.com/about3m/pioneers/fry.jhtml, accessed November 20, 2001.

29. Ibid.

30. "3M History." *3M* Accessed 4 May 2016. http://solutions.3m.com/wps/portal/3M/en_US/3M-Company/Information/Resources/History/

31. Collins, J.C., and J.I. Porras, "Built to Last: Successful Habits of Visionary Companies," New York: Harper Collins, 1994.

32. Barney, J., "Looking Inside for Competitive Advantage," *Academy of Management Executive 9*, no. 4 (1995): 50.

33. Ibid, 50.

34. Ibid, 56.

35. Ibid, 7.

Chapter 5

The External Audit

It is a strange and challenging time for the world's largest retailer, Wal-Mart. At the beginning of its 2017 fiscal year, Wal-Mart reduced its sales growth projections to a modest 3-4 percent increase. This followed a disappointing fiscal year 2016 in which the company's overall sales decreased by 0.7% and its operating revenue decreased by 11.2%, Wal-Mart's worst sales performance since 1980.[1] Wal-Mart also warned its investors in Fall 2015 to expect revenue decreases for the next two years. In addition to the financial shortfalls, the retail giant announced that it would close 269 underperforming stores worldwide in 2016, including 154 stores in the United States. The store closings would impact 10,000 employees.[2] What is happening to the world's largest retailer? The answer, at least in part, is that Wal-Mart's external environment has changed and the retailer has to adjust its strategies to adapt.

While Wal-Mart does have multiple e-commerce platforms in various countries, the retailer has not yet fully integrated them into its core business practices. In his 2016 letter to Wal-Mart's shareholders, CEO Doug McMillion recognized that changing technology is disrupting the retail industry.[3] Online retailers, especially Amazon, have been able to harness technology to redefine the shopping experience and have changed customers' expectations. "Customers used to compare us with the store down the street," said McMillion, "now they compare us with the best online shopping experience."[4] Wal-Mart began to address its deficiency in online sales in 2016 as it announced plans to invest $1 billion in global e-commerce initiatives, including further developing its mobile pay app feature and its click-and-collect pick-up service for groceries and home goods.[5] Wal-Mart announced that its ShippingPass membership will offer free two-day delivery and cost $49 a month.[6]

While Amazon has chipped away at Wal-Mart's dominant position in the retail sector, brick-and-mortar retailers are also viable competitors fighting for more market share. Dollar stores, such as Dollar General and Dollar Tree, attract price-conscious consumers with their small sizes ideal for quick shopping. Mid-tier stores, like Target, offer various incentives to customers, like 5% off all purchases and free shipping on online orders if customers pay with their REDcard. Higher end retailers, like Costco and Kroger, tempt customers with high-end, brand-name food, appliances, and designer clothes at competitive prices. McMillion alludes to this competition in his letter to shareholders by saying: "Retail is not just about putting items on a shelf anymore. It's about fighting for our customers, cutting out the hassles and the headaches and advocating for them on price, too. We're moving beyond just selling products to being the brand customers rely on to make their lives simpler and more meaningful as they save money. The winners in this time of change will be those who put the customer first."[7]

In addition to technology changes and competitive threats, Wal-Mart has been impacted by social and political pressure and by macro-economic conditions in the form of wage increases and foreign currency fluctuations. Amid a well-publicized national campaign by social activists and civil rights reformers to raise the minimum wage across the country, Wal-Mart increased its starting wage to $9 in 2015 and raised it again to $10 in 2016. In total, Wal-Mart invested $2.7 billion in higher hourly wages and more education and training, a boost for employees but an increased expense nevertheless.[8] In addition, Wal-Mart global sales were squeezed by the strength of the U.S. dollar. In fact, Wal-Mart lost $4.7 billion in global sales due to foreign currency fluctuations in fiscal year 2016, impacting revenues from Wal-Mart's subsidiaries in the United Kingdom, Canada, Chile, Japan, and Mexico.[9] These changes in Wal-Mart's external environment are creating new threats and new opportunities for the retail giant.

In the previous chapter, we discussed the internal audit, one component of a situation analysis. The purpose of this chapter is to describe the second component of a situation analysis—the external audit. The Strategic Management Framework shown in Figure 5-1 indicates the position of the external audit in the strategic management process and identifies questions addressed in this chapter.

The purpose of the external audit, as we will discuss in this chapter, is to identify the external opportunities and threats faced by the firm. In the case of Wal-Mart in the opening vignette above, changes in the external environment have undermined Wal-Mart's dominance in the market. Wal-Mart's senior management team, however, recognizes the importance of adapting to the changes and aligning Wal-Mart's strategies with the new realities of its external environment.

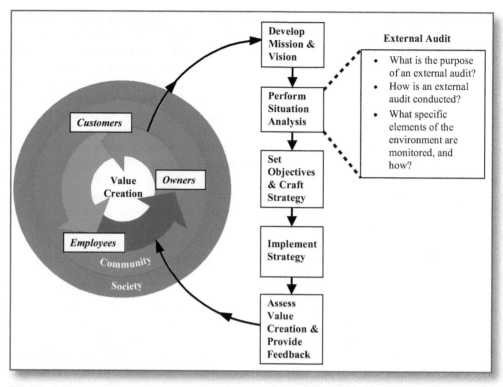

Figure 5-1
The Strategic Management Framework

Several key external forces are mentioned in the Wal-Mart example above, beginning with technology and competition. Wal-Mart measures its performance against its competitors around the world, not taking the competition for granted and always being alert. Technology has altered the way consumers shop and changed their buying expectations. Political and social trends, such as the "Fight for 15" to raise the national minimum wage, are also impacting Wal-Mart. Macro-economic forces such as the value of the dollar are also an uncontrollable variable in Wal-Mart's external environment. All of these forces influence Wal-Mart decisions about top management team composition, new products, store locations, levels of advertising expenditures, and cost control initiatives. In turn, Wal-Mart's actions and strategies influence competitors, customers, and suppliers. Wal-Mart is aware that in forming its strategies for the future, it must continue to be aware of this give and take relationship with its external environment.

An *external audit,* also known as *environmental scanning,* is a systematic, ongoing process of analyzing the external environment to identify *opportunities* and *threats* facing an organization. A firm uses its strengths and avoids or overcomes its weaknesses by formulating strategies that take advantage of opportunities and/or mitigate threats. It is a basic premise of strategic management that organizations shape or fit their strategies in the context of their external environment.[10] For example, Wal-Mart can neither stabilize the economy, nor control customer demands, nor rid itself of competitors. When these forces were identified as threats, Wal-Mart revised its market growth strategy to counter the negative effects and take advantage of any positive trends.

Research has found that when firms achieve an environment-strategy fit, financial performance levels are consistently better.[11] Thus, the external audit coupled with the internal audit informs decisions about mission, vision, objectives, strategy and implementation. In the next section we explore why an external audit is crucial to value creation.

ENVIRONMENT-ORGANIZATION RELATIONSHIP

Organizations are *open systems,* meaning that they interact with and respond to their external environments, taking in inputs (human, informational, physical, and financial resources) and producing outputs (goods and services). Resources that are indispensable to a firm's current and future operations come from the external environment. Additionally, the environmental context is a source of change and uncertainty, affecting organizational decisions. In the open systems perspective, organizations are not just passive entities that react to the environment; they also try to shape and influence the environment through their strategies. [12]

The *external audit* becomes important in understanding how to secure resources, reduce uncertainty, avoid surprises, and create the future. There is ample evidence that inattention to external forces can be risky, if not fatal to an organization. For a century, Eastman Kodak Company was the preeminent name in film photography, with a near monopoly on cameras, film, and film development. Unfortunately, the company failed to capitalize on the growing popularity of digital photo imaging. After filing for Chapter 11 bankruptcy in 2012, Kodak has slipped out of the public eye and now primarily serves as a digital printing and graphics company for commercial films.[13]

Goals of an External Audit

Since organizations are open systems, it is not difficult to see that an external audit is critical to a firm's future, limiting as well as creating strategic options. The goals of an external audit are to: 1) identify and analyze important current issues and trends; 2) articulate or forecast likely emerging issues and trends; 3) foster strategic thinking and action throughout the organization; and ultimately to 4) identify opportunities and threats for planning purposes.

Through the external audit process, current data and information is gathered, aggregated and classified. Ways to evaluate issues as opportunities or threats must also be set up. In addition to the identification of current issues, the external audit process attempts to detect signals that may identify emerging issues. Strategic managers must go beyond the known and speculate on the future nature of the external environment. This process often stimulates creative thinking concerning the organization's present and future products and services. When all levels throughout the organization are cognizant of the relationship of the organization to its environment, a higher level of responsiveness and proactiveness is likely. Strategic thinking fosters adaptability and openness to change.[14]

Challenges of an External Audit

There are several important challenges of the external audit process. First, environmental change is accelerating and the significance of changes may be difficult to determine. Second, an external audit is time consuming. Third, an external audit cannot foretell the future. Fourth, pertinent or timely information may be difficult or impossible to obtain. Fifth, managers' strongly held beliefs inhibit detection and rational interpretation of issues and organizational limitations.

The external environment is a source of uncertainty, so even the most comprehensive and well-organized external audit process will not detect all of the changes in that environment. Perhaps the most limiting factors though, are the preconceived beliefs of management. Often, what managers already believe about the external environment inhibits their ability to perceive or accept signals for change. There is often a need to unlearn or forget the past.[15] For example, in the early stages of the smartphone market, leaders at Blackberry did not believe that the touch screen of the iPhone was a feature they needed to add to their smartphones. Similarly, Budweiser, Miller, and Coors did not see craft brewer Samuel Adams as a viable threat for market share. A rigorous external audit process that questions current worldviews is essential to creating a vision of the future. Despite the challenges of doing an external audit, this process is critical to the value creation cycle.

Before we look at the steps for conducting the external audit, it is important to define the factors that make up the external environment. What specific external elements do we examine in an external audit?

THE SEGMENTS OF THE EXTERNAL ENVIRONMENT

There are two main segments of the external environment: the *macro environment* (also known as the *general environment*) and the *task environment* (also known as the *industry environment*). The macro environment includes four clusters of general forces outside the control of the organization: economic, demographic/sociocultural, political/legal, and technological. The task environment includes those groups of variables that directly affect and are affected by an organization's operations, such as competitors, suppliers, customers, substitute products, new entrants, and other stakeholders (e.g., communities, creditors, labor unions, special interest groups, and trade/professional associations).

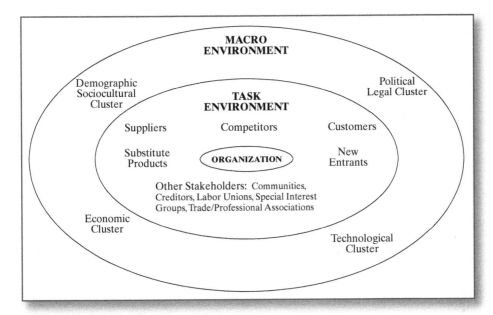

Figure 5-2
The External Landscape

Figure 5-2 depicts the external environment and its relationship to the organization. What we can't depict in a diagram, but which is critical to understand, is that this is a dynamic, interactive landscape. Trends in the external environment have significant and unequal effects on firms in different industries and in different locations. After we look at each of the external environment segments in detail, we'll discuss a process for dealing with this dynamic environment.

Defining the Macro Environment

The macro environment includes four forces, each with multiple variables that are largely uncontrollable by the organization but may directly affect it. We assess whether these forces have either a positive impact (opportunity) or negative impact (threat) on the potential attractiveness of strategic decisions, on organizational operations, and on organizational performance. Let's look at each of the four forces in detail.

Economic Forces

Economic Forces consist of a set of variables that measure the levels and patterns of economic activity in areas such as industrial output, consumption, income and savings, investment, and productivity.[16] For example, Gross Domestic Product (GDP) is a measure of all production located in a specific country calculated by adding up the contributions to final output of every firm in the economy. Often, GDP is expressed as a rate of growth from year to year, as well as on a per capita basis (derived by dividing the total value of GDP by the population). GDP indicates the size of national markets, while per capita GDP is a measure of living standards. Another important economic variable is *purchasing power*, measured as disposable income per capita. Disposable income

Table 5-1   Key Economic Variables

Availability of Credit	Disposable Personal Income
Consumer Debt Levels	Money Market Rates
Consumer Price Index	Monetary Policies
Currency Values/Exchange Rates	Per Capita Income
Government Budget Deficit	Price Fluctuations
Gross Domestic Product (GDP)	Savings Rates
Gross National Product (GNP)	Stock Market Trends
Housing Starts	Trade Balances
Industrial Investments	Tax Rates
Inflation Rates	Unemployment Rates
Interest Rates	Workforce Productivity

is the amount of current personal income minus personal income taxes that households have to spend or to save divided by a nation's population. Table 5-1 identifies economic variables often assessed for evidence of opportunities or threats.

Some industries are particularly vulnerable to interest rate fluctuations. The interest rate is the price paid to borrow capital, and there are many different kinds of interest rates, such as long-term Treasury bill rates, and corporate bonds. While it may be difficult to predict the direction of future interest rates, we know some of the relationships of interest rates with other factors. For instance, interest rate fluctuations affect strategic decisions about expansion because as long-term interest rates rise, funds for capital expansion become more costly and may result in projects being rejected or put on hold. Interest rates also affect sales. Rising mortgage rates decrease sales of new homes (a threat to a real estate company), but increase sales in the home repair market (an opportunity for Home Depot and Lowes) because people fix up or expand their current homes rather than move to new ones.

Demographic/ Sociocultural Forces

Demography is the study of the characteristics of the human population, including age, rate of growth, racial, ethnic or religious composition, and education levels. Shown in Table 5-2 are examples of important demographic variables.

Sociocultural forces pertain to societal traditions, values, attitudes, beliefs, tastes and patterns of behavior in a nation or region. Table 5-3 provides examples. Changes in demography or social values can create either opportunities for new products/ services and markets or threats to product/service offerings or to the very existence of the firm.

Monitoring shifts in demographic and sociocultural forces is part of the external audit process. Let's take the case of the growing Latino/Hispanic population in the United States. As shown in Table 5-4, the Hispanic population is the largest minority population in the United States, representing about 17.4% of the total US population

Table 5-2 Key Demographic Variables

VARIABLE	TYPICAL CATEGORIES
Age distributions	Under 6, 6–11, 12–19, 20–34, 35–49, 50–64, 65–75, 76+
Gender	Female, Male
Family Size	1–2, 3–4, 5+
Family Life Cycle	Young, single; young, married, no children; young married, youngest child under 6; young, married, youngest child over 6; older, married, with children; older, married, with no children under 18; older, single; other
Income	Under 25,000; 25,001–50,000; 50,001–75,000; 75,001–100,000; over 100,000
Occupation	Professional and technical; managers, officials, proprietors; clerical, sales; craftsmen, foremen; operatives; farmers; retired; students; unemployed; other
Education	Grade school or less; some high school; high school graduate; some college; college graduate; post college education
Religion	Catholic; Protestant; Jewish; Muslim; Hindu; None; Other
Race	White; Asian; Hispanic; African American; Native American; Other

Table 5-3 Key Sociocultural Variables

Attitudes toward saving and investing	Importance of social responsibility
Attitudes towards material goods	Importance of technology
Attitudes towards business	Life-styles
Attitudes toward women and minorities	Quality of life issues
Attitudes toward work and careers	Regional tastes and preferences
Attitudes toward product/service quality	Value placed on short term versus long term
Attitudes toward leisure time	Value of education
Gender roles	Value of individual freedom
Importance of environmental issues	Willingness to accept change
Importance of family and religion	

in 2014.[17] The US Census Bureau projects that the Hispanic population in the U.S. will grow by 86% from 2015 to 2050 and number 119 million by 2060.[18] Also, the Census Bureau estimated that the median age for Hispanics is 29 years old, the youngest median age of all major ethnic groups in the United States. The Pew Research Center reports that the rate of smartphone ownership in the Hispanic population is equal to the overall rate.[19]

In order to adapt to the country's changing demographics, Wal-Mart has launched Hispanic formats in stores across the country, but primarily in densely

Table 5-4 Projections of Racial Composition in the United States (%)

PERCENT OF TOTAL POPULATION	2015	2020	2030	2040	2050	2060
TOTAL	**100.0**	**100.0**	**100.0**	**100.0**	**100.0**	**100.0**
White Alone	61.7	59.6	55.5	51.3	47.3	43.7
Hispanic (of any race)	17.7	19.0	21.6	24.1	26.5	28.6
Black Alone	12.4	12.4	12.6	12.7	12.8	13.0
Asian Alone	5.3	5.8	6.7	7.6	8.4	9.1
All other races[1]	2.9	3.2	3.6	4.3	5.0	5.6

[1] American Indian, Alaska Native, Native Hawaiian, Other Pacific Islander, and Two or More Races

From *Percent of the Projected Population by Hispanic Origin and Race for the United States: 2015 to 2060* (2014), by permission of the U.S. Census Bureau.

populated Hispanic regions. The majority of these stores are located in eight states with most of them concentrated in Texas, California, Florida, Arizona, and New Mexico. The new stores offer products that appeal specifically to this demographic group as market research shows that Hispanics outspend total market households by 40% or better in several product categories, including hair care products, cooking oil, baby food, diapers, grooming aids, women's fragrances, electronics, and carbonated beverages.[20] The 39,000-square-foot stores are called *Supermercado de Wal-Mart* and are located in former Neighborhood Market stores. As previously mentioned, a large proportion of Hispanics own smartphones, which signifies an area where Wal-Mart can promote its reconstructed e-commerce platform to this promising demographic.

Political/Legal Forces

Political/Legal Forces represent power relationships, national stability, constraining and protecting laws, and administrative, regulatory, and judicial institutions at the federal, state, and local levels.[21] It is important to keep track of current and potential legal, regulatory, and political changes in any country in which an organization does business or is considering doing business. In looking at the example of Wal-Mart, the recent national push to raise the minimum wage put pressure on Wal-Mart to raise its hourly wage to $10 in 2016. A summary of key political and legal variables for evaluation as opportunities or threats is in Table 5-5.

An important regulatory consideration for any organization is Human Resource (HR) legislation. Table 5-6 gives some examples of U.S. labor laws. Let's look an example from the Occupational Safety and Health Administration (OSHA) established by The Occupational Safety and Health Act of 1970. In conjunction with

Table 5-5 Key Political/Legal Variables

Government regulations or deregulations	Tariff regulations
Consumer laws	Trade treaties/alliances
Local, state, and national elections	Location and severity of terrorist activities
Judicial system	Number, severity, and location of government protests
Level of defense spending	Patent and copyright laws
Level of government subsidies	Tax laws
Political systems	Environmental protection laws
Political stability	Human Resources laws
Government agencies	Quality of life laws
Voter participation rates	Local, state, or regional laws
Attitudes toward the legal system	Antitrust legislation and merger approval process
Size of government budgets	Attitudes toward intellectual property
Government fiscal and monetary policy	

Table 5-6 Examples of Significant U.S. Human Resource Legislation

OCCUPATIONAL SAFETY AND HEALTH ACT OF 1970
Requires employers to provide a working environment free from hazards to health.

EQUAL EMPLOYMENT OPPORTUNITY ACT OF 1972
Forbids discrimination in all areas of employer-employee relations.

WORKER ADJUSTMENT AND RETRAINING NOTIFICAITON ACT OF 1988
Requires employers with 100 or more employees to provide 60 days' notice before a facility closing or mass layoff

AMERICANS WIH DISABILITIES ACT OF 1990
Prohibits employers from discriminating against individuals with physical or mental disabilities or the chronically ill; also requires organizations to reasonably accommodate these individuals.

CIVIL RIGHTS ACT OF 1991
Reaffirms and tightens prohibition of discriminations; permits individuals to sue for punitive damages in cases of intentional discrimination.

FAMILY MEDICAL LEAVE ACT OF 1993
Grants 12 weeks of unpaid leave each year to employees for the birth or adoption of a child or the care of a spouse, child, or parent with a serious health condition; covers organizations with 50 or more employees.

Table 5-7 Key Technological Variables

Biotechnology	Superconductivity
Consumer electronics	High-definition graphics
Robotics and artificial intelligence	Number of patents
Handling industrial/chemical waste	Lasers
Food additives	Biogenetics
Satellites and satellite imaging	Wireless technology
Total Federal spending for R&D	Changes in telecommunications
Changes in information technology	

Drive Safely Work Week, OSHA began an education campaign calling on employers to prevent work-related distracted driving, with a special focus on prohibiting texting while driving. "Year after year, the leading cause of worker fatalities is motor vehicle crashes," said Assistant Secretary of Labor for OSHA, Dr. David Michaels. "There's no question that new communications technologies are helping businesses work smarter and faster. But getting work done faster does not justify the dramatically increased risk of injury and death that comes with texting while driving."[22] While business and government disagree on the extent of the problem, the correct solution, and the annual cost of compliance, it is clear that OSHA considers this an important workplace issue. Firms will either consider it an opportunity to proactively improve workplace conditions or a threat and react only as far as required by law.

Technological Forces

The concept of technology relates to the development and application of knowledge. Technology can have an enormous impact on products, such as those in healthcare, pharmaceuticals, and consumer electronics, and in the marketing and selling of those products or services in the retail industry (as in the case of Wal-Mart discussed above). Listed in Table 5-7 are examples of technological forces.

A common mistake in analyzing technological forces is to focus only on end-product changes. However, we need to be alert to inventions, innovations, and diffusions as shown in Table 5-8. *Inventions* are basic research into principles and relationships in nature resulting in increased knowledge of how the world works. Transforming basic knowledge into trial products is *Innovation*. *Diffusion* occurs when many people adopt the innovation. Inventions, innovations, and diffusions can radically alter the entire external environment and make a company's products and services obsolete. For example, from its peak of over 9,000 stores in 2004, Blockbuster Video filed for bankruptcy protection in 2010 as new technologies rendered its business model obsolete.[23]

Let's consider a few examples of the impact of technology on business. Technological changes are radically changing the healthcare field. Magnetic resonance imaging (MRI), electronic patient records, DNA mapping, protein-based and biotech

Table 5-11 Industry Comparison for Supermarkets and Drugstores

Ticker	Company	Yr. End	Return on Revenues (%)					Return on Assets (%)					Return on Equity (%)				
			2013	2012	2011	2010	2009	2013	2012	2011	2010	2009	2013	2012	2011	2010	2009
FOOD RETAIL‡																	
CASY	§ CASEY'S GENERAL STORES INC	# APR	1.7	1.7	1.8	1.8	2.8	6.3	5.9	6.9	6.3	8.8	20.3	20.0	25.7	15.4	15.1
KR	‖ KROGER CO	# JAN	1.5	1.5	0.7	1.4	0.1	5.6	6.2	2.6	4.8	0.3	31.7	36.6	13.0	22.0	1.4
SWY	‖ SAFEWAY INC	DEC	0.6	1.3	1.2	1.4	NM	1.5	3.8	3.4	3.9	NM	5.3	17.1	11.9	11.9	NM
SVU	† SUPERVALU INC	# FEB	0.0	NM	NM	NM	1.0	0.1	NM	NM	NM	2.3	NA	NA	NA	NA	14.4
WFM	WHOLE FOODS MARKET INC	SEP	4.3	4.0	3.4	2.7	1.8	10.2	9.7	8.3	6.2	3.3	14.3	13.7	12.8	12.0	7.6
DRUG RETAIL‡																	
CVS	‖ CVS CAREMARK CORP	DEC	3.5	3.2	3.3	3.6	3.8	6.7	6.0	5.5	5.6	6.0	12.2	10.3	9.2	9.4	10.6
WAG	§ WALGREEN CO	AUG	3.4	3.0	3.8	3.1	3.2	7.1	7.0	10.1	8.1	8.4	13.0	12.9	18.6	14.5	14.7
FOOD DISTRIBUTORS‡																	
ANDE	§ ANDERSONS INC	DEC	1.6	1.5	2.1	1.9	1.3	4.0	4.1	5.5	4.3	3.0	13.9	14.2	19.5	15.3	10.3
SPTN	§ SPARTANNASH CO	DEC	0.0	1.1	1.2	1.3	1.0	0.1	3.6	4.2	4.3	3.5	0.2	8.4	10.1	11.2	10.2
SYY	‖ SYSCO CORP	JUN	2.2	2.6	2.9	3.2	2.9	8.0	9.6	10.6	11.5	10.4	20.1	23.9	27.0	32.4	30.8
UNFI	† UNITED NATURAL FOODS INC	JUL	1.8	1.7	1.7	1.8	1.7	6.7	6.3	5.8	5.9	5.5	10.4	9.9	10.2	11.6	11.6
HYPERMARKET § & SUPER CENTERS‡																	
COST	‖ COSTCO WHOLESALE CORP	AUG	1.9	1.7	1.6	1.7	1.5	7.1	6.3	5.8	5.7	5.1	17.6	14.0	12.8	12.5	11.3
WMT	‖ WAL-MART STORES INC	# JAN	3.4	3.6	3.5	3.7	3.5	7.8	8.6	8.4	8.7	8.6	20.9	23.0	22.5	22.0	21.2
OTHER COMPANIES RELEVANT TO INDUSTRY ANALYSIS																	
DG	‖ DOLLAR GENERAL CORP	# JAN	5.9	5.9	5.2	4.8	2.9	9.7	9.5	8.0	6.8	3.8	19.7	19.7	17.6	16.9	10.9
DLTR	‖ DOLLAR TREE INC	# JAN	7.6	8.4	7.4	6.8	6.1	21.6	24.4	20.7	17.0	14.8	42.1	41.1	34.8	27.5	23.9
FDO	‖ FAMILY DOLLAR STORES	AUG	4.3	4.5	4.5	4.6	3.9	12.5	13.3	13.0	12.3	10.6	30.6	35.4	31.0	25.0	21.6
FRED	§ FREDS INC	# JAN	1.3	1.5	1.8	1.6	1.3	4.0	4.6	5.4	5.1	4.2	5.9	6.9	7.9	7.2	6.0
FWM	FAIRWAY GROUP HOLDINGS	# MAR	NM	NM	NM	NM	NA	NM	NM	NM	NM	NA	NA	NA	NA	NA	NA
NAFC	NASH FINCH CO	DEC	NA	NM	0.7	1.0	0.1	NA	NM	3.4	5.0	0.3	NA	NM	9.2	14.0	0.8
RAD	# RITE AID CORP	# FEB	1.0	0.5	NM	NM	NM	3.4	1.5	NM	NM	NM	NA	NM	NA	NA	NA
RNDY	‖ ROUNDY'S INC	DEC	0.9	NM	1.3	1.2	1.3	2.4	NM	3.2	3.2	NA	16.5	NM	29.3	27.4	NA
SFM	SPROUTS FARMERS MARKET	DEC	2.1	1.1	NM	NA	NA	4.5	2.1	NM	NA	NA	11.4	6.0	NA	NA	NA
TRM	† FRESH MARKET INC	# JAN	3.4	4.8	4.6	2.4	5.7	11.9	18.1	17.7	9.3	21.0	22.4	39.5	52.4	33.3	92.7
WMK	WEIS MARKETS INC	DEC	2.7	3.1	2.7	2.6	2.5	6.4	7.8	7.5	7.2	7.1	8.8	10.7	10.3	9.6	9.3

Note: Data as originally reported. ‡S&P 1500 Index group. ‖Company included in the S&P 500. †Company included in the S&P MidCap 400. §Company included in the S&P SmallCap 600. #For the following calendar year.

Reprinted from *S&P CAPITAL IQ* (August 2014), by Standard and Poors.

Geographical scope pertains to whether to treat physically separate markets as served by the same industry or distinct industries. For example, does it make more sense to talk of the U.S. pharmaceutical industry or the global pharmaceutical industry? Interdependence across markets is high for pharmaceutical companies, suggesting that defining the pharmaceutical industry at a global level is logical. As global connectivity accelerates, thanks in part to advances in telecommunications and cross-border mergers, more and more industries are being defined globally. The beer industry is an excellent example. Since the start of the new millennium, the beer industry has had multiple cross border mergers. One occurred in 2005 when the Canadian brewery, Molson, merged with the American brewery, Coors, to form Molson Coors Brewing Company. In 2008 iconic American brewery, Anheuser-Busch, merged with InBev, which itself is the product of a 2004 cross-border merger between Belgian InterBrew and Brazilian AmBev, to form Anheuser-Busch InBev. In 1998, American automaker, Chrysler, and German auto manufacturer, Daimler Benz, merged to form Daimler Chrysler. The marriage did not last long, as Daimler Benz sold Chrysler to Cerebus Capital Management firm in 2007 for a meager $7 billion. The merger failed for many reasons, including that the companies clashed on accepted quality standards for automobiles.[32]

Competitor scope looks at the additional complexities arising if competitors differ significantly in terms of their revenues, breadth of products or services, or some other identifiable dimension. We may want to use *strategic group maps* which are conceptual clusters formed to facilitate understanding and analysis of the industry. *Strategic groups* within an industry are sets of firms competing in similar ways for similar customers and interacting more directly within each group than with competitors drawn from other strategic groups in the industry.[33] It is possible to define strategic groups along any dimensions that seem relevant (age of capital equipment and level of diversification; price and image; price and service level, etc.).

Figure 5-4 illustrates a *strategic group map* for chain restaurants in the United States based on price and service level dimensions. We can see which competitors cluster together because they are similar in price and service level. For example, Panera Bread, Chipotle Mexican and Five Guys offer moderate price, fast casual dining. We can also see that there are some spaces in the map where there are no major chain restaurants in the United States; a potential *strategic window* of opportunity.

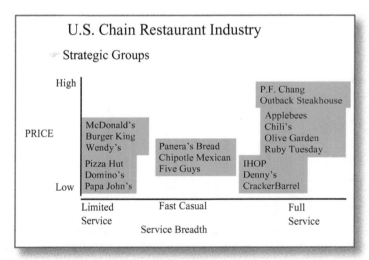

Figure 5-4
Strategic Group Map of U.S. Restaurant Chain Industry
Adapted from: J. David Hunger and Thomas L. Wheelen, *Essentials of Strategic Management*, second edition, Prentice Hall, Upper Saddle River, NJ. 2001, p 44.

These simple charts convey a great deal of information, such as the selection and partial understanding of an industry's critical structural characteristics, competitive dynamics, evolution, and areas of "white space."[34]

Five Forces Model of Competition

Another tool for identifying and assessing the industry environment is Michael Porter's Five Forces Model.[33] The Five Forces Model expanded the definition of task environment to include not only *rivalry among direct competitors*, but also the *power of suppliers, power of customers*, threat of *substitute products* or services, and threat of *entry of new competitors*. Together these five forces determine the nature and extent of competition in an industry and shape the strategies of firms by limiting options (such as pricing) and affecting performance. The underlying premise is that the weaker the five forces, the more attractive the profit potential of the industry. Thus, when the forces are judged weak, it is an opportunity, allowing for greater profit potential, through either lower costs, increased prices, or a combination of both. On the other hand, when the forces are strong, it is a threat, because firms may encounter higher costs, lower prices, or both.

Stakeholder Model of Competitive Forces

Another useful model for understanding and evaluating the task environment is the Stakeholder Model. The Stakeholder Model complements the Five Forces Model by recognizing the impact on industries of stakeholders not specifically considered in the Five Forces Model, such as communities, creditors, labor unions, special interest groups, and trade and professional associations.[36] In certain industries, these stakeholders are especially important. Labor unions play a critical role in the airlines industry. Special interest groups keep a close watch on energy companies. Figure 5-5 combines the Five Forces and Stakeholder models.

Strategic leaders focus on identifying the most appropriate and defensible strategic positions and selecting strategies that maintain or improve positions in each

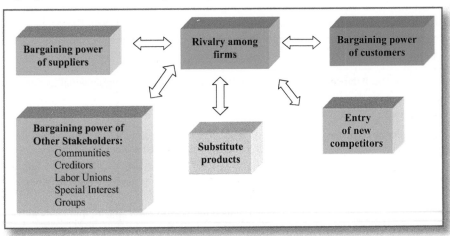

Figure 5-5
Forces Driving Industry Competitiveness
Adapted from: Michael E. Porter, *Competitive Strategy, Techniques for Analyzing Industries and Competitors*, The Free Press, 1980.

industry in which a firm competes. Different forces take on prominence in shaping competition in each industry. Analyzing these forces also is helpful when considering a diversification strategy into new industries or industry segments. Let's examine each force more closely.

Rivalry Among Firms

Head-to-head competition between direct competitors is perhaps the most obvious of the competitive forces. Examples include Wal-Mart versus Target, Coke versus Pepsi, Ford versus Toyota, Apple versus Samsung, McDonald's versus Wendy's, and Nike versus Adidas. It helps determine the dissipation of value created by the industry in the competitive effort. Price competition, product/service differentiation, product/service innovation, and/or advertising battles are the common forms of competitive moves. Porter relates the intensity of the rivalry among the firms to the presence and intensity of a number of factors such as those listed in Table 5-12.

Bargaining Power of Suppliers

When organizations supplying raw materials or services to an industry can affect the profitability of the buying industry by either raising prices or reducing the quality or quantity of goods or services, they have *supplier power*. Powerful suppliers are obviously a threat to the buying industry. A supplier or supplier group may gain power when:

- There are few suppliers.
- Satisfactory substitute products/services are not available.
- Industry firms are not a significant customer for the supplier group.
- Suppliers' goods are critical to the customer's marketplace success.
- The effectiveness of suppliers' products create high switching costs.
- Suppliers are a credible threat to integrate forward into the customer's industry.

Table 5-12 Factors involved in firm rivalry

RIVALRY FACTORS	RIVALRY INTENSIFIERS
Concentration and balance of competitors	Competitors are numerous or roughly equal in size.
Industry growth	Slow growth; market share battles.
Product or service characteristics	Product or service is very similar no matter which firm sells. Customers can switch easily.
Fixed or storage costs	High fixed costs and perishable products encourage price-cutting to either cover the fixed costs or salvage sales before spoilage.
Capacity	New plants often lead to overcapacity that leads to price-cutting.
Exit barriers	High costs to leave the industry, for example, specialized assets and management loyalty.

The profitability of the major airlines, for example, is vulnerable to fuel costs. The prices of sugar and coco have a major impact on the profitability of confectionary companies like Tootsie Roll, Hershey and M&M Mars. In the case of both candy and airfare, the price sensitivity of consumers means that commodity price increases cannot simply be passed on to consumers in the form of higher prices.

Bargaining Power of Customers

The power of customers influences the terms and conditions of a sale. When the balance of power favors buyers, they can capture more of the value created in an industry by bargaining for lower prices, better quality at the same prices, and/or additional services. Thus, powerful customers are a threat to the supplying industry. A customer or customer group may gain power when:

- A customer purchases a large proportion of the seller's product or service.
- Alternative suppliers are plentiful because the product is undifferentiated.
- Changing suppliers is not costly (i.e., low *switching costs*).
- A customer has the potential to integrate backward by producing itself.
- The customer industry has large firms.

Wal-Mart can negotiate favorable contracts with manufacturers such as Hershey, Procter and Gamble and Mattel because Wal-Mart stores account for such a large percentage of the manufacturers' sales. Hershey, for example, simply cannot afford to lose the Wal-Mart account without suffering a huge loss of sales. In this case, the retailer has bargaining power over the manufacturers.

Entry of New Competitors

New competitors can bring new capacity, new rivalry for market share, substantial resources, and increased diversity, thus disrupting the established patterns of competition. The threat of new entrants depends on the *entry barriers* that existing firms have erected to protect their positions in the industry and the attractiveness of the industry. The lower the barriers, the greater the threat of new entrants, assuming, of course, the industry is attractive. Starting your own house painting business is easy, and therefore more competitive and less profitable than starting your own environmental law firm. Entry barriers for the latter are much higher than the former. Examples of entry barriers are listed and explained in Table 5-13

Sometimes, despite barriers to entry, new firms enter an industry with lower prices and or better ways to distribute the product. The threat of new entrants in the U.S. biopharmaceutical market has grown as non-U.S. pharmaceutical companies look to make a splash in the U.S. market. Indian pharmaceutical companies have been buying up smaller U.S. drug companies to develop and sell more sophisticated high-powered painkillers and cancer treatments.[37] The expiration of long-standing patents of major drug companies is an enticement for new entrants in a market. For example, Johnson & Johnson's patent for its rheumatoid arthritis drug, Remicade, is set to expire soon. This will allow for other pharmaceutical companies to develop and market knockoff versions or "biosimilars" of the original drug.[38]

Substitute Products

Substitute Products put an upper price limit on an industry's products or services because consumers will switch to other less expensive substitute products/services

Table 5-13 Entry barriers

BARRIERS TO ENTRY	EXPLANATION
Economies of scale	Cost advantage due to large size of production, research, marketing
Product Differentiation	Customer loyalty to the brand
Capital Requirements	Requirements to do business in the industry, not only for fixed facilities but also for R&D or marketing
Disadvantages other than size	Familiarity with the industry (learning & experience curve); relationships with suppliers, favorable locations
Distribution Channels	Access to wholesale or retail channels
Regulation and/or Licensing Requirements	Special approvals needed before being permitted to compete in an industry

if these satisfy the same need. For example, glass containers for beverages are much less common today than years ago, due to less expensive plastics. Similarly, less expensive molded plastics have replaced steel fenders on cars.

Competitive pressures arising from substitute products/services also come from technological advancements or deregulation. Examples are downloadable online music replacing CDs and tape cassettes, and mobile application based transportation services, like Uber and Lyft, competing with conventional forms of public transportation.

Bargaining Power of Other Stakeholders

Other stakeholders may also influence the nature of competition in an industry, by limiting strategic options, or increasing compliance costs, for example. The intensity of the effects varies widely across industries. Let's take a look at some examples of the stakeholder forces.

Local *communities* differentially exert influence on industries depending on the nature of the products/services. For example, in industries such as chemicals, paper and forest products, metals and mining, and utilities and power, communities may exert pressure on organizations to respect the environment and comply with federal and local environmental laws. In other industries, such as food, banking, and discount and fashion retailing, communities are often less powerful forces. Even here, though, community-zoning laws and regulations often restrict organizations.

The power of *creditors* to influence profitability in an industry is contingent upon the need for debt financing. Debt financing is most often significant in capital-intensive industries, such as power generation and airlines, or if equity financing is not an option (non-profits and privately held firms).

Labor Unions may limit management options and increase the cost structure of companies. The power of labor unions to influence the competitive environment within industries depends on the number and variety of unionized firms in an industry and the size of the unions. US Airways, for example, must negotiate with several strong unions, including the Airline Pilots Association (ALPA), the Association of Machinists, and the Association of Flight Attendants (AFA).

Non-government Organizations (NGOs) lack official power of government agencies, so they exert influence by using the media to call attention to their positions. Prominent interest groups in the United States include the American Association of Retired Persons (AARP) the National Rifle Association (NRA), the National Association for the Advancement of Colored People (NAACP), the U.S. Chamber of Commerce, the League of Women Voters, and People for the Ethical Treatment of Animals (PETA). Nike, Gap, and most other leading U.S. garment manufacturers continue to be sensitive to anti-sweatshop activists who work for full disclosure of working conditions in garment and shoe factories around the world.[39]

Trade/Professional Associations are voluntary organizations. They often have power over business transactions in an industry by setting performance, output, and quality standards. OPEC is an example of a powerful trade association. The International Electronic and Electrical Engineers (IEEE) association has considerable power in the electrical and electronics industry.

Individual Citizens. Through the power of the Internet, individuals from around the globe band together to influence not only companies, but political events as well. Through social media websites and apps, like Facebook, Instagram, Twitter, SnapChat, and Vine, blogs and popular websites, like You-Tube, power is exerted to affect changes. These "net-groups" are most often informal and temporary, coming together for specific issues. Recent socio-political movements, like the Fight for 15, have used these online avenues to promote their messages to affect change.

Assessing the Overall Competitiveness of the Industry

With the information gathered in the Five Forces Model of Competition it is possible to make an assessment of the strength of each force and then an overall assessment of the competitiveness of an industry (broad scope) or segment of an industry (narrow scope). You should recall that the stronger the forces, the more upward pressure on costs and the higher the costs, the less potential for profits, thus the less attractive the industry or segment is. Using this tool helps strategic decision makers decide whether to grow the existing segments, enter new segments, exit industries or segments, or maintain those segments. For example, Hansen Natural competes in both the natural drinks and energy drinks segments (NAICS #312111). Using a Five Forces Model, strategic decision makers can weigh the attractiveness of its current segments, as well as compare these segments to a new segment Hansen's might consider entering, natural foods (NAICS #311340). An example of this type of assessment is shown in Table 5-14.

Now that we have defined the macro and task environments, let's discuss how to conduct a competitor analysis.

Competitor Analysis

Studying industry trends and assessing the attractiveness of industries provides valuable information to strategic decision makers. However, it is important to remember that firms can perform better than industry averages due to the strategic decision choices made by top management. For example, in the grocery industry, a five-year average return on sales is around 2%. Wal-Mart, has averaged a return on sales closer to 3.4%.

Table 5-14 Applying the Five Forces Model of Competition (Hansen's Natural, Spring 2010)

PORTER'S MODEL	(NAICS # 312111) ENERGY DRINK INDUSTRY	(NAICS #312111) NATURAL—DRINK INDUSTRY	(NAICS #311340) NATURAL FOODS INDUSTRY
Degree of Rivalry • **Number of competitors** • **Industry Growth** • **Product Differentiation** • **Exit Barriers**	• Moderate amount of competitors • Growing market; still being built • Price competition is crucial • Marketing for brand recognition is high • Exit barriers are low	• Large amount of competitors • Established market • Price competition is crucial • Product differentiation for sales is high • Few large competitors	• Moderate amount of competitors • Growing market; new niche of consumers. • Product differentiation is high • Advertising for brand recognition is high • Exit barriers are low.
RATING	Medium	High	Medium
Threat of Entry • **Economies of Scale** • **Brand Identity** • **Access to Distribution** • **Switching Costs** • **Government Policy**	• Economies of scale and scope is crucial • Brand identity is high • Switching costs are low • Some federal regulation about launching new beverages	• Economies of scale and scope is crucial • Brand identity is medium • Switching costs are low • Some federal regulation about launching new beverages	• Economies of scale and scope is crucial. • Brand identity is medium. • Switching costs are low. • High federal regulation about food safety issues.
RATING	High	High	Medium
Threat of Substitution • **Functional Similarity** • **Price/Performance Trend** • **Product Identity**	• Few energy drinks meet the same functional needs • Pricing and success in industry is very similar • Product identity is very high	• Natural-drinks can meet various functional needs, for example, artificial drinks or tap water. • Pricing and success in industry is very similar • Product identity is medium	• Few organic, energy bars meet the same functional needs • Pricing and success in industry is pretty similar • Product identity is fairly high
RATING	Medium	High	Medium

(continued)

Table 5-14 Continued

PORTER'S MODEL	(NAICS # 312111) ENERGY DRINK INDUSTRY	(NAICS #312111) NATURAL—DRINK INDUSTRY	(NAICS #311340) NATURAL FOODS INDUSTRY
Bargaining Power of Suppliers • **Supplier Concentration** • **Number of Buyers** • **Switching Costs** • **Substitute Raw Materials**	• Suppliers in numerous different locations • Number of buyers is high • Switching costs are low • Substitute raw materials is high	• Suppliers in numerous different locations • Number of buyers is very high • Switching costs are low • Substitute raw materials is high	• Suppliers in numerous different locations. • Number of buyers is low • Switching costs are low • Substitute raw materials is medium
RATING	Low	Low	Low
Bargaining Power of Buyers • **Buyer Concentration** • **Number of Suppliers** • **Switching Costs** • **Substitute Products**	• Brand loyalty of buyers very important • Many alternative retailers • Switching costs are low	• Brand loyalty of buyers is moderate to low. • Many alternative retailers • Switching costs are low	• Brand loyalty of buyers is fairly low. • Several alternative retailers • Switching costs are medium
RATING	Medium	High	Medium
Overall Assessment	The energy-drink industry is still an expanding market; Porter's forces are moderate, so profit potential is moderate.	The natural-drink industry is a relatively stable market; Porter's forces are strong, so profit potential is lower.	The natural-foods industry is still a high-growth niche market; Porter's forces are moderate, so profit potential is moderate.

As we investigate competitors, one of the first questions we ask is how do we identify which firms to study? It is more relevant to think of a competitive set, looking at competition at a broad, mid and narrow scope within each segment. In the narrow scope, we examine competitors with the largest market share, those most similar, the fastest growing, and the most profitable while also being sure to keep companies in the mid and broad scope on our radar screen. Wal-Mart started out as a discount department store and moved into the grocery store segment, blindsiding traditional grocery stores. Wal-Mart competes as a grocery store against traditional grocery companies such as Kroger, Ahold, Albertson's, Safeway and numerous regional chains such as Publix, Wegman's and H.E. Butt Grocery. It also competes against discount department stores, such as Target and Kohl's, as well as deep discounters like Dollar General and warehouse club stores like Costco. With its investment in its supply chain and logistics to bolster its e-commerce capabilities, Wal-Mart also seeks to compete head-to-head with online retail leader Amazon.

Once the competitive landscape is defined, several types of data should be collected on a routine basis, including but not limited to objectives, strategies, competencies and financial performance. If the competitors are publically traded, Security and Exchange Commission (SEC) filings such as quarterly (10Q) and annual (10K) reports provide valuable information. Also, external databases, such as those mentioned in previous sections are useful, as are company websites.

Now that we have defined the macro and task environments, let's look at the external audit process.

THE EXTERNAL AUDIT PROCESS

During the external audit, the organization monitors or *SEES* the external environment. SEES represents the four steps of the external audit process as shown in Figure 5-6:

- <u>S</u>canning to collect i nformation about the environment,
- <u>E</u>stimating the future direction of the external forces,
- <u>E</u>valuating the information to identify the opportunity or threat potential of each issue,
- <u>S</u>haring the information.

Scanning the External Environment

Scanning is the process of continuously searching the external environment for current and emerging information and organizing that information into useable

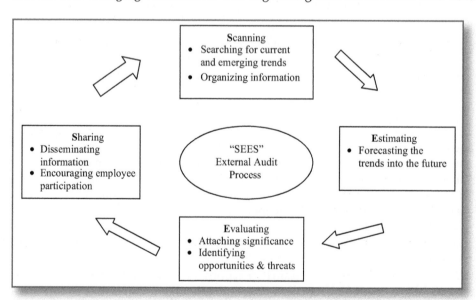

Figure 5-6
The External Audit Process: SEES

formats or categories. Imagine a radar screen or instrument panel where monitoring of the external environment is constant.[40] A dynamic, ongoing process is ever alert and vigilant for patterns and changes in both the macro and task environments. Companies tap into an extensive array of digital sources. You can sign up with newsgroup services that will deliver news items to your smartphone on pre-selected topics. Companies have Facebook pages, Linked-In profiles, Instagram, Pinterest, and Twitter accounts. Some organizations hire vendors, such as Dun and Bradstreet and a number of consulting firms, to scan for them. Panels of in-house experts and outside consultants receive inputs about changes in the external environment and often monitor blogs. The amount of information available may depend on the industry. In industries dominated by large, public firms (e.g., automotive), detailed and complete industry figures abound. In smaller and less mature industries or product lines (e.g., picture framing), statistics may be very difficult to obtain.

Asking questions in critical areas can guide the scanning process. Table 5-15 offers some frequently asked questions to frame the search for current and emerging trends in the macro and task environments.

Estimating the Future Impact

Estimating is a process of forecasting the future impact of the trends, developments, dilemmas, and events that the organization is monitoring. Both quantitative and qualitative techniques are available for this task. Outside experts or published reports by the organizations generate estimates. For example, *The Futurist*, a journal of the World Future Society, has published forecasts, trends, and ideas about the future since 1962 and TechCast.com provides forecasts focused on technology.[41]

Quantitative forecasting techniques are most appropriate when historical data is available and when there is expected stability in relationships among the key variables. As the historical relationships become less stable, quantitative forecasts become less reliable. Commonly used *quantitative forecasting* techniques are econometric models such as regression analysis and trend extrapolation. Advancements in both hardware and software have made quantitative forecasting techniques faster, more reliable, and less expensive.

Qualitative forecasting approaches may also be important. These approaches typically involve collecting and analyzing the opinions and judgments of customers, experts, or other key groups of people. Some qualitative approaches include:

- focus groups—bringing together ten to fifteen key individuals to discuss, develop, evaluate, and reach conclusions regarding future trends or issues.
- opinion surveys of either customers (current or potential) or experts
- scenario analysis—a story about the future based on a number of plausible alternative futures.[42]
- Delphi Technique—anonymous collection of individual opinions on a selected topic going through several rounds until consensus is reached.[43]
- brainstorming—group members are encouraged to present any ideas that occur to them. Ideas are recorded, but not criticized.
- Blogs—A blog (a blend of the term web log) is a kind of website or part of a website. Individuals maintain blogs, but there are also corporate sponsored blogs as

Table 5-15 Scanning Process Questions

A. Macro Environment
  1. What are the relevant segments of the macro environment?
     a. Which clusters are most important?
     b. Which variables within each cluster are most important?
     c. Which geographic areas are important?
  2. What are the current and emerging trends and patterns?
     a. What are the emerging trends or patterns?
     b. What are the indicators (measures) of these trends or patterns?
  3. What is the historical trend or pattern to these indicators?
  4. What is the degree of change?
     a. Is the degree of change minor or major?
     b. Does the change need monitoring or require immediate action?

B. Task Environment
  1. How is the industry defined?
     a. What is the horizontal, vertical, geographic, and/or competitive scope?
  2. What is the financial performance of the industry?
     a. What is the approximate size of the market in dollars and/or volume? Growth rate?
     b. What is the average level of profitability?
     c. How much does it vary from year-to-year?
     d. What are the important industry-specific indicators of performance?
  3. Who are our competitors? In which markets?
     a. What share of the defined market does each have? How is it changing and at what rate?
     b. Who is the market leader (largest share)?
     c. Who is the most profitable competitor?
     d. Who is the competitor most like us?
     e. Who is the fastest-growing competitor?
     f. Who do outside sources consider our competitors to be?
  4. What do we analyze about our competitors?
     a. Sales
     b. Profits
     c. Objectives
     d. Strategies
     e. Competencies
  5. What is the relative importance and strength of the forces of competition?
     a. Current rivalry?
     b. Entry of new competitors?
     c. Substitute products?
     d. Bargaining power of suppliers?
     e. Bargaining power of customers?
     f. Bargaining power of other stakeholders?
  6. Who are our customers?
     a. How are they changing?
     b. What needs do our products/services serve?
     c. How are these needs changing?

well. Most blogs are interactive, allowing visitors to comment and message each other and it is this interactivity that separates them from other static websites. Several blog search engines are used to search blog contents, such as Bloglines, BlogScope, and Technorati. Technorati, which is among the most popular blog search engines, provides current information on both popular searches and tags used to categorize blog postings.[44]

Evaluating the Information

The third step of the external audit is *evaluating,* the process of making sense and attaching significance to the information gathered in the scanning and estimating processes. The critical or strategic issues are identified and the labels of *opportunity* or *threat* are often given to these issues. As we have stated, an opportunity is a positive trend or force that the organization can take advantage of and a threat is a negative trend or force that the organization needs to defend against.

In the evaluation process, most often a group interprets and assesses the information. Collected or generated information is already complex and fraught with uncertainty and the group decision making complicates the situation. Different decision-makers, even when evaluating identical issues, may assess meaning quite differently. The perceptions, values, and experiences of decision-makers influence the evaluating process.

A common form of group decision making takes place face-to-face. However, face-to-face groups often censor and pressure individual members toward conformity. The *nominal group technique* and *group decision support systems* (GDSS) are two ways to reduce many of the problems inherent in face-to-face decision making. When using the nominal group technique, participants identify and evaluate in writing their view of the important external trends and issues, then present all ideas without discussion. There is time for questions, and then ranking of the evaluations is last. The final evaluation is determined by the highest aggregate ranking.[45] GDSS are configurations of computer hardware and software that generate messages displayed on a central public projection screen. Ideas are presented anonymously and a skilled facilitator guides the session.[46]

Worksheets and decision matrices, such as the one shown for Wal-Mart in Table 5-16, may also be useful for organizing and evaluating environmental data. As illustrated in the table, the process includes the identification of external forces by cluster, the consideration of current and future trends, and the designation of the trend as an opportunity or threat. Not all forces present opportunities or threats. For example, the political stability in the United States forecasted in Table 5-16 is neither an opportunity nor threat for Wal-Mart.

Sharing Information

The final step of the process is *sharing,* or disseminating the audit results throughout the company, especially to key decision makers. Sharing also involves encouraging employee involvement in scanning, estimating and evaluating the environment. The size of the organization influences the sharing process. In a small or medium-sized organization, employees may be in closer contact to both the external environment and to senior managers, making information sharing easier to achieve. In larger organizations, the sharing process will be more complicated and may involve many people. An important component of this step is encouraging employees in closest contact with the environment to share information. Customer representatives who often have the most up-to-date information on customer needs often have the most to share, but are not encouraged to do so. A culture of sharing is critical for a successful external audit process.

Table 5-16 External Audit Worksheet for Wal-Mart in the U.S.

Region or Country: United States

Forces	Current (C) Year	Forecast C+1	C+2	C+3	Opportunity	Threat
Economic Force:					✓	
1. Gross Domestic Product (% Change)	2.2%	2.3%	2.3%	2.2%		
Demographic Force:					✓	
1. Hispanic population in U.S. is growing	17.7% of total U.S. population	Will grow to 19.0% of population				
Sociocultural Force:					✓	
1. Strong Hispanic culture and identifiable taste profiles	Spices and family recipes important	Trend expected to continue				
Political/Legal Force:						✓
1. Political stability	Stable	Will continue				
2. Wages	Not stable	Social and political pressure to raise wages				
Technological Force:					✓	
1. Growth of e-commerce sales	Q2 of 2016= $97.3 billion; 15.8% increase over Q2 of 2015	Growth expected to continue				

From the U.S. Census Bureau.

CONCLUSION

Organizations need a continuous, systematic external audit process. This process includes an understanding of the macro and task environments. The macro environment includes four clusters of forces (economic, demographic/sociocultural, political/legal, and technological). The task environment encompasses industries defined along horizontal, vertical, geographical, and/or competitor scopes and in which dynamic forces of competitors, suppliers, customers, new entrants, substitute products/services, and other stakeholders interact.

Conduct the external audit process in four steps (SEES). Scanning is a process of continuously searching for current and emerging information and organizing that information into useable formats or categories. Estimating is a process of extending the trends, developments, dilemmas, and events into the future. Evaluating is a process of making sense and attaching significance to the information gathered. Sharing is a process of circulating the information and encouraging all employees to participate in the external audit process.

KEY TERMS AND CONCEPTS

After reading this chapter, you should understand each of the following key terms:

- External Audit
- Macro Enviornment
- Task Environment
- Opportunity
- Threat
- Economic Forces
- Demographic/sociocultural forces
- Political/legal forces
- Technological forces
- Blogs
- Industry
- NAICS codes
- Horizontal scope
- Vertical scope
- Geographical scope

- Competitive scope
- Strategic groups
- Five Forces Model
- Rivalry among firms
- Competitor Analysis
- Entry of new competitors
- Substitute Products
- Power of Suppliers
- Power of Customers
- Power of Stakeholders
- Open System
- SEES
- Quantitative Forecasting
- Qualitative Forecasting
- Goals and challenges of an External Audit

DISCUSSION QUESTIONS

1. What are the two segments of the external environment and how do they relate to each other?
2. What kind of variables are included in the economic, demographic/sociocultural, political/legal, and technological clusters?
3. How has the definition of 'industry' changed? How do you think the definition of industry might change in the next five years?
4. Choose an industry in which you would like to compete. Use the expanded Five Forces Model to explain why you find the industry attractive.
5. Discuss the following statement: Major opportunities and threats usually result from an interaction among key external trends rather than from a single external event.
6. What are the steps of the external audit process of SEES? How would you rate the importance of each component?
7. Discuss the impact of the Internet on environmental scanning.

EXPERIENTIAL EXERCISE

Perform an External Audit of an International Business. Either in teams or individually, select an organization that competes in international markets and conduct a complete analysis of its macro environment in the United States, using the format suggested in the table below. Identify the most important opportunities and threats faced by the organization. Cite your sources of information.

Next, repeat the process for one of the organization's most important international markets. Compare the results of the U.S. and international audits. What are the implications for the firm's strategy?

REGION OR COUNTRY:							
			FORECAST				
FORCES	CURRENT (C) YEAR	C+1	C+2	C+3	OPPORTUNITY	THREAT
Economic:							
Demographic:							
Sociocultural:							
Political/Legal:							
Technological:							

ENDNOTES

1. Oyedele, Akin. "Walmart expects virtually no sales growth this year." *Business Insider.* 18 February 2016. Web. 29 April 2016.
2. Nassauer, Sarah. "Wal-Mart Surprises Market With Dim Outlook." *WSJ.* 14October 2015. Web. 27 April 2016.
3. "2016 Wal-Mart Annual Report." Accessed 26 April 2016. p.6.
4. Ibid. p.6
5. Ibid. p. 16.
6. Stevens, Laura; Nassauer, Sarah. "Wal-Mart Takes Aim at Amazon." *WSJ.* 12 May 2016. Web. 12 May 2016.
7. "2016 Wal-Mart Annual Report." Accessed 26 April 2016. p.7.
8. Nassauer, Sarah. "Wal-Mart Surprises Market With Dim Outlook." *WSJ.* 14October 2015. Web. 27 April 2016.
9. "2016 Wal-Mart Annual Report." Accessed 26 April 2016. p. 30.
10. Powell, T.C., "Organizational Alignment as Competitive Advantage," *Strategic Management Journal*, Vol. 13, 1992, pp. 119–134.
11. Jan, J. J., and R. J. Litschert, "Environment-Strategy Relationship and Its Performance Implications: An Empirical Study of the Chinese Electronics Industry," *Strategic Management Journal*, Vol. 15, 1994, pp. 1–20; W. M. Tsai, I. C. MacMillan, and M. B. Low, "Effects of Strategy and Environment on Corporate Venture Success in Industrial Markets," *Journal of Business Venturing*, Vol. 6, January, 1991, pp. 9–28; N.Venkatraman, and J. E. Prescott, "Environment-Strategy Coalignment: An Empirical Test of Its Performance Implications," *Strategic Management Journal*, Vol. 11, January, 1990, pp. 1–23.
12. Barnard, C., *The Functions of the Executive* (Harvard University Press, Cambridge, MA, 1938); R.B. Duncan, "Characteristics of Organizational Environments and

Perceived Uncertainty," *Administrative Science Quarterly*, Vol. 17, 1972, pp. 313–327; F. E. Kast and J. E. Rosenzweig, "General Systems Theory: Applications for Organizations and Management," *Academy of Management Journal*, December, 1972: pp. 447–465; P. R. Lawrence and J. W. Lorsch, *Organization and Environment: Managing Differentiation and Integration. Division of Research*, (Harvard Business School, Boston, 1967); J. Pfeffer and G. R. Salancik, *The External Control of Organizations: A Resource Dependence Perspective* (Harper & Row, New York, 1978); P. R. Varadarajan, T. Clark and W. M. Pride, "Controlling the Uncontrollable: Managing Your Market Environment," *Sloan Management Review,* Winter, 1992, p. 39.

13. McCarty, Dawn; Jinks, Beth. "Kodak Files for Bankruptcy as Digital Era Spells End to Film." Bloomberg Technology. Bloomberg. 19 January 2012. Web. 14 May 2016.

14. Hamel, G., and C. K. Prahalad, *Competing for the Future* (Harvard Business School Press, Boston, MA, 1994).

15. Ibid

16. Agnese, J. Industry Surveys: Supermarkets & Drugstores. Standard & Poor's, pp. 12–13.

17. Krogstad, Jens Manuel; Lopez, Mark Hugo. "Hispanic population reaches record 55 million, but growth has cooled." *Pew Research Center*.25 June 2015. Web. 16 May 2016.

18. Krogstad, Jens Manuel . "With fewer new arrivals, Census lowers Hispanic popula-tion projections" *Pew Research Center*. 16 December 2014. Web. 16 May 2016.

19. Krogstad, Jens Manuel; Lopez, Mark Hugo. "Hispanic population reaches record 55 million, but growth has cooled." *Pew Research Center*. 25 June 2015. Web. 16 May 2016.

20. Souza, Kim. "Wal-Mart to focus more on Hispanic shoppers." *The City Wire*. 20 March 2013. Web. 12 May 2016.

21. Narayanan V. K., and L. Fahey, Macroenvironmental Analysis: Understanding the Environment Outside the Industry. In *The Portable MBA in Strategy*, eds., L.Fahey and R.M. Randall.

(John Wiley & Sons, Inc. New York, 1997), pp. 195–223.

22. http://www.osha.gov/pls/oshaweb/owa-disp.show_document?p_table=NEWS_ RELEASES&p_id=18432 Accessed March 13, 2011

23. De la Merced, M. "Blockbuster, Hoping to Reinvent Itself, Files for Bankruptcy," The New York Times, SEPT. 23, 2010. Accessed September 16, 2016.

24. http://www.internetworldstats.com/ stats.htm. Accessed March 13, 2011.

25. Collis, D., and P. Ghemawat, *Industry Analysis: Understanding industry structure and dynamics* in the Portable MBA in Strategy, eds. L. Fahey and R. M. Randall (John Wiley & Sons, Inc. New York, 1997), pp. 171–194.

26. United States Census Bureau, 2007, www.census.gov.

27. http://www.mscibarra.com/products/ indices/gics/. Accessed March 13, 2011.

28. Hoover's Inc. "Hoover's Online, the Business Network, 2006, www.hoovers. com.

29. Agnese, J. Industry Surveys: Supermarkets & Drugstores. Standard & Poor's Net Advantage Industry. http://sandp.ecnext. com/coms2/page_industry. Accessed March 13, 2011.

30. "2016 Wal-Mart Annual Report." Accessed 26 April 2016. p. 22.

31. Collis, D. and P. Ghemawat, *Industry Analysis: Understanding industry structure and dynamics* in the Portable MBA in Strategy, eds. L. Fahey and R. M. Randall (John Wiley & Sons, Inc. New York, 1997), pp. 171–194.

32. Mateja, Jim. "How Chrysler marriage failed." *The Chicago Tribune*. 15 May 2007. Web. 15 May 2016.

33. Hunt ,M.S., *Competition in the major home appliance industry*, 1960–1970 (doctoral dissertation, Harvard University, 1972); M. Porter, *Competitive Strategy* (Free Press, New York, 1980), p. 129; R. K. Reger and A.S. Huff, " Strategic groups: A cognitive perspective," *Strategic Management Journal*, Vol. 14, 1993, pp. 103–123.

34. Nath, D. and T. Gruca, "Convergence across alternatives for forming strategic groups," *Strategic Management Journal*, Vol.

18, 1997, pp. 745–760; K. G. Smith, C. M. Crimm and S. Wally, "Strategic groups and rivalrous firm behavior: Towards a reconciliation," *Strategic Management Journal*, 18, 1997, pp. 149–157.

35. Porter, M., *Competitive Strategy* (Free Press, New York, 1980).

36. Donaldson, T. and L. E. Preston, "The Stakeholder Theory of the corporation: Concepts, evidence, and Implications," *Academy of Management Review*, Vol. 20, pp. 65–91; R. E. Freeman, *Strategic Management: A stakeholder approach* (Pitman, Boston, 1984).

37. Bhattacharya, Suryatapa. "India's Drugmakers Step Up U.S. Investment." *WSJ*. 25 February 2016. Web. 15 March 2016.

38. Loftus, Peter. "Panel Recommends FDA Approval of Knockoff of Remicade." *WSJ*. 9 February 2016. Web. 7 March 2016.

39. Bernstein, Aaron., "A Major Swipe At Sweatshops," *Business Week* (May 23, 2005): 98–100.

40. Slywotzky, A. J., *Value Migration* (Harvard Business School Press, Boston. 1996).

41. The World Future Society, www.wfs.org, accessed March 14, 2011. TechCast, http://www.techcast.org/, accessed on March 14, 2011.

42. Schoemaker, P. J. H., " Multiple Scenario Development: Its Conceptual and Behavioral Foundation," *Strategic Management Journal*, March, 1993, p. 195; A. Schriefer, "Getting the Most Out of Scenarios: Advice from the Experts," *Planning Review*, Vol. 23, No. 5, 1995, pp. 33–35.

43. Lutz, S., "Hospitals Reassess Home-Care Ventures," *Modern Healthcare*, Vol. 20, No. 37, September 17, 1990, pp. 22–30.

44. http://en.wikipedia.org/wiki/Blog. Accessed March 14, 2011. http://technorati.com/. Accessed March 14, 2011.

45. Robbins, S. P., *Essentials of Organizational Behavior*, 5th ed. (Prentice Hall, Upper Saddle River, NJ, 1997), p.105.

46. Jessup, L. M., and J. S. Valacich, *Group Support Systems* (Macmillan Publishing Company, New York, 1993).

Chapter 6

Setting Objectives and Making Strategic Choices

CHAPTER LEARNING OBJECTIVES

After studying this chapter, you should be able to

- Explain the relationship between objectives and strategies and know the SMART format for writing objectives;
- Understand and be able to apply various tools and models for strategic choice at the corporate and business levels;
- Integrate ethical considerations and analyses into strategic choices;

- Understand the dynamic nature of competition and its impact on strategic choice;
- Appreciate the increased complexity of strategic choice in a global environment.

*W*hen Microsoft was founded in 1975, the communications and computing industry was a fledgling industry, just a fraction of the size and complexity that it is today. Throughout the 1980s and up to the mid-1990s, the focus was on developing the most advanced and all-encompassing PC on the market. From the late 1990s to the mid-2000s, the goal was to leverage the endless possibilities of the Internet. Today, the primary point of emphasis is on cloud computing to support the global proliferation of mobile devices for both individuals and enterprises. Microsoft has created a new technical platform, the Azure cloud, for all of its products to communicate and share information with one another. Azure is available in 140 countries with the most datacenters (20) of any public cloud platform. China is one of those 140 countries, making Microsoft the first multinational company to operate a public cloud in China.[2] Despite its success in cloud computing, some of Microsoft's legacy businesses have struggled. For example, Microsoft's smartphones, most notably their Lumia phones, have yet to break up the stranglehold held by Apple and Android phones in the market. Microsoft faces important strategic decisions about investing in new cloud technologies while contemplating its commitment to its traditional core or "legacy" businesses.

The third step in the Strategic Management Framework, shown in Figure 6-1, is setting objectives and choosing a strategy. Microsoft is an example of a company that is in transition, reconsidering its objectives and strategies in light of key challenges from the external environment. As a firm's internal or external situation changes, its objectives and strategies may also have to change.

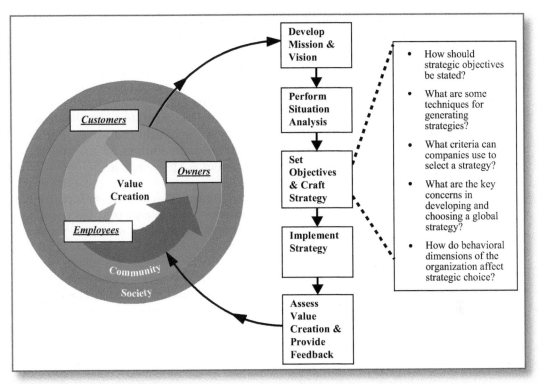

Figure 6-1
The Strategic Management Framework

In this chapter, we will discuss tools and methods for setting strategic objectives and generating, evaluating, and choosing strategies. These approaches will emphasize the importance of creating strategic objectives and crafting strategies that address the key challenges and strategic issues faced by the organization. This includes an emphasis on understanding the impact of competitive dynamics on the choice of strategy. Tools for strategic choice at both the corporate and business levels of strategy are introduced and discussed. In addition, strategic choice in a global business setting is examined. The influence of ethical considerations and behavioral dimensions of strategic choice is also considered. After reading this chapter, you should be able to answer each of the questions posed in Figure 6-1.

FOCUSING ON STRATEGIC ISSUES

Setting strategic objectives and making strategic choices are vital activities that require tight integration with the analysis assembled in the previous steps in the strategic management framework. Strategic selection is a complex process that needs to carefully weave the core attributes that define the corporation with the opportunities and threats derived from the audit of the external environment. Unfortunately, the selection of the appropriate strategic objectives and strategies is not a linear and straightforward progression that follows the completion of the situation analysis. There is no general model or formula that would ensure making the right choices. Rather, we need to thoroughly understand both the priorities and context of the organization in order to guide and inform the process of making strategy choices. To facilitate this selection process, it is valuable to identify and focus on the strategic issues facing the organization. *Strategic issues* are the critical challenges, opportunities, problems or questions the organization needs to address for the sake of its future. Identifying and focusing on these key issues is a prerequisite for determining the strategic priorities of the organization.

A decision-making framework, shown in Figure 6-2, can help to identify the strategic issues. The framework links the mission, vision and core values of the organization with the results of the internal and the external audits of the firm, and is useful for understanding both the strategic priorities and constraints of the organization and in guiding strategy selection. By examining the strategic issues, we are able to more directly connect the strengths and weaknesses developed in the internal audit to the opportunities and threats found in the external audit. The decision-making framework allows us to put the pieces together in a way that makes sense for creating value for customers, employees and shareholders. This process helps to identify strategic objectives and strategic initiatives that meet the following conditions:

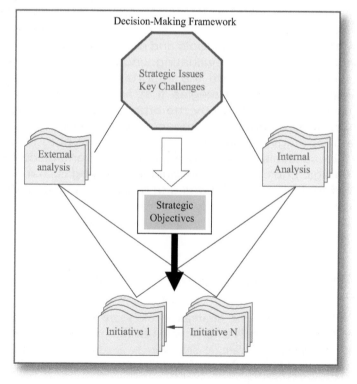

Figure 6-2
A Decision-Making
Framework

Chapter 6   **Setting Objectives and Making Strategic Choices**

- fit with company mission, vision, and objectives;
- are consistent with the realities of the external audit;
- are feasible given the firm's internal audit and its competencies and resources;
- are able to leverage and build upon competitive advantage;
- reduce vulnerability to changes in the environment;
- increase potential rewards (i.e., the return);
- establish an appropriate level of risk for the company.

Reflection is critical for identifying and articulating the right strategic issues implicit in a business situation. The business world is littered with correct answers to the wrong questions. Reflection leads to the continuous examination of whether the best questions are being asked. Although not necessarily a standard practice, it is a good practice to state a strategic issue in the form of a question that captures what is important in the situation analysis (internal and external audit) and brings focus to the strategic actions that the company needs to consider. Similarly, we should avoid framing strategic issues as numerous fragmented bullet points or as a list of weaknesses or threats. Rather, a strategic issue is an explicit statement or question that links opportunities or threats identified in the external environment with the relevant factors inside the organization. This helps the organization understand its main challenges or opportunities and highlights the gap between where the organization currently is and where it could or should be to create more value. The proper definition of a strategic issue reveals a new insight that was not obvious before.

At first, we may not understand or have enough information to identify the root cause(s) of a particular problem or strategic issue. But we could go back and re-examine the diverse internal and external factors that may underlie and lead to the emergence of these particular challenges. This process of using the decision-making framework and framing the strategic issues helps us to identify root causes and leads to a higher level of understanding of the problems that the organization is facing. It also fosters a deeper understanding of the main priorities, drivers, and constraints in the strategic choices faced.

Senior executives are often called to solve contradictions and reconcile positions that may seem incongruous. Top managers should be capable of developing a higher-level conceptualization that provides a thorough understanding of the strategic issues that the company faces. The decision-making framework can provide the common theme that links all pieces together and provides a synthesis useful for the formulation of strategic objectives and strategic choice. This tool can help organizations diagnose the strategic issues they face and answer the questions implicit in those challenges.

SETTING STRATEGIC OBJECTIVES

Strategic objectives define the fundamental goals that the corporation wants to achieve and link the mission of the organization to organizational actions. Strategies or strategic initiatives represent the specific pathways by which the organization will achieve the objectives. Strategic objectives are targets set to both focus and direct organizational activity. These objectives represent critical performance levels the organization wishes to achieve, within a defined time frame, as well as standards of performance against which the company can evaluate its progress in achieving the organizational mission and vision. Strategic objectives reflect the priorities of the company, and if set properly, should help to create coordination of activities across functions and activity centers, thereby fostering synergies. An organization without strategic objectives is an organization without a specific direction, one that will drift aimlessly toward an end that is uncertain. These objectives should both update and translate the mission, vision, and values of the company to the context in which the company is operating.

Sometimes a distinction is made between the terms "goal" and "objective." For example, some view goals as specific performance targets at intermediate levels of the firm while objectives are seen as more overriding, corporate targets.[3] We will use these terms interchangeably.

Strategic objectives broadly specify the major direction of the organization and link the mission of the organization to organizational actions. The specific numbers are derived from past performance or based on the external and internal audits. Strategies are then developed to achieve the long-term objectives. The longterm objectives also form the basis for strategy implementation, especially when used to set shortterm objectives.

Long-term objectives are stated for a planning period of more than 1 year, such as 3 years or 5 years or longer depending on the circumstances. In industries where the pace of change tends to be much faster than for the economy as a whole, such as information technology, strategic objectives must necessarily be set for a shorter time horizon, such as 3 years or less. For example, in 2015, Microsoft set goals for fiscal year 2018 to achieve $20 billion in revenue from its commercial cloud services and to serve 1 billion active Windows devices per month.[4] Objectives set for periods longer than this are rendered fundamentally meaningless by the pace of change in such industries.

Short-term or annual objectives establish specific performance targets for a period of one year. They may focus on the rate of sales growth, market share targets, profitability measures, or other targets. For example, an automobile company may set a specific one-year goal in terms of the number of vehicles that it intends to sell in that year. A university identifies a specific number of incoming freshmen to be recruited for a given class. Short-term objectives must contribute specifically to the achievement of long-term objectives.

Short-term objectives can also be set for periods shorter than a year, such as a specific promotional period. A retailer with a backlog of accumulated inventory might offer an inventory reduction sale and set specific targets for the amount of merchandise, in terms of both units and dollars, that it wants to move during the sale period.

Writing Objectives

Objectives can be effective in their various roles only if stated properly. The *SMART* format is one way to state objectives in a clear, action-oriented way. Objectives must be:

- Specific
- Measurable
- Aggressive
- Realistic
- Time-bound

The SMART format reflects the fact that objectives must be stated for specific dimensions of performance (e.g., ROI, sales, market share), in quantitative terms, if possible (e.g., 10 percent, plus 15 percent, increase by 2 share points), and for a defined time period (e.g., over the next 3 years, by the end of the fiscal year). Stating objectives such as "our company will increase our share in the children's outerwear category by 3 percentage points by the end of 2019" allows a firm to determine if objectives have been achieved or not, and to use objectives as standards by which to evaluate performance. In addition, objectives should be realistic or attainable given our asset and resource base and with a reasonable level of effort, yet challenging, and motivating. We can only "get to the next level" if we reach beyond what we have accomplished up to the present time.

Pinterest, the social sharing service that allows its members to "pin" their favorite images, videos and content to their "pinboard," announced the following operational and financial objectives in 2015 for the short and long term:

- Total revenue from ad sales will reach $3 billion by 2018.
- Total percentage of international Pinterest members will be 50% by the midpoint of 2016.[5]

Pinterest's objectives meet the SMART format test.

Performance Areas

Managers set strategic objectives in several key performance areas, including profitability, productivity, growth, market position, shareholder wealth, technological position, employees, organizational reputation, and social responsibility. These are graphically depicted in Figure 6-3. The specific metrics within each performance area will vary depending upon the size and type of organization (profit, nonprofit,

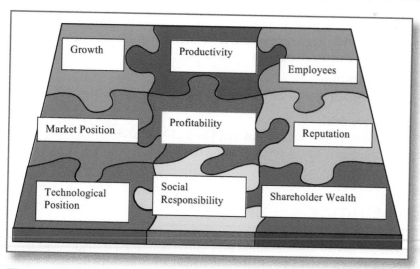

Figure 6-3
Long-term Objectives—Common Performance Areas

government) and its core values. Businesses of any size will almost always set strategic objectives on an annual basis for sales and profitability.

Examples of common objectives include the following. Notice that many, but not all, of the objectives are evaluated based on financial metrics.

1. **Growth:**
   - Achieve sales growth of 11 percent annually.
   - Triple international revenues from 5 to 15 percent of total revenues in five years.

2. **Productivity:**
   - Lower cost of goods sold from 57 percent to 52 percent by the end of next year.

3. **Employees:**
   - Increase annual employee retention rates to 80 percent within three years.

4. **Market position:**
   - Increase market share of the family-sized pie and cake category to 20 percent within three years.

4. **Profitability:**
   - Increase net profit margin from 11.3 percent in 2017 to 17.8 percent in 2020.
   - Increase Return on stockholder's equity (ROE) from 15.2 percent in 2017 to 16.9 percent in 2019.

6. **Reputation:**
   - Move from number 53 to the top 25 on the Fortune Magazine list of "Most Admired Companies" within the decade.
   - Become the number one rated school in our region in the next Business Week ranking of best regional universities.

7. **Technological position:**
   - Increase number of patents applied for and granted by 10 percent by 2019.
   - Increase the percentage of revenue generated by products introduced within the past two years to 30 percent by next year.

8. **Social Responsibility**
   - Donate 7.5 percent of after-tax profits to charities each year (e.g., Ben & Jerry's) [6]

9. **Shareholder Wealth**
   - Increase earnings per share from $1.48 to $1.60 by 2018.
   - Increase dividends by 15 percent in the next year.

STRATEGIC CHOICE

Once the strategic issues are identified and corresponding strategic objectives are set, the firm can begin to consider alternative strategies to achieve the objectives, and address the issues. This sequence of steps is shown in Figure 6-4 below.

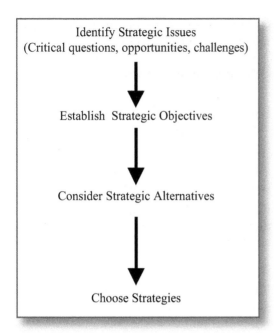

Identify Strategic Issues
(Critical questions, opportunities, challenges)

Establish Strategic Objectives

Consider Strategic Alternatives

Choose Strategies

Figure 6-4
The Sequence of Strategic Choice

Strategic choice involves identifying alternative courses of action designed to move the firm toward its strategic objectives, and ultimately, selecting a strategy from among various courses of action deemed most appropriate. These courses of action are known as *strategic initiatives* or *strategic alternatives*. This process requires translating the strategic objectives into viable courses of action that enable the organization to achieve its fundamental goals. The search for strategic alternatives is guided, constrained and interactive, yielding a set of options not all of which we either can or want to implement. These alternatives do not just materialize; the company's existing strategies, mission, vision, and its understanding of both the internal and external environments influence the choice of strategic issues to address which, in turn, inform the strategic objectives, which guide the creation of strategies as shown in Figure 6-4.

Strategic choice requires a consideration of six elements or dimensions of strategy.[7] The first four of these apply to any business while the remaining two apply to organizations with more than one business unit. In order to craft a strategy, we must make choices regarding:

1. The product market in which the business will compete, which defines not only the markets it wishes to serve but the competitors with whom it will compete.
2. The level of investment made in a business, which can vary from the significant investment required to enter or grow a market, to investment to maintain current position in a market, to investment designed to maximize short-term profit while preparing to exit the business.

3. The functional area strategies needed to compete in a market, such as product positioning, pricing, sourcing, manufacturing, distribution, and information technology.
4. The strategic assets or competencies that underlie a strategy and provide sustainable competitive advantage.

For organizations with multiple businesses, two other decision areas remain, which are

5. The allocation of financial and non-financial resources over the business units.
6. The development of *synergistic effects* across businesses, that is, the creation of value by having business units that support and complement one another.

Choosing or crafting a strategy involves generating feasible strategic alternatives, evaluating these alternatives, and selecting a strategy that will create value. While strategic choice should be based on specific criteria, it is not strictly the result of analytical thinking. Strategies are also influenced by factors such as the firm's culture, the characteristics of the strategic management team, politics in the company, ethical considerations and social responsibility. In addition, boards of directors are exercising more control over strategic choice in today's organizations. These behavioral dimensions of strategic choice will be discussed in more depth later in this chapter.

CORPORATE LEVEL STRATEGIC CHOICE

In Chapter 1, we stated that corporate or organizational level strategy focuses on two major issues: determining the organization's business scope (i.e., the choice of business(es) in which to compete in), and allocating organizational resources to these businesses. In Chapter 3, we studied several types of strategies affecting the business scope of the corporation. In virtually every organization, an underlying bias toward growth exists and drives the corporate level strategic choice, at least in the long run. Diversification strategy enables corporate managers to modify the scope of the businesses of the organization by entering and exiting new industries. Firms that follow a related diversification strategy observe a common theme among their business-units, while unrelated diversified firms (or conglomerates) lack clear commonalities in their business portfolio.

One of the fundamental questions that corporate managers need to answer is which activities should be conducted internally by the organization itself, and which activities can be done by external partners such as suppliers and distributors. Hence, vertical and horizontal integration and the formation of alliances, partnerships, and joint ventures are key aspects of corporate strategy decisions.

Let's examine how companies can make corporate strategy choices that are consistent with value creation. One goal of corporate strategy is to create synergistic effects among business units within the company, such that the whole is greater than the sum of the business unit parts.

This synergy may be elusive to achieve and the coordination among business units required by diversification can add significant administrative costs. For example, consider the 2015 merger of Kraft Foods and Heinz. Prior to the merger, Kraft sales were stagnant in 2014 and 2015 due in part to declining sales of products such as Cheez Whiz and Miracle Whip. The taste preferences of U.S. consumers were shifting away from fattier, highly processed foods.[8] The merger between the two companies was orchestrated by the owners of Heinz, 3G Capital and Berkshire Hathaway in July 2015. While Heinz owners invested $10 billion, Kraft shareholders received 49% of the stock in the merged company and a cash dividend of $16.50.[9] From the beginning, 3G and Berkshire planned to cut costs at Kraft as they announced a $1.5 billion restructuring plan after the deal was completed.[10]

While it is premature to analyze the long-term results of the merger, Kraft Heinz posted positive Q1 2016 financial results:

- Adjusted EBITDA increased by 27.3%
- Adjusted diluted earnings per share (EPS) increased by 37.7% to $0.73.[11]

Michael Porter has developed a model for assessing the value of diversification. This model suggests that for diversification to create value it must pass three tests:

1. The *attractiveness* test: Diversification must be directed towards industries with attractive (or potentially attractive) structural conditions. The presence of an attractive industry enhances the likelihood of long-term growth and profitability.
2. The *cost of entry* test: The cost of entry must not compromise the future profits of the corporation or the business unit. In the case of mergers or acquisitions, the entry costs refer to the price paid to complete the financial transaction. In the case of internal development, the cost of entry refers to aggregate value of investments made by the corporation to enter a given industry.
3. The *better-off* test: Either the new unit must gain competitive advantage from its links with the corporation, or vice-versa. What synergies exist between the core business and the new business?[12]

The Kraft-Heinz merger was assessed favorably on each of the three tests. Both companies are in the same market but many of their products are non-competing, creating opportunities for synergy. Industry analysts see the food manufacturing sector as mature but steady and growing. The cost of the merger was $3 billion but management believes that the two companies combined can operate with greater efficiency, particularly by eliminating any overlaps and inefficiencies between the production processes of the two companies.[13] Finally, the better-off test showed considerable potential for both companies in the merger. For Kraft, the addition of 3G and Berkshire Hathaway provides a corporate team with a proven track record in the food industry and for Heinz, the merger provides access to a viable supply chain system and better brand recognition in the United States.[14]

The Kraft-Heinz merger illustrates that top management must promote cooperation among business units in order to achieve synergy and improve the overall position of the organization. This example also shows that a merger of this magnitude comes at a high cost. While the restructuring process has not concluded, jobs may be cut and plants may be closed in order to make sure the newly merged company operates more efficiently. Next we will examine tools to assess value creation at the corporate level. These tools include portfolio models, transferring competencies and sharing activities, and restructuring.[15]

Portfolio Models

Portfolio models of strategic management rely on certain principles from the finance discipline as tools of strategic choice. For example, portfolio models treat business units as investments, and therefore can be used to guide decisions related to allocation of investment capital and other organizational resources, and the overall achievement of a balanced portfolio.

The business literature includes several portfolio models, the two most popular of which are the Boston Consulting Group (BCG) Matrix and the GE-McKinsey Business Screen. Portfolio models use a two-dimensional grid, with dimensions representing internal and external factors, to define and position business units so that relationships between and among different units can be easily noted. These dimensions are either single criterion dimensions, as in the case of the BCG Matrix, or composite dimensions, as in the case of the GE-McKinsey Model. The positioning of the organizational units in the matrices has specific strategic implications, as we will explain below.

The Boston Consulting Group (BCG) Matrix

The BCG Growth-Share Matrix uses single criterion dimensions of market growth rate and relative market share. *Market growth rate* is defined as the growth rate of the *industry* (not the company). Market growth rate is a surrogate indicator of the attractiveness of an industry. Analysts use different cut-off points to indicate high or low market growth rates depending on the circumstances. In some versions, the midpoint of the market growth rate axis is zero; in others, market growth rates that exceed the growth rate of the economy as a whole are considered high growth. The second dimension of the matrix, *relative market share*, is defined as the ratio of the firm's share of market to that of its largest competitor in the industry. It is an internal variable and is a surrogate indicator of the strength of the business. Again, different cut-off points can be used in the model. For example, some analysts consider a relative market share of 1.0 as the distinction between high and low share. The model uses relative instead of absolute share because a given share of market, say 20 percent, has much different implications for business strength if the leading competitor has a 40 percent share as opposed to a 10 percent share.

Businesses are measured on both the relative market share and market growth dimensions, and then they are positioned in a two-by-two matrix as shown below in Figure 6-5.[16] The model portrays each business unit or SBU as a circle, with the size of the circle corresponding to the proportion of total revenue generated by the business unit. Some versions of the model also show the percentage of corporate profits generated by the business as a pie-shaped wedge in the circle. Based on its position on the two dimensions, a business is placed into one of four categories with the colorful labels of stars (high growth, high share), cash cows (low growth, high share), question marks (high growth, low share), and dogs (low growth, low share).

Figure 6-5 shows the outcome of a BCG analysis for a corporation with four business units. Its largest business unit is a cash cow, followed by a star. It also has two smaller units - one star and one dog. This mix of businesses represents a fairly balanced portfolio, and thereby would be considered attractive (all other things being equal).

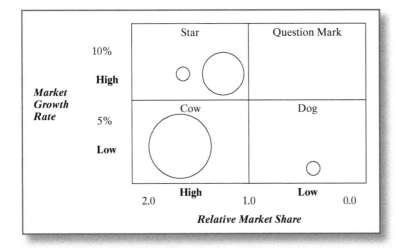

Figure 6-5
Boston
Consulting
Group Matrix
Adapted from:
Boston Consulting
Group, *Perspectives*
on Experience, Boston,
MA: The Boston
Consulting Group,
1974.

Businesses with high relative share typically achieve high margins and high profits, and produce significant amounts of free cash flow. Empirical data from the PIMS project (Profit Impact of Marketing Strategies, an initiative of the Marketing Science Institute in Cambridge, MA) has shown that there is a significant positive correlation between relative market share and return on investment. Conversely, businesses with low relative share tend to generate lower profits. High growth rate businesses require investments in cash to fuel additional growth that may in turn lead to cost advantages relating to scale economies of manufacturing and distribution experience. Low growth rate businesses, which may be in the mature stage of the life cycle, require only maintenance levels of investment.

Implications

Businesses labeled as stars are in high relative share positions in high growth markets, implying that while such businesses are profitable, they need heavy infusions of investment capital to continue strengthening their competitive position and taking advantage of possible cost economies due to both scale and experience. As the industry matures, the star will move down and become a *cash cow*, provided that the business maintains its relative market share. The cash cow moniker represents a business with high relative share in a low growth industry, leading to high profits and low demand for cash. As the term suggests, such a business generates cash that can be used to fuel businesses in high growth arenas (i.e., stars and question marks).

Question marks are businesses that have a relatively weak position in high growth industries, suggesting three alternative strategies. Firms can invest in these businesses to move them into more dominant, and therefore more potentially profitable, competitive positions. Alternatively, firms can redefine the market and use a niche strategy to gain a strong position in a smaller business. Finally, firms can prepare to exit the business, sometimes using a harvesting strategy to reap available profits before liquidating or selling the business. A *harvesting strategy* suggests minimal investment in a business to reap maximum short-term returns. It is important to remember that too many question marks will consume a lot of cash, so firms may wish to divest any question mark without significant long-term growth potential.

Dogs (low share, low growth businesses) represent potential cash traps due to the fact that they typically absorb cash with little return. Dogs can sometimes bounce back from poor performance with a turnaround or retrenchment strategy. In addition, a business labeled a dog may actually generate stable and respectable profit margins for a company.

Prudent judgment must be exercised when choosing a strategy for a business regardless of where it is positioned in the BCG model. Keep in mind that many business units may be in slow-growth categories, and thereby be considered either cash cows or dogs. Choosing "cookie cutter" strategies based solely on the positioning of a business in the BCG Matrix is unwise and potentially lethal; it is also an abdication of corporate management's responsibility.

The GE-McKinsey Business Screen

The GE-McKinsey Model, shown in Figure 6-6,[17] is also known as the market attractiveness-business strength matrix. This model is similar to the BCG Matrix in

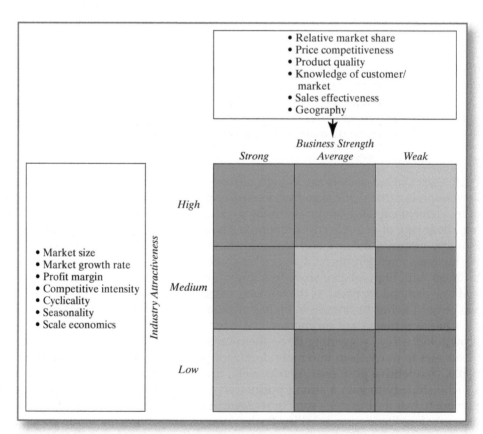

Figure 6-6
The GE McKinsey Business Screen
Reprinted from *The Manager's Guide to Competitive Marketing Strategies, Second Edition* (1999), by Norton Paley, by permission of General Electric, Inc.

theory but uses composite dimensions and a three-by-three matrix for a more comprehensive analysis of both internal and external factors.

The *market attractiveness* dimension of the model is a function of market size and growth, customer satisfaction levels, the quantity and nature of competition, price and margin levels, technology, regulation and sensitivity of the category to economic trends. The second dimension of the matrix, *business strength*, evaluates the ability to compete in a market and is a function of the size and growth rate of the firm, market share by segment, customer loyalty, margins, distribution channels, technology skills, patent positions, marketing skills, and organizational skills. The dimensions may be modified depending on what internal and external factors are considered most relevant to the business.

The two dimensions are used to plot each business unit in the matrix. Similar to the BCG model, the size of each circle can represent the proportion of total revenues generated by the unit, while a shaded wedge of the circle represents the unit's proportion of corporate profits. The cells of the matrix can be colored-coded as in Figure 6-7 to signify go (growth strategies), caution (stability or maintenance

		Business Strength		
		Strong	*Average*	*Weak*
Industry Attractiveness	**High**	Premium—Invest for Growth: • Provide maximum investment • Diversity worldwide • Consolidate position • Accept moderate near-term profits • Seek to dominate	Selective—Invest for Growth: • Invest heavily in selected segments • Share ceiling • Seek attractive new segments to apply strengths	Protect/Refocus—Selectively Invest for Earnings: • Defend strengths • Refocus to attractive segments • Evaluate industry revitalization • Monitor for harvest or divestment timing • Consider acquisitions
	Medium	Challenge—Invest for Growth: • Build selectively on strengths • Define implications of leadership challenge • Avoid vulnerability—fill weaknesses	Prime—Selectively Invest for Earnings: • Segment market • Make contingency plans for vulnerability	Restructure—Harvest or Divest: • Provide no unessential commitment • Position for divestment *or* • Shift to more attractive segment
	Low	Opportunistic—Selectively Invest for Earnings: • Ride market and maintain overall position • Seek niches, specialization • Seek opportunity to increase strength (for example through acquisition) • Invest at maintenance levels	Opportunistic—Preserve for Harvest: • Act to preserve or boost cash flow • Seek opportunistic sale *or* • Seek opportunistic rationalization to increase strengths • Prune product lines • Minimize investment	Harvest or Divest: • Exit from market or prune product line • Determine timing so as to maximize present value • Concentrate on competitor's cash generators

Figure 6-7
Strategy Options Using GE McKinsey Business Model

Reprinted from *Strategic Marketing Planning* (1982), by Bernard Rausch, by permission of American Marketing Associations, Extension Institute.

strategies) and stop (retrenchment, turnaround or exit strategies) as a way of making the model more illustrative of appropriate strategies.

As with the BCG Matrix, each cell of the GE-McKinsey model suggests a different investment strategy for the business. Suggested strategies are shown in Figure 6-7.[18]

Summary and Evaluation

The BCG model highlights the cash flow, investment needs and performance of various business units. Strategists can use the model to identify how corporate resources can best be deployed to maximize future growth and profitability.[19] The approach is relatively simple to understand and to use, which is both an advantage and a disadvantage. The notion of a balanced portfolio, defined in terms of the use of cash from businesses in slow growth markets to fuel businesses in high growth markets, is both useful and intuitively logical. However, the BCG model tends to be overly simplistic, relying on single criterion dimensions to guide significant investment decisions. Many businesses tend to fall in the middle of the matrix and this leads to ambiguous implications for strategy. Also, if the market is defined too broadly, businesses that have strength in small segments may be misidentified as dogs.

The relationships posited by the BCG model between relative share and cash generation are predicated on the assumption that firms could achieve significant cost advantages through both experience and scale effects. The experience curve posits a relationship between cumulative output and unit cost. Experience effects suggest that firms invest heavily in building market share and expanding output in order to achieve a cost advantage that will grow with accumulated experience. However, production technologies, such as the availability of computer aided design and computer aided production, have rendered experience effects inoperable in many situations, thereby invalidating the relationship between relative share and profitability.

Finally, the model potentially leads to self-fulfilling prophecies with damaging results. For example, a BCG analysis may show declining sales in a category leading to the conclusion that a business has entered the mature stage of its life cycle and cash should be pulled back and redeployed in other businesses with higher growth rates. The model may be reacting to a false signal created by some extraneous or short-term event, but the mere fact of pulling back on the cash to support a business will lead to declining, sales and profits.

The GE-McKinsey model is more comprehensive than the BCG model, but is more subjective and qualitative. Both models suffer from the same drawback in that the performance analysis is static—a view of internal and external factors at one point in time. Portfolio models treat businesses as relatively independent units. In reality, firms with multiple business units typically require some type of organized process to facilitate exchanges of technologies, skills, assets and people across functions and divisions.

Portfolio models first came into vogue as strategic planning tools in the 1970s, an era of much unrelated or conglomerate diversification. As a result of companies becoming increasingly diversified in unrelated businesses, it became important to manage the firm as a set of investments, similar to the way one would manage a financial portfolio. Over time, corporate strategy has evolved and the name of the game currently is for companies to focus their activities in related businesses that

Table 6-1 Advantages and Limitations of Portfolio Models

Advantages:

- Encourages top management to evaluate each business individually; to set objectives and consider resources
- Helps managers to recognize the inherent financial relationship between different business units
- Requires the use of external data to supplement managerial judgment
- Graphic representation makes interpretation and communication straightforward

Limitations:

- The analysis is static in that it is based on a view of internal and external factors at a point in time
- Market definitions can be somewhat arbitrary and therefore misleading
- Understanding the success requirements for an industry is not always easy
- Using standardized strategies or a cookie-cutter approach to strategic choice is overly rigid and may lead to both missed opportunities and impractical or even dangerous strategies
- Portfolio analysis may give strategists an illusion of scientific rigor and objective analysis when in fact much intuition and qualitative assessment is necessary to use portfolio models
- Some of the posited relationships that drive portfolio models have questionable validity given changes in production technology

build upon and extend core competencies and assets. This trend has resulted in substantially less unrelated diversification. Nevertheless, portfolio models continue to be utilized to help guide strategic choice.

Overall, these models are useful as analytical tools to help guide corporate and business unit strategy. The visual representation of business units reveals some useful insight. But the weaknesses of portfolio analysis mean they should be used along with other considerations and tools, and should not be relied upon in isolation. Advantages and limitations of portfolio models are summarized in Table 6-1.

Transferring Core Competencies and Sharing Resources

One of the key mechanisms for achieving value creation at the corporate level is the transfer of core competencies and the sharing of resources across business units. Resource sharing across business units allows greater efficiencies by enabling scope economies. *Economies of scope* refer to the cost advantages a firm achieves when combining activities rather than having independent and specialized companies complete them. Economies of scope may provide greater ability to differentiate by sharing resources among different business units.

The linkages across the value chain activities of different business units within a company can foster a corporate advantage based on the transfer of core competencies. The company needs to decide which competencies have become sources of competitive advantage and decide whether it wishes to retain control. Companies with strong brand equity and reputation have incentives to share this valuable resource by expanding into other market segments. The transfer of these core competencies and resources across distinct businesses units is facilitated by common ownership. The company needs to be able to monitor and control the transfer of its core competencies into other businesses. It must also develop appropriate coordinating mechanisms and incentive systems that promote cooperation among distinct business units.

Value can be created when the benefits of transferring competencies and sharing resources across business units outweigh the greater coordination costs that are required to enable these linkages. Honda originally developed its core competency in engine technology by manufacturing and selling motorcycles, but eventually was able to transfer these skills to the more profitable car segment. Honda has been able to use its engine competencies by expanding into the lawn mower, electric generator, and snow blower industries worldwide. Similarly, Amazon has become not only the largest online retailer, but a global leader in supply chain management. Amazon has applied its unique innovative culture to its supply chain to offer faster and more efficient deliveries, using technologies such as Amazon Dash (Wi-Fi-enabled push button to refill an order), Amazon Prime Air (deliveries by drone), and Prime Now (deliveries within one hour, but limited to major metropolitan areas).

In the case of mergers and acquisitions, the transfer of skills and resources can complement and enhance the competitive advantage of the receiving business. For example, Microsoft's strategy after acquiring Skype, the web application that allows for video chat and video call services, has been to integrate the service into its family of new products and services, such as the recently released 84-inch touchscreen display monitor, Surface Hub, and the not yet released HoloLens headset, which is a set of virtual reality head-mounted smartglasses.[20]

Restructuring

Restructuring creates value at the corporate level by identifying business units or firms performing below their potential and then taking the appropriate actions to increase profitability. These actions imply acquiring management control of the underperforming unit by purchasing a majority of its ownership. The restructuring company then takes the corrective actions to restore profitability. Restructuring implies shaking up the way the company operates and usually entails cutting costs and finding new ways to increase revenues.

The restructuring strategy works in the presence of capable managers who are able to pinpoint what is wrong with the company and execute a strategy that increases profitability. Restructuring is consistent with the cost of entry test since the underperforming company is purchased at a discount price. After the company has stabilized and shows signs of growth, it is not unusual for the acquiring firm to sell its shares and realizes a significant premium over the original acquisition price.

Google restructured in 2015, creating a new umbrella company, Alphabet, Inc. Since its founding in 1998, Google had branched into many diverse sectors, such as smartphones, drone technology, and biological R&D. In an effort to consolidate its various businesses, Alphabet was formed to serve as the parent company for seven other business units (Calico, the biological R&D company focused on prolonging human life; Nest, offers smart home products like thermostats, smoke detectors, and

Motorola, and McDonald's strengthens the brand and creates a cross-cultural understanding of what these brands represent. Global brand associations have become even more important with the growth of the Internet and consequent worldwide access to information. Of course, we must make sure that any words we use in advertising slogans translate properly. Many examples exist of slogans that when translated take on unintended, unfortunate and sometimes comical meanings. For instance, Chevrolet's "Nova," when translated into Spanish became "doesn't go," and Pepsi's slogan, "come alive," when translated into Chinese became "brings your ancestors back from the dead" (creating significant challenges for truth in advertising). In the United States, people "pin" their favorite things to their tack board, and it has translated well for American Pinterest users. However, the concept of "pinning" something to one's "board" is not common in Brazil and "pins" are more commonly associated with fasteners on a diaper. So in 2015, the Pinterest changed the feature to "saving" photos to the user's "folder."[42]

The opportunity to source products from low-cost locations has been one of the prime reasons for the growth of global strategies. Major league baseballs and other sporting equipment are manufactured in countries such as Haiti and Korea where labor costs are much lower than in the United States. As we know from Chapter 1, ethical concerns may arise from off-shore manufacturing. Nike has suffered negative publicity because of alleged problems in their Asian contract manufacturing plants.

Countries such as Ireland have established significant economic incentives for companies to locate manufacturing, distribution, and sales operations there. These incentives take the form of low cost land acquisition, tax breaks, and even cash payments. Ireland is home to a number of pharmaceutical and health care companies, including Merck, Abbott, Pfizer, Lilly, Novartis, Roche, and GlaxoSmithKline. Together, these companies help make Ireland the number two exporter of medicines in the world. Japanese auto companies have located production plants in the United States, staffed by Americans, not only to reduce transportation expenses, but also to avoid tariffs on cars imported into the United States. Finally, companies in wireless communication have found Eastern Europe to be a particularly enticing market due to the relatively low level of penetration of wired telephones.

The global growth of users of the Internet and corresponding growth of e-commerce have bolstered global strategies. As discussed in Chapter 5, Internet usage has grown everywhere but has particularly accelerated in Asia, Africa and Latin America. English language users now account for 25.9% of global Internet usage with Chinese speakers representing 20.9% of Internet users. From 2000 to 2015, the number of Chinese speaking Internet users increased by 2080.9% while English speaking Internet users increased by 520.2%.[43] Forrestor Research predicts that online sales will reach $523 billion by 2020, growing by 9.32% each year from 2015 to 2020.[44]

Standardization Versus Customization

Companies that compete globally face two types of potentially conflicting competitive pressures: pressures for cost reductions and pressures to be locally responsive.[45] Pressures for cost reductions cause companies to seek out low-cost locations for value-added activities, and to standardize products and marketing tactics across countries in order to achieve scale and experience efficiencies. Pressures for local responsiveness lead to differentiation of products and marketing tactics in order to meet individual country demand patterns as well as market and competitive conditions, distribution channels, business practices and government policies. Differentiation involves smaller levels of and duplication of activities, which in turn lead to higher costs.

As a result of the conflicting pressures toward both cost reduction and local market responsiveness, one of the key issues in global strategy is that of standardization or *globalization* versus customization or *localization*. Firms that standardize product design, production processes, brands and marketing approaches can achieve significant cost savings research and development activities can be spread over a larger base of business. Standardized product design leads to efficiencies in the supply chain, manufacturing, and after-the-sale service. Use of the same brand name and advertising strategies from country to country helps create impact due in large part to the amount of international travel and global access to information.

While global tastes and preferences in many product categories have increasingly converged, customization is often mandated by significant differences in topography, climate, language, culture, customs and regulations that exist between countries. For example, U.S. automobile companies must not only provide for increased fuel efficiency in overseas markets where gasoline prices far exceed those in the United States, but they must conform to local customs, such as driving on the left side of the road in Japan and the United Kingdom. The technology platform for electronics products differs between Europe and the U.S. Companies that customize a brand name or marketing approach may find that the higher cost is more than offset by being perceived as a "local player." Plus, products that deliver significant benefits in one country may not work at all in another country. Currently, any food manufactured from a genetically modified seed will have a very poor reception from the European Union or in Japan.

Certain guidelines exist to help managers make decisions on standardization versus customization. In general, commodity products, capital-intensive processes, and technology platforms favor some degree of standardization. At the same time, advances in the technology of design, manufacturing, distribution, and advertising have made it easier for companies to customize offerings without experiencing significant cost disadvantages.

A framework for assessing the globalization versus localization question is presented in Figure 6-9. The framework shows that some industries, such as aerospace, chemicals, and consumer electronics, are well suited for a global strategy. These industries are characterized by customers whose needs are relatively homogenous around the world. This means that products and services do not need to be customized for the local market. Other industries, such as food retailing, banking, and legal services, require products and services that are tailored to the needs of the local market, and are better suited for a multinational strategy Some industries, such as pharmaceuticals and automobiles, require a mixed strategy to gain the efficiencies of a standardized approach and to adapt to and accommodate local market needs. For example, Lipitor, Pfizer's drug for elevated cholesterol, may be the same throughout the world, but how that drug is priced, promoted, distributed, and sold will depend on varying country regulations and market conditions.

In situations where pressures toward globalization are high and pressures toward localization are low, such as in high-technology products with high costs of

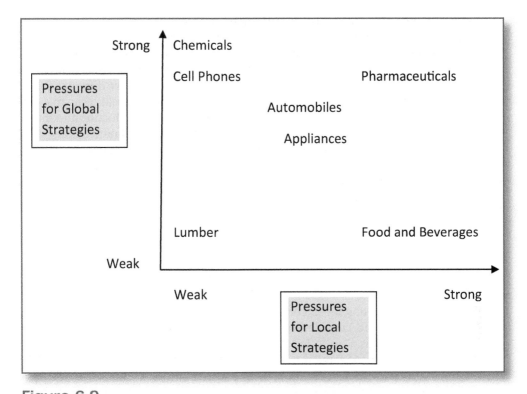

Figure 6-9
The Global-Local Matrix
Source: Adapted from Henzler, Herbert and Wilhelm Rall. "Facing Up to the Globalization Challenge."
The McKinsey Quarterly, Fall 1986.

research and development, there is a strong argument for a global strategy. Hybrid strategies are also available. When Dell entered India, for example, it did not want to alter its build-to-order model for doing business. However, competition from HP and Lenovo forced them to change their strategy slightly. Indian customers were waiting almost a month for delivery of their computers. By opening a factory in India, Dell cut its delivery time by almost half. Customers were also struggling with the idea of not seeing the computer before they purchased it. To address this complaint, Dell opened exclusive stores across India by partnering with local retailer Tata Infotech.[46]

Where pressures toward globalization are low and pressures toward localization are high, such as in low-value consumer packaged goods that must appeal specifically to local tastes and preferences, there is a strong argument for a localized strategy. For products in the other cells or toward the middle of the matrix, the strategic implications are not so clear. For example, McDonald's benefits by standardizing the back-of-the-house production and assembly of foods, but customizes specific items as well as the taste profile to appeal to local food preferences, like offering the McArabia Chicken flatbread at its Middle Eastern locations, adding macarons to its French menu, and featuring McSpaghetti at its Filipino locations.

Pharmaceutical companies spend upwards of $500 million to develop a new drug and gain regulatory approval, but the cost of goods is minimal. So the key to profitability is to expand distribution globally in order to write off the investment over a larger market base. Local customs and medical practices affect the industry. For example, Japan is very concerned with safety and minimization of side effects, even to the extent that the Japanese will trade efficacy for safety, thus calling for lower dosages. Similarly, different countries with different cultures require different colors and shapes of both the pills and the packaging. Global pharmaceutical companies deliver these different products and packages, despite the inherent production and marketing inefficiencies, to both meet local needs and to help protect the brand against generics.

Competing on a global basis is complex and difficult. Differences in culture, language, business customs, economic and political systems, and regulations abound, and firms must gain insight into the far-reaching implications of these differences to understand and control the uncertainties inherent in global competition.

BEHAVIORAL ASPECTS OF STRATEGIC CHOICE

Strategic choice on any level (corporate, business, functional, international) requires the contribution and consideration of people inside the organization. As a result, human behavior has a profound influence on strategy. For example, the characteristics of the senior management team, the organization's culture and its beliefs about ethics and social responsibility come into play in strategic choice, as they shape how individuals in the firm behave and what the firm seeks to achieve. Human behavior must also be considered when choosing strategies because as explained in Chapter 9, people are a critical part of the implementation of any strategy.

In this section, we turn to two of the behavioral aspects of strategic choice—organizational culture, and ethics/corporate social responsibility—and discuss how each factor relates to the strategic choice process.

Organizational Culture

Every organization possesses a unique **organizational culture**, consisting of "shared values, beliefs, attitudes, customs, norms, personalities and heroes that describe a firm."[47] Culture is learned, shared, and passed down from generation to generation within the firm. Culture shapes the behavior of both individuals that make up the firm and the firm itself. For example, one can easily observe the differences in culture between a high-tech Silicon Valley firm and a major metropolitan bank in several dimensions: the appearance, dress and language of employees, the schedules kept by employees, even the design and decor of company facilities.

Culture binds the organization and provides an identity for its people. Culture helps give meaning to the work that people do for the firm. People who do not share cultural values and norms find very quickly that there is a lack of fit or comfort in the environment. On the other hand, those that share core values derive inspiration and a sense of commitment to move the organization ahead. As a result, culture is important to strategic choice as it impacts the ability and willingness of employees to carry out the strategy chosen by management.

No two organizational cultures are the same. Cultures differ from one another in many ways. Some common factors that distinguish cultures are the extent to which they exhibit the following characteristics:

- Innovation
- Risk-taking
- Team Orientation
- People Orientation
- Technological Sophistication
- Attention to detail
- Aggressiveness
- Stability

In fact, there is ample evidence from the business world to support the notion that blending different organizational cultures, such as that of Chrysler and Daimler-Benz discussed in Chapter 5, proves to be one of the most vexing issues involved in mergers. Other failed mergers due to clashing corporate cultures are New York Central Railroad and Pennsylvania Railroad (1968-1970), AOL and Time Warner (2000-2008), and Sprint and Nextel (2005-2012).[48]

Strategies and other organizational initiatives that fall within the accepted range of behavior will likely be supported and embraced by managers and employees. Strategies that violate corporate norms will be very difficult to implement. Companies that experience a significant downturn in financial performance often must significantly alter organizational direction to adapt to a changing environment. One of the most difficult aspects of moving in a different direction is getting the people that make up the organization to respond positively to the change, because the change may not fit the existing culture.

UPS was founded in 1907, giving the firm a 64-year head start on FedEx. But it was Frederick Smith, founder of Federal Express, who formed the idea of overnight package delivery in 1971, forever changing the package delivery business. UPS did not create its own overnight service until 1988. The explanation may lie in its corporate culture. UPS had a rigid, military-like culture from its earliest days as a messenger service. This culture did not breed risk-taking. But within the company, speed was valued above all other virtues. So while it took UPS a number of years to pull even with FedEx, UPS has moved ahead on many fronts, largely because UPS has created logistical systems for its customers that save time and money.[49]

Because cultures are so multifaceted, they are difficult to understand. Ideally, a culture can be understood by spending time inside it and observing what the organizational members value and how they behave. Cultures can sometimes also be understood through classic stories told by people in the company. For example, it is an age-old legend in the Ford Motor Company that its founder, Henry Ford, used to remind his people when they disagreed with him that it was his name on the building. Company rituals can also give one a sense of its culture. For example, many companies have celebrations for employees like annual Christmas parties and company picnics.

Some organizations do not have a strong sense of culture; employees do not share common values. Oftentimes, these organizations have subcultures. *Subcultures* are smaller groups of people in an organization bonded together by a set of common values that are different than the values held by the majority of the people in the organization. An example of a subculture could be a sales team that focuses on customer needs and earning commissions.

Ethics and Social Responsibility

We know that organizations have a responsibility to create value for and serve the interests of customers, employees and shareholders. This obligation includes the need to make a profit and secure the long-term survival of the firm, to provide products or services that satisfy customer needs, and to provide employment opportunities that are rewarding. But do organizations also have a responsibility to go beyond financial obligations? Do they have more direct and fundamental ethical responsibilities to their stakeholders?

Some economists such as Milton Freidman contend that the firm's only responsibility is to make profits for investors, and that companies ought to adopt policies that treat others well and respond to their interests only insofar as they help the company generate a profit. This view sees ethics as a means to the goal of profit. Others disagree with Freidman, emphasizing the fundamental obligation of organizations to act in ethical and socially responsible ways. In this view, the ethical obligation is not adopted merely as a strategy to make profits, but because it is the morally right thing to do. Perhaps the ethical transgressions of companies such as Enron, WorldCom, Global Crossing and Arthur Andersen support this latter view and underscore the need for a renewed commitment to ethical behavior in business.

The decisions and outputs of organizations impact the communities in which they operate and may also reverberate to the broader society. For example, companies provide significant benefits to communities—employment, tax revenues, and intellectual capital, among others—but can also create adverse impacts on the aesthetics of the community or create traffic, congestion, and pollution problems. Managers need to understand how to analyze ethical issues and make decisions. Various approaches or frameworks for doing so are introduced and explained below.

The organizational culture is influenced by the personal ethics of the people inside it. *Personal ethics* are the moral principles that define the behavior that a person believes is acceptable or right. One person's ethics often differ from another person's ethics, as people tend to bring different experiences and values to the workplace and consider situations differently. This does not suggest, however, that everything is relative and there is no way to determine right from wrong.

Business ethics are the moral principles that define the behavior that the organization as a whole views as acceptable. What is considered morally acceptable or unacceptable may vary from one company to the next, but experience proves that not all organizational decisions and actions are ethically defensible. In fact, business ethics and personal ethics are both subject to critical assessment through the use of the ethical frameworks described below. These frameworks attempt to provide resources for organizing, evaluating, justifying and adjudicating between ethical beliefs. Some frameworks are:

- Utility view—it is ethical if it represents the greatest good for the greatest number of people.
- Rights view—it is ethical if it protects and respects basic human rights.
- Justice view—it is ethical if it treats people fairly based on basic standards, rules, and laws.

These ethical norms, which are further discussed below, are in contrast to a norm of *individualism* that suggests an action is ethical if it serves one's own self-interests, and *relativism* which suggests that there is no way to determine right from wrong since it all depends on the situation and every situation is unique. Relativism and individualism are criticized as ways to justify almost any type of action or behavior.

Business ethics drive an organization's sense of **corporate social responsibility**, which is the obligation that it feels towards its stakeholders. As in the cases of personal and business ethics, corporations differ in their sense of corporate social responsibility. All organizations tend to concern themselves with economic responsibilities. *Economic responsibilities* refer to an organization's obligation to be profitable and stay in business. This focuses on keeping jobs for employees and satisfying customers. Most organizations also concern themselves with *legal responsibilities*, which refer to an organization's obligation to obey the law and other external regulators.

Organizations should go beyond economic and legal responsibilities to emphasize ethical responsibilities. *Ethical responsibilities* refer to a company's obligation to focus not only on making a profit or obeying the law, but to respond to situations based on what it believes is right, just, and fair. Ethical responsibilities may overlap with economic and legal responsibilities. For example, the responsibility to look after the investors' money is a responsibility of all three sorts. The responsibility to investors is economic if the reason given is the need to stay in business; it is legal if it pertains to the fiduciary duties of management; it is ethical if the reasons given are that management has a fundamental duty to either not harm or protect specific interests of those affected by corporate decisions.

Some organizations go further still and focus on *voluntary responsibilities*. Firms that adopt voluntary responsibilities also focus on doing what is right, just, and fair. The difference, though, is that when an organization takes on voluntary responsibilities, it is not just responding to situations. The organization is not only proactively trying to be a good corporate citizen by attempting to advance the well-being of individuals, organizations, communities, and society, but also going "above and beyond the call of duty." That is, the voluntary responsibilities are good works or policies that the company freely chooses to support, rather than acts or policies that it is required by legal or moral principles to adopt. For example, some organizations encourage their employees to volunteer with non-profit or community service organizations and provide them with compensated time to do so.

Before making a commitment to a strategic choice, managers need to assess the ethical dimensions of the strategy. Does the strategy pass the ethics test? Some companies ask themselves, "Will we be comfortable reading about ourselves and this strategic choice in a front-page newspaper article?" Figure 6-10 presents a three-stage process for analyzing the ethical aspects of a strategic choice. In stage one, the facts and evidence about the strategy are gathered. What is the strategy; what resources will it consume; what stakeholders will it impact; what are its intended and unintended consequences?

In stage two the strategy is analyzed according to various ethical frameworks and moral principles described above. The *utility* analysis seeks to identify the various stakeholders impacted by the strategy and the relative costs and benefits of the strategy for each. The utilitarian approach emphasizes consequences and aims to assess the aggregate welfare that the strategy produces. The better strategy is the one that produces the most overall benefit for stakeholders. Some inherent problems with this approach include the practical difficulty of predicting and measuring consequences of strategies and the possibility that even a strategy that benefits many stakeholders can violate the fundamental rights of a particular stakeholder.

To counteract these inherent problems, a *rights*-based analysis can be conducted. This approach recognizes the basic rights of stakeholders such as respect for property rights and personal dignity, and the duty of the organization to respect those rights. The Golden Rule, "Do unto others as you would have them do unto you," is a rights-based principle, emphasizing the norm that a decision or act is ethical if it results in implications for others that you would not mind for yourself.

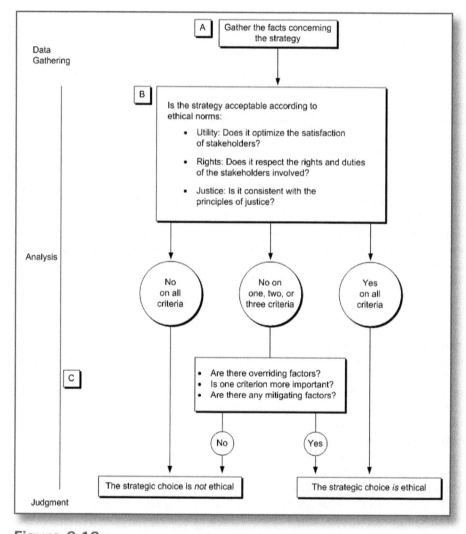

Figure 6-10
A Framework for Ethical Analysis of Strategic Choice
Source: Adapted from Cavanagh, G. F. (2006). *American Business Values : A Global Perspective* (5th ed.). Upper Saddle River, NJ: Pearson/Prentice Hall.

Let's consider an example. Suppose a major food retailer is considering a strategy to open a supermarket in the middle of an impoverished and under-served urban neighborhood. The new store may be very appealing to local consumers who would gain access to more grocery and nonfood products at lower prices, and to potential employees who might be hired to staff the new store. The company could justify the strategy based on the good it will do for the neighborhood and for shoppers, a utilitarian argument. But does this aggregate good outweigh the rights of local homeowners whose homes are located on the property where the supermarket wants to open? Do the rights of a few homeowners outweigh the potential benefits of a new supermarket to many stakeholders or does the aggregate good outweigh the homeowners' rights? This example illustrates that rights may impose constraints on utilitarian arguments for the aggregate good.

Similar to the rights approach, the *justice* approach evaluates the strategy based on principles of fairness and justice. The justice approach might apply to issues such as setting executive compensation versus workers salaries, equal opportunity for women and minority candidates, sweat shops, and the question of a living wage. In the example of the supermarket above, a justice approach might also be applied to assess ethical considerations. For example, is it fair for supermarkets (or other retailers) to avoid impoverished neighborhoods? Do companies, in this case food retailers, have any obligations to serve consumers in poor communities? If so, how are those obligations balanced against the obligation to be profitable and create value for stockholders? Some companies are turning conventional wisdom upside down and finding creative and profitable ways to serve the poor as consumers. These strategies not only respect and promote the dignity of the poor but also create value for stockholders.

As Figure 6-10 shows, the third and final stage of ethical analysis is to make a judgment as to whether the strategic choice is ethical. Strategies that pass the ethics test are ready to be considered for the next steps of the strategic management process as described in the following chapters.

Conclusion

Strategies are the actions organizations want to take in order to reach predetermined objectives. Objectives should be stated in terms that are actionable and measurable, and must be set so that the achievement of a sequence of short-term objectives will move the firm toward achievement of long-term objectives. For multiple business firms, strategies are established at the organizational as well as the business unit level. At the organizational level, portfolio models provide guidance for strategy creation. At the business unit level, techniques such as the SWOT Matrix and scenario planning help managers create strategies that are appropriate given the organization's situation analysis.

Microsoft is an example of a firm that operates beyond the boundaries of its home market and therefore must think globally in generating and choosing strategies. Global strategies involve choices regarding whether to standardize (globalize) or customize (localize) specific activities and processes. Firms must consider the various pressures toward both globalization and localization in setting strategy.

Strategic choice is subject to a number of competitive, ethical and behavioral dynamics. Financial tools for strategic choice are the focus of the next chapter.

KEY TERMS AND CONCEPTS

After reading this chapter you should understand each of the following terms.

- Strategic Objectives
- The SMART Format for Objectives
- Portfolio Models
- The BCG Matrix
- The SWOT Matrix
- Scenario Planning
- Global strategy
- Globalization
- Behavioral aspects of strategic choice
- Personal ethics

- Strategic issues
- Rights-based approach to ethics
- Long-term and Short-term objectives
- Multinational strategy
- The GE-McKinsey Business Screen
- Competitive Advantage
- Localization
- Organizational Culture
- Corporate Social Responsibility
- Utilitarian approach to ethics

DISCUSSION QUESTIONS

1. You have just been appointed Vice President of Baseball Operations for the most longsuffering franchise in major league baseball—the Chicago Cubs, a team that has not won a world championship since 1908. Using the SMART Format discussed in the chapter, develop a set of both long-term and short-term objectives for the franchise.

2. Compare and contrast the BCG and GE-McKinsey portfolio models in terms of (a) how they are constructed and (b) their implications for strategic choice.

3. Assume you are the president of a company with 3 major product divisions. Division A is in a low growth market, and has a low market share position. Divisions B and C are both market share leaders in their respective markets. Division C is in a high growth market and Division B is in a market that is growing at a rate of 2 percent per year. Sales and income figures for the three Divisions are shown below. Use the Boston Consulting Group Matrix to diagram your portfolio of product divisions and discuss the implications of your diagram (identify any assumptions you find necessary). Label your axes.

Product Division	Sales (in millions $)	Operating Profits (in millions $)
A	250	25
B	200	35
C	50	10

4. Kodak is a company that exemplifies how fundamental change in technology can severely affect corporate performance. Using the business periodical literature, perform a SWOT analysis for Kodak's photography business, and use your SWOT matrix to generate four strategies that Kodak might pursue to enhance the firm's ability to create value for its customers, employees and shareholders.

5. The genesis of Nike was collaboration between Bill Bowerman, who knew how to create high-performance running shoes, and Phil Knight, who understood

how offshore production could yield a major cost advantage. Discuss Nike's current global strategy and the extent to which Nike is/should be globalizing/standardizing or localizing/customizing its strategies.

6. What is the relationship between the behavioral aspects of strategic choice and value creation for employees, customers, and shareholders?

EXPERIENTIAL EXERCISE

Microsoft has embarked on a number of new strategic initiatives including Windows 10, Surface Hub, and HoloLens. Using the current business periodical literature, describe these and other new strategic initiatives of Microsoft. Assess each of these initiatives (1) with respect to the extent to which each leverages and enhances a competitive advantage and (2) according to the criteria for evaluating strategies specified in this chapter.

ENDNOTES

1. "2015 Microsoft Annual Report." *Microsoft*. Accessed 13 May 2016.
2. Ibid
3. Hunger, J. D., and T. L. Wheelen. *Strategic Management*. 5th ed. Reading, MA: Addison-Wesley Publishing Company, 1996, 12.
4. Op cit, "2015 Microsoft Annual Report."
5. Koh,Yoree. "Pinterest Works to Pin Down Path to Wider International Audience." *WSJ*. 23 March 2016. Web. 9 April 2016.
6. Ben & Jerry's was acquired by Unilever in April 2000. Part of the acquisition agreement specified that Ben & Jerry's could continue their annual practice of donating a percentage of after-tax profits to charities.
7. Aaker, D. *Strategic Market Management*. New York: John Wiley & Sons, Inc., 1999, 4–5.
8. Gasparro, Annie. "Kraft Heinz Is Still Taking Shape After Its Own Merger." *WSJ*. 5 August 2015. Web. 9 May 2016.
9. Giammona, Craig; Boyle, Matthew. "Kraft Will Merge With Heinz in Deal Backed by 3G and Buffett." *Bloomberg*. 25 March 2015. Web. 10 May 2016.
10. Op Cit, Gasparro, A.
11. "Kraft Heinz Reports First Quarter 2016 Results." *Business Wire*. Berkshire Hathaway. 4 May 2016. Web. 10 May 2016.
12. Porter, M. E. "From Competitive Advantage to Corporate Strategy," *Harvard Business* Review (May–June 1987): 46.
13. Heneghan, Carolyn. "Merger update: Kraft Heinz zeroes in on efficiencies, synergies." *Food Dive*. Industry Dive. 25 April 2016. Web. 11 May 2016.
14. Ibid.
15. These tools were adapted from Porter, M. E. "From Competitive Advantage to Corporate Strategy," *Harvard Business Review* (May–June 1987): 46.
16. Boston Consulting Group, *Perspectives on Experience*. Boston: The Boston Consulting Group, 1974.
17. Paley, N. *The Manager's Guide to Competitive Marketing Strategies*. 2nd ed. Boca Raton, FL: CRC Press, 1999, 154.
18. Paley, N. *The Manager's Guide to Competitive Marketing Strategies*. 2nd ed. Boca Raton, FL: CRC Press, 1999, 155.
19. Hill, C. W. L., and G. R Jones. *Strategic Management Theory: An Integrated Approach*. 3rd ed. Boston: Houghton Mifflin, 1995, 308.
20. Warren, Tom. "Skype is everywhere in Microsoft's latest vision for the future." *The Verge*. Vox Media. 18 March 2015. Web. 11 May 2015.
21. Kelly, Heather. "Meet Google Alphabet-Google's new parent company." *CNN Money*. CNN. 11 August 2015. Web. 11 May 2016.
22. Hill, C. W. L., and G. R. Jones. Strategic *Management Theory: An Integrated Approach*. 3rd ed. Boston: Houghton Mifflin, 1995, 171.

23. Weihrich, H. ,"The TOWS Matrix: A Tool for Situational Analysis," *Long Range Planning 15,* no. 2 (April 1982): 54–66.

24. "2015 Starbucks Annual Report." *Starbucks.* Accessed 30 April 2016.

25. "Starbucks and PepsiCo to Bring Starbucks RTD Beverages to Latin America." *Starbucks Newsroom.* Starbucks. 23 July 2015. Web. 12 May 2016.

26. Aaker, D. *Strategic Market Management.* New York: John Wiley & Sons, Inc.,1999, 32.

27. Wysocki, B., Jr., "Power Grid: Soft Landing or Hard? Firm Tests Strategy on 3 Views of Future-Most Likely, Duke Energy Decides, Is a Growth Era of "Flawed Competition," *The Wall Street Journal,* July 7, 2000, Al.

28. Schumpeter, J.A. *The Theory of Economic Development.* Cambridge, MA: Harvard University Press, 1934.

29. D'Aveni, R., *Hypercompetion.* New York, NJ: Free Press, 1994.

30. Smith, K.G., C..M. Grimm, and M.J. Gannon. *Dynamics of Competitive Strategy.* Newbury Park, CA: Sage Publications, 1992.

31. Chen, M. J., "Competitor Analysis and Interfirm Rivalry: Toward a Theoretical Integration," *Academy of Management Journal 21* (1996): 100–134.

32. Warren, S., "Move to Denver Signals Threat To Southwest's Low-Cost Model," *The Wall Street Journal,* November 29, 2005, A1.

33. Griffin, G., "Spirit Airlines to Drop Flights from Denver to Detroit, Fort Lauderdale, Fla." *Knight Ridder Tribune Business News,* July 8, 2004, 1.

34. Derfus, P.J., P.G. Maggitti, C..M. Grimm, and K.G. Smith. "Firm Action, Rival Action, and Firm Performance: Understanding the Effect of Competitive Interdependence." *Academy of Management Conference* (2005).

35. Gimeno, J. "Reciprocal Threats in Multimarket Rivalry: Staking Out 'Spheres of Influence' in the U.S. Airline Industry." *Strategic Management Journal 20* (1999): 101–128.

36. Chen, M. J., "Competitor Analysis and Interfirm Rivalry: Toward a Theoretical Integration," *Academy of Management Journal 21* (1996): 100–134.

37. Smith, K.G., W.J. Ferrier, and H. Ndofor. "Competitive Dynamics Research: Critique and Future Directions." In Handbook of Strategic Management, eds. M. A. Hitt, R.E. Freeman, & J.S. Harrison, Oxford, U.K.: Blackwell Publishers, 2001, 315–361.

38. "Who Are Uber's Biggest Competitors?" Zacks. Zacks Investment Research. 18 February 2016. Web. 13 May 2016.

39. Ferrier, W. J., K.G. Smith, and C.M Grimm. "The Role of Competitive Action in Market Share Erosion and Industry Dethronement: A Study of Industry Leaders and Challengers." *Academy of Management Journal 42* (1999): 372–383.

40. Ibid.

41. Aaker, D. *Strategic Market Management.* New York: John Wiley & Sons, Inc.,1999, 255.

42. Koh,Yoree. "Pinterest Works to Pin Down Path to Wider International Audience." *WSJ.* 23 March 2016. Web. 9 April 2016.

43. "Top Ten Languages Used in the Web - November 30, 2015" *Internet World Stats.* Web. Accessed 12 May 2016. http://www.internetworldstats.com/

44. Lindner, Matt. "Online sales will reach $523 billion by 2020 in the U.S." *Internet Retailer.* Vertical Web Media. 29 January 2016. Web. 13 May 2016.

45. Hill, C. W. L., and G. R. Jones. *Strategic Management Theory: An Integrated Approach.* 3rd ed. Boston: Houghton Mifflin, 1995, 299.

46. Prasad, Anurag, "How Dell Conquered India," *Fortune,* February 10, 2011.

47. David, F. R. *Concepts of Strategic Management.* 6th ed. Upper Saddle River, NJ: Prentice Hall, 1997, 196.

48. Ruesink, Megan. "Top Corporate Mergers: The Good, The Bad & The Ugly." *Rasmussen College.* 28 September 2015. Web. 28 April 2016.

49. Haddad, C., and J. Ewing. "Ground Wars," *Business Week* (May 21, 2001): 65–68.

Chapter 7

Strategic Choice: A Contingency Approach

CHAPTER LEARNING OBJECTIVES

After studying this chapter, you should be able to

- Understand how strategic choices are influenced by industry characteristics;
- Apply the Five Forces model to various stages of the industry lifecycle;
- Recognize the essential aspects of technology and innovation in strategic management;
- Determine the best entry mode for firms expanding to new countries;

- Understand that successful non-profit organizations must also manage financial performance;
- Recognize that with some modification, non-profit organizations pursue the same rules of strategy as businesses.

Strategic choices are based on context. That is, the right strategies for a firm depend on the firm's situation. This "contingent" relationship between strategic choice and firm context is reflected in the Strategic Management Framework shown in Figure 7-1. Throughout the book we have emphasized the importance of "strategic fit," that is, analyzing the firm's internal and external environments to ensure that the strategies selected fit the context of the firm. In this chapter, we identify and explain several specific and unique cases of contingency variables that affect strategic choice. After reading this chapter you should be able to answer each of the questions listed in Figure 7-1.

For years, Amazon.com's founder and CEO, Jeff Bezos (see Figure 7-2), has driven investors mad due to his insistence on prioritizing growth opportunities over improving profitability, thus disappointing Wall Street analysts on earnings performance while posting sizable growth in sales.[3] Yet over the past ten years, Amazon.com's stock has wildly outperformed the overall market. How can this be?

This is because in high-growth markets like those pursued by Amazon.com, earnings are secondary. Size is imperative; the secret is to capture market share now in order to reap profits later, after these markets begin to mature. Senior managers of Amazon.com continue to believe that there is extraordinary growth potential in e-commerce, and have been willing to defer profits until growth opportunities wane. Investors generally approve, driving up Amazon.com's share price.

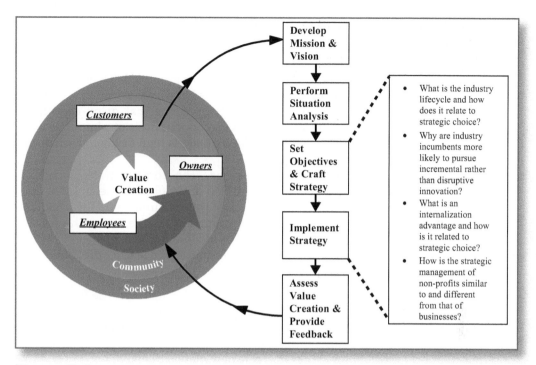

Figure 7-1
The Strategic Management Framework

Figure 7-2
Jeff Bezos
Courtesy of epa european pressphoto agency b.v/Alamy.

A Contingency-based View
of Strategic Choice

A frustrated former U.S. President, Harry Truman, once grumbled "Give me a one-handed economist. All my economists say, 'on the one hand ... on the other.'"[4] When making this comment, President Truman was complaining that many economic theories are contingency-based. That is, the correct economic decision almost always depends upon something, such as whether employment is high or low, or whether consumer confidence is rising or falling.

Strategic choices are also contingency-based. The correct strategic choice depends upon the financial and operating condition of the firm, the behavior of the firm's competitors, and the conditions within the firm's environment. This chapter provides a brief overview of contingency-based strategic choice, using the firm's environment and the firm's overall mission as the moderating variables.

Let's start by considering some of the important contingencies that strategic decision-makers must consider:

- In new or embryonic markets, barriers to entry can be high, because few if any firms have the knowledge required to compete in these nascent areas, and customer demand is poorly understood. Savvy firms in these markets prioritize capturing market share in promising market segments, and improving quality, reliability and credibility in order to create new market demand.

- As highlighted in the brief case of Amazon.com above, higher rates of growth are easier to achieve in growth markets. This is because new customers are entering these markets at a relatively fast clip, so incumbent firms face relatively lower competitive rivalry. Smart managers know how to exploit this situation by capturing as much share as possible and creating a sustainable competitive advantage that can serve as a barrier to future competitive entry.

- In markets undergoing shakeouts, some sorting takes place. Growth begins to slow and competitive rivalry begins to take shape. Firms that entered the market but failed to develop a sustainable competitive advantage may fail.

- In mature markets, growth slows, barriers to entry increase, and rivalries among competitors intensify. By now, the best firms exploit their sustainable competitive advantage in order to defend their market positions, and to manage profitability.

- In declining markets, weaker firms, or firms with more attractive prospects elsewhere, exit the industry. Now is the time for the strongest firms to consolidate their positions, and reap considerable profits.

- High-tech markets follow very different, sometimes surprising rules. For example, firms that are focused on high-tech products or services are highly susceptible to being overtaken by new forms of innovation. Despite their best efforts, incumbent firms in high-tech industries may get caught by surprise by new forms of innovation. Highly-innovative firms also often *share information with each other*. This seems to be foolish—maybe even anti-competitive. In fact, smarter firms know that they can learn from their competitors and innovate faster than them.

- Strategic choice in international markets is still poorly understood. For example, a common view is that firms must build their own facilities and hire their own employees overseas. Quite often, this foreign direct investment (FDI) is not necessary.
- In non-profit organizations, unique aspects in mission, sources of funds, the end-users of the product/service provided, employee motivation, and leadership styles complicate the strategic process. Particularly challenging to management is balancing the needs of clients who many times do not pay directly for the cost of a product/service with a diverse set of funding stakeholders who many times have priorities that are unrelated to the mission of the organization. Another vexing dilemma is controlling the productivity of a workforce that is frequently more wed to the cause than the organization addressing the cause.

Following is a more careful consideration of a contingency-based model of strategic choice emphasizing the impact of the Industry Lifecycle Model, and important characteristics of high-tech industries, international markets, and non-profit markets on strategic choice.

STRATEGY BY INDUSTRY LIFECYCLE STAGE

Industry Life Cycle and the Five Forces Model

As you recall from Chapter 5, the Five Forces Model of Competition determines the nature and extent of competition in an industry and influences the strategies of firms by limiting their options (such as pricing) and affecting their financial performance. Firms competing in industries with relatively stronger collective forces face significant challenges in creating economic value and generating profit. Firms competing in industries with relatively weaker collective forces are more likely to create financial value.

An important view is that the five forces that shape the competitive environment change over time in predictable ways. One way to understand how these forces change is to consider the Industry Life Cycle Model.

The Industry Life Cycle Model was introduced in the 1970s,[5] with a generally accepted version developed by 1980.[6] The model describes industry evolution in five distinct phases, ranging from embryonic through growth, shakeout, mature and decline (see Figure 7-3 below). In each of these phases, industry characteristics change in important ways. Astute strategic managers adapt their firm's strategy to accommodate these changing industry conditions.

Embryonic Stage

Sometimes it is hard to remember that wireless telephones have been available for sale since the mid-1980s. Why didn't wireless take off until about ten years later in the mid-1990s? The reason is because in the early years, mobile service was lousy, prices were outrageously high, and few people knew how to use these cumbersome devices (see Figure 7-4). This is typical of an industry in an embryonic stage.

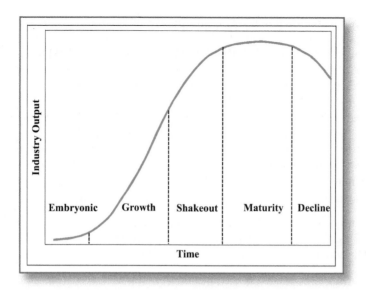

Embryonic / Growth | Shakeout | Maturity | Decline

Industry Output

Time

Figure 7-3
The Industry Life
Cycle Model

Figure 7-4
Early Wireless Phone
Courtesy of Roman Vukolov/Shutterstock.

During the embryonic stage, the industry is only beginning, and growth is generally quite slow. High prices, low quality, and lack of familiarity usually hinder growth. Prices are high because no one competitor has economies of scale, quality is low because the industry is using developing, unproven technology, and the essential newness of the product or service means that few people even know that it exists.

Figure 7-6
Whither The Flying Car?
Courtesy of United Archives GmbH/Alamy.

When flying cars do finally become available, it is unlikely they will be introduced by General Motors. How do we know that? We know because the flying car will destroy the value of General Motors' competencies. GM has invested over a century in mastering the development and manufacturing of car suspensions, braking systems, and engines and transmissions ideally suited to travel on roads. These competencies will fall in value if we adapt to personal air travel. The flying car would be GM's worst nightmare.

The same logic explains why telecommunications firm AT&T was so slow to embrace internet protocol (IP) technology. Despite being the first, largest and most sophisticated telecommunications services company in the U.S., few if any innovative internet services were introduced by AT&T. Compuserve became an internet service provider in 1979, more than a decade before AT&T offered the same service.[8] In 2003, Vonage offered voice over internet protocol (VoIP) services for pennies on the dollar compared to AT&T's voice services.[9] Today, AT&T's plain old telephone service (POTS) is an insignificant portion of the firm's revenues.

This has happened many times in the digital storage industry. Clayton Christensen of the Harvard Business School observed the dominant players in the digital storage industry were frequently overtaken by challengers from outside the industry.[10] In the early to mid-1980s, insurgent firms such as Shugart Associates, Micropolis, Priam and Quantum destroyed the 14 inch disk drive market by introducing an all-new 8 inch storage disk drive. Soon after, all but one of the firms providing 8 inch drives had failed, as a new market entrant named Seagate offered the 5.25 inch disk drive. Only Micropolis survived because they were able to get into the 5.25 inch disk drive market.

Seagate's fortunes soured as the 3.5 inch disk drive dominated the burgeoning personal computer market by yet *another* outside entrant, Connor Peripherals, leaving only the shrinking minicomputer market to Seagate. Where is Connor today? They were acquired a long time ago. Currently, flash memory is the standard for data storage; few if any users require magnetic disk drives today.

How could so many market incumbents be overtaken by outsiders? It is not because incumbents like AT&T, Shugart, or Connor were dumb or lazy. It is because, to some extent, incumbent firms in high-tech industries are held hostage by their current customers. Incumbents are focused on keeping their customers happy, and that usually means constantly improving current products and services. By contrast, challengers from outside the industry are not bound by any current customer requirements. As a result, they are free to innovate more aggressively and develop path-breaking, disruptive technologies.

Incumbents in high-tech industries are also saddled with old technologies, and can be committed to extend the "shelf life" of their existing capabilities. Incumbent firms can't afford to scrap all they have developed. AT&T had invested billions of dollars into an older technology (the circuit-switched network) that was poorly adapted to the internet age. To AT&T, the emergence of the internet was sure to destroy their outdated investments; they were motivated to resist the new technology, and even to defend the old one.

Over the past few decades, we have made great progress in understanding the strategic implications of high-technology industries. Following is a brief discussion of the most important contingencies in these markets.

Disruptive vs. Incremental Innovation

Scholarly research has confirmed what we described above in the stories about the internet and digital storage. Incumbent firms generally produce 'incremental' innovations.[11] That is, they focus an enormous amount of effort on refining existing technological competencies. Challengers, firms from outside the industry, tend to produce 'disruptive' innovations.[12] This happens because challengers have nothing to lose. Outsiders are not particularly concerned if they destroy the way things proceed within an industry. In addition, challengers are confronted with various barriers to entry, which makes competitive entry into established markets quite difficult.

We now know that a disruptive innovation that will overtake a current form of technology is likely to originate outside the industry, and that disruptive innovation is likely to destroy industry incumbents. So how do incumbents prepare themselves for this form of disruptive competitive attack?

One way that the best firms cope with disruptive innovation is by employing a "real options framework." In the world of finance, an option is the right, but not the obligation, to make a transaction in the future. Clever strategists hold a set of *strategic* options. That is, they create situations where they have the ability, but not the obligation, to make a future transaction. In response to his first book on the challenges of dealing with disruptive innovation, Clayton Christensen and his co-author describe a way that firms can create a set of options that will enable them to cope more effectively with future technologies.[13]

Incumbent high-technology firms know that the next disruptive innovation will originate outside the industry, but they don't know precisely *where*. If the incumbent firm knew where this threat would originate, they would be able to react more effectively. In order to improve their awareness of the status of disruptive innovations, incumbent firms create friendly relationships with startup firms in industries from which the disruption can occur. High-tech firms can take a set of small equity positions in startup firms that show particular promise in order to improve their awareness of the viability of new, potentially disruptive innovations.[14] The incumbent firm is now in a better position to monitor the range of innovations that may disrupt the usual way of proceeding in the future. In this situation, the high-tech firm has created a set of "options." It now has the ability, but not the obligation, to make an offer to acquire a startup that is on the verge of creating a commercially viable new innovation.

> In high-technology industries where disruptive innovations can threaten incumbent market positions, strategically adept incumbents will create a set of real options that will enable them to acquire or cooperate with the disruptive innovation once it becomes commercially viable.

First-mover and Fast-Follower Advantages

In early 2007, Apple Inc. introduced one of the first smart phones, this one with a large touchscreen, and changed the world of communications. Many of us are familiar with the lines outside of Apple stores on the night before a new product is launched. Customers can't wait to see what's new on each fresh device.

It may surprise some to learn that Apple holds less than 14% of the smart phone market.[15] The rest of the market is held by late-coming products that run on the Android operating system. Among Android phone vendors, Samsung dominates with over 21% market share.[16]

While market observers shower accolades on Apple for its ability to lead the market by introducing innovations first, Samsung has done an impressive job of carving out a fast-follower strategy. Indeed, research has shown that fast-followers can outperform first-movers in some contexts.[17] While Apple has made many pioneering mistakes by inventing and offering failed technologies (like the Apple Newton—a personal digital assistant that was met with disdain in the late 1990s), Samsung mimics only the most successful products offered by Apple, saving money. (A notable exception to its ability to avoid mistakes was Samsung's defective battery in its Galaxy Note 7 phones). While Apple educates the market through their highly effective promotional events that explain the value of owning a smart phone, Samsung quietly benefits by attracting the majority of customers who want a smart phone but can't afford Apple's prices.

A common view is that high-tech industries are simply in an innovation race— a race to be first to market with the next exciting offer. That is not always the case.

> In high-technology markets, first-movers can capture the lion's share of the early market, and command higher prices from customers who value cutting-edge innovation. Fast-followers can develop a superior cost structure by benefitting from the consumer education conducted by the first-mover, avoiding pioneering mistakes, and mimicking only the most successful products and services.

Geographic Clustering of Innovation

Why does so much innovative software development occur in Silicon Valley outside of San Francisco, California? Significant innovation in biotechnology occurs along Route 128 in Boston. Southern Germany has a geographical cluster of innovation within the high-precision instrument industry. Why is cutting edge innovation often locally concentrated?

Innovative activity clusters geographically because the cutting-edge knowledge that is required to innovate is *tacit* in nature. Tacit knowledge is known by relatively few people, and can only be transmitted in face-to-face settings.[18] Tacit knowledge is easier to protect from competitors because of the difficulty involved in transmitting it from one person (or place) to another.

R&D-based knowledge travels locally, and is embedded in local labor networks.[19] To get access to the newest, most valuable innovative knowledge, firms co-locate near each other in order to get access to the locally-embedded specialists who work in these towns, and to learn from each other.

However, simply being in a technological cluster does not ensure success. In order to engage in knowledge *exchange*, firms must be willing to share knowledge with potential competitors. So the idea is to ensure that your firm benefits *more* from that exchange of information. Thus, knowledge-based competition takes the form of "learning races" within technology clusters. The highest performing firms not only locate within technological clusters, but also invest in "absorptive capacity."[20] R&D not only generates new information, but also enhances the firm's ability to assimilate and exploit existing information. A firm's absorptive capacity refers to the firm's ability to capture and leverage publicly available information. Firms develop more absorptive capacity as they conduct more R&D.[21]

> The best firms within high-technology industries not only locate technical specialists within geographic technology clusters, but also invest heavily in R&D to improve their own knowledge, so that their scientists can learn more from other firms located within the cluster.

STRATEGY IN INTERNATIONAL MARKETS

Let's say I have a very successful brew pub. I brew, market, distribute and sell my own craft beer at my restaurants in several U.S. metropolitan markets. Let's say my market research indicates that my beer might catch on in Brazil. Should I build a brewery, hire a labor force, become a local distributor, and open brew pubs in Brazil? The answer is perhaps, but not right away.

A common view is that in order to enter international markets, a domestic firm should make a foreign direct investment (FDI). That is, the domestic firm should go overseas, create and run the foreign operation directly. That is not always the case. In fact, it is often not the case. In this section, we will explore how the best firms expand internationally—in clever stages that minimize investment and mitigate risk.[22]

Exporting

A sensible way to expand my hypothetical brewing business internationally would be to begin with exporting. Using exporting, I would manufacture my product in a central location and ship it to foreign markets. In this way, I minimize risk by avoiding heavy investments in foreign infrastructure while gaining knowledge about how international consumers react to my product.

However, exporting brings about many problems. My brewing cost structure is likely to be extremely high, as lower cost manufacturing locations likely exist in Brazil. In addition, the cost of shipping a relatively low-priced, heavy product like beer will be prohibitively expensive. Tariffs imposed by countries to which I export may make my cost structure even worse. In addition, I would have no control over the quality of the product handling, marketing or distribution in the foreign market, so my brand equity could be damaged if foreign importers handle my products inappropriately. I can start with exporting, but this is not sustainable.

Licensing

Once I become confident that my craft beer can sell in Brazil, I should look for alternatives to exporting. One option is licensing. Under a licensing arrangement, my brewing firm grants the authority to another firm to manufacture, market, and distribute my products in the foreign market in exchange for royalty fees. This solves two problems. It eliminates the onerous costs of shipping and tariffs, while enabling me to avoid the risk of investing in manufacturing and distribution infrastructure overseas.

Licensing also has drawbacks. I continue to lack control over my product overseas, so the wrong licensee could seriously damage my brand equity. Perhaps more importantly, by licensing my capabilities to a licensee, I create a potential competitor for my firm by sharing all of the proprietary know-how required to brew and distribute my craft beers. While licensing is right for some firms considering international expansion, it may not be right for a brewing company.

Franchising

One way to mitigate the risk associated with poor quality is to engage in franchising. Under a franchising arrangement, my brewing company will grant rights similar to licensing to a foreign firm to manufacture, market and distribute my product in exchange for royalty fees. However, in addition, the franchisee is required to use specific methods and procedures that are specified by the franchiser. My firm's franchising agreement with a Brazilian franchiser can specify how my product is manufactured, marketed and distributed, which can mitigate the risk to my brand equity. This is the reason that so many McDonald's restaurants, owned by thousands of different franchisees, all look and feel the same.

In general, franchising presents fewer problems, but they still exist. Although the franchising agreement may obligate the foreign franchisee to adhere to certain operating standards, the geographical distance of the foreign market may make monitoring that franchise difficult. Quality problems may continue to exist. In addition, my firm continues to run the risk of losing its proprietary knowledge of brewing and distribution to potential competitors. This may not be the best option for my brewing company.

Foreign Direct Investment

A "full" foreign market entry is called Foreign Direct Investment, or FDI. By undertaking FDI, my brewing firm directly participates in the creation and operation of the entity in a foreign market. There are two different FDI entry modes: via a joint venture or via a wholly-owned subsidiary.

Creating a joint venture with a foreign partner has several important advantages. My brewing company can benefit from the local knowledge and reputation of my joint venture partner, which may reduce the new venture's liability of newness. My firm also benefits by sharing the startup investments with a partner.

Joint ventures have some familiar disadvantages. Proprietary knowledge can continue to spill over from one partner to another, creating future potential competitors. Further, control of the joint venture can become problematic, as the two independent companies that own the joint venture may undermine each other's efforts in order to assert more control over the joint venture.

Finally, my brewing company could create a wholly-owned subsidiary in which my brewing company owns 100% of the foreign entity. My firm can accomplish this by acquiring an existing brewing company, or by undertaking a greenfield launch of a brand new company from the ground up.

In the brewing industry, acquisition is a common form of FDI. In 2015, major brewers improved their presence in the burgeoning American craft brewery segment. Belgian mega-brewer Anheuser-Busch InBev purchased five U.S. based craft brewers; Dutch-based Heineken International acquired Lagunitas; and Spanish brewer Mahou-San Miguel acquired a major stake in Anchor Brewers, with a stated intent to acquire more. At least 24 acquisitions took place in the craft brewing industry in 2015.[23]

While this form of market entry eliminates the risks of knowledge spillover and lack of control, new risks are present. Under this entry mode, my subsidiary may make critical mistakes due to a lack of understanding of the foreign market, or it may suffer from a lack of local reputation. Further, my firm now assumes all of the risk and expense of entering this market.

After reviewing these entry modes, readers can appreciate that FDI may in fact be a small portion of all international market entry. That is the way it should be. In fact, FDI is a highly specialized form of market entry that should be chosen only under very specific conditions.

The "eclectic paradigm" or "O-L-I Framework" is an economic theory that explains how firms can best undertake foreign market entry.[24] OLI is an acronym for Owenership, Location and Internationalization. The O-L-I Framework posits that firms possess three types of advantage.

- Ownership advantages—the firm must have ownership of specific components of competitive advantage, such as patents, trademarks or proprietary knowledge.
- Location advantages—it must be beneficial for the firm to locate its operations in the foreign market. For example, if a firm can manufacture practically weightless microprocessor chips and mail them to its customers in foreign markets, there may be no need for that firm to move to the foreign market. On the other hand, if the firm can eliminate costly shipping charges (as in our brewing example above) by locating in the foreign market, then FDI may be in order.
- Internalization advantage—the firm must possess proprietary knowledge that it wishes to protect. If licensing or franchising arrangements will permit proprietary knowledge to spill over to potential competitors, then FDI may be the appropriate entry mode.

Table 7-1 A Model for Foreign Market Entry Mode

		CATEGORIES OF ADVANTAGES		
		OWNERSHIP ADVANTAGES	INTERNALIZATION ADVANTAGES	Location advantages
Form of market entry	Licensing	Yes	No	No
	Export	Yes	Yes	No
	FDI	Yes	Yes	Yes

Economists John Dunning and Matthew McQueen pulled all of this together to create a normative model for foreign entry mode (see Table 7-1).[25]

Here we see that firms must only possess ownership advantages in order to engage in licensing. That makes sense, since it implies that firms can license their patent, trademark, or any other piece of intellectual property to a foreign firm. Firms must possess an ownership advantage and an internalization advantage in order to engage in exporting. This is also intuitive; I will not license my knowledge or technology to another firm if there is a danger that it can use it against me as a future competitor. Firms must possess ownership, location and internalization advantages in order to engage in FDI. This is the case of our brewing company above; in order to eliminate excessive shipping charges and tariffs (location), in order to prevent potential competitors from learning about my processes (internalization), and in order to exploit my great beer recipes (ownership), my brewing firm should ultimately enter foreign markets via FDI.

> The best form of international market entry depends upon the types of competitive advantage the firm possesses. Only firms with ownership, internalization and location advantages should engage in foreign direct investment.

STRATEGY AND THE NON-PROFIT ORGANIZATION

From a strategic perspective, non-profit organizations (NPOs) are commonly viewed as "different" than their for-profit counterparts. In reality, the strategic management principles and techniques prescribed for the business world in this book are applicable to all organizations, regardless of product or service rendered or financial orientation.

In this section, an analysis of strategic decision-making in the NPO environment is explored. We will see that 1) "non-profit" does not mean "no-profit" or breakeven, and 2) with some modification at times, the same rules of the game are in play.

Most strategic management courses, as well as the text books utilized in these courses, are heavily oriented toward large, publicly traded organizations. Little mention of the existence, role or functioning of the NPO is made. With the exception of an occasional specialty course on the topic, this same shortcoming is found throughout the entire curricula of most business schools. As a result, most students have little to no idea about this sizable portion of the U.S. economy. Let's examine this sector.

NPOs are generally recognized as organizations that provide goods and/or services that, while creating benefits for an entire society or some subset of society, typically are not profitable and thus are not included in the for-profit segment of an economy. NPOs include such diverse organizations as churches, soup kitchens, charities, political associations, business leagues, sororities, fraternities, sports leagues, colleges and universities, hospitals, cultural organizations, credit unions, and labor organizations.[26] These organizations enjoy tax-exempt status as long as they satisfy Internal Revenue Service (IRS) standards, predominantly under sections 501(c)(3), which define a public charity, and 501(c)(4), categorized as a social welfare organization. Two major IRS requirements for the granting of non-profit status are that a) none of the proceeds generated by the organization benefit any private shareholder or individual and b) the NPO cannot attempt to influence legislation or participate in political campaign activities.[27]

The impact of NPOs on the economy cannot be overstated. Consider the following statistics:

- In 2015, there were 1,571,056 non-profit organizations in the United States, including 1,097,689 public charities, 105,030 foundations, and 368,337 "other" NPOs.[28]
- In 2014, non-profits comprised 5.3% (approximately $1 trillion) of U.S. gross domestic product (GDP). In 2013, public charities had $1.74 trillion in total revenues, $1.63 trillion in total costs, and over $3 trillion in total assets. [29]
- In 2012, 11.4 million jobs or 10.3% of private sector employment was provided by NPOs.[30]
- The number of NPOs, as well as number of employees and total wages of NPOs grew steadily from 2007-2012 (even during the recession of 2007-2009). Private sector employment during the same period declined by 3.0% and wages and number of firms grew at a slower pace.[31]

In light of these statistics, excluding NPOs from any consideration of strategic management techniques is a serious oversight indeed.

MISCONCEPTIONS ABOUT THE NPO

Now that we understand the importance of the NPO to society and the economy, let's examine the common misconceptions about these organizations.

NPOs strive for breakeven operating results
Perhaps the most common misperception about the typical NPO revolves around the concept of profit, in particular the false idea that these organizations consider

breakeven performance as the mark of success. Nothing is further from the truth. Indeed, NPOs cannot fulfill their missions if they cannot pay their bills. While it is true that their financial accounting may not contain the word "profit," their income statements utilize the phrase "revenues in excess of expenses" as the bottom line. Although it is difficult to summarize the financial results of the myriad of groups that are housed under the non-profit label, the following statistics are indicative of the successful financial performance of this sector of the economy:

- The 38.2% of registered non-profit organizations that are required to file an IRS Form 990 reported $2.3 trillion in revenue and assets of $5.5 trillion in 2016.[32]
- Public charities reported $1.7 trillion in revenue, $109.5 billion in net income (a 6.3% return) and fund balances of $2 trillion in 2013.[33]
- Private foundation charities reported $107 billion in revenue, $33.1 billion in revenue in excess of expenses (a 30.7% return) and fund balances of $734 billion in 2013.[34]

In light of this level of "profitability," it is clear that in total, non-profit organizations achieve financial performance in excess of breakeven operations and in some cases meet or exceed the metrics recorded by their for-profit counterparts.

The CEO model for strategic management does not apply in the NPO environment

Given the lack of attention paid to the non-profit environment in traditional strategy textbooks, it may seem quite reasonable to surmise that NPOs operate under a different set of rules than mainstream business organizations. Again, nothing is further from the reality confronting the NPO. Although there are unique aspects of the non-profit environment which will be discussed below, the same steps navigated throughout the CEO model equally apply in both organizational settings.

1. **Value Creation:** the CEO model postulates that strategy must create value for the customers, employees, and owners of an organization. This value creation triad is as important for the NPO as it is for the general business world. Although the customers are not always directly "buying" the product or service, there is the expectation that the NPO is addressing a customer or client need. Sometimes this need is of an intangible nature and is as much of a social contract as it is an actual product. As examples, a medical center provides a health care product; a library satisfies educational and recreational services. In both cases, society expects that a certain level of quality that is difficult to measure is maintained. For employees, job satisfaction is the main value sought, although as we will see below, the value proposition for determining employee value can vary in the non-profit environment. The fact that the NPO does not have shareholders complicates the owner value equation, however. For-profit organizations have various types of investors such as shareholders, banks, and venture capitalists who demand to receive value in the form of profits, dividends, and interest payments. NPOs have multiple stakeholders such as clients, patrons, and partner organizations who seek non-financial returns from their interaction with the NPO.[35,36] Thus, the ability of the NPO to generate value is as critical to the long-term viability of the NPO as it is for the profit motivated organization.

2. **Internal and External Environmental Assessment:** No organization, regardless of financial orientation, will survive without a thorough understanding of its internal and external environments. From an internal perspective, Porter's Value Chain model introduced in Chapter 4 remains applicable in the NPO environment. Although its origins are rooted in the manufacturing sectors, the value chain has been successfully modified for use in service and non-profit industries. Figure 7-7, for example, is the value chain for the health care industry as envisioned by some researchers.[37] The factors may change, but the concept of the identification and thorough analysis of the primary and support activities required for creating a product or service is critical for the NPO. The goal is to accurately (and many times courageously) define the strengths and weaknesses of the organization.

The same applies to the tools introduced in Chapter 5 for conducting an external audit. The economic, political/legal, technological, and socio/demographic factors found in the external environment, as well as the industry and competitive environmental factors utilized by for-profit firms, can be applied virtually without change by NPOs. The key is to identify the opportunities and threats confronting the organization.

If diligently and honestly tackled, the result of the internal and external audits is a realistic SWOT analysis which the NPO can then use to craft future strategies.

3. **Strategic Alternatives, Strategy Selection, Implementation, and Evaluation:** The strategy selection, implementation and evaluation steps of the Strategic Management Framework (see Figure 7-1) are virtually unchanged whether in the for-profit or non-profit environments. The SWOT matrix should yield multiple strategic alternatives, all of which are potential strategies. Given that it is not possible to adopt all of these strategies due to fiscal, organizational culture, or other stakeholder

Support Activities			
Firm Infrastructure Organizational structure, financial management, strategic planning, managed care networks			**Profit Margin**
Human Resource Management Recruiting, training, benefits administration			**or**
Procurement Office and medical supplies, technology acquisition, physician recruitment			**Excess of Revenue over Expenses**
Primary Activities			
Pre-Service Network integration, mix of services, advertising, pricing strategy, payor relationships	**Service Delivery** Clinical operations, network transfers, non-clinical and physical plant functions	**Post Service** Clinical aftercare, medical records, billing, public relations	

Figure 7-7
Value Chain Analysis: Health Care Provider Industry
Source: Adopted from Linda Swayne, W. Jack Duncan, and Peter Ginter. Strategic Management of Health Care Organizations, 5th edition (2006). Malden, MA: Blackwell Publishing, p. 155.

constraints, a final decision on the selected strategies is made. The strategies are then implemented and ultimately evaluated for effectiveness. Since results achieved often do not match the predicted performance, the strategies are monitored and reevaluated using the components of the Strategic Management model.

Thus, for NPOs, the steps of the Strategic Management Framework are completed in the same sequence as followed by the for-profit organization.

UNIQUE ASPECTS OF NPO STRATEGY

Although the same CEO model is followed, there are several distinct characteristics that require consideration when managing non-profit strategy.

Mission statements

"The American Red Cross prevents and alleviates human suffering in the face of emergencies by mobilizing the power of volunteers and the generosity of donors."[38]

"The mission of the United States Air Force is to fly, fight and win in air, space and cyberspace. Our rich history and our vision guide our Airmen as we pursue our mission with excellence and integrity to become leaders, innovators and warriors."[39]

As noted in Chapter 2, there is no one formula that defines the perfect mission statement. Perhaps the greatest difference between the for-profit and NPO approach is the diminished focus on a profit motive for the NPO. Indeed, most non-profit mission statements, particularly for those groups providing human services, emphasize the services offered and the compassion of those individuals who perform the

Figure 7-8
American Red Cross

Figure 7-9
U.S. Air Force

services.[40] Notice how the two mission statements above follow this guideline. Both identify the services provided and the zeal required for their members to carry out these services. The Air Force mission also indicates its perspective on the theatres and conduct of future warfare.

End users of the products/services

In the typical business transaction, the buyer is the actual user of a product or service and is expected to pay the full price for the good. Not necessarily so for the NPO, whose user may receive the group's output at a reduced price or not pay for the service at all. Many human service groups, such as clinics or missions, provide service at no charge. Others, such as libraries and museums, may charge fees that reflect only a portion of the true costs of creating the service. Still other groups, such as health care and public service organizations, sometimes can mitigate the actual financial impact of their services on the end user through subsidies such as food stamps and public and private health insurance programs. As a result, the demand for below market priced services by end users or clients can challenge the ability of the NPO to provide the services in the volume or quality needed.

Sources of funds

If the users/clients are not supplying the full cost of the services provided, how does the NPO receive its funding? The sources will vary based upon the type of service, and are a mixture of public and private, internally and externally generated revenue. Although creativity in finding funding venues is an ongoing effort, the following activities are mainstays of the revenue-generating process:[41]

- Self-generated fees for service
- Charitable contributions
- Corporate philanthropy
- Federal, state, and local governments
- Federated funds such as United Way campaigns
- Grants
- Corporate, Family, and Community Foundations
- Capital campaigns and Planned Giving programs

External revenue sources, while critical for organizational survival in many cases, can represent a vexing challenge for the NPO. These stakeholders may not directly utilize the services performed by the NPO, but can exert pressure on the types and delivery of these services. Thus the NPO must balance the needs of the clients served with the wishes of the patron donors, who at times may seek diverse benefits unrelated to or in conflict with the mission of the NPO. The dilemma becomes even more acute when the donor is also a member of the board of directors.[42] Most NPOs maintain or are strongly encouraged to develop a detailed conflict of interest policy that addresses not only donor conduct, but employee and IRS concerns as well.[43]

Management of Employees

One of the most difficult challenges of any organization, either for-profit or NPO, is maintaining a motivated, productive workforce. Studies show that employment in the NPO sector is growing. A 2014 survey reported that 46% of non-profits increased staff while 17% reported fewer employees and that 20% of the job openings were generated by employee resignations. Thus, employee turnover is a major challenge faced by NPOs.[44]

So what motivates the NPO worker? Compensation may be a factor, but non-profits have the reputation of underpaying and overworking employees.[45] A 2015 study by the Unemployment Services Trust (UST), a group dedicated to helping NPOs lower turnover, found that employee job satisfaction and engagement were most closely linked to a strong affinity for the NPO's mission, a sense of purpose from the work performed, and the culture of the organization.[46] Compensation is important, but NPO employees are often more motivated by the cause of the organization. They may be willing to accept lower salaries in exchange for their commitment to the mission of the organization, especially if benefits such as health insurance, telework, casual dress, and on-site day care are available.

Strong leadership is key for successful employee management in all organizations, regardless of financial status. For the NPO, optimizing the fit between the employee and the culture of the organization is especially critical because key decisions often involve mission and values achievement over financial priorities. In the for-profit venue, strong compensation can "buy" employee loyalty, at least in the short run. The NPO typically does not have this luxury. Studies have demonstrated that the transformational leader, that manager who can facilitate employee motivation by converting the dream of the mission into observable strategies, decisions, and actions, creates a culture of more harmonious employee relationships and lower levels of stress and turnover than the transactional leader, who merely gives orders and expects a high level of compliance.[44,47] This leadership effect is not limited to U.S.-based NPOs; it is an almost universal characteristic of non-profit organizations around the world.[48]

CONCLUSION

In this chapter, we established that the correct strategic choice depends heavily upon context. The appropriate strategy is determined by the stage of development in which the industry operates, the extent to which technology and innovation drive competition, and whether the firm is seeking to grow internationally.

The CEO model of strategic management analyzed in this textbook is equally applicable to organizations both in the for-profit and non-profit sectors of the economy. Despite some unique aspects in mission, sources of funds, end users of the product/service provided, and employee motivations, the NPO is well-served by adhering to a systematic, well-developed strategic management process. Perhaps even more so than in the for-profit world, inadequate long-term planning by NPOs results in organizational failure.

KEY TERMS AND CONCEPTS

After reading this chapter you should understand the following terms:

- Industry Lifecycle Model
- Contingency-based strategic choice
- Not-For-Profit entities
- Disruptive versus incremental innovation
- Geographic technological clusters

- The O-L-I framework
- Exporting
- Licensing
- Franchising
- Foreign Direct Investment

DISCUSSION QUESTIONS

1. How do the Five Forces in an industry change over the industry lifecycle?
2. Why are industry incumbents more likely to pursue incremental innovation, and industry outsiders to pursue disruptive innovation?
3. How are non-profit organizations similar to traditional for-profit firms? How are they different?
4. Under what conditions is exporting the best form of foreign market entry?
5. What is an internalization advantage and how is it related to knowledge spillovers in licensing or franchising models?
6. What are some common misconceptions about non-profit organizations?

EXPERIENTIAL EXERCISE

In what stage of the Industry Lifecycle Model is the electric car industry? How can we expect the Five Forces to change in this industry over the next ten years?

ENDNOTES

1. "2015 Amazon.com Annual Report." *Amazon.com.* Accessed 21 September 2016.
2. Ibid, p 6.
3. Stone, B. "Amazon employees, not investors, will have to pressure Jeff Bezos to slow down." *Bloomberg* (October 23, 2014), http://www.bloomberg.com/news/articles/2014-10-23/amazon-employees-not-investors-will-have-to-slow-jeff-bezos-down. Accessed July 6, 2016.
4. *The Economist.* "The one-handed economist". (November 13, 2003.) http://www.economist.com/node/2208841. Accessed July 6, 2016.
5. Utterback, J. and W. Abernathy. A dynamic model of process and product innovation." Omega 3 (1975):639–656.
6. Porter, M. Competitive Advantage. Free Press: New York, 1980.
7. Keiser, G. "Microsoft writes off $7.6B, admits failure of Nokia acquisition." *Computerworld* (July 8, 2015) http://www.computerworld.com/article/2945371/smartphones/microsoft-writes-off-76b-admits-failure-of-nokia-acquisition.html. Accessed July 6, 2016.
8. Tweney, D. "September 24, 1979: First online service for consumers debuts." *Wired* (September 24, 2009) http://www.wired.com/2009/09/0924compuserve-launches/. Accessed July 6, 2016.
9. Vonage Corporation. "About Us." (2016) http://www.vonage.com/corporate/about_timeline.php. Accessed July 6, 2016.

10. Christensen,C. *The Innovator's Dilemma.* Boston, Massachusetts: Harvard Business School Press, 1997.

11. Banbury, C. and W. Mitchell. "The effect of introducing important incremental innovations on market share and business survival." *Strategic Management Journal* (1995) 16(1): 161–182.

12. Reinganum, J.F. "Uncertain innovation and the persistence of monopoly." *American Economic Review* (1983) 73:741–748.

13. Christensen, C. and M. Raynor. *The Innovator's Solution: Creating and Sustaining Successful Growth.* Boston, Massachusetts: Harvard Business School Press, 2003.

14. From an ethical and legal perspective, it is important to state that the incumbent and startup firms have a clear understanding of the nature and intent of this equity investment. This is not intended to be a form of secret "espionage"; rather, this occurs between two firms who would be willing to cooperate in the future.

15. IDC Corporation. *Smartphone OS Market Share* (2016) http://www.idc.com/prodserv/smartphone-os-market-share.jsp. Accessed July 6, 2016.

16. IDC Corporation. *Smartphone Vendor Market Share* (2016) http://www.idc.com/prodserv/smartphone-os-market-share.jsp. Accessed July 6, 2016.

17. Mitchell, W. "Dual clocks: Entry order influences on incumbent and newcomer market share and survival when specialized assets retain their value." *Strategic Management Journal* (1991) 12(2): 85–100.

18. Zucker, L., M. Darby and J. Armstrong. "Commercializing knowledge: university science, knowledge capture, and firm performance in biotechnology." *Management Science* (2002) 48(1): 148–153.

19. Almeida, P. and B. Kogut. "Localization of knowledge and the mobility of engineers in regional networks." *Management Science* (1999) 45(7): 905–917.

20. Cohen, W.M. and D.A. Levinthal. "Innovation and learning: the two faces of R&D." *Economic Journal* (1989) 99: 569–596.

21. Mudambi, R. and T. Swift. "Professional guilds, tension and knowledge management." *Research Policy* (2009) 38: 736–745.

22. McDonald, F., F. Burton and P. Dowling. *International Business.* Cengage Learning EMEA, 2002.

23. Furnari, C. "Editor's Note: 2015 a Year of Deals, Rumors, Preemptive Denials, and Lots of Cash". Brewbound. (December 23, 2015). Accessed August 12, 2016. http://www.brewbound.com/news/editors-note-2015-a-year-of-deals-rumors-preemptive-denials-and-lots-of-cash

24. Dunning, J. "Toward an Eclectic Theory of International Production: Some Empirical Tests". *Journal of International Business Studies* (1979) 11(1): 9–31.

25. Dunning, J. and M. McQueen. "The Eclectic Theory of International Production: A Case Study of the International Hotel Industry." *Managerial and Decision Economics* (1981) 2(4): 197–210.

26. Legal Dictionary. *Non-profit organization legal definition.* http://legal-dictionary.thefreedictionary.com/nonprofit. (2016). Accessed June 15, 2016.

27. IRS (2016) (a). *Exemption Requirements-501(c)(3) Organizations.* (2016) https://www.irs.gov/charities-non-profits/charitable-organizations. Accessed June 13, 2016.

28. NCCS: National Center for Charitable Statistics. *Quick Facts about Nonprofits.* (2016) http://nccs.urban.org/statistics/quickfacts.cfm. Accessed on June 13, 2016.

29. Urban Institute. *The Nonprofit Sector in Brief: Public Charities, Giving, and Volunteering.* (2015) http://www.urban.org/research/publication/nonprofit-sector-brief-2015. Accessed on June 13, 2016.

30. Bureau of Labor Statistics. *Nonprofits account for 11.4 million jobs, 10.3 percent of all private sector employment.* (2014) http://www.bls.gov/opub/ted/2014/ted_20141021.htm. Accessed June 15, 2016.

31. Monthly Labor Review. *Nonprofits in America: new research data on employment, wages, and establishments.* (2016) http://www.bls.gov/opub/mlr/2016/article/nonprofits-in-america.htm. Accessed on June 15, 2016.

32. Internal Revenue Service b). *Registered Nonprofit organizations by Level of Total Revenue*. (2016) http://nccsweb.urban.org/. Accessed on June 23, 2016.

33. NCCS (a) Core File (Public Charities). 501(c)(3) *Public Charities: Financial Activity by Level of Total Expenses*. (2013) http://nccsweb.urban.org/. Accessed June 23, 2016.

34. NCCS (b) Core File (Private Foundations). 501(c)(3) *Private Foundations: Financial Activity by Level of Total Expenses*. (2013) http://nccsweb.urban.org/. Accessed June 23, 2016.

35. Dainelli, F., G. Manetti, and B. Sibilio. *Web-Based Accountability in Non-profit Organizations: The Case of National Museums*. ISTR Vol (2013) 24, pp. 649–665.

36. Jones, K. and L. Mucha. *Sustainability Assessment and Reporting for Nonprofit Organizations: Accountability "for the Public Good"*. ISTR Vol (2014) 25, pp. 1465–1482.

37. Swayne, L., W.J. Duncan, and P. Ginter. *Strategic Management of Health Care Organizations*, 5th edition. Malden, MA.: Blackwell Publishing, 2006.

38. American Red Cross. *Our Mission*. (2016) http://www.redcrossblood.org/about-us/our-mission. Accessed June 13, 2016.

39. U.S. Air Force. *Mission*. (2016) http://www.airforce.com/mission. Accessed June 24, 2016.

40. Mission Statements.com. Non-Profit Mission Statements. (2016) https://www.missionstatements.com/nonprofit_mission_statements.html. Accessed June 13, 2016.

41. Fritz, J. *Where Do Nonprofits Get their Revenue?* (2015). http://nonprofit.about.com/od/fundraising/a/fundraising101.htm. Accessed June 13, 2016.

42. Moscowitz, J. "Understanding Conflict in Nonprofit Organizations." *Acresolution*, (2007)Fall/Winter, pp. 22–23.

43. Dierks, L. Crash Course in Conflict of Interest. Spokes Resources for Nonprofits. (2016) http://www.spokesfornonprofits.org/crash-course-in-conflict-of-interest. Accessed June 25, 2016.

44. Otten, L. Smart Hiring. *The Nonprofit Center*. (2014) http://lasellenonprofitcenter.org/smart-hiring. Accessed June 13, 2016.

45. Beckbridge, L. "Keys to Nonprofit Employee Retention." *Nonprofit HR*. (2014) http://www.nonprofithr.com/employee-retention. Accessed June 13, 2016.

46. Maulhardt, M. and J. Smith. *2015 UST Nonprofit Employee Engagement & Retention Report*. (2015). http://www.ChooseUST.org. AccesseD June 24, 2016.

47. Jaskyte, K. "An Exploratory Examination of Correlates of Organizational Culture." *Administration in Social Work*, (2010) 34: 423–441.

48. McMurray, A., M. Mazharul Islam,jj. Sarros, and A. Pirola-Merlo. "The impact of leadership on workgroup climate and performance in a non-profit organization." *Leadership & Organization Development Journal* (2012) 33 (6): 522–549.

Chapter 8

Financial Tools for Strategic Choice

CHAPTER LEARNING OBJECTIVES

After studying this chapter, you should be able to:

- Understand how the firm is capitalized;
- Recognize the alternative sources available to finance strategic initiatives;
- Identify various financial tools used to inform strategic choice;
- Estimate the value of a public or private firm;
- Apply financial tools in the task of selecting between competing strategies.

The Walt Disney Company continually searches for growth opportunities. Among Disney's most prominent growth initiatives were its 2009 acquisition for $3.96 billion of Marvel Entertainment with prominent movie franchises such as *Iron Man*, *X-Men*, *The Avengers*, and *The Guardians of the Galaxy* and its 2012 acquisition of Lucasfilm with its iconic *Star Wars* franchise for $4.1 billion.[2] When these deals were first made, there was debate over whether Disney could maintain the franchises' quality and profitability. Since becoming part of Disney in 2009, Marvel has produced eleven interconnected movies and four television shows in the Marvel Cinematic Universe with an aggregate score of 89.4% on Rotten Tomatoes. Four of those movies surpassed the $1 billion threshold for worldwide box office revenue.[3]

The Lucasfilm deal is being heralded as possibly the deal of the century for Disney CEO Robert Iger. Disney paid now-retired George Lucas $4.1 billion for Lucasfilm, special-effects art house Industrial Light & Magic (ILM), Skywalker Sound, and the video game company LucasArts.[4] The first *Star Wars* movie under the Disney regime, *Star Wars: The Force Awakens*, did not disappoint as it became the highest grossing *Star Wars* movie of all time, the highest grossing North American movie ever, and the fastest movie to earn $1 billion in box office revenue.[5] Disney plans to release a new installment of the *Star Wars* saga every two to three years while releasing ancillary movies in between to further develop its own cinematic universe. Overall, the movie grossed more than $2 billion worldwide in box office revenue.

Movies are just one element of Disney's growth strategy. In his 2015 letter to shareholders, Iger indicated that the company has explored opportunities to add *Star Wars* theme park attractions to their Disneyland and Disney World resorts and to further develop the *Star Wars* merchandise platform to grow and enhance the company.[6] Hasbro reported a 35% sales increase in its boys' segment during the 2015 holiday season due in large part to a new wave of *Star Wars* merchandise, such as action figures, BB-8 replica toys, backpacks, lightsabers, and more. The toy company has the brand rights to *Star Wars* and reported revenues of $1.47 billion for the 2015 holiday season (Q4), which is a 13% increase year-over-year.[7] Growth strategies such as these require substantial investments of capital before they generate a single dollar of revenue from sales. For example, the Shanghai Disney Resort which opened in Spring 2016 cost $4.4 billion to construct and was in the planning, development, and building phases for almost 20 years before its grand opening.[8]

The purpose of this chapter is to help you understand the critical role of the finance function in the strategic management process. We focus on four paramount issues: (1) understanding how the cost and form of the firm's sources of investment capital impact the firm's appetite for risk (2) describing financial tools that are useful for making strategic choices (3) exploring various approaches to valuing a firm, and (4) forecasting the financial results of a strategy. These issues are inherent in Disney's strategic choices described above. After reading this chapter you should be able to answer each of the questions listed in Figure 8-1. The figure shows that the questions posed for this chapter pertain to strategic choice and implementation, the third and fourth steps of the strategic management process.

THE FINANCE FUNCTION IN STRATEGIC MANAGEMENT

Financial management is concerned with the investing, funding, and cash operations aspects of the firm and, as such, is an essential subset of the overall management function. It also focuses on generating financial information and applying tools that can be used to improve decision-making and strategic choice. As we know, strategic management focuses on value creation for key stakeholders of the enterprise. The finance perspective contributes to the focus of value creation by zeroing in on value for owners or shareholders.

What does The Walt Disney Company tell its owners and employees ("cast members") about its financial objectives? Management states that "Allocating

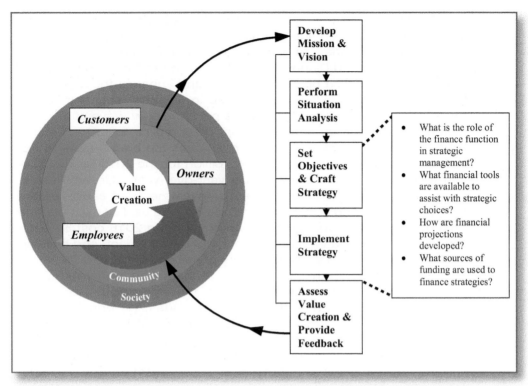

Figure 8-1
The Strategic Management Framework

capital profitably and managing our day-to-day operations in a way that maximizes Disney's opportunity for both creative and financial success are the most important ways that we serve the owners of our company."[9] Sound financial management practices play a critical role in achieving the firm's strategic objectives.

Consider an example. Suppose top management has identified the need in the marketplace for a new product. Should the firm go ahead with the new product project? Is it an attractive strategic choice? The decision cannot be made without a check on the project's long-term financial viability. However, before that can be assessed, a more immediate set of questions must be answered. How will the firm pay for the project? What will it cost? Where will the money come from for retooling the machinery? How will the firm pay for the supplies, labor, and raw materials needed to manufacture the new product? Who will supply the funds to package and ship the item? And, of course, marketing dollars will be needed to make consumers aware of the firm's willingness to satisfy their needs for this product.

All of these issues are an important part of the finance function. No strategic initiative moves forward without consideration of financial management issues. Before beginning our discussion of financial tools applied in the strategic choice process, let's consider some key financial concepts and terms that we use throughout this chapter.

Acquiring Funding
for Strategic Initiatives

When faced with the need to raise cash, management has several options. Each option must be evaluated within the context of the overall strategy of the firm. Let's look at ways firms can raise cash, both from within the firm and from outside investors.

Capitalization of the Firm

The term *capital structure* generally is used to describe the permanent, or long-term, sources of financing used by a company. As we will describe in more detail later in this chapter, firms use both *internal funding sources* and *external funding sources* to satisfy cash needs; they draw on cash from operations as well as debt and equity sources.

Do capital structure and the mix of financing sources make a difference in creating value? Certainly! As we will see below, acquiring funds to implement strategic plans—as well as to carry out day-to-day operating activities—costs money. In addition, acquiring funds adds an inherent element of risk to the firm's very existence. There is uncertainty in nearly every strategic choice, just as there is risk in the choice of financing the enterprise.

At the outset, it is important to note that firms, and their owners, prefer to finance new investments with internal sources of funding. For simplicity, we define *internal sources* as resources that management can obtain on its own without going to the financial marketplace. Acquiring funds from the external investment community is costly, time consuming, and it adds risk to the firm. Most firms hire financial services firms (such as investment bankers) to issue new debt or equity. Understand, too, that existing investors prefer not to add new investors to the firm, since that will dilute their ownership or reduce their influence.

After making any additions desired to working capital, excess *internally generated funds* are either distributed to owners or used to acquire new long-term productive assets. Thus, firms use unallocated financial resources within the firm to fund new initiatives before going outside for financing. In addition to using internally generated funds from operating cash flows to fund new investments, we consider two main sources of internally generated funds: divestment of assets and deliberate retrenchment.

Divestment Followed by Reinvestment

Financing for a new strategy can be obtained by selling a division or segment of the company. Instead of generating sales from consumers, the business raises cash by selling a piece of its operations—whether that is identifiable assets or stock owned in a subsidiary entity.

As mentioned in Chapter 3, GE used this financing scheme when it sold its white goods (appliance) division to Haier for $5.4 billion to begin its transition to a digital industrial company. GE will now focus on writing code for its jet engine, power turbine, and medical equipment divisions. GE's April 2016 announcement of the construction of a new $73 million data-driven manufacturing plant in Greenville, SC is an example of divestment followed by reinvestment. The plant will be operated by GE Power, which produces gas turbines, jet engines, wind turbine blades and other power industry parts and products. However, the new plant will also house digital technologies, such as big data software, Internet of Things applications, and 3D printing and modeling machines, to create data streams which will link traditionally isolated industrial processes and systems. GE refers to this stream as a "Digital Thread." According to GE's Chief Information Officer, the goal of leveraging these technologies at this new plant is "to develop tools to more quickly adjust to input from across the supply chain and other external sources, use insights drawn from the data to fine-tune production on the fly, and get new parts and products to market faster." GE also plans to invest $327 million more in the facility over the next few years. Funded by a recent divestment, this new plant represents GE's future.[10]

Retrenchment

Compare the divestment-with-reinvestment actions of GE with a retrenchment-downsizing strategy. Here, at least in the short-term, the strategic path taken involves getting smaller. This shrinking of the firm may be for defensive purposes—as when a division is sold, with the proceeds distributed to owners to fend off an unwanted corporate suitor. Alternatively, the proceeds may be used to pay down debt. In another instance, there may be a genuine interest in closing down part of the business, as has been seen in some financial services industry companies. Increased risk, government regulation, or another external force may press the strategic management team to adopt this type of plan. Whatever the driving force, retrenchment will result in internal generation of funds that can be used for investment or returned to owners.

The sources of external funding from debt and equity comprise the firm's capital structure, and are a critical determinant of the firm's strategic capabilities. One reason that managers carefully determine the firm's capital structure is that debt and equity investors have different investment objectives. By purchasing bonds, debt investors are making a loan to the firm; the return to that investment is the interest paid by the firm to the bond holder. Since debt holders earn a fixed interest payment from the firm in which they invest, they receive no benefit from firm profitability that exceeds the threshold required to meet the firm's operating expenses and interest payments. Yet firms can default on interest payments to debt holders if firm profitability falls below levels necessary to meet current obligations. Of course, debt holders want to avoid risk that can threaten earnings performance; they place a high priority on the firm's ability to pay interest on its debt and to repay loans as they mature. In order to secure the lowest possible interest rate on its borrowings, firms must demonstrate to the investment community their ability to repay loans plus interest. Firms that acquire external funds via debt financing must show stable, dependable earnings that will more than cover the contractual debt commitments.

In contrast, equity investors—those who purchase shares of company stock—seek higher returns than debt holders; they are willing to assume higher levels of risk to achieve a better investment yield. Equity investors prefer returns in the form of dividends paid by the firm to shareholders out of profits and from growth in the firm's value that is reflected through an enhancement of the firm's share price. Generally, to increase overall enterprise value and, therefore, its share price, firms must grow revenue and earnings. Investing large sums of money in growth strategies is inherently riskier than simply managing the status quo. With a growth strategy, outcomes are uncertain and firms may need years for free cash flows to recoup a strategic investment.

Investment returns from any growth strategy also must exceed the total cost of all investor dollars obtained (both debt and equity) in order to create greater enterprise value. Here we see the link between a firm's capital structure and strategies. Firms that want to undertake riskier growth strategies must consider the investment objectives and preferences of both equity and debt investors who provide funds. These investors place limits on the strategic flexibility of the firm.

The Firm's Cost of Capital

Regardless of the type, source, or timing of acquiring funds, somebody will demand compensation for being without her/his own money or property. The firm's *cost of capital* is the average return that it must pay to attract and retain its debt and equity investors. In the long run, if the firm fails to return at least its cost of capital to investors, those investors will go elsewhere and the firm will die from lack of funding for growth.

A common theme of any discussion of strategic choice is the cost/benefit trade-off associated with obtaining financing and compensating suppliers of funds. Research has shown that the firm can minimize the cost of capital by using an ideal mix of debt and equity financing. The ways that firms determine this preferred position are beyond the scope of this book. We deal here with the cost of capital as if it were a known commodity and one that is fixed. That is a simplification adopted only so that we can focus the discussion on the models and tools used by the strategic management team in making choices and assessing outcomes. Suffice it to say that undertaking initiatives that earn at least the firm's *weighted average cost of capital* is necessary to create and maintain value for the firm. The cost of capital is determined by the mix of debt and equity funding used by the firm.

Valuation of Strategic Decisions: Capital Budgeting

To support organic or internal growth, managers make decisions every day that involve the fundamental trade-off between cash flows earned now and cash flows receivable in the future. For example, Disney must evaluate the trade-off between negative cash flow created by the costs of building new theme parks and the expected future positive cash flow that should result from gate receipts. Disney managers must determine whether the cash outflow is justified by the anticipated inflows from future revenues. Most often these choices involve acquisition of long-term operating assets for the purpose of growing revenue, profits, and cash flow. Examples of such acquisitions include buildings, machinery and equipment, software, and intellectual property rights. These are fundamental examples of *capital budgeting decisions*.

FINANCIAL TOOLS FOR STRATEGIC CHOICE

Before describing the various financial tools used in strategic choice, we must set the stage with a review of four basic components common to all business investment decisions. To judge the value-creating attractiveness of a strategy, we must consider:

- the amount expended—we'll call this the *net investment;*
- the potential benefits—the *net operating cash inflows;*
- the time period involved—the strategic initiative's *economic life;*
- end-of-project recovery of capital—the *net salvage value, or residual value.*

These elements are not difficult to understand. However, our analysis must consider both the dynamic and interactive effects of them. We will see this through a discussion of examples using several related techniques that can assist us in making strategic choices.

Payback Period

How soon will I get my investment back? That is not an unreasonable or uncommon question for an investor to pose. The strategic manager *is* an investor. She or he (more likely, though, a <u>team</u> of professionals) proposes to allocate some of the firm's scarce resources to an initiative that is expected to create additional value for the firm. A simple, somewhat unsophisticated rule of thumb we can use to help answer this question is the *payback period.*

This technique compares forecasted cash inflows from a strategic initiative to the project's net investment. Let's look at a straightforward example.

Suppose the strategic management team is presented with a proposal to acquire a new distribution warehouse. This state-of-the-art facility would be located at a new site and will significantly reduce the cost of processing orders and getting the product to customers. The net investment is $10 million. Annual net savings of $1 million in distribution expenses are expected. (We ignore here, for the sake of simplicity, the obvious potential for more or larger orders that could result from better customer service.)

We can say that as long as the expected savings from the new warehouse last for ten years, we ought to consider implementing this strategic investment. How do we know that? Because the payback period is ten years!

Payback = Net investment/Annual cost savings.
In our case: $10 million/$1 million = 10 years.

The result from this uncomplicated exercise is the number of periods required for the initial outlay to be repaid. It is a rough-and-ready test of whether the cost of a strategic initiative can be recovered within its expected economic life span. For the firm that is presented with multiple investment opportunities, it can be particularly important to know how long an investment will tie up cash.

Unfortunately, recouping the net investment really isn't enough for our value creation-minded strategic management team. Their concern is with payback that <u>exceeds</u> the input cost. Furthermore, they must consider a basic fact: dollars of payback that arrive in future years are not equivalent in purchasing power value to those dollars invested in a strategic initiative today. In order for the firm to create value for its owners, it must recover the initial investment plus a return equal to or greater than its *cost of capital*, adjusted for the time value of money.

There also is a third consideration. The payback period is not really a "break-even" position, for if the net investment in the chosen project had been placed instead in a secure savings account, at least a minimal amount of interest above the initial investment would have been earned. Note, too, that this simple payback period analysis implicitly assumes level annual operating cash inflows. This insensitivity to variations in cash flow can be a serious shortcoming for certain new product introductions and physical asset replacement decisions.

All of this is not to say that payback period is not usable, just that its shortcomings limit the weight we ought to assign to it in making strategic choices. Payback is easy to understand and compute. As long as we recognize its limitations, payback will suffice as a quick way to decide whether a strategic initiative should be given more sophisticated analysis. Some of the pros and cons of using payback period as a strategic choice tool are listed in Table 8-1.

Table 8-1 Payback Period

ADVANTAGES	LIMITATIONS
• Easy to compute and understand • Provides a preliminary quantitative analysis of strategic alternatives • Allows managers to quickly discard projects that have little chance to create value	• Does not account for the time value of money • Assumes a constant level of forecasted cash inflows • Does not account for opportunities forgone by choosing the strategy in question

Time Value of Money Concept

The payback period method of making financial decisions on strategic projects is a simplistic technique that gives first-level indications. It is useful to set the stage for analysis by making a connection between a strategy's cost (net investment) and benefit (net operating cash inflows or net savings in cash outflows).

As we have stated, strategic choices entail tradeoffs that weigh economic consequences of current costs against probable future cash flow benefits (i.e., inflows or cost savings). Given an appropriate period for analysis, this assessment requires an understanding of the *time value of money*. Before moving to several techniques used in helping strategic managers analyze the time value of money, we must review this important concept.[1]

---

[1] *You have undoubtedly encountered the concept of time value during your study of basic accounting principles and fundamental corporate finance. If, after the review given to the topic in this chapter, you are still uncomfortable with its application, dust off those old texts and review the concept anew, for you will be using it throughout your business career!

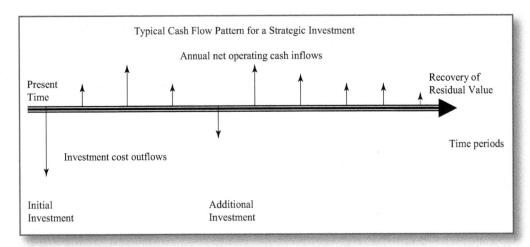

Figure 8-2
Time Value of Money

Strategic decisions are <u>always</u> forward looking—they are about investment for future value creation. Given this prospective orientation, the simple axiom that a dollar received today is worth more than a dollar received one year from now takes on added relevance. The chance to invest profitably a dollar received today is postponed, or forgone, in anticipation of cash inflow later. This lost opportunity is a cost associated with the strategic choice to trade investment today for future operating cash inflows.

A dollar spent now cannot be invested to earn any additional return. Similarly, postponement of spending a dollar until a year from now means that dollar can earn a return in the meantime. So the time value concept relates to both the investment (outflow now or later) decision and the opportunity to earn a return (current inflows or future inflows).

Let us consider an illustration. Look at Figure 8-2. Concentrate your attention on the *timing* of the cash flows generated by the initial strategic investment.

The figure shows that the initial outlay for a strategic initiative takes time to earn a return. Disney's $4.4 billion investment to build and open the Shanghai Disney Resort was decades in the making before the park welcomed its first paying customers. Nike might spend $10 million this year to design a new running shoe that will not generate any sales until 18 months from now. Campbell Soup's development of a new line of snack crackers by its Pepperidge Farm group might cost $2 million now, but not yield a single sales dollar for a year. Merck might spend $500 million to create and test a new pharmaceutical product that will require ten years from project initiation to market introduction. Similarly, it will take South Eastern Pennsylvania Transit Association (SEPTA) years of design and construction before a new train line is operational.

It is not enough to ask, as we did in the previous section, "When do I get my initial investment back?" For every period in which any portion of our initial outlay is not available, earning *potential* is lost. As important as getting back the initial outlay is, the timing of its return—future inflows of cash—is critical to the strategic choice. Those dollar inflows in the future have less value than the dollar spent today.

All of the future cash inflows must be "brought back" in time to the present so they can be matched fairly—that is, in the same purchasing power units—with the present cost of the strategic initiative. The methodology to do this is called *discounting*. It is the standard practice for expressing future dollars in the form of equivalent present dollars. It is the basis for all contemporary techniques of investment and valuation. Determining the *present value* of expected future inflows (or cost savings) is the foundation for any serious financial analysis applied to inform strategic choice decisions.

To be certain that you understand the time value concept, consider the following example. And, to be safe in our explanation, let's do this in several steps.

Step 1: Suppose you have $1,000 to invest and choose to place this sum in a bank savings account that earns interest at the annual rate of 5 percent. In a year, you will have $1,050. The amount of your return would be $50; the rate of return is the previously stated 5 percent. (You can compute this rate just as we did above: amount of return/initial investment, or, $50/$1,000—that's 5 percent.) Suppose, also, that your friend has $1,000 to invest, but being uncertain about the financial viability of local banks, simply puts the cash in a shoebox under the bed. For your friend, the chance to earn $50 is lost. This is the *opportunity cost* we previously described.

Step 2: The *future value* of your $1,000 investment in our example is its initial "cost," $1,000, plus the interest earned, $50 ($1,000 at 5 percent for a year), or $1,050. The future value of your friend's investment (or, in this case, non-investment) is just $1,000: there was no return on that initial amount.

Step 3: Looking into the future from the time (today) when you and your friend made the decision on how to invest, you expect to have $1,050 of future value and he/she expects to have $1,000. Certainly, you expect to be better off. Your friend's strategic choice entails a missed opportunity to be better off.

Step 4: The *present* value of your strategic choice is known to be $1,000. How is that related to the *future* value of $1,050 (see Step 2)? Consider that the future value is the initial value plus the return: $1,050 = $1,000 + $50. Note that the future value divided by the initial investment is nothing more than 1 plus the earnings rate: $1,050/$1,000 = 1.05. And, finally, see that if we *discount* the future value by the factor of 1.05, we convert the future value into the present value: $1,050/1.05 = $1,000. In other words, when the interest rate is 5 percent the present value of $1,050 expected a year from now is the same $1,000 initial investment with which we started this example.

Step 5: But, what about your friend? The method of analysis doesn't change! The promise to receive $1,000 from the shoebox in a year, when we could earn 5 percent in the bank, is $952.38: nothing more than the future value discounted by 1.05 ($1,000/1.05 = $952.38).

Let us summarize. Without question the sum of $1,000 offered to someone (your friend) a year from now is less valuable than the same amount of $1,000 offered today. The simple reason is that with the money in hand now, you can invest it to have a future value that is larger than the initial sum available, and certainly larger than the promised $1,000 one year hence.

This exercise demonstrates that with an assumed earnings rate of 5 percent the expected receipt of $1,000 a year from now is "worth" only $952.38 today. The analysis is meant to reflect the economic reality of the trade-off between dollars received today and dollars to be received in the future. Further, it is intended to show that in the context of strategic choices a dollar committed today must be returned at a larger absolute amount if a positive rate of return is expected. Conversely, strategic managers will commit fewer present-value dollars to receive the same number of future-value dollars. How much less will we pay for a dollar in the future? That all depends upon the earnings rate involved and the time at which the future dollars will be received.

Net Present Value

Strategic managers must decide what dollars to commit today with some expectation of receiving dollars in the future. The senior management team at Southwest Airlines has to choose whether to commit $60 million for two new Boeing jetliners that can serve new markets. What justifies today's dollar outlay for these aircraft? Of course: future cash inflows from ticket sales. However, those future ticket sales dollars are not equivalent to the current cash outlay. Today's dollars are worth more than the "promised" dollars of the future. We know this to be the case from the simple shoe-box example in the prior section. What's the strategic manager to do when faced with this situation? He or she must "convert" future dollars to equivalent present-day dollars. In other words, the future inflows must be *discounted* to today's dollars. Future value must be translated into present value.

The *net present value* (NPV) technique weighs the cash flow trade-off among initial investment outlay, future benefits, and potential net salvage value in equivalent present value terms. This will allow the strategic manager to see whether the net balance of these values is favorable or not.

To use this tool, a rate of discount that represents the required return on investment demanded by the firm's investors (or the firm's cost of capital) first must be specified. Then the present value of each and every cash outflow and inflow associated with the strategic initiative over its entire expected useful economic life can be computed. With everything in time-adjusted terms, the present value of inflows (positive amounts) and outflows (negative amounts) can be combined. The result will be the net (inflows minus outflows) present (current dollars) value.

The NPV number indicates whether the strategic initiative, considered over its expected economic life, will achieve the earnings rate applied in its calculation. A positive NPV indicates that the cash flows generated by the strategic initiative over its economic life will:

- recover the initial outlay;
- recover any additional capital costs included in the analysis;
- earn the desired/required rate of return on the investment; and
- provide a cushion in case the future differs from expectations.

Conversely, a negative result suggests that the strategic initiative will not achieve an outcome that meets the earnings standard expected of new projects and is

Enterprise Value versus Share Value

The measure of any enterprise's value (we'll denote this as V_{ENT}) is the total value of benefits derived from all the operations and assets of the firm, which create, maintain and grow value for all investors' capital claims. In other words, V_{ENT} determines the value of debt holders' capital (V_D), plus the residual value of shareholders' equity (V_{EQ}). Thus, we can think of the firm's *enterprise value* as:

$$V_{ENT} = V_D + V_{EQ}$$

Knowing the value of any two of these components would allow us to compute the third one. It is no coincidence that this equation is similar to the accounting truism:

Assets = Liabilities plus Owners' Equity

Thus, if we calculate the estimated total *enterprise value* (V_{ENT}) or the value of the benefits associated with all assets and then subtract the value of debt (V_D) we can estimate the *intrinsic value* of owners' equity in total (V_{EQ}), and by dividing by number of shares outstanding, compute the value per share. The total value of debt (V_D) is the value of all firm debt that carries regular interest payments, excluding current "spontaneous" debt such as accounts payable, wages payable, taxes payable and similar items that are not investor claims and are part of net working capital. For simplicity in our discussion, let us assume that the value of debt can be approximated by using the book value of debt shown on the firm's balance sheet.

Survey of Methodologies

In corporate valuation, there is more than one method for valuing the enterprise (V_{ENT}). (Notice we didn't say "stock," so if you still are not sure of the difference, re-read enterprise value *versus* share value above). The choice of method is likely guided by the purpose or circumstances of the valuation itself. Often several methods are used, with the results compared. However, to quote Mr. Buffet again: "Managers and investors alike must understand that accounting numbers are the beginning, not the end, of business valuation." And: "The investor of today does not profit from yesterday's growth."[14]

Corporate enterprise valuation starts with accounting results to estimate the firm's value. Three broad methods, and a number of approaches to each, are in common use. The three are the *Cost method*, the *Income (or DCF) method*, and the *Market method*. These three methods will sometimes be done concurrently and "triangulated," that is, compared to each other to establish a range of probable value.

Cost Method: Here, the central focus is on the enterprise balance sheet:

1. **Book value:** This approach uses historic accounting numbers. It requires no calculation and no market values are indicated (except where the accounting policies say that market value is being used to value an asset, such as the firm's marketable securities). The obvious disadvantage of this approach is that book value is neither forward-looking nor necessarily reflective of market value.

Table 8-5

1. Cost Method—Liquidation Value

UNIVTECH CO.	BOOK VALUE 12/31/2016	ADJUSTMENT TO MARKET	LIQUIDATION VALUE	ADJUSTMENT EXPLANATION
Assets				
Cash and cash equiv.	$ 15,272		$ 15,272	
Accounts receivable	$ 86,740	–$17,348	$ 69,392	80% realizable
Inventories	$ 48,720	–$36,540	$ 12,180	25% realizable
Other current assets	$ 3,492		$ 3,492	
Total current assets	$154,224	–$53,888	$100,336	
Property and equipment, net	$213,408	$25,609	$239,017	Mark real estate to market at 112%
Intangibles	$225,860		$225,860	Patents, trade marks
Other assets	$ 4,444		$ 4,444	
Total assets	$597,936	–$28,279	$569,657	
Liabilities and Shareholder's Equity				
Accounts payable	$ 62,950		$ 62,950	
Accrued salaries	$ 13,068		$ 13,068	
Other accrued liabilities	$ 9,294		$ 9,294	
Total current liabilities	$ 85,312	$ 0	$ 85,312	
Long-term Debt	$ 81,933	$12,290	$ 94,223	Mark debt to market 115%
Other Liabilities	$ 5,383		$ 5,383	
Total liabilities	$172,628	$12,290	$184,918	
Net Assets (V_{ENT}, V_{EQ})	$425,308	–$40,569	$384,739	(a)

2. **Liquidation value:** This approach estimates the immediate "quick-sale" or auction value at market of each balance sheet item. This may be appropriate when a company ceases operations, is in bankruptcy or is no longer considered to be a viable going concern. Assumptions such as bulk sale value (i.e., an entire factory) can yield very different answers than piecemeal value and also may be heavily influenced by the appraiser's knowledge and experience. An example of a liquidation valuation is shown in Table 8-5.

3. **Replacement value:** In this method, the cost to replace long-lived productive assets is determined. It is often difficult or nearly impossible to determine reliably these values, as new technology replaces old or the cost to duplicate physical facilities may be based on much higher (i.e., inflated) rates.

Income (or Discounted Cash Flow) Method. Analysis for this approach to valuation centers on the free cash flow that is generated from the firm's assets and operations. In contrast to the cost method, an income method focuses on both present and future benefits. Therefore, this approach assumes that the firm is a going concern. The value assessed is the summation of the present value of future free cash flows using a discount rate representing the firm's weighted average cost of capital (WACC).

Free Cash Flow

In the income approach, analysts forecast the residual cash flow from the firm and estimate the value of the firm as the present value of this stream of cash inflows. While many definitions of cash flow have been used, it is best to use free cash flow (FCF) in this approach.

The firm's FCF is the cash flow available to all investors (debt holders and stockholders) after paying all cash expenses and making all necessary investments in working capital and long-lived operating assets. This represents the cash flow after all reinvestment by the firm, but before any payments to both debtholders and stockholders. An example of a free cash flow calculation is found in Table 8-6.

The income method makes use of discounted cash flow (i.e., present value) approaches. There are several variations in use, including perpetuity and two-stage growth. For the purposes of this discussion, we will focus on the second method since it also includes the first method. The computation involves forecasting FCF and discounting this forecast for each future period at an appropriate discount rate. Typically, the weighted average cost of capital is applied as the discounting factor. The important difference here, in comparison to a project-type investment, is that since a corporation is presumed to have an indefinite life, a value-in-perpetuity calculation is added as the "terminal value" (this really is a misnomer, as it means "continuing value" forever!). The terminal value is an estimate of what the firm will be worth at the end of the FCF forecast.

The formula (Gordon Model)[15] for the present value of free cash flows into perpetuity is:

$$\text{Terminal Value (TV)} = FCF_N \ (1 + g)/(K - g)**$$

**g is the growth rate into perpetuity, usually the expected GDP growth; K is the discount rate.

The sum of the present values of the FCF forecast plus the terminal value equals the *enterprise value* (V_{ENT}) of the firm. This represents the *intrinsic value* of the enterprise. However, this may not be the value that the acquiring firm can appropriate for themselves. Why? Because the acquired firm may have outstanding debts. Therefore, we subtract debt (V_D) from V_{ENT} in order to arrive at the value of the firm's equity (V_{EQ}); this is the value attributable to the prospective new owners.

Market Method

This method is based upon observable market value metrics for the stock of a comparable public company or group of companies, or transactions values (multiples) of M&A transactions of similar companies, applied to the company to be valued.

Comparable Companies

Experience tells us that firms in similar markets during the same time period exhibit fairly stable relationships between firm value and firm performance. Therefore, as a quick rule of thumb, we often multiply the proposed target company's performance by the ratio of value to performance of comparable companies in order to estimate

Table 8-6

2. Income (DCF) Method				
	2016	2017	2018	EXPLANATION
UnivTech Co.				
EBIT	$ 31,904	$ 38,867	$ 52,803	From income Statement
Tax (@ 40%)	$(12,762)	$(15,547)	$(21,121)	Marginal Tax Rate
NOPAT	$ 21,158	$ 25,337	$ 33,700	
Adjustments:				
Changes in net working capital	$ (1,598)	$ (1,582)	$ (2,045)	Net working capital growth
Capital expenditures	$ (5,865)	$ (6,721)	$ (6,845)	Investment in LT assets
Depreciation/amortization	$ 20,714	$ 23,975	$ 25,440	Add back noncash charge (income stmt)
Free Cash Flow (FCF)	$ 34,409	$ 41,009	$ 50,250	
Terminal Value (TV)			$603,946	Continuing FCF Value (Perpetuity)
Total FCF	$ 34,409	$ 41,009	$654,196	
Present Value (PV) of FCF	$ 30,896	$ 33,063	$473,581	
V_{ENT}	$537,539	$537,539		Sum of Present Values of FCF
Less: LT debt	$(94,223)			LT debt Market Value
V_{EQ}	$443,316			
Assumptions:				
g	2.82%		Long-term growth in GDP	
K_{EQ}	13.03%		K = 4.62 + 1.529 × (10.12 – 4.62) [CAPM]	
W_D	17.53%		Market value debt / (Market value debt + market value equity)	
W_{EQ}	82.47%		Mkt value eq (100k × 6.45)/mkt. value debt + mkt value eq.	
K(WACC)	11.37%		WACC = (0.0588 × (1 – 0.4) × 0.1753) + ((0.1205) × 0.8247)	
TV	$603,946		$(FCF_3 × (1 + g))/(K – g) = (66,232 × (1 + 0.03))/(0.1095 – 0.035)$ [Gordon Model]	

a valuation. In this approach, analysts use some key ratios in which stock price is compared to various measures of firm performance, such as earnings before interest and taxes (EBIT), earnings before interest taxes depreciation and amortization (EBITDA), earnings per share (EPS), or even total sales, and then the "best" ratio is applied to the EBIT, EBITDA, EPS or total sales of the subject company. This method is very much dependent upon finding a comparable (country, product, market, size, etc.) company or group of companies. That selection process often is difficult to do. When the firm's share price is used as the measure of firm value, one must add debt to the result in order to find enterprise value (V_{ENT}).

Comparable Transactions

In this approach, analysts identify recent M&A transactions that are similar to the transaction being considered to find comparable multiple values (often multiples of EBITDA). Of course, this technique depends upon truly comparable recent transactions being uncovered. Even then, this method is often not reliable because the information is incomplete: there is no information regarding a premium or discount that may have been included in the comparable transaction as a result of negotiations over deal price.

"Triangulation" and a Value Conclusion

Valuation is still regarded as a combination of an art and an application of scientific methodology. By looking at all the methods, comparing them, and picking a mid-point, we "minimize the error." In this way, one can develop a good sense of the range and probable intrinsic value of the firm.

The following table provides a summary of market multiple and triangulation methodologies.

The Role of Synergies

Often an acquiring firm pays more than the market value for the firm it acquires. How can this be? Are they crazy? An acquisition's value to the acquiring firm is its contribution to sustainable profits and free cash flow. However, the acquiring firm often has conceived of ways to improve the acquired firm once the acquisition is complete. This usually requires that total costs be reduced, revenues be increased, operating assets be more efficiently deployed (or sold), and some improvement be

Table 8-7

3. Market Multiple (Comparable Companies Method)

	2016		EXPLANATION
UnivTech EBIT	$31,904		2016
Avg Mkt Mult	13.0		Average of comparables
Total V_{EQ}	$414,752	(c)	
Add: debt	94,223		Mkt value of debt
Total V_{ENT}	$508,975		

4. Triangulate Methodologies—Value Conclusion

UNIV TECH CO.	V_{ENT}	V_{EQ}	REFERENCE
1. Liquidation value	$384,739	$384,739	(a)
2. DCF value	537,539	443,316	(b)
3. Market multiple	508,975	414,752	(c)
Average	$477,084	$414,269	
Per share		$ 4.14	

made in tax costs or overall financing costs. Our intrinsic value formula for estimating enterprise value must be expanded to reflect synergies:

$$V_{ENT} = V_D + V_{EQ} + V_{Synergies}$$

It is no accident that M&A announcements often include a reference to expected synergies, the catchword for these improvements. This presupposes that strategies must be crafted to bring about cost savings, revenue improvements, and so forth. These improvements are captured in enhanced free cash flow forecasts that drive the valuation and can be significant determinants of intrinsic value. The returns from these synergy-based strategies must meet or exceed the cost of capital for funding the acquisition. In other words, the deal must be "accretive" to earnings.

Finally, we can explain why acquiring firms will pay more than the market value to complete an M&A transaction. Acquiring companies will often be required to pay a "control premium" (often 15-30%) over the value quoted for a single share in order to buy enough shares to have the right to take control of the firm. (As an aside, a so-called "merger of equals" does not require such a premium). The impact of a premium, when it exists, is to cause us to expand our value equation to:

$$V_{ENT} = V_D + V_{EQ} + V_{Synergies} + V_{Control}.$$

How do acquiring firms afford all this "extra" value they have to pay for? By creating enough synergistic value to make up for the premium paid for the acquired firm while also covering the required return on the cost of capital of the acquiring firm. This is difficult!

FORECASTING THE FINANCIAL OUTCOME OF STRATEGIC CHOICES

An important concern for strategic managers is the question of what the organization's financial reports—its accounting statements—will look like if a particular strategic choice is made. In effect, we are interested in estimating the future financial position of the firm under alternative scenarios regarding strategic initiatives. This requires a future-looking process of turning prospects for profit into actual value creation. That course of action starts with development of forward-looking or projected financial statements.

Projected Financial Statements

The heart of the firm's financial plan is contained in its *forward-looking* or *projected financial statements*. These statements, sometimes referred to as pro forma statements, are estimates or forecasts of the firm's future financial picture. Projected statements—the balance sheet, income statement, and statement of cash flows—are enormously versatile accounting reports that can serve at least three important purposes:

- estimate future free cash flows and cash needs;
- project financing requirements for new strategies and projects;
- develop targets for performance and assessment of achievements.

Financial projection is a useful simulation of the likely results of management's broad assumptions about the future and the expected consequences of its strategic plans. The relative ease with which future-looking financial statements and cash flow projections can be developed makes them attractive tools for strategic decision-making.

Assumptions About the Future

To begin the process of assessing where the firm will be in the not-too-distant future, strategic managers must develop a realistic and supportable set of assumptions about how the factors that impact financial performance are expected to change.

Think back to our discussion about the external environment in Chapter 5. Before we can honestly deal with how our company will fare in the future, we must ask questions about the forces in the external environment that affect us. For example, is there specific government regulation on the horizon that will impact our business (or that of our competitors)? Do changing demographics have important effects on our ability to generate revenues? Will technological innovation, consumer tastes, or general economic conditions impinge on the firm's ability to accomplish its mission and create value?

The external audit process will help us answer these questions and identify factors that we will need to consider in the process of estimating the firm's financial future. Our projection of the firm's future financial health depends on the validity of the assumptions we make about the external environment. These assumptions must be fully developed and assessed.

Financial and Operating Relationships

The most important ingredient for successful projection of the firm's financial position into the future is a thorough understanding of the fundamental relationships that drive or create the financial outcomes. While the use of sophisticated computer models and planning spreadsheets is a great boon to the process discussed here, nothing takes the place of management's insight and expertise regarding the actual operation of the firm.

Projecting the Income Statement

There is no magic formula that assures we will be successful in developing projected financial statements. The income statement, however, is normally the first to be developed, for a number of reasons. The operating lifeblood of every business is dollars from sales revenue. Furthermore, the bottom line, net income, is of the utmost concern to business owners. Finally, the connection between sales and all the items that intervene and shrink top-line revenue into bottom-line profit are the major focus for the estimation process. All of these suggest that we tackle the income statement first in the development of our projections.

Sales Forecasts

To start the estimation process we need to forecast future sales. This figure is crucial because many items in the projected statements will be derived from the sales forecast based on their historical relationship to sales along with assumptions about the future. Using sales to derive expense numbers, which we deal with in detail below, is known as the *percent of sales method*.

Sales can be estimated in a number of ways—from sophisticated market and customer studies to simple extrapolation of prior trends. Most sales projections require the use of a mixture of approaches. Every approach uses some combination of past trends and future expectations. The assumptions about the future come from our analysis of the external environment coupled with our intended strategies. The overall sales forecast is based on a trend analysis, adjustments for anticipated changes in the firm's external environmental, and the projected impact of new strategies on sales.

Assuming you have accurate historical data and a valid and reliable projection of trends in current markets, you can make reasonable projections of sales for "steady state" situations, meaning no change in products offered and markets served. The challenge occurs when environmental conditions are in a state of flux and therefore unpredictable. When this is the case, you should use a type of contingency planning, and project sales for best case, most likely and worst case scenarios.

Trend analysis uses past performance to project future performance. In its simplest form, trend analysis determines the historic growth rate and applies it to current sales to forecast future sales. For example, if the annual revenue growth rate is 5 percent and current annual sales are $100,000, we would project $105,000 ($100,000 × 5% + $100,000) for next year and $110,250 for the following one ($105,000 × 5% + $105,000). Unfortunately, it is rarely this simple! These projections assume that nothing changes in the environment—a truly unusual occurrence.

Our base sales projection needs to be adjusted for the positive and negative impact of changes in the environment. For example, the oil industry's sales revenue increases as a result of an increase in oil prices. Gasoline prices go up. Retailers earn more revenue from each gallon sold and they sell the same (or almost the same) number of gallons, since consumers do not adjust their driving habits in the short-run. So a simple trend projection would dramatically understate actual gasoline sales revenues.

If there are no positive or negative environmental impacts on sales, then the trend projection becomes our base sales projection. We now have to add the impact of our proposed strategies on sales revenue.

Forecasting the impact of new strategies on sales is both art and science. We first must identify a basis on which to project sales that we expect will result from our strategic initiative(s). For example, if we are a retailer opening stores in a new market, the average sales per square foot of our existing stores (total sales/total square footage of current stores) may be a good place to start. We would take the computed average sales per square foot and multiply it by the number of square feet in the new stores. If we are a consumer packaged goods company expanding into a new market, our existing market may be a good basis. We would compute our market share (our sales/total market sales for our product) and multiply market share by the available market in the new area. We have to be careful here, since we may not gain traction in the market immediately since we will have to build consumer awareness and compete for share with existing products in the market. So, we may decide to use 50 percent (or some other conservative number) of our current market share to estimate our initial position in the new market. If our strategy is successful, our market share will build over time.

Understand that our strategy may have a negative impact on our base sales. For example, if we are a retailer opening additional stores in an existing market, the new stores might take some sales from existing stores as our regular customers begin to shop at a more convenient new location. Similarly, a company launching a new product into an existing market may draw some of the new item's sales from the sales of existing items in the company's line, so we have to allow for some cannibalization of current sales in addition to net new sales gained from competitors' shares or from growth of the category.

Also note that we only want to estimate sales for the period of time our new strategy is in place. This may seem obvious, but it still bears remembering as we project the strategy's impact on revenue. As an example, if our strategy is to expand distribution into a new market and sales of the product in this market will not begin for six months into the fiscal year, we can expect one half of the annual projected sales for that strategy.

The rate of growth of sales from new strategies may outpace the existing sales trend. This is because strategic impact often starts slowly and gains momentum as promotion takes hold, distribution increases, and customer awareness expands. So if our historical growth rate is 5 percent, sales increases from new strategies may be two or three times that rate.

As an example of sales forecasting, consider ActionVision, a hypothetical company in the electronic gaming business. Let's assume that senior managers of the company have chosen a new growth strategy - to expand into eSports, a rapidly growing business. In February 2016, Forbes called eSports "the next big thing in marketing." Most commonly, eSports take the form of organized video game competitions involving multiple players. Professional tournaments now engage thousands of players and spectators.

In addition to entering the eSports market, a second element of ActionVision's strategy is to develop a sponsorship arrangement with some of the major eSports competitions. ActionVision plans to invest in a sponsorship of the ESL Pro League next year (plan year 1), adding additional sponsorships in plan years 2 and 3. The sponsorships are designed to create additional awareness in the electronic gaming community of the portfolio of ActionVision's products and encourage both veteran and rookie gamers to become ActionVision game players.

Table 8-8 shows how these three forecasting components tie together to create an estimate of future sales for ActionVision. Current year sales equal $24.2 million. The table (line one) shows a historical growth rate of ten percent per year for its existing business, assumed to remain constant for the next three years as no major changes are forecast for the industry. Line two shows the impact of the market growth in online gaming driven by the increasing interest in eSports, which the industry estimates at five percent per year. Line four shows the impact of ActionVision's entry in eSports. In year one, ActionVision will launch new products, for which consumer awareness and interest will build (at a constant rate) during the year, so that the total for the year is half of the projected annual sales figure of $8 million, or $4 million. In year two, as the growth of the category continues and ActionVision has established a position in the market, growth is targeted at 30 percent of the $8 million annual sales for the new eGaming products, and that growth rate is expected to continue during year three.

Table 8-8 Forecasting Sales: ActionVision

	ActionVision **Three Year Sales Projections** (000 omitted)			
	CURRENT YEAR [C]	C + 1	C + 2	C + 3
Base Sales (10% annual growth trend)	$24,200.0	26,620.0	29,282.0	32,210.2
Environmental Impact (5% annual market growth)		1,210.0	1,331.0	1,464.1
Impact of New Strategies				
New Products		4,000.0	10,400.0	13,520.0
Sponsorships		484.0	798.6	878.5
Yearly Sales Revenues	24,200.0	32,314.0	41,811.6	48,072.8

The final component of the overall sales forecast is shown on line five and reflects the impact of an expanding sponsorship position over the three years of the analysis. In year one, ActionVision's sponsorship of the ESL Pro League, based on similar results gained by other companies in the industry, should generate a two percent increase in current year sales. In years two and three, selected additional sponsorships should yield net sales increases of three percent of base sale, reflecting the effect of the expanding presence of and increased affinity for ActionVision in the eSports market. By combining each of the three components of the sales forecast, we estimate that sales will increase to $32.3 million in plan year one (i.e., C + 1), $41.8 million in year two, and 48.1 million in year three.

Expense Forecasts

Next we turn to expenses, beginning with cost of sales. The essential elements here are direct labor, direct materials, and overhead. Cost of sales is typically estimated as a percentage of sales (i.e., the percent of sales method).

Fortunately, the relationship between sales and cost of sales tends to be rather stable, with changes occurring only slightly over time. Much of this stability has to do with the fact that the firm may be able to control the mix of input factors, but only rarely can have any significant effect on the prices it pays for these inputs. In the longer run (not generally relevant to this estimation exercise, unless it is the actual focus of the strategic initiative under consideration) substitution of basic input factors—capital or technology for labor, as an instance—may alter the sales to cost of sales relationship, and therefore deserves consideration.

Generally, the percent of sales method also is applied to obtain the estimates for nearly all the operating expenses described on the income statement as "general and administrative." There tends to be much more variability and discretion, though, with selling expenses. These items may need a projection method that is not a linear extrapolation of the current or prior periods' association with sales.

Below the line of net income from operations, there are two important elements for consideration. Interest expense is related to the amount of debt carried by the firm and its specific rate structure for credit. There is no expected relationship of these interest costs to dollar volume of sales. Income taxes are also not directly related to sales but rather to the amount of income before taxes and the prevailing tax rates.

Before attempting to connect the income statement and balance sheet, the issue of distributions of profits to owners should be considered. For U.S. corporations, there tends to be a very stable, almost rigid, view taken toward dividend policy. In the projection process, unless there is substantial evidence to the contrary, most strategic managers expect that the *payout ratio* (i.e., the proportion of earnings distributed to owners) will change little over time.

Forecasting the Balance Sheet

With the income statement projected, we can move to the balance sheet. The link between the company's income statement and its balance sheet is net income for the period. It is still beneficial to project the basic elements of assets and liabilities on the basis of prior proportions as well as relationship to sales. For example, if the firm routinely sells only on credit and historically collects 95 percent of its receivables within 45 days, we have a straightforward way of estimating the balance sheet number once sales have been projected. Likewise, if the company's payables are mainly related to material inputs, and are typically paid within 30 days of purchase, the elements for estimation based on sales are available. As a final example, if there is no plan to change the financing structure of the firm in the near term, then the future debt in the projected balance sheet will be known.

When we turn to the balance sheet in this projection process, we have the freedom to solve for either a cash balance or a financing component item (typically, long-term debt). In other words, the balancing nature of this particular accounting report provides us with the opportunity to have the forward-looking statements generate the cash or debt requirement. As we noted earlier, this is a very useful purpose served by a set of projected financial statements.

Cash Flow Projections

The statement of cash flows is a report that highlights the results of management's financing, investing, and operating decisions by showing the results of cash movements over a period of time. The cash flow statement also is extraordinary in its ability to act as a bridge between the operating statement and the balance sheet. Of course, the best part of all this is that once the other two forward-looking statements are completed there is no additional projection work to do—just the conversion of operating, financing, and investing activities to the cash-flow basis for display.

To summarize, forward-looking or projected statements are an important way to present estimations of the company's financial performance. They can be helpful in determining cash and financing needs. These statements depend on and are only as good as the assumptions and reasoning on which they are based. Reasonable assumptions about the impact of the external environment on the firm and solid reasoning about the financial relationships among the categories in the accounting reports are required. The reward for developing estimated statements is a view of the future that strategic managers can use to plan the path for achieving value creation.

Format and Presentation of Projected Statements

Let's consider two additional important questions about the development and presentation of projected financial statements. First, how far ahead should we estimate? General rules are difficult to give on this issue, but most analysts would like to project five years, but are willing to settle for three. As the future unfolds it tells us about the validity of the assumptions that underlie our forecasts. That means that projected statements require adjustment, refinement, and revision as the unknown future turns into the certain present and as the present becomes unchangeable history. Just as with strategic management itself, the development of estimated financial outcomes from strategy alternatives is a continuous and on-going process.

The second question is: How will we present the expected impact of new strategies on the projected statements? Most strategic managers want to see an estimation of the future *without* changes compared to each of the viable strategy alternatives being considered for implementation. For example, top management needs to know what the projected profit will be if no changes are made, if Strategy A is implemented, and if Strategy B is chosen. Strategies A and B might be complementary, mutually exclusive, or scalable in a way that both can be implemented. Today's desktop computing capabilities allow managers to consider many "what if" scenarios before a choice is made.

Figure 8-3 shows the format and presentation of a projected income statement for the Pro Forma Company, a hypothetical company operating in the United States. The projected statement is based on the assumptions identified in the footnotes shown. For the sake of simplicity, we suppose that the company expects stable growth in revenues and expenses until year 3, when a new market development strategy is to be implemented. The strategy is to expand beyond the domestic borders for the first time, with entry into the Mexican market. This new strategy means added growth in sales, but also higher selling expenses and new debt, as reflected in the year 3 figures.

Notice the format of Figure 8-3. It begins with actual numbers from Pro Forma's current period. It is helpful to express these numbers both in nominal units (i.e., dollars) and as a percentage of sales (i.e., common size). Another useful way to present the projections is in percent change format, which is not shown in Figure 8-3. From the actual figures, Pro Forma's analysts have projected three years into the future. A remarks column or detailed set of footnotes also accompanies the statement to identify and explain the assumptions underlying the projections.

The forecasted statement of operations helps us to evaluate the strategic choice of expanding into Mexico. If our estimates are reasonable, the projection suggests that expansion into the Mexican market does not create value, at least not right away. We come to this conclusion not only because our net income declines in year 3 (from $529,000 to $507,000), but also because our net profit margin, or return on sales, drops from 11 percent to 9.8 percent. This does not mean we should reject the strategic alternative, however. Notice that we have projected only the first year revenues and expenses for our expansion strategy. Many strategies do not pay off in their first year, as we know. We need to evaluate this strategy over a longer time horizon. The financial tools described previously in this chapter can assist us in that task.

Pro Forma Company, Inc.
Projected Income Statement

	CURRENT YEAR (C)		C + 1	C + 2	C + 3
	AMOUNT '(000)	COMMON SIZE (%)	AMOUNT '(000)	AMOUNT '(000)	AMOUNT '(000)
Sales revenue	$4,350	100%	$4,568.00	$4,796.00	$5,180.00
Cost of goods sold:					
Labor, materials, and overhead	$2,536	58.3	2663	2796	3020
Depreciation	144	3.3	151	158	171
Gross profit	1,670	38.4	1,754	1,842	1989
Selling expenses	$430	9.9	452	475	622
General & administrative expenses	352	8.1	370	388	420
Net Operating Income	888	20.4	932	979	947
Interest expense	0	0.0	0	0	8
Profit before taxes	888	20.4	932	979	939
Income taxes	408	9.4	429	450	432
Net income	480	11.0	503	529	507

Assumptions:
- Sales growth is forecasted at a rate of 5 percent in years 1 and 2, followed by 8 percent in year 3 when a new market (i.e., Mexico) is entered (these forecasts would be supported by research and analyses).
- Cost of goods sold remains constant. Therefore, the gross profit margin rate does not change (38.4 percent of sales) over the three years.
- Selling expenses increase to 12 percent of sales in year 3 due to the added costs of entering the Mexican market. All other operating expenses remain constant.
- To finance expansion into Mexico, a $100,000 loan will be taken in year 3 to defray the costs of purchasing new vehicles for product distribution. The vehicles will have a 10-year useful life. All of this amount could be financed at 8 percent interest. Prior to year 3, Pro Forma has no debt.
- The effective income tax rate holds at 46 percent of pre-tax profit.

Figure 8-3 A projected income statement

CONCLUSION

Value creation is ultimately what the strategic management process is all about. The financial management function supports this value-creating focus. In this chapter we have reviewed the finance function in the firm and various tools that are available to assist managers in making strategic choices. An important part of strategic choice is to project a financial view of the firm as it might appear under alternative strategic choices. Forward-looking financial statements are an effective way to do so.

As always, benefits come at a cost. Financing for the strategies selected might be from internal or external sources. External financing sources will involve public and private securities sales. More likely than not, when external financing is sought it will be from creditors—either individual investors or financial institutions—or private lenders.

Once our strategies have been selected, we face the challenging task of implementation. This is our focus in the next two chapters.

KEY TERMS AND CONCEPTS

After reading this chapter you should understand the following terms.

- Financial structure
- Payback period
- Net Present Value (NPV)
- Internal financing
- Capital structure
- The cost of capital

- Present value payback
- External financing
- Capital budgeting
- Time value of money
- Forward-looking financial statements
- Synergy value

DISCUSSION QUESTIONS

1. What is the role of the finance function in strategic management?
2. What financial tools are available to assist with assessing strategic choices? What are the pros and cons of the various tools?
3. What is the purpose of forward-looking financial statements? How are they developed and presented?
4. What sources of funding are available to finance strategies? How has use of the various sources shifted over the past two decades? Why?
5. Do you agree or disagree with the following statement: The Present Value Payback technique is the best way to assess the attractiveness of a strategic choice.
6. How can a firm justify acquiring another firm for 20 percent more than its fair market value?

EXPERIENTIAL EXERCISE

Developing a Projected Income Statement. Develop a revised projected income statement for Pro Forma, Inc. (PFI) based on the following information.

PFI is a manufacturer of air filters for lawn mowers. The company has developed the following projected income statement for the period ending June 30, 2018 based on the assumption of no new products and a continuation of current trends and growth rates.

	6/30/18			
	AMOUNT (000)		COMMON SIZE (%)	
Sales revenue		$4,350		100.0
COGS				
Labor, materials, and overhead	$2,536		58.3%	
Depreciation	144	$2,680	3.3%	61.6%
Gross profit		$1,670		38.4%
Selling expenses	$430		9.9%	
General and administrative expenses	352	$782	8.1%	18.0%
Profit before taxes		$888		20.4%
Income taxes		$408		9.4%
Net income		$480		11.0%

Assume that the strategic management team is considering a strategy to extend PFI's product line by manufacturing fiber elements for truck and automobile oil filters, and wants to know the projected impact of the strategy on the financial results projected for fiscal year 2018 (see table above). The new product would be done on a contract basis for a manufacturer of one of the leading oil filter brands now in the marketplace.

The project team provides these data and assumptions on the proposed strategy:

1. A contract could be negotiated for initial yearly output of 1 million fiber elements at 50 cents per unit beginning in 2018. Sales would grow by 3% in both 2019 and 2020 for the entire company.

2. New equipment, with a 10-year useful life with no salvage value, would be needed for production. Installed cost would be $500,000. All of this amount could be financed at 9% interest.

3. Based on engineering and manufacturing estimates, labor, material, and overhead costs of the new product would be approximately 57 % of the unit selling price.

4. To handle the additional administrative burden of this contract, another office worker would be hired. The yearly employee cost (wages, benefits, taxes) would be $45,000. This cost is in addition to the existing general and administrative common sized overhead.

5. The growth rate of free cash flows after 2020 is 2%.

6. Net working capital is estimated at 2% of sales.

7. The company's weighted average cost of capital is 15%.

8. Unless otherwise stated above, assume all historical cost relationships are constant.

STUDENT EXERCISE

1. Construct new proforma income statements for the years 2018, 2019 and 2020 with the addition of the new assumptions.
2. Calculate the free cash flow (FCF) for each set of proformas.
3. Calculate the NPV for the new strategy, including the terminal value.

Note—The solution to this exercise is presented in the Appendix to this chapter.

ENDNOTES

1. "About The Walt Disney Company." *Walt Disney Company*. Web. Accessed 15 May 2016.

2. Ingram, Matthew. "Six years later, Disney's acquisition of Marvel looks smarter than ever." *Fortune*. Time, Inc. 8 October 2015. Web. 14 May 2016. And Krantz, Matt; Snider, Mike; Della Cava, Marco; Alexander, Bryan. "Disney buys Lucasfilm for $4 billion." *USA Today*. Gannett Company. 30 October 2012. Web. 12 April 2016.

3. Tartaglione, Nancy. "'Captain America: Civil War' Crossing $1B Global Box Office Today; #1 Movie Of 2016." *Deadline Hollywood*. Penske Business Media. 20 May 2016. Web. 21 May 2016.

4. Krantz, Matt; Snider, Mike; Della Cava, Marco; Alexander, Bryan. "Disney buys Lucasfilm for $4 billion." *USA Today*. Gannett Company. 30 October 2012. Web. 12 April 2016.

5. Baidawi, Adam. "Star Wars, Marvel, Pixar: Why Disney bought them all."

Intheblack. CPA Australia Ltd. 1 April 2016. Web. 12 April 2016.

6. "2015 The Walt Disney Company Annual Report and Letter to Shareholders." *The Walt Disney Company*. Accessed 11 May 2016.

7. Ziobro, Paul; Hufford, Austen. "'Star Wars' is the force behind strong Hasbro sales." *WSJ*. 8 February 2016. Web. 9 March 2016.

8. Op Cit, "2015 The Walt Disney Company Annual Report and Letter to Shareholders."

9. The Walt Disney Company, 2005 Annual Report

10. Loten, Angus. "New Plant Designed to Push GE Further Into Digital." *WSJ*. 22 April 2016. Web. 10 May 2016.

11. Bershire Hathaway, 2008 Letter to Shareholders, p. 5.

12. The Essays of Warren Buffet: Lessons for Corporate America (2001), p. 200.

13. Fortune Magazine, April 3, 1995.

14. The Essays of Warren Buffet: Lessons for Corporate America (2001), p. 183.

15. Gordon, Myron J. (1959) "Dividends, Earnings and Stock Prices." *Review of Economics and Statistics* 41 (2): 99–105.

Appendix

Table 8-9 Solution to Exercise

Solutions for Experiential Exercise

Baseline Proforma	Amount (000) 6/30/18		Common Size %	Amount (000) 6/30/19		Common Size %	Amount (000) 6/30/20		Common Size %
Sales revenue	$ 4,350		100.0%	$ 4,481		100.0%	$ 4,615		100.0%
COGS									
Labor, material & overhead	$ 2,536		58.3%	$ 2,612		58.3%	$ 2,690		58.3%
Depreciation	$ 144	$ 2,680	3.3% 61.6%	$ 144	$ 2,756	3.2% 61.5%	$ 144	$ 2,834	3.1% 61.4%
Gross Profit		$ 1,670			$ 1,724			$ 1,780	
Selling Expenses	$ 430		9.9%	$ 443		9.9%	$ 456		9.9%
General & Administrative Expenses	$ 352	$ 782	8.1% 18.0%	$ 363	$ 805	8.1% 18.0%	$ 373	$ 830	8.1% 18.0%
Profit before Taxes		$ 888	20.4%		$ 919	20.5%		$ 951	20.6%
Income Taxes		$ 408	9.4%		$ 423	9.4%		$ 437	9.5%
Net Income		$ 480	11.0%		$ 496	11.1%		$ 513	11.1%
Add Back Depreciation		$ 144			$ 144			$ 144	
OCF		$ 624			$ 640			$ 657	
Changes In NWC		$ -			$ 13			$ 13	
Changes in Fixed Assets		$ -			$ -			$ -	
FCF		$ 624			$ 627			$ 644	

Proforma with Strategy	6/30/18 Amount (000)		6/30/19 Amount (000)		6/30/20 Amount (000)	
Sales revenue						
Existing Sales	$ 4,350		$ 4,481		$ 4,615	
New Sales	$ 500		$ 515		$ 530	
Total Sales Revenue		$ 4,850		$ 4,996		$ 5,145
COGS						
Labor, material & overhead						
Existing	$ 2,536		$ 2,612		$ 2,690	
New	$ 285		$ 294		$ 302	
Depreciation						
Existing	$ 144		$ 144		$ 144	
New	$ 50	$ 3,015	$ 50	$ 3,100	$ 50	$ 3,187
Gross Profit		$ 1,835		$ 1,896		$ 1,959
Selling Expenses	$ 480		$ 494		$ 509	
General & Administrative Expenses	$ 437	$ 917	$ 449	$ 943	$ 461	$ 970
EBIT		$ 918		$ 953		$ 988
Interest Expense		$ 36		$ 36		$ 36
EBT		$ 882		$ 917		$ 952
Income Taxes		$ 406		$ 422		$ 438
Net Income		$ 512		$ 531		$ 550
Add Back Depreciation		$ 194		$ 194		$ 194
OCF		$ 706		$ 725		$ 744
Changes In NWC		$ 50		$ 15		$ 15
Changes in Fixed Assets		$ 500		$ -		$ -
FCF		$ 156		$ 710		$ 729

	6/30/18	6/30/19	6/30/20	Terminal
FCF Attributable to new Strategy	$ (467)	$ 83	$ 85	$ 615.23
NPV	$ 102			

Chapter

9

Strategy Implementation: Leading People & Managing Change

CHAPTER LEARNING OBJECTIVES

After studying this chapter, you should be able to

- Understand the strategy implementation process and a model for implementation;
- Identify common barriers to strategy implementation and understand approaches to overcome the barriers;
- Apply principles for leading change and overcoming employee resistance;
- Appreciate the importance of leadership and corporate culture in the strategic management process.

256

Amazon.com

amazon

Recall from our discussion in Chapter 7, the Seattle-based Amazon.com, was founded by Jeff Bezos as an online bookstore. It has grown into the world's largest online retailer as it earned more than $100 billion in revenue for 2015.[1] Amazon's three core businesses are its online marketplace (Amazon.com), delivery service (Amazon Prime), and enterprise web services (Amazon Web Service). The web giant has its hands in everything from space exploration and artificially intelligent drone development to grocery delivery, mobile devices and its own original television shows and movies. To learn more about Amazon, visit www.amazon.com.

*N*amed after the world's largest river, Amazon.com has grown into a company that sells products and services ranging from A to Z, as its logo implies. Amazon was founded as an online bookstore and it revolutionized the industry in the late 1990s. Some competitors, including Barnes & Noble, emulated Amazon with its own website, while others, like Borders, failed to adapt to the seismic change brought by Amazon.

As Amazon grew, it broadened its offerings to include an expansive list of products such as compact disks, kitchenware, toys, electronics, and more. It further expanded by establishing a platform for companies and individuals to sell second-hand products in its digital marketplace. Amazon implemented this strategy by purchasing online retail service companies to expand product offerings and by overhauling its supply chain management system to account for the growth of product offerings. Amazon acquired Junglee Corporation and Planet All to widen its product lines in the late 1990s. Then, at the start of the 21st century, Amazon opened eight new order fulfillment centers (five in the U.S. and three in Europe) to build a larger and more efficient supply chain.[2] These investments in capacity and infrastructure have continued for Amazon which now operates 109 warehouses around the world and offers over one billion products.[3]

Today, Amazon is a behemoth with three central focuses: Marketplace, Amazon Prime, and Amazon Web Services. The story behind Amazon's growth is a story of a company that has transformed itself by responding to changes in technology and consumer demand while also recognizing how to create long-term growth. It is a story of a company that grows and adapts not only by developing new strategies but also by being able to *implement* these new strategies.

Up to this point in the book we have emphasized the importance of strategy formulation—the steps for developing and choosing effective strategies. The success of the strategic management process depends in large part on effective strategic choice. But that is not the end of the process. A well-conceived strategy must also be implemented, or put into action. And this is often where strategic management breaks down and fails. According to research, the inability to get things done, to have ideas and decisions implemented, is widespread in organizations today. It is, moreover, a problem that seems to be getting worse in both public and private sector organizations.[4]

Many factors influence the success of strategy implementation. It is possible to group the factors into two broad categories—the human or people issues and the organizational issues. The purpose of this chapter is to discuss the implementation phase of strategic management, focusing on the *people* issues of managing change. This includes the management style and skills of the leaders, the role of middle managers in the process, overcoming resistance to change, as well as aligning the culture of the organization with its new strategy. We will examine common reasons for failure of strategy implementation and identify principles of effective implementation. After reading this chapter, you should understand the human side of implementation and be able to answer each of the questions listed in Figure 9-1. The organizational side of implementation is discussed in Chapter 10.

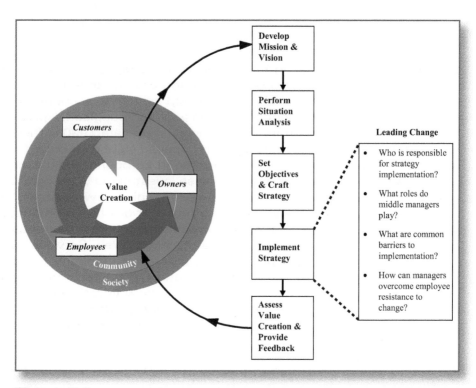

Figure 9-1
The Strategic Management Framework

WHO IS RESPONSIBLE FOR STRATEGY IMPLEMENTATION?

One of the prime functions of a strategic manager is to cope with changes in a firm's external environment in order to ensure its survival and long-term growth.[5] Changes in the organization are often needed to adapt to these external changes. Hence, the simple answer to the question of who is responsible for strategy implementation is—everyone. In most organizations, just about everyone plays a role in implementing strategy and creating change within the firm.

In large and diversified companies, corporate strategies at the top of the organization must be supported by business-level strategies, which in turn are bolstered by functional-level strategies. From top to bottom of the organization, everyone contributes in some way to the effort. Corporate executives team up with Vice Presidents or senior managers of the divisions to translate corporate objectives into business-level priorities. The division managers, in turn, will work with their direct reports (subordinates and peers) to take business-level objectives to the functional level. Plans will be developed, programs established, and budgets created. Within each division, functional managers, supervisors, and operating employees have specific goals and responsibilities. Whereas the strategy may have been formulated by a select group of top managers or by a team of representatives of several or all levels of the organization, the task of implementation usually rests on the shoulders of all employees.

The Roles of Middle Managers

Middle managers play a particularly important role in strategy implementation for two reasons: (1) they are a key source of information for top managers regarding the internal and external environments of the organization, and (2) they are often most directly responsible for overseeing the implementation process within their functional areas. In recent years, the number of middle managers in organizations has been reduced due to the advent of new information and communications technologies and the corresponding flattening of organization structures.[6] As organizations become flatter and less hierarchical, however, the strategic importance of middle managers in the implementation of strategies is likely to increase.

Figure 9-2 identifies four roles played by middle managers in strategic management. As the link or liaison between corporate officers and frontline workers, middle managers have the opportunity to exercise their influence either upward or downward in the implementation process. This is reflected in the "direction of influence" axis in Figure 9-2. The second axis of the figure focuses on the "expected activities of middle managers." These activities are categorized as either *traditional*, whereby middle managers focus on their conventional roles as senior management's agents for strategy implementation, or *entrepreneurial*, where middle managers are more active and creative in both developing and implementing strategies and essentially become change agents.[7]

Using these dimensions, we obtain four roles played by middle managers. Synthesizing information and implementing deliberate strategies are both traditional roles of middle managers. In the *synthesizing information* role, middle managers

Direction of Influence ↓	Expected Activities of Middle Managers	
	Traditional	Entrepreneurial
Upward	Synthesizing Information	Championing Strategic Alternatives
Downward	Implementing Deliberate Strategies	Facilitating Adaptability

Figure 9-2
Strategic Roles of Middle Managers
Adapted from Floyd & Wooldridge (1994).

assist top managers in constructing the world around them through data gathering and labeling the data as either opportunities or threats[8] so that top managers can analyze the situation in a strategic fashion. *Implementing deliberate strategies* is the most traditional role of middle managers where they take a master strategy created by top managers and lead the frontline workers to execute the envisioned strategies.

In the role of *championing strategic alternatives,* middle managers act more proactively and help to shape the strategies and direction of the organization by using upward influence on senior managers. This role allows middle managers to experiment with new ideas among frontline employees. Similarly, in the *facilitating adaptability* role, middle managers take the strategy from top managers but become innovative in fostering the implementation. They encourage broad-based participation by employees and seek ways to overcome employee resistance to change. These entrepreneurial activities and roles are further discussed later in this chapter.

THE STRATEGY IMPLEMENTATION PROCESS

Implementation is a complex and sometimes muddled process. It may require major changes in the systems, structure, leadership style, employee behaviors, and resources of the organization, as well as the identification and creation of new core competencies and organizational culture. These change efforts may require a considerable length of time.

Implementation is commonly viewed as a mechanical process where action plans are deduced and carried out by middle managers from a master strategy conceived by top management. Research suggests that the reality is considerably more complex: "Even in fairly stable situations, priorities must be revised as conditions evolve and new information unfolds. Implementation, therefore, is best characterized as an ongoing series of interventions which are only partly anticipated in top management plans and which adjust strategic directions to suit emergent events.[9]

Let's consider an example of successful implementation before introducing a strategy implementation model.

Amazon's Strategy Implementation: A Continuous Example

For the better part of two decades, Amazon has sailed along as the undisputed industry leader in online retail and services. For insights into this success, consider how the online retailer implemented strategies for its two other business segments: Amazon Prime and Amazon Web Services.

Amazon Prime was introduced in 2005 as a $79 per year service that provided subscribers free two-day delivery for one million in-stock items.[10] That service has expanded to become the same free two-day delivery on 20 million items along with access to Prime Instant Video (unlimited streaming of movies and television shows), Kindle Owner's Lending Library (unlimited access to thousands of books, unlimited photo storage), and Prime Music (unlimited access music service).[11] The cost of Prime membership service, including all of the new features added in the past ten years, is $99 per year or $10.99 per month.[12]

According to analysts, Prime membership grew by 51% in 2016 year over year, nearly 33% of U.S. households now have a Prime subscription, and the estimated number worldwide is 65 million.[13] On the day after Christmas 2015, Amazon reported 10 million new customers registered for Prime subscriptions.[14] Customer Intelligence Research Partners reported that Prime subscribers spend $1,100 a year while non-subscribers spend $600 a year and that the company has retained approximately 80% of its original 2005 subscribers.[15] These outcomes reflect not only a good strategy, but its successful implementation. Amazon's overarching goals of customer intimacy/growth, customer retention, and brand growth are all being achieved by the Amazon Prime segment.

Another example of successful strategy implementation is Amazon Web Services (AWS). Introduced in 2006, AWS offers IT infrastructure services to businesses in the form of web services, commonly known as cloud computing. With the AWS Cloud, businesses no longer need to plan to procure servers and other major IT infrastructure months in advance. With AWS companies can instantly tap into thousands of servers to deliver faster results. AWS is a highly reliable, scalable, low-cost infrastructure cloud platform that powers thousands of businesses in 190 countries around the world with notable customers like Netflix, Salesforce.com, and the Central Intelligence Agency.[16] With data center locations in the U.S., Europe, Brazil, Singapore, Japan, and Australia, customers across all industries are taking advantage numerous features of AWS such as application hosting, website configuration, backup and storage, content delivery, enterprise IT, and database curating.[17]

As discussed in Chapter 7, Amazon is not known for its profitability as the company has historically deferred profits to invest in its supply chain and innovation departments. In Spring 2016, however, Amazon delivered record financial results, including 28% sales growth year over year, its highest growth since 2012, and an operating margin of 3.7%, its best in more than five years. This financial success is due in part to AWS. The unit's sales for the first quarter of 2016 increased by 64%, reaching $2.57 billion and CEO Jeff Bezos expects AWS sales to reach $10 billion by the end of 2016. While $2.57 billion is a fraction of Amazon's total sales of $29 billion for the first quarter of 2016, 67% of Amazon's operating income in that time period came from the AWS segment. Operating margins in the segment were 23% compared to 1.8% in Amazon's other retail segments.[18] These financial results reflect a strong and well executed strategy. Still, the question remains: what were the reasons for Amazon's success with implementing these strategies in its Prime and AWS segments?

A Strategy Implementation Model

In some ways, strategy implementation is like a puzzle. The challenge is to fit the pieces together to support the organization's strategy. Figure 9-3 is a model of the strategy implementation process and illustrates the challenge. A strategy is first set and people and organizational factors are fashioned around it. For instance, employees are hired or promoted based on their ability to contribute to the strategy. The design of the organization takes shape around the strategy. When the strategy and objectives are changed to take the organization in a new direction there may be a clash between the old structure and systems and the new strategy. This clash creates a tension in the organization that may result in administrative problems and weakening organizational performance. As employees, structure and systems adjust and adapt to the new strategy, performance improves, and implementation is enhanced.

The case of Amazon illustrates the importance of the concept of "fit" or alignment in the implementation process. With Amazon Prime, according to Global VP, Greg Greely, the original goal was to create the ultimate in convenience and bargain shopping.[19] To deliver low prices to customers and high quality service, Amazon needed to build highly efficient supply chain and logistics divisions, so

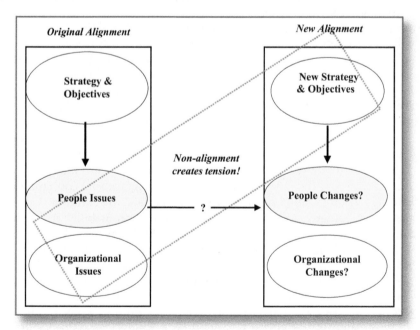

Figure 9-3
An Implementation Model

the company invested heavily in warehouse expansion and new fulfillment center construction. Fast and free shipping on a global scale is made possible with 109 fulfillment centers.[20] To keep operating costs as low as possible, Amazon also struck a deal to lease twenty planes to shuttle merchandise around the U.S., installed robotic assistants in its warehouses, opened new storage facilities closer to urban centers, and began delivering more of its own packages to customer doorsteps.[21] Likewise, Amazon developed new and innovative features to retain Prime subscribers. The online retailer increased its spending on technology and original content by 28% to $3.56 billion in the first quarter of 2016. Much of this spending included producing original content for new television series along with other popular content such as "Transparent," "Mozart in the Jungle" and "The Man in the High Castle."[22]

Amazon launched its very profitable Web Services segment to leverage its thousands of servers to provide cloud services to enterprise clients. AWS was a pioneer in the cloud computing market due to its sheer scale, its unique services, and its format. As AWS Senior Vice President, Andy Jassy, explained, strong demand for AWS services required Amazon to buy more IT infrastructure, which created economies of scale and reduced Amazon's per unit infrastructure costs. These reduced infrastructure costs allowed Amazon to lower its prices for customers, which, in turn, increased demand. Jassy refers to it as the "Virtuous Circle." As more services and features are added by AWS and more companies are added as customers, the Virtuous Circle spins faster and faster, and allows for prices to be lowered even further. From 2006 to 2014, AWS's prices were lowered 23 times. Another strategic element of the implementation of AWS has been its pay-as-you-go scheme. Rather than forcing customers to pay a large sum of money for capacity they may not end up utilizing, AWS allows customers to decrease their fixed costs and pay based on their usage, making AWS all the more attractive.[23]

Figure 9-4 illustrates the Virtuous Circle that Jassy referred to when describing strategy implementation for Amazon Web Services. Failure to align the implementation factors for both Prime and AWS would have undermined Amazon's strategy

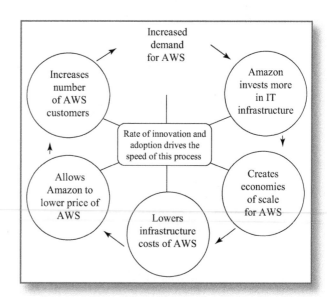

Figure 9-4
Amazon Web Services'
Implementation: Virtuous
Circle

and weakened the unit's financial results Instead, the alignments were made and Amazon's strategy succeeded.

The Role of Organizational Culture in Implementation

Recall from Chapter 6 that an organization's culture represents the shared values of its members. Culture expresses the underlying beliefs and attitudes of the organizations' members, and drives their behavior.

Organizational culture also plays an important role in strategy implementation. For example, consider the case of a merger of two firms where the success of the strategy depends on whether the merging firms can successfully integrate their cultures. When the two cultures clash, implementation is very difficult.

Although culture can be a barrier to implementation, it can also be a facilitator in some cases. A strong organizational culture, where norms, values and beliefs are clear and shared widely, may make it easier for firms to get the employee buy-in needed to implement strategic changes. Employees are often more willing to embrace the new strategy because a broad consensus within the firm already exists concerning the direction of the firm.[24] On the other hand, when a strong culture becomes rigid and inflexible, it is unable to accommodate change and becomes an impediment to implementation. The implication for managers is that culture is a key implementation variable that must be monitored, managed and aligned with the strategy to improve its likelihood of success.

WHY DOES IMPLEMENTATION FAIL?

Between the ideal of strategic alignment described above and the reality of successful implementation lie many difficulties. Research shows that some of the most common barriers to implementation are related to people issues, including:[25]

- Unclear strategy or poor communication of strategy
- Top-down or laissez-faire senior management style
- Poor coordination across functions, business activities, or national borders
- Employee resistance to change or inadequate preparation for change

Any one of these factors can be an implementation killer. Let's examine each one and some remedies for avoiding or overcoming the barriers.

Unclear Strategy or Poor Communication of Strategy

Lacking a clear vision and/or strategy and not effectively communicating a strategy are two different problems, but they both can result in failed implementation. In either case, employees are confused and uncertain about what really matters. Priorities are muddled or inconsistent and no clear sense of direction and purpose exists.

An example of this barrier to implementation was described by John Kotter, an expert on managing organizational change. One company developed a four-inch-thick notebook describing its strategic change, complete with procedures, goals and deadlines. What was lacking, however, was a clear and compelling statement of where this new strategy was leading—the new vision of the future. Instead of inspiring change and rallying the employees, the notebook of details created confusion and frustration.[26]

The problems of miscommunication can take several forms. A common example is when top management believes that one meeting or one announcement of the new strategy is sufficient. This is rarely the case. This mistake is based on the assumption that if top management pronounced the change, it is understood and will be supported. Another common example is when top management fails to "walk the talk." In this case the number and variety of communication efforts may be sufficient to get the message across but senior managers undermine the power of the message by decisions and actions that fail to support the new strategy. When this occurs, actions speak louder than words, and the real message being sent is antithetical to the new strategy.[27]

To overcome these implementation barriers, strategic managers need to use a variety of communication channels to promote the change—memos, meetings, public speeches, the company newsletter, formal and informal interactions, press releases, and e-mail announcements. In short, strategic managers should look for every opportunity to broadcast and reinforce the message of change and the underlying need for change. Repetition and variety are important.

In addition, managers must lead by example. As we know, communication comes in both words and deeds. Behavior from senior managers that is incongruent with the new strategy can overwhelm all other communication efforts.

Two-way communication is also an important principle of successful strategy implementation. This is discussed in the next section.

Top-Down or Laissez-Faire Senior Management Style

Another barrier to implementation of strategy can be the management style of senior executives. Two common obstacles are a top-down style, which imposes strategic change on employees without adequate attempts to get their buy-in, and a laissez-faire style whereby executives are too isolated and disengaged from the implementation process. A company known for its top-down management style is the Hyundai Group. Hyundai employees were once required to wear soldier-like uniforms and forced to put 30% of their wages into a savings account. Hyundai's leader, Chung Ju-Yung, made most managerial decisions without any input from his management team. Subordinates were even fearful to speak to Chung, who was known to grab employees by their neckties.

Change is a process that needs to be managed. It takes time. Implementation almost always requires the support of employees to carry out the new strategies. Fiats from corporate executives to "change or else" can be an abdication of management's responsibility to take the time to manage change as a process. The same point is true of a hands-off style of management.

Consider the example of a successful mid-sized consulting firm that recently hired a new division manager. The new manager came from a competitor where he had established a strong and successful track record. On arriving at his new company, the division manager (DM) was instructed by the company president to seek growth opportunities for the division. Revenue growth was strong in some segments but had fallen drastically, by almost 50 percent, in one of the division's core markets.

To achieve the growth expected by the president, the new manager embarked on the development of a series of new consulting services and programs based on his experience in the industry and his knowledge of emerging trends. At first the changes were supported by employees, albeit somewhat reluctantly. But when the manager continued to push for more and more new programs, employees began to push back. They resisted for a variety of reasons, but one of the most important ones was their sense of frustration with the manager's top-down style. They felt they had no voice in the strategy process and believed their legitimate concerns about rapid or undisciplined growth and inadequate resources to support the growth were either unheard or ignored. The division manager was astute enough to recognize the warning signals being sent, so he stepped back, slowed down and listened. This recognition marked the beginning of a change in his management style.

Building a shared vision of the future and an organization-wide commitment to strategic change is not a simple task, nor a task that can usually be accomplished by mandates from senior managers. Two-way communication in the planning process and involvement by employees throughout the organization, and not just at the top, helps to overcome this barrier to implementation. Peter Senge, a leading author and management thinker, contends that the task of designing ongoing processes in which people at every level of the organization can speak openly and participate meaningfully in the planning process is critical since it ultimately determines the quality and the power of the results. "A true shared vision cannot be dictated; it can only emerge from a coherent process of reflection and conversation."[28]

High Involvement Strategic Planning

These notions of employee participation make sense in theory but are they practical? Is it really possible to involve middle managers and operating employees in the strategic management process? New planning tools and techniques are an attempt to do just that. For example, *high-involvement planning*, also known as *direct participation planning*, is an inclusive approach to the strategic management process.[29] The approach is achieved by moving away from the top-down, control-oriented model of planning to a process that encourages the participation and ideas of middle managers and front-line employees such as sales representatives, engineers, and operating employees.

By engaging larger numbers of employees in the planning process, high involvement planning seeks to achieve the goals of better strategy by tapping into the creative ideas of employees, and better implementation by fostering employee buy-in to the outcomes of the process. Furthermore, the process views front-line employees as vital strategic resources instead of mere factors of production. It is based on the premise that corporate executives cannot afford to be isolated from the people in their organizations if they are to compete in today's ever-changing world of business.[30]

Including all employees in the process may not be realistic, due to the prohibitive costs, in time and money, of full participation, and the lack of enthusiasm for participation by some employees. Instead, the goal is to create "a hierarchy of imagination."[31] The conventional view is that strategic decision-making is the domain of top management but the hierarchy of imagination concept stresses the importance of including key people from each level of the organization in the planning process,

to increase the chances of an effective and productive working relationship. The three-step process encourages the American to realize that culture matters and that she may be well served by taking the time up front to establish a good personal rapport and positive working relationship with her Dutch counterpart.

Knowledge of Hofstede's cultural dimensions is important but not necessarily sufficient for cultural competence. Other cultural variables may also play a role in achieving cross-cultural cooperation. Take the case of Germany. The American and German managerial models are very different in some ways, although these differences are not primarily reflected in the cultural dimensions in Table 9-1. The German model of "codetermination" requires employee participation on the company's board of directors and representation in the board's decision-making. As a result, German managers must eschew autocratic directives in favor of consensus among bosses and workers. Mergers, acquisitions and strategic alliances and other forms of partnership between German and U. S. companies must take these differences into account.

Employee Resistance to Change or Inadequate Preparation for Change

The fourth and final barrier to implementation discussed in this chapter is employee resistance to change or lack of preparation for change. This problem may be the result of an autocratic, top-down management style, the second barrier discussed above, or it may surface despite senior management's best efforts to involve employees using a more participative management style. In any case, the end result is the same—incomplete and flawed implementation.

Research suggests that employee resistance is not an inevitable by-product of change. It is, however, a common response, especially when the change is large scale, ambiguous, or threatening. Reasons for resistance are many, and include:

- loss of control
- fear of the unknown
- lack of confidence to adapt to the new demands of the change
- an ever increasing workload
- past resentments and distrust toward management
- loss of status or job security for the employee[38]

Consider the following example. Robert was an accountant specializing in corporate tax for a large firm. He had been with the same firm for eight years, since his college graduation. He was a respected employee who had steadily advanced within his firm. One night after a tiring day at work, he sat down to relax and watch the late news. What he learned was anything but relaxing—it was reported that his firm had agreed to merge with an equally large competitor. The consolidation of the industry was an ongoing trend, and mergers were commonplace. But this was different. For the first time it was his firm and involved him personally. Furthermore, the announcement was completely unexpected; he had no prior knowledge of the merger.

Robert felt numb. "It couldn't be true", he told himself. "We're a strong and successful firm. We don't need to merge. It's all a mistake. It won't happen. I'm sure it will fall through." It didn't take long for Robert to realize that it wasn't a mistake—it was real. It was several days before he overcame his initial shock. When he did he was angry. "How could they do this?" he muttered to himself. "Can't they see they're going to ruin the firm? This is ridiculous!" After a few weeks Robert's anger and frustration eventually dissipated and were followed by a period of reflection. His mindset changed from anger to questioning. "What will I do? What does the merger mean for me and my future here at the firm? Is there still a place for me and can I continue to advance? Should I update my resume and explore new opportunities?"

Robert's reaction to the merger is an example of resistance to change and inadequate preparation for change. It is also a typical reaction to unwanted change. Research shows that people often experience a predictable emotional and psychological response to threatening change. This four-phase response—avoidance, resistance, exploration and commitment—is shown in Figure 9-7.[39]

Of course, not all change is resisted—in fact, it is sometimes welcomed and embraced. But when it comes to threatening and unexpected change, this four-phase response is common. The first phase is *avoidance*. As in our example of Robert above, avoidance is characterized by withdrawal, and by a feeling of numbness and a sense of denial. Avoidance is a passive form of opposition while the second stage, *resistance*, is more active. Negative emotions run high in the resistance phase, including anger, frustration, disgust, anxiety, and in extreme cases, even hostility. During these first two phases, the individual continues to focus on the past, on what was and how it might be preserved. A breakthrough occurs in the third stage when the employee begins to accept that the future will be different and trying to cling to the past is a fruitless effort. Robert entered the *exploration* phase when he began to question the impact of the merger on his future with the firm. Confusion and a lack of clear focus remain but at least an awakening to a new reality has set in. During resistance and exploration, the individual's focus turns inward—on the personal impact of change. During the final phase, *commitment*, the focus shifts outward—to the causes and effects of change throughout the organization. The employee's focus is much clearer and broader. He or she is now ready to accept the change, adapt and move forward.

When faced with threatening change, most people will move through each of these stages, though not necessarily in strict sequence or at the same pace. Some people will bounce back and forth between stages. Furthermore, the timing of the

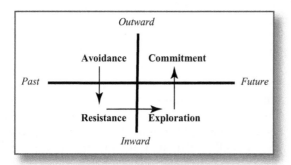

Figure 9-7
A Four-Phase Reaction to Change
Source: Adapted from *The Transition Grid*™, part of the Change Programs, Managing the Human Side of Change, by Flora/Elkind Associates, San Francisco. and C. Scott and D. Jaffe, *Managing Organizational Change: A Practical Guide for Managers* Crisp Publications, Inc, Menlo Park, CA, 1989, 26.

movement may be different for each person. Some will transition through rather quickly in days or even hours, while others may get bogged down for weeks or more in a particular phase.[40] To complicate the transition even further, the manager(s) in charge of leading the change may be struggling with the same emotional reactions.

Leaders of strategic change, at all levels of the organization, play a key role in determining how quickly the transition from avoidance to commitment occurs. Fortunately, there are actions managers can take to facilitate the process. For example, during avoidance, communicate openly and often with employees. Let them know that the change will happen, what to expect, and how they might adjust. Provide as much information as possible, as soon as possible. Lacking information, employees often assume the worst. Anxiety, stress and frustration will only build if information is withheld.

During the resistance phase, give employees some freedom to express their concerns and fears. Talk to them in person—do not rely exclusively on memos, e-mail and other impersonal means of communicating during a difficult change. Listen carefully and respond with empathy as employees work through their anxieties. Insist that employees understand the reasons for the change and its expected benefits.

In the third phase, exploration, employees begin to realize their need to adjust and adapt, but they may be unclear about how to do so. Managers of change can help by working with employees to establish priorities and short-term goals. Seek ways to regain the team's focus. If the change means that employees need to acquire new skills and knowledge, programs for training and development should be discussed and planned. Involving employees in these discussions may help to allay their fears and send the message that the company wants to invest in their future.

Finally, in the commitment phase, employees have moved on to accept the change. New behaviors and practices have been established; cooperation and teamwork are evident. This is a victory worth celebrating. Recognize and appreciate the employees who have made the transition. They have learned and adapted. They have successfully overcome one of the most difficult barriers to implementation—employee resistance to change.

Thus, leaders of change need good coaching skills. With good coaching and appropriate training programs (if necessary), most employees will adapt to change, even major and threatening change. It may be necessary, however, to hire new employees and/or replace those who cannot or will not commit to change. Organizations must learn and adapt to survive. Employees who refuse to change despite appropriate efforts by leaders of change are jeopardizing the organization and their own future in it. They do so at their own risk.

SUCCESSFUL STRATEGY IMPLEMENTATION: THE PEOPLE ISSUES

In the previous section we emphasized a variety of barriers to strategy implementation and mentioned several ways to deal with the barriers. Strategy implementation is a bad news-good news scenario. The bad news is that implementing change can be a complex, time-consuming and challenging process, as we have stated. Even successful change efforts are fraught with surprises and frustrations. But the good news is that there are principles for managing people through the change process that leaders can rely on to facilitate implementation. In this section we discuss those principles.

Organizational change is typically viewed as a three-part process known as "unfreezing, changing, and refreezing."[41] During the *unfreezing* phase, the organization must disengage from its past, understand the reasons for change and prepare itself for transformation. Next, the organization creates and embraces a new vision of the future, and takes steps necessary to achieve that new vision. In the *refreezing* state, new policies, practices, systems and structures are put into place to institutionalize the change.

A stream of research studies over a period of decades has resulted in a set of principles or steps for managing the transition from unfreezing to refreezing.[42] These principles have become recommended procedures for any organization attempting to implement significant strategic change. Let's take a closer look at several of the principles (see Table 9-2).

Table 9-2 Principles for Implementing Change

- Establish a sense of urgency—Analyze and explain the need for change. If the situation is urgent, let people know. Identify and discuss crises, potential crises, or major opportunities. If it is not urgent, however, don't attempt to create a false sense of urgency.
- Communicate early, often and in person—Whenever possible, communicate openly. Full disclosure may not always be possible but it is the ideal.
- Involve people in the process—Form a guiding coalition with enough power to lead the change effort. Encourage the group to work together as a team. Give employees a personal stake in the outcome of the change and provide employees with the training they need. Consider using a high involvement planning process.
- Create and communicate a shared vision of the future—Develop a statement of strategic direction that articulates the links between the organization's competitive environment, its new strategies, and the organizational changes needed to realize the goals of the strategies. Use every vehicle possible to communicate the new vision and strategies.
- Develop an implementation plan—Define roles, responsibilities, deadlines and resource requirements for change. Work with employees to establish the plan and to develop a sense of partnership.
- Anticipate and remove barriers to change—Encourage new ideas and behaviors and change systems, policies and structures that undermine the new strategies. Hire, promote, and develop employees who can implement the new strategies.
- Reinforce and institutionalize new approaches—Articulate the connections between the new behaviors and corporate success. Plan for and create short-term wins. Recognize and reward employees involved in the improvements.

This list was adapted from three sources: John P. Kotter, Leading change: Why transformation efforts fail, *Harvard Business Review*, March-April 1995, pp. 59–67; and Rosabeth Moss Kanter, B. A. Stein and T. D. Jick, The challenge of execution: Roles and tasks in the change process, *The Challenge of Organizational Change*, Free Press, New York, NY, 1992, pp. 369–394; and Michael Beer, and R. A. Eisenstat, The silent killers of strategy implementation and learning, *Sloan Management Review*, Summer 2000, pp. 29–40.

Since change is inevitable in today's dynamic and competitive business environment, managers would do well to understand and practice these principles for implementing change. While the list is not exhaustive, it does identify many steps that can mean the difference between implementation success and failure.

In applying the principles to their organizations, leaders of change will need to consider the unique circumstances they face, and adapt accordingly. For instance, consider the first principle in Table 9-2, creating a sense of urgency. There are many ways this can be accomplished. One way is to circulate data about customer satisfaction and financial performance to more managers and employees, especially information that demonstrates weaknesses. Similarly, organizations could insist that more employees speak directly with dissatisfied customers or disgruntled stockholders. Providing people with information on future opportunities and on the organization's current inability to pursue those opportunities, or exposing organizational weaknesses relative to key competitors can also raise the sense of urgency within the organization.[43] As we have consistently emphasized, value creation is the barometer of successful strategic management. Failure to create value should trigger a sense of urgency in the organization.

CONCLUSION

Amazon.com continues to adapt to changes in technology and customer tastes by transforming its strategies for its three business segments—Marketplace, Amazon Prime, and Amazon Web Services. Amazon's new strategies have been supported by major investments and large-scale realignment of both people and organizational systems within the company. In this chapter, we have identified and discussed the people side of implementation. In the next chapter we turn our attention to the organizational issues.

KEY TERMS AND CONCEPTS

After reading this chapter you should understand each of the following terms.

- High Involvement Planning
- Individualism
- Power Distance
- Exploration
- Corporate Culture
- Hierarchy of Imagination
- Uncertainty Avoidance

- Avoidance
- Commitment
- Cultural Competence
- Competitiveness
- Resistance
- Unfreezing and Refreezing

DISCUSSION QUESTIONS

1. Who is responsible for strategy implementation? What roles do middle managers play in implementation?
2. Discuss the importance of alignment in strategy implementation. Identify the people factors to be aligned.

3. Discuss how the management style of senior executives can be a barrier to implementation, and what can be done to overcome this barrier.
4. What is high involvement planning and under what conditions is this approach most likely to succeed?
5. Identify and explain Hofstede's four dimensions of culture and how they may be used to facilitate implementation across national borders.
6. Why is employee resistance to change a common implementation barrier? What can be done to address this barrier?

EXPERIENTIAL EXERCISE

Managing Strategic Change Research a company that attempted—either successfully or unsuccessfully—to transform itself by developing and implementing a major change in strategy. Provide all relevant details. Critique the implementation efforts and approach used by the company. What does your analysis tell you about effective strategy implementation?

ENDNOTES

1. "2015 Amazon.com Annual Report" Accessed 20 May 2016.
2. Hansell, Saul. "Amazon.com Is Expanding Beyond Books." *New York Times*. The New York Times Company. 5 August 1998. Web. 23 May 2016.
3. "Amazon Investor Relations" Accessed 21 May 2016. http://phx.corporate-ir.net/phoenix.zhtml?c=97664&p=irol-irhome
4. Pfeffer, J. *Managing with Power*. Boston, MA: Harvard Business School Press, 1992, 7.
5. Chandler, A. D. *Strategy and Structure: Chapters in the History of the American Industrial Enterprise*. Cambridge, MA: MIT Press, 1962; Lawrence, P. R., and J. W. Lorsch, *Organization and Environment: Managing Differentiation and Integration*. Homewood, IL: Richard D. Irwin, 1969.
6. Floyd, S.W., and B. Wooldridge, "Dinosaurs or Dynamos? Recognizing Middle Management's Strategic Role," *Academy of Management Executive* 8, no. 4 (1994): 47–57.
7. Joshi, M. P. "Implementing Strategic Change: Styles Used by Middle Managers." Unpublished Dissertation, Fox School of Business and Management, Temple University, Philadelphia, PA, 1996.
8. Floyd, S.W., and B. Wooldridge, "Dinosaurs or Dynamos? Recognizing Middle Management's Strategic Role," *Academy of Management Executive* 8, no. 4 (1994): 47–57.
9. Floyd, S.W., and B. Wooldridge, "Dinosaurs or Dynamos? Recognizing Middle Management's Strategic Role," *Academy of Management Executive* 8, no. 4 (1994): 51.
10. Weise, Elizabeth. "Amazon Prime is big, but how big?" *USA Today*. Gannett Company. 3 February 2015. Web 22 May 2016.
11. Tsukayama, Hayley. "What Amazon's learned from a decade of Prime." *The Washington Post*. Nash Holdings. 3 February 2015. Web. 22 May 2016.
12. Bensinger, Greg. "Amazon Ups the Ante on Streaming Video, Challenging Netflix." *WSJ*. Wall Street Journal. 18 April 2016. Web. 3 May 2016.
13. Hook, Leslie. "Amazon's Prime challenge is international growth." *WSJ*. Wall Street Journal. 4 March 2016. Web. 28 March 2016.
14. Op cit, Tsukayama, Hayley
15. Op cit, Hook, Leslie.

16. McMillan, Robert. "Salesforce Bases New Service on Amazon's Cloud." *WSJ.* Wall Street Journal. 10 May 2016. Web. 21 May 2016.

17. "About AWS." Amazon.com, Inc. Accessed 22 May 2016. https://aws.amazon.com/about-aws/

18. Bensinger, Greg. "Cloud Unit Pushes Amazon to Record Profit." *WSJ.* Wall Street Journal. 28 April 2016. Web. 22 May 2016. And Gottfried, Miriam. "Amazon's Cloud Cover Makes It a Bigger Threat." *WSJ.* Wall Street Journal. 20 May 2016. Web. 24 May 2016.

19. Tsukayama, Hayley. "What Amazon's learned from a decade of Prime." *The Washington Post.* Nash Holdings. 3 February 2015. Web. 22 May 2016.

20. Tsukayama, Hayley. "What Amazon's learned from a decade of Prime." *The Washington Post.* Nash Holdings. 3 February 2015. Web. 22 May 2016.

21. Bensinger, Greg. "Cloud Unit Pushes Amazon to Record Profit." *WSJ.* Wall Street Journal. 28 April 2016. Web. 22 May 2016.

22. Ibid.

23. Capistrano, Jon. "The History of Cloud Computing in Amazon Web Services." *XENlife.com.* XEN Systems. 23 October 2014. Web. 23 May 2016.

24. Joshi, M. P., and R. D. Hamilton. "The Use of Participative Style by Middle Managers in Implementing Strategic Change: The Role of Organizational, Economic, and Individual Perceptual Factors," working paper series 01–03, 2001, Saint Joseph's University, Haub School of Business.

25. Beer, M., and R. A. Eisenstat, "The Silent Killers of Strategy Implementation and Learning," *Sloan Management Review* (Summer 2000): 29–40

26. Kotter, J., "Leading Change: Why Transformation Efforts Fail," *Harvard Business Review* (March–April 1995): 63.

27. Ibid, 63.

28. Senge, P.M., C. Roberts, R. Ross, B. Smith, and A. Kleiner. *The Fifth Discipline Fieldbook: Strategies and Tools for Building a Learning Organization.* New York: Doubleday/Currency, 1994.

29. For a good description of how one large company, Chevron Corporation, used the direct participation approach, see Ellis, C. M., and E. M. Norman, "Real Change in Real Time," *Management Review* (February 1999): 33–38.

30. Bartlett, C. A., and S. Ghoshal, "Changing the Role of Top Management: Beyond Systems to People," *Harvard Business Review* (May–June 1995): 142.

31. Weisbord, M. *Discovering Common Ground.* San Francisco: Berrett-Koehler, 1992.

32. Jacobs, R. W. *Real Time Strategic Change: How to Involve an Entire Organization in Fast and Far-Reaching Change.* San Francisco: Berrett-Koehler, 1994. Robert Jacobs published a book entitled *Real-Time Strategic Change,* which extols the benefits of high-involvement planning. The book emphasizes that high-involvement planning is built on principles that address several of the keys to successful change management.

33. Op cit, Weisbord, M.

34. Op cit, Weisbord, M.

35. This example is based on a case study found in Brake, T., and K. Sullivan, *Doing Business Internationally: The Cross-Cultural Challenges.* Princeton, NJ: Princeton Training Press, 1992, 2–26.

36. Thurm, S., and J. S. Lublin, "Peter Drucker's Legacy Includes Simple Advice: It's All About the People," *The Wall Street Journal,* November 11, 2005, B1.

37. Hofstede's research on the cultural dimensions of management has extended over many years. His studies include Hofstede, G., "National Cultures in Four Dimensions: A Research-Based Theory of Cultural Differences Among Nations," *International Studies of Management & Organization* 13, no. 1–2 (1983): 46–75; and Hofstede, G., "Cultural Constraints in Management Theories," *Academy of Management Executive* 7, no. 1 (1993): 81–94.

38. Kanter, R. M., B. A.Stein, and T. D. Jick. *The Challenge of Organizational Change.* New York: The Free Press, 1992, 380.

39. This pattern is illustrated and described in video and text form by Scott, C., and D. Jaffe, *Managing Organizational Change: A Practical Guide for Managers.* Menlo Park, CA: Crisp Publications, Inc., 1989.

40. Scott, C., and D. Jaffe, *Managing Organizational Change: A Practical Guide for Managers.* Menlo Park, CA: Crisp Publications, Inc., 1989, 26.

41. The three-part model was originally developed and explained in Lewin, K., "Frontiers in Group Dynamics," *Human Relations* 1 (1947): 5–41. Since the time of this publication the model has been developed and expanded and new terminology has been used to describe the three parts of the process. The essence of the model, however, has remained relatively unchanged.

42. For a good overview of this stream of research on change management, see Kanter, R. M., B. A. Stein, and T. D. Jick. *The Challenge of Organizational Change.* New York: The Free Press, 1992.

43. Kotter, J., "Leading Change: Why Transformation Efforts Fail," *Harvard Business Review* (March–April 1995): 63.

Chapter 10

Strategy Implementation: Managing the Organizational Issues

CHAPTER LEARNING OBJECTIVES

After studying this chapter, you should be able to

- Understand the organizational challenges inherent in strategy implementation;
- Use project management tools to facilitate implementation;
- Explain the role of organizational alignment in implementation;
- Understand the various types of organizational structures and their role in strategy implementation.

Southwest Airlines

Southwest's success with implementation of its low cost strategy has helped to make it the largest U.S. carrier based on domestic passengers. What began as a small Texas airline, has grown to become one of the largest airlines in the United States. Today, Southwest Airlines flies more than 100 million passengers a year to 97 destinations with more than 3,900 flights a day. The company's ability to integrate systems with strategy makes it a model for success. To learn more about Southwest, visit **www.southwest.com**

Since 1971 Southwest Airlines has grown from 195 employees and three planes that flew between three cities within Texas, to one of the largest U.S. domestic carriers with over 49,000 employees and over 700 Boeing 737 aircrafts, serving seven countries plus the United States.[1] Southwest is consistently ranked in *Fortune's* Top Ten most admired corporations and was ranked 7th overall in 2015.[2]

Southwest's success in being a lean, mean flying machine is attributed to its ability to successfully implement its low cost strategy and provide a service that customers value.[3] This chapter will help you understand Southwest's success with implementing its strategy.

In the previous chapter, we examined the people issues of strategy implementation. The purpose of this chapter is to focus on the organizational side of implementation, emphasizing the need for project planning, strategy-systems alignment, and the role of organizational structure and design. International aspects of strategy implementation are also examined.

We proceed by first discussing the importance of project management in strategy implementation. Next, we consider the importance of various functional areas in carrying out the programs, policies, and plans that support a company's overall strategy, and help in creating value for the customers. The concepts of vertical (across levels) and horizontal (across functions) alignment, and their roles in successful strategy implementation are discussed. Later, we look at how strategy is successfully implemented through a compatible organizational design that helps coordinate activities effectively throughout the organization. The relationship between strategy and structure is emphasized. Lastly, we examine different ways of creating international alliances for successful implementation of strategy. After reading this chapter, you should be able to answer each of the questions listed in Figure 10-1 regarding strategy implementation.

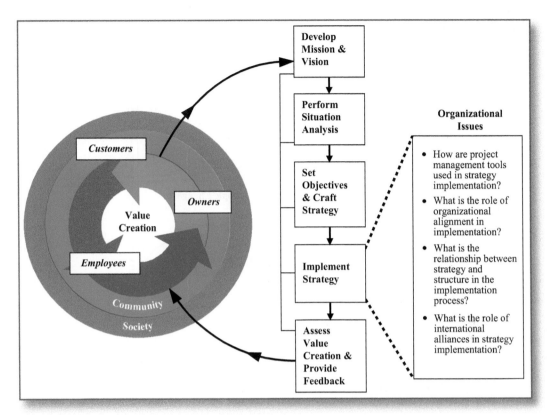

Figure 10-1
The Strategic Management Framework

KEYS TO SUCCESSFUL IMPLEMENTATION: THE ORGANIZATIONAL ISSUES

In Chapter 9, we introduced the model of implementation shown in Figure 10-2, emphasizing the people issues of the process. As Figure 10-2 suggests, successful implementation also requires attention to organizational issues, the focus of this chapter. Let's take a closer look at these issues.

Consider the example of Federal Express (FedEx), whose average daily volume in 2016 exceeded 11.5 million shipments.[4] Some of the organizational systems and arrangements that FedEx uses to achieve its strategic goal of providing fast and reliable service to its customers include careful choice and deployment of technology, effective design of package delivery systems, and tight coordination across the company. Each of these factors, among others, must be aligned to support the FedEx strategy.

To achieve a record of more than 99 percent accurate, next-day delivery, FedEx designed its package handling system after a hub-and-spoke network

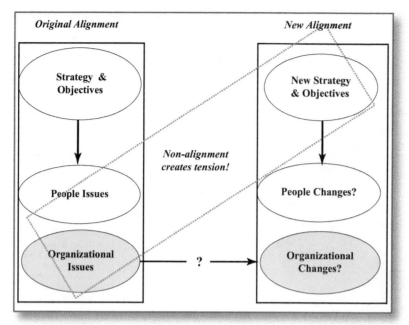

Figure 10-2
An Implementation Model

arrangement. The first hub was located in Memphis, Tennessee—an airport with a near-perfect record for good flying conditions. Today, FedEx has 33 ground hubs and ten air express hubs which are complemented by approximately 3,700 freight service centers and more than 1,800 FedEx Office centers.[5] To achieve speed and accuracy in package tracking, FedEx couriers use "PowerPads" to provide near real-time, wireless access to the FedEx network. FedEx's wireless global strategy allows dispatchers to schedule deliveries more efficiently, and couriers to send and receive real-time information when away from their delivery vans. The PowerPad technology includes electronic signature capture, electronic pickup manifest, hands-free data transmission through the use of Bluetooth, and automatic scan transmission.[6]

Of course, people (FedEx employees) also play a key role in successful implementation. The company's human resources department recruits and retains highly energetic, enthusiastic, and intelligent employees who sort over a million pieces of mail in a short period of four hours.

As the FedEx example suggests, successful implementation depends on effective management of both people and organizational issues. In this chapter, we emphasize the organizational side of implementation, highlighting the role of three factors:

- project management—planning, scheduling, monitoring, and control
- organizational alignment
- organizational structure and design

PROJECT MANAGEMENT

The task of strategy implementation can be viewed as a project with a specific purpose and desired results. Like any project, strategy implementation requires a group of employees to implement a logical sequence of interrelated activities within a given timeframe, and without exceeding the available resources. A successful execution of such a project involves project planning, scheduling, and monitoring and control.

Project Planning is required to establish a set of directions in sufficient detail to tell the implementation team exactly what must be done, when it must be done, and what resources to use for successful implementation. The purpose of planning is to facilitate successful implementation or accomplishment of the goals. Project planning requires organizing the team and linking needs with timed project activities.

Project plans are developed by identifying the activities of a project and organizing them in a logical sequence from start to finish. The Apple Watch, Apple's most recent foray into wearable device technology, was the result of extensive planning by cross-functional teams, including the design, technology, and human interface departments, as well as senior executives within Apple.[7] As with most new product launches, this project required the coordination of many cross-functional activities. Stage 1 typically involves defining and refining the project concept. This includes identifying consumer needs, a target market and potential benefits, and developing product descriptions, and manufacturing processes. Stage 2 consists of designing the product and preparing the market launch, including project commitment and design readiness. Later stages might focus on marketing and manufacturing implementation, including market introduction and sales.

These stages and activities can be broken down further into tasks and subtasks by functional area. For example, the marketing department at Apple would need to develop an implementation plan for the marketing mix of the new Apple Watch. Marketing managers would consider the types of questions posed in Table 10-1. For each element of the marketing mix, a series of questions must be analyzed to determine its role in the successful implementation of the overall plan. A similar type of analysis and planning would be necessary within each functional area that supports the new product launch.

The project plan, as the Apple Watch example shows, needs to specify exactly what is to be done, by whom, and when. A simple method to assist in planning all this detail in a hierarchical manner is called an *even planning processs*[8] which starts with making an ordered list of major activities necessary to complete a project. Each of the first level activities is then broken down into second level tasks, ranging between 2 and 20. Each of the second level tasks is then split into 2 to 20 subtasks. The end result of this planning process is an *action plan* that identifies the set of activities required to meet the project objectives, the person(s) responsible for each activity, the time required to complete each activity, the predecessor activities, and the resources. *Predecessor activities* are tasks that must be finished before the new task can begin. An action plan for the launch of a sample new product is presented in Table 10-2.

Table 10-1 Marketing Planning and Launch

Product	– Who is your target customer? What product attributes are important to your customer? Your competitors' customers? Why?
	– How are you positioned on these attributes? How are your competitors positioned?
	– What can you do to improve your position on these attributes or make other attributes more salient? What could your competitors do?
Place	– How and where does your customer purchase the product? Does it have to be this way? Can you improve it or do it differently? What about your competitors?
	– What are the dominant channels for distribution? Are these changing? Should they? Are the same forces impacting your competitors?
Promotion	– Where does your customer get information about the product? Are they getting the right information in the right way? How about your competitors' customers? Do you have a compelling message for them?
	– How can you improve the effectiveness of this effort? Have you explored all options—standard and creative? Can you communicate effectively to your competitors' customers?
Price	– How important is price to your customer? To your competitors' customers? If it has great importance, will your cost structure allow you to compete?
	– How can you change your cost structure or add value to make price less important to your customers or to your competitors' customers?

Project Scheduling involves placing an action plan on a time scale with relative and specific times for activities. Some commonly used techniques for project scheduling are Program Evaluation and Review Techniques (PERT) and Critical Path Method (CPM). PERT was developed in the late 1950s through the joint efforts of the U.S. Navy Special Projects Office, Lockheed Aircraft, and a consulting firm (Booz, Allen & Hamilton) to manage the Polaris missile project. PERT has been credited with delivering the Polaris missile project two years ahead of schedule. During the same time period, DuPont, Inc. and Remington Rand Corporation developed CPM to manage maintenance projects in chemical plants.

A major difference between the two techniques is their orientation to the time elements of projects. PERT was designed to handle *probabilistic* time estimates of activities, and to aid in determining the probability of completion of a project by a given date. The probabilistic time estimates are subject to variation. CPM, on the other hand, used deterministic time estimates—time estimates that are fairly certain.

Both techniques help identify the *critical path* in the project—the set of tasks that control the duration of the project. Every project has at least one critical path. The tasks or activities on the critical path are called *critical activities*—any delay in these activities will result in a delay for the entire project. Managers find it extremely helpful to know which activities are critical and which activities have slack, so they can

Table 10-2 Action Plan

OBJECTIVE: LAUNCH THE NEW PRODUCT BY JUNE 15*

STEPS	TIME (DAYS)	RESPONSIBILITY	PRECEDENT
1. Preliminary investigation	60	Marketing	—
1. Market assessment	90	Production	
2. Technical assessment			
2. Evaluate sales & customer reaction	15	Marketing	1.1, 1.2
3. Detailed Investigation	30	Marketing	2
1. Market research	45	Production	2
2. Technical appraisal	15	Finance	2
a. Manufacturing appraisal			
b. Financial analysis			
4. Development Stage	15	Marketing, Production	3.1, 3.2
1. Prototype	15	Marketing	4.1
2. Customer feedback	30	Marketing	4.2
3. Develop market launch plans	40	Production	4.2
4. Develop production plans			
5. Testing and Validation	15	Marketing, Production	4.1
1. In house product tests	15	Marketing	4.2
2. Field trials	15	Production	4.2, 5.1, 5.2
3. Pilot production	20	Marketing	5.3
4. Trial sell			
6. Pre-commercialization Analysis	7.5	Finance, Production	4.4, 5.4
1. Review operations plan	5	Marketing, Distribution	4.3, 5.4
2. Review marketing plans			
7. Full production and market launch	30	Purchase, Production, Marketing	6.1, 6.2

*Based on the information in "Developing New Products for a Changing Marketplace," edited by A.L. Brody and J.B. Lord, Technomic Publishing Co. Inc., Lancaster, PA, 2000; and "Winning in New Products," Second Edition, by R.G. Cooper, Addison Wesley, Reading, MA 1993.

concentrate on the critical activities to ensure a timely completion of the project. If an organization can implement its intended strategies ahead of time, it can start reaping the benefits sooner.

The use of scheduling techniques has increased with the proliferation of project management software packages, such as Microsoft Project, Smartsheet, Mavenlink, and Time Line. A project schedule serves as the basis for monitoring and controlling project activity.

Project monitoring and control includes collecting information about project performance, comparing actual progress to the plan, and taking action to bridge any difference between the desired plan and the actual results. The common formats used to present a schedule and monitor progress include Gantt charts and network diagrams. A Gantt chart is a horizontal bar chart with an embedded time scale that helps identify the start and completion of activities.

It is a useful tool for indicating the current status of activities compared to the planned progress for each. A network diagram is composed of a number of arrows and nodes. The arrows represent the activities, and the nodes indicate the start and completion of an activity. A network diagram better illustrates the interdependence of activities as compared to a Gantt chart.

From the information in the action plan, a Gantt chart as shown in Figure 10-3 was produced using Microsoft Project, a project management software. Task names for summary activities, such as preliminary investigation, are in bold. The critical tasks are distinguished from the non-critical ones. The vertical line in the chart is the project status line and indicates that, as of the date noted, the preliminary investigation (including market and technical assessment, evaluation of sales & customer reaction, market research, and financial analysis) has been completed. Technical appraisal is partially completed since manufacturing appraisal, a sub task, is incomplete (see Figure 10-3). This is a critical task, and any delay in its completion is going to affect timely completion of the entire project.

Resource Allocation

The task of managing a project involves deploying resources to achieve the desired goals. The Gantt chart in Figure 10-3 has resources noted for each task. Resources usually are limited and they can have a significant effect on the timely completion of a project. In our product launch example, the marketing department seems to be heavily engaged in certain quarters of the project. To know the exact requirement of the marketing group in a particular quarter on a daily or weekly basis, we could obtain a time-based resource usage profile from the project management software. If the time-based profile indicates the project needs more resources than are available, the management has the option of either making additional resources available or pushing back the completion date of the project. In some cases, it may also be possible to transfer resources from non-critical activities to the critical activities.

THE ROLE OF ORGANIZATIONAL ALIGNMENT IN STRATEGY IMPLEMENTATION

Organizational alignment is the process of linking and coordinating discrete activities within the organization. Alignment requires a shared understanding of organizational goals and objectives by managers at various levels and within various units of the organizational hierarchy. A firm's ability to seek and maintain a competitive advantage rests upon its ability to acquire and deploy resources that are coherent with the organization's competitive needs. The two forms of organizational alignment are:

- Vertical alignment
- Horizontal or lateral alignment

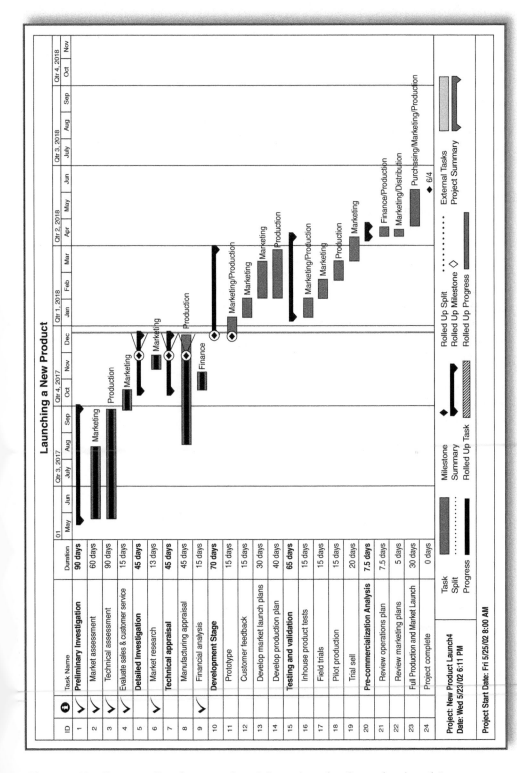

The table/chart content:

ID	●	Task Name	Duration
1	✓	**Preliminary Investigation**	**90 days**
2	✓	Market assessment	60 days
3	✓	Technical assessment	90 days
4	✓	Evaluate sales & customer service	15 days
5		**Detailed Investigation**	**45 days**
6	✓	Market research	13 days
7		**Technical appraisal**	**45 days**
8		Manufacturing appraisal	45 days
9	✓	Financial analysis	15 days
10		**Development Stage**	**70 days**
11		Prototype	15 days
12		Customer feedback	15 days
13		Develop market launch plans	30 days
14		Develop production plan	40 days
15		**Testing and validation**	**65 days**
16		Inhouse product tests	15 days
17		Field trials	15 days
18		Pilot production	15 days
19		Trial sell	20 days
20		**Pre-commercialization Analysis**	**7.5 days**
21		Review operations plan	7.5 days
22		Review marketing plans	5 days
23		Full Production and Market Launch	30 days
24		Project complete	0 days

Launching a New Product

Project: New Product Launch4
Date: Wed 5/23/02 6:11 PM

Legend:
Task ▬▬
Split ....
Progress ▬▬
Milestone ◆
Summary ▬▬
Rolled Up Task ▬▬
Rolled Up Split ....
Rolled Up Milestone ◇
Rolled Up Progress ▬▬
External Tasks ▬▬
Project Summary ▬▬

Project Start Date: Fri 5/25/02 8:00 AM

Figure 10-3
Gantt Chart for Launching a New Product

Chapter 10   Strategy Implementation: Managing the Organizational Issues   287

Vertical Alignment

Vertical alignment refers to the alignment of strategies, objectives, action plans, and decisions throughout the various levels of the organization. Recall from Chapter 1 that there are three levels of strategy—corporate, business, and functional—which we refer to as Levels 1, 2 and 3, respectively, in Figure 10-4. In addition to coordinating activities and priorities across each of these three levels, vertical alignment depends on coordination at a fourth level—the decision areas within each function. Figure 10-4 shows this hierarchy of relationships. Strategic management is an iterative process that starts with the development of an overall strategy at the corporate level to guide the entire organization. Strategy implementation is effectively carried out in a bottom-up fashion, with an aim to make lower level decisions consistent with the decisions at the upper levels. When this consistency is achieved, vertical alignment has been realized.

At Level 4, the specific actions or decisions made within each function should support that function's strategy. For example, the decisions made in the operations function (e.g., production capacity and scheduling, technology utilization, plant location, work force management, performance measures) should be made in line with the Level 3 operations strategy of the company. Similarly, the promotion or pricing decisions should be consistent with the marketing strategy. Further, each functional strategy should support the competitive advantage (overall low cost or differentiation) pursued by each business unit (Level 2). Each business unit, division

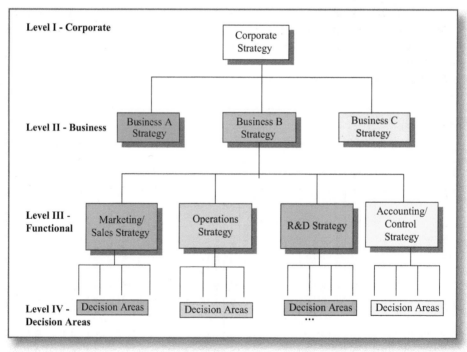

Figure 10-4
Vertical Alignment of Strategy

or SBU (Strategic Business Unit), in turn, supports the company's overall mission and corporate strategy (Level 1).

Consider an example. General Motors Company (GM) made a conscious corporate level decision (Level 1) to remain in the automobile manufacturing and financing business after its Chapter 11 bankruptcy filing in 2009. Consistent with its corporate strategy, GM established five strategic business units (SBUs): GM North America (GMNA), GM Europe (GME), GM International Operations (GMIO), GM South America (GMSA), and GM Financial. Each SBU has various divisions (Level 2) within it. For example, GMNA primarily operates the following four divisions: Buick, Cadillac, Chevrolet, and GMC. Each of the divisions focuses on a specific market segment or a subsegment with minimal overlap. For example, GM marketing executives describe GMC as its "professional grade" brand while Cadillac is viewed as its prestigious luxury brand.[9] The GM Financial division deals with the financing of all types of automobiles made and sold by GM. At Level 3, within each of GM's divisions, different functional areas—marketing, operations, finance, HR, and R&D—implement functional strategies that support the corresponding SBU strategy.

Vertical Alignment and Cost Leadership

A manufacturer pursuing a business-level strategy of cost leadership should focus on establishing tight cost control, strictly enforcing rules to control product or service costs, and ensuring proper utilization of resources in various functional areas.[10] Each functional area will then translate these objectives into function-specific action plans which support the business strategy.

For example, to align with the low cost strategy of an SBU, the decisions made within the operations function regarding technology, capacity, location, and work force management should support the functional strategy objectives of efficiency, machine utilization, and labor productivity. An SBU with an emphasis on low cost should opt for a line type of process technology if it is a discrete product manufacturer, such as a TV manufacturer, or a continuous process technology for products like fertilizer, sugar, oil or cement. A *line process* is characterized by a product-focused grouping of machines and workstations, which are set up in a sequence dictated by the steps required for manufacturing the product. When a line process is used to manufacture non-discrete products in bulk, such as sugar and fertilizer, it is termed as a *continuous process*. Further, it would locate its plant(s) near resources to minimize transportation costs, among other things. The management practices used by the operations managers would stress monitoring and control[11] to make sure the resources (people, materials, machines and equipment) were being efficiently utilized.

Vertical Alignment and Differentiation

The approach used to achieve vertical alignment for a business strategy based on differentiation would look much different. Suppose an SBU sought competitive advantage based on delivery, speed, and product flexibility in a make-to-order setting. Operations managers in this case should opt for a job or batch process technology with multi-purpose machinery that can handle varying needs of its customers. A *job process* is characterized by a function- or process-focused grouping of machines and workstations. A job process is well suited for the production of a wide variety of small-size (low volume) customer orders. A *batch process* is an intermittent production process like a job shop, but can handle relatively large quantities of a set mix of products. The quantities produced per batch are generally predetermined based on the proportion of setup costs to inventory holding costs.

Even though developments in information technology have rendered distances less consequential, such plants should be located near customers or near freeways and airports to promote easy and fast access. Operations managers should demonstrate participative and relationship-oriented workforce management practices, such as consulting, delegating, and team building.[12] For example, managers would often need to consult with employee teams before making delivery commitments or promising an alteration or a design change to their customers. To ensure a speedy delivery, the employee teams would also be empowered to make certain decisions on their own. These decisions and approaches which work to achieve vertical alignment are summarized in Table 10-3.

Is Vertical Alignment a Reality?

Despite the numerous anticipated benefits of aligning decisions within an organization, not all organizations manage to achieve vertical alignment. In fact, research shows mixed evidence regarding the prevalence of vertical alignment. One study involving thirty-nine manufacturing managers found a close match between business strategies and manufacturing priorities.[13] In two other studies of manufacturing strategy, however, perceived strategies across the business and functional levels were found to be misaligned.[14] Researchers in the marketing field also observed misalignment between marketing executives and their sales managers with regard to specific product strategies.[15] One of the factors related to misalignment, identified in a study of ninety-eight manufacturers, was the length of association between managers.[16] As the years of association between managers increases, misalignment decreases. Another misalignment factor was found to be the differing responsibilities and

Table 10-3 Achieving Vertical Alignment: Cost Leadership Versus Differentiation

STRATEGY/ DECISION AREA	COST LEADER	DIFFERENTIATOR: DELIVERY SPEED/ PRODUCT FLEXIBILITY
Operations strategy	• Strictly enforce rules to control product or service costs • Focus on efficiency, machine utilization, labor productivity	• Reduce rigidity in systems • Promote ability to switch from one product to another quickly • Reduce processing lead time
Process choice or technology	Line or Continuous	Job or Batch shop
Work force management practices in operations	Monitoring, controlling, problem solving	Consulting, delegating, team building
Location	Near raw materials	Near customers

perspectives of managers at different levels of the organization. For example, senior managers seem to emphasize externally focused priorities, such as meeting customer demand and counteracting competitive challenges. Functional managers seem to have an inward focus, on issues such as cost control and manufacturing flexibility.

These studies suggest the need for organizations to foster more interaction and exchange among managers at different levels and across functions. Organizations should develop new and better ways to communicate to ensure that strategies and competitive priorities are understood uniformly across all levels and the benefits of vertical alignment may be achieved.

Horizontal Alignment

Horizontal alignment refers to coordination of efforts across the organization and is primarily relevant to the lower levels in the strategy hierarchy. Horizontal alignment can be defined in terms of *cross-functional* and *intra-functional integration*. Cross-functional integration connotes the consistency of decisions across functions (Level 3) so that activities and decisions across marketing, operations, HR, and other functions complement one another. Intra-functional integration is achieved through coherence across decision areas (Level 4) so as to achieve synergy within each function. For successful implementation, decisions within a function (Level 4) should be aligned vertically with that function's strategic objectives, as well as, laterally—across decision areas within a function.

The process of horizontal alignment requires exchange and cooperation among various functional activities, as depicted in Figure 10-5 below.

Horizontal Alignment and Cost Leadership

Let's consider a business, such as Southwest Airlines, that strives to be a cost leader. As mentioned before, a cost leadership strategy requires establishment of tight cost control and strict rule enforcement throughout the organization to control product or service costs. Cost leaders should also ensure proper utilization of resources in various functional areas. Each functional area needs to translate these objectives into

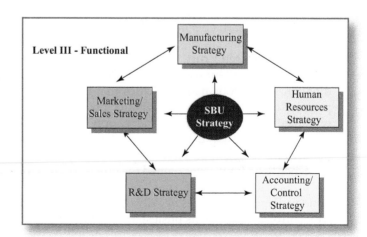

Figure 10-5
Horizontal Alignment through Cross-Functional Integration

function-specific action plans to support the business strategy. The operations function, for example, will attempt to cut costs through efficiency, machine utilization, and labor productivity. R&D will strive for standardized product designs to contain costs. Marketing will offer a limited variety of products and promise minimal options or design changes to accommodate customers' desires. Human resources will focus on job specialization.

Horizontal Alignment and Differentiation

On the other hand, an SBU that seeks to differentiate itself on product flexibility would seek to promote the ability to offer several products and to easily modify them to accommodate customer needs. To achieve its intended business strategy, the business unit should work towards reducing rigidity in its systems, promoting the ability to switch from one product to another quickly, and reducing the processing lead time.

To support the above business objectives, the R&D function should consider a custom design approach. If this objective is combined with delivery speed, the strategy could include the ability to put together quickly a wide variety of products through various permutations and combinations of the basic product modules. For example, some watch manufacturers use this approach by having a few common base designs, and a variety of dials, straps and colors to create several combinations that appear different to the customer.

The R&D department and the marketing department should work in unison to lead in new product development and new product introduction. Marketing's promotion plan should be based on product variety, and could use a price premium for customization. Manufacturing should develop the ability to produce in small batches and to switch quickly from one product to another.[17] The SBU's assembly operation should be able to process a wide variety of products in a short period of time, without having to spend too much time in changeovers. Human resources should focus on hiring multi-skilled workers, and should also foster job rotation. Purchasing may need to develop a base of reliable suppliers in the vicinity to be able to procure materials in small quantities quickly and reliably. Table 10-4 summarizes these relationships.

Horizontal Alignment at Papa John's

When John Camaro opened his first Papa John's Restaurant, he made a commitment to quality and the use of quality ingredients. His pizzas are made with all-natural sauce, hand-tossed crust, fresh-cut vegetables, and real meat and cheeses. Papa John's is an excellent example of horizontal alignment and cross-functional coordination. It has four main activities that must be coordinated in order to meet its promise of "better ingredients, better pizza"—warehouse management, inventory optimization, transportation, and supply chain intelligence. Papa John's believes that its operating and distribution systems are what help it to achieve superior food quality and customer service.

Since Papa John's was named the official pizza sponsor of the Super Bowl in 2010, the pizza restaurant anticipates preparing roughly 1 million pizzas each Super Bowl Sunday. Papa John's relies heavily on its distribution centers as QC Centers, or Quality Control Centers, on its busiest day of the year. The Indiana-based pizza purveyor

Table 10-4 Achieving Horizontal Alignment: Cost Leadership Versus Differentiation

FUNCTIONS	COST LEADER	DIFFERENTIATOR: DELIVERY SPEED/PRODUCT FLEXIBILITY
Operations	• Focus on efficiency • Machine utilization • Labor productivity	• Promote ability to switch from one product to another quickly • Reduce processing lead-time
Marketing	• Offer a limited variety of products • Promise minimal options or design changes to customers	• Offer product variety • Price premium for customization • Lead in new product introduction
R&D	• Standardized product design	• Custom design approach • Lead in new product development
Human Resources	• Job specialization	• Foster job rotation • Focus on developing multiple skills

requires that all franchises order their supplies from these QC Centers to ensure that they are using the freshest ingredients. In preparation for each Super Bowl Sunday, Papa John's forecasts the amount of ingredients it most likely needs and relays that information to its suppliers. The organization accomplishes this through the use of inventory optimization software. It then has to arrange the timely delivery of those ingredients to all of its franchises via its ten domestic QC Centers. For Super Bowl XLVI, Papa John's had to coordinate the delivery of 2 million pounds of cheese and 350,000 pounds of pepperoni.[18] Overall, the Super Bowl sponsorship has resulted in more profitable first and fourth quarters for Papa John's as Q1 2015 and Q4 2015 accounted for more than half of Papa John's total revenues for that year.[19]

Consequences of Weak Horizontal Alignment

The lack of cooperation and exchange across functions, on the other hand, could lead to suboptimal decisions. Consider the example of a supermarket that competes on the basis of price, and encourages cost cutting throughout the organization. Accordingly, the purchasing manager decides to save money for the organization through bulk purchase of sugar. He orders two truck loads of sugar to take advantage of a ten percent price discount. He fails to consult with other functional managers, however, about the ramifications of his decision. When the sugar arrives, the operations manager is asked to unload and stack it in the store warehouse. Due to limited space availability, the operations manager is unable to unload the sugar, and, in turn, decides to rent and keep the trailers in the parking lot for a couple of weeks, thus incurring rental expenses. When the accounting department is presented with an invoice from the trucking company for rental, it summons the operations manager. After hearing the operations manager's side of the story, the accounting manager decides to get rid of the sugar fast so as to save on truck rental and contacts the marketing department to launch a half-price sale for sugar. Thus, a cost-saving strategy without adequate cross-functional consultation on the part of a purchasing manager turned out to be a loss-making endeavor for the organization.

Horizontal Alignment Within a Function

Coordination across decision areas within a function is also important for effective implementation. As shown in Figure 10-6, alignment across decision areas within a function, such as operations, contributes to improved performance. The decision areas in the operations function are broadly classified under structural and infrastructural decision areas.[20] The *structural decisions* relate to the physical structure of the facility, such as location, technology, and capacity. The *infrastructural decisions* are about the operating systems, such as manufacturing, planning and control, work force management, quality management, organizational design, and performance measurement systems.

Let's examine how decisions in various areas within a function, such as operations, can be coordinated. To develop the ability to produce in small batches and to switch quickly from one product to another, a company has opted for a batch manufacturing process. To facilitate production in batches, the company should buy general-purpose machinery and equipment that offers the ability to switch quickly from one product to another with minimal setup time. To support the ability of the manufacturing process (to offer variety and still deliver on time) the company should use a *lead capacity* strategy, that is, it should have surplus capacity, some of which will be necessary because of underutilization due to changeovers.

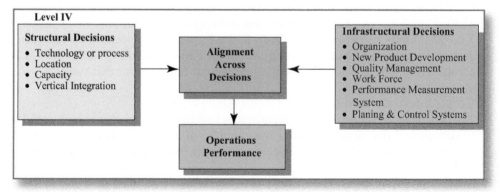

Figure 10-6
Horizontal Alignment within the Operations Function

The decisions regarding infrastructure, such as organization structure and workforce management, should also complement the structural decisions—technology and capacity. Thus, in the above example, the workforce management practices that complement technology and capacity decisions would include encouraging employees to work in self-managing teams that are empowered to make routine decisions and to fix problems as they arise without having to wait for approvals and intervention from the bosses.[21] Researchers contend that linking decisions within a function leads to improved performance.[22]

Enterprise Resource Planning (ERP): A Way of Achieving Horizontal Alignment

Enterprise Resource Planning (ERP) integrates decisions and resources across various functional areas using a common database. Enterprise-wide integration is possible through the use of a common database, which reduces duplication of effort and forces various functions to coordinate their activities. For example, in an ERP system, marketing and production work together to develop a common forecast, which is then used by the finance department as a basis for raising capital, or making funds available, and by the HR department to make available the required number of people with requisite skills.

In the absence of an integrated system, various functions might have generated their own forecasts, perhaps, using different approaches and arriving at different conclusions. The integrated ERP systems eliminate redundancy and duplication of information, while making real-time information accessible to the entire organization. These systems also facilitate coordination on a global basis—with customers, suppliers, or other units of the same company—through the availability of current information on a common database that is accessible anywhere in the world at any time. Managers in various functions or in different geographic regions now take a business perspective rather than a functional perspective, and make sure that their decisions are aligned with the decisions of others in the organization.

STRATEGY AND ORGANIZATIONAL DESIGN

A successful implementation effort also hinges on a compatible *organizational design*, that is, the structure and control systems that help a company achieve its intended strategy. Organization structure is a key component of design.[23] The *organization structure* specifies the reporting relationships between different offices and employees, the lines of authority, and the channels of communication and information flow.

The organizational design provides a vehicle to coordinate the activities of various functions, and to ensure that they are in line with the overall strategy of the business unit, as well as, the strategy of the corporation. Since each function develops and pursues its own strategy—of course, in unison with the business strategy—it needs a structure to exploit the skills and capabilities of its employees, and to control and coordinate the activities of its employees to achieve the desired functional goals and objectives. An organization needs to create a mechanism that coordinates the activities of different functions and divisions to effectively pursue the organizational strategy, yet affords sufficient autonomy to various functions in achieving their functional goals.

The elements of organization structure include chain of command, span of control, and form or degree of centralization. The principle of *chain of command* suggests that an employee should report directly to one supervisor. Early researchers argued that employees reporting to two or more bosses might have to cope with conflicting priorities. The principle is easy to follow in traditional organizational structures and many contemporary organizations as well. There are some specific situations, discussed later in the section, when strict adherence to the principle creates some inflexibility in the organization, and it has to be violated.

Span of control pertains to the number of subordinates directly reporting to a supervisor. Some studies suggest that a supervisor can effectively manage six direct reports,[24] but in practice, effective span of control varies depending upon several factors, such as the managerial level in the organization, the training and experience of subordinates, and task complexity. The *degree of centralization* refers to the distribution of decision-making authority at various levels in the organization. In a highly centralized organization, decisions are mostly made at the top, whereas in a more decentralized organization, employees at lower levels are empowered to make decisions. In organizations that have a relatively simple task structure and a focus on cost control, such as a fan assembly operation, a greater degree of centralization affords efficient use of employees and control. An organization that competes on the basis of delivery speed or product flexibility is better served through employee empowerment, that is, higher decentralization. Authorizing employees to make decisions on the spot reduces the need for unnecessary approvals by senior managers that hinder speed.

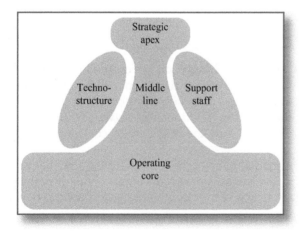

Figure 10-7
The Components of an Organization
Reprinted from "Organization Design: fashion or fit?" by H. Mintzberg, *Harvard Business Review* (Jan-Feb 1981), by permission of Harvard Business Publishing.

Five Components of an Organization Structure

An organization can be divided into five distinct components, as shown in Figure 10-7.[25] The top management is called the *strategic apex* and is primarily responsible for creating a vision for the organization. The employees that do the front line work of the organization constitute the *operating core*. The managers who mediate between the top management and the working core form the *middle line*. The staff people responsible for the planning and control of the organization are called *technostructure*; and the staff personnel that provide indirect services to the entire organization, such as administrative assistants and mail room employees, form the *support staff*. The configuration that results from putting these components together is called an *organization structure*.

The Structure—Strategy Relationship

Organizational design decisions are not static but dynamic in nature. An organization needs to revisit and, perhaps, change its structure as it changes its strategy. As seen in Figure 10-8,[26] changes in strategy may lead to administrative problems. As an organization grows or expands as a result of its opportunities and needs (created by changing population demographics or technological advancements), the new strategy may present additional administrative burdens for the existing structure. The organization's neglect of the administrative challenges could lead to inefficiency or ineffectiveness, and could have financial implications for the organization.

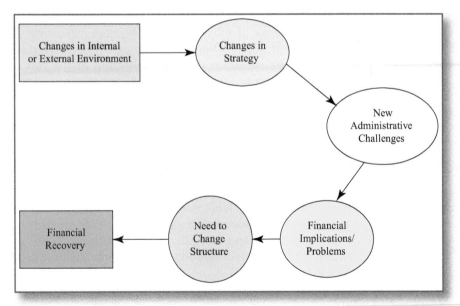

Figure 10-8
Structure and Strategy
Adapted from: Chandler, A. D. Jr., 1962. Strategy and Structure: Chapters in the History of the American Industrial Enterprise. The M.I.T. Press, Cambridge, MA.

Types of Organization Structure

The need and relative importance of the five components of structure vary from organization to organization, depending upon the nature of the work being done and the degree and type of coordination of activities required. The components may be configured into several distinct types of organizational structure which have been found to be suitable in different situations. The types of structure are:

- Simple
- Functional
- Divisional
- Matrix
- Network

Simple structure

In a young and small entrepreneurial firm, the top manager—often the owner and president/Chief Executive Officer—creates a vision for the organization and carries it out by directly supervising the operating core, with little or no need for any staff or middle line managers. Such an arrangement is called a *simple structure*.[27] It offers flexibility for simple innovation, low overhead, and high responsiveness to customers. There is little formalization or standardization of tasks and processes. The control is centralized with almost all decision-making power resting at the strategic apex with the chief executive. Some examples of simple structures include dot com companies, and Mom and Pop stores.

Functional Structure

As a business grows, so does its range of activities, which become increasingly difficult to manage through a simple structure. One way to manage the expanded range of activities is to group employees based on their specialization or the task they perform. For example, all information technology specialists are grouped together, as are all accountants, human resource specialists, and so on. This way of grouping specialists together is called a functional structure, and leads to hierarchies within each function. Figure 10-9 shows a generic functional structure. Such hierarchies provide a clearly defined career path for individuals within each function, and afford managers greater control of activities.

A functional structure facilitates information sharing and learning among specialists. For example, if a tool and die specialist discovered a more efficient way of exchanging dies for a plastic molding machine, the same knowledge could be easily disseminated to other specialists in the manufacturing function. Such structures promote a high degree of standardization and formalization, which leads to efficiency and consistency. A functional structure is well-suited for an organization pursuing an overall low cost strategy.

Divisional Structure

Another way to solve the coordination problem arising from the expanded range and scope of tasks associated with growth and diversification strategies is to use a divisional structure. The divisions could be formed on the basis of products, geography

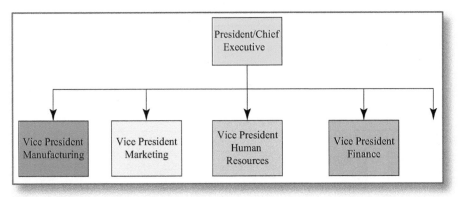

Figure 10-9
A Functional Organization Structure

or customers served. Each division may have functional subdivisions, but divisional lines separate functional specialists from one another. Top management, through its headquarters managers, maintains control over the divisions by setting quantifiable goals for each division. The divisional managers are held responsible for the performance of their unit, which is measured through performance and control systems. The organization typically creates a small technostructure to design and implement these control systems, and a central support staff to provide common services, such as public relations and legal counsel, to the divisions.[28] Top management also maintains a degree of direct supervision through periodic visits to each division.

A divisional structure facilitates functional integration or horizontal alignment within each division. For example, an R&D engineer is more likely to learn quickly about the feasibility of a design and the availability of materials from a manufacturing manager and a purchasing manager if they are in the same division than he or she would if they operated in a functional organization.

Figure 10-10 presents a SBU/divisional structure of a large automobile company such as General Motors. At Level 2, General Motors is organized into SBUs based on geography (GMNA, GMSA, GME, and GMIO) and a product (GM Financial). Under each of the geographic SBUs, the divisions are based on automobile brand. For example, GMNA's brands include Cadillac, Buick, Chevrolet, and GMC. Each of these automobile divisions enjoys considerable autonomy in its management of day-to-day affairs.

The major advantages of the divisional structure include its focus on results, better allocation of corporate resources and enhanced control, ease of accommodating growth and diversification, and freeing up of corporate staff from operating responsibilities so they can focus on strategic issues.

The major disadvantages of the divisional structure are the duplication of resources and activities, and competition among divisions for corporate resources. For example, each division may have its own human resources department. If the human resources function were centralized, as in a functional organization, those activities could be done at a fraction of the cost. The second problem is competing

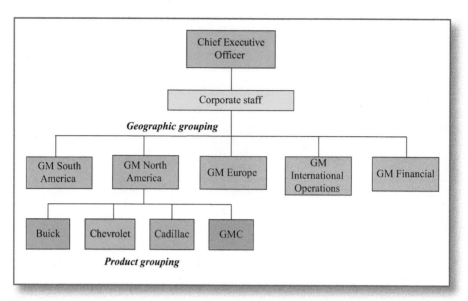

Figure 10-10
Divisional Structure of an Auto Manufacturer (Modeled after GM)

for resources may lead to rivalry among divisions and reduced interdivisional coordination.

The internal competition fostered by the divisional structure has a positive side; it forces divisions to consider differentiating from one another. The Cadillac division differentiates itself from Chevrolet, GMC, and Buick based on product design, product performance, and customer service (various dimensions of quality). Further, as the divisional managers enjoy a considerable degree of autonomy, it makes it easier for them to pursue the differentiation strategy. For example, a division could easily pursue delivery speed strategy for its products or services since it does not have to consult with the headquarters for operating decisions. Employee empowerment and having to deal with fewer administrative layers within a division speeds up the decision-making process and cuts back the processing lead time.

Matrix Structure

The Matrix structure combines the advantages of specialization that a functional structure offers, and the focus and accountability that a divisional structure affords.[29] Figure 10-11 illustrates a matrix structure. This kind of structure has a dual focus on functional and product or project considerations. Employees in this structure have at least two bosses: a product or project manager, and a functional manager. The project manager has the responsibility and commensurate authority to coordinate the project team's activities to achieve the project's goals. The functional manager is responsible for the team member's annual reviews, salary and promotion recommendations. The two managers must communicate regularly to effectively coordinate the work of product or project team members drawn from various functions.[30]

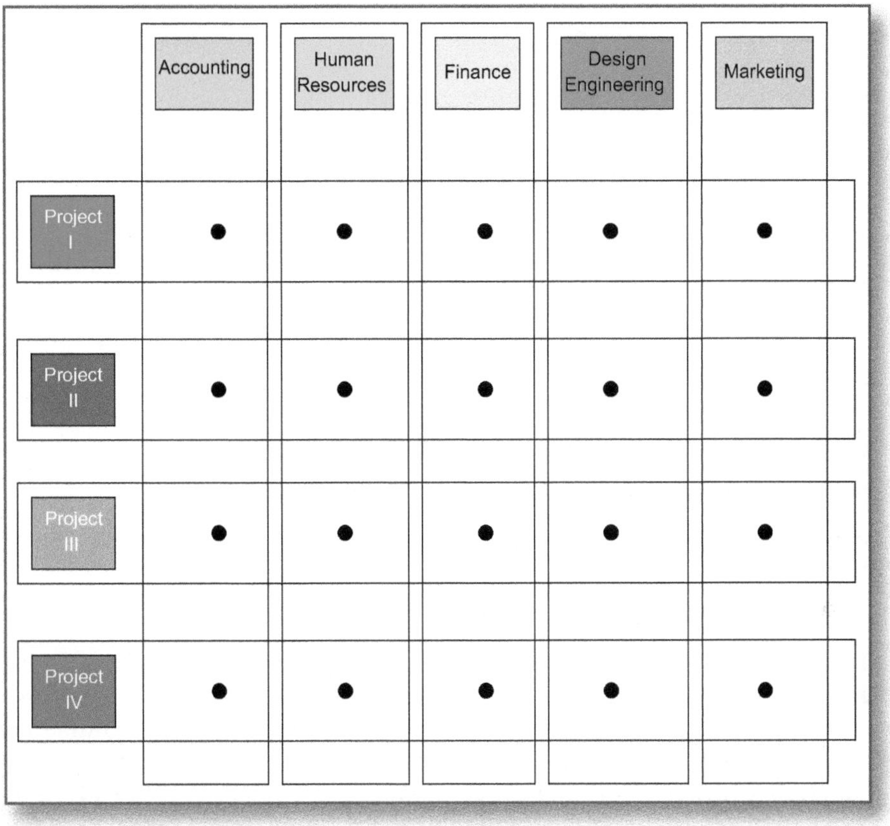

Figure 10-11
Matrix Structure

A primary advantage of the matrix structure is that it affords the flexibility to handle complex and interdependent projects while still maintaining the benefits that result from keeping experts grouped under various functions. A potential disadvantage of this type of structure arises from the violation of the chain of command principle. If the product or project managers fail to coordinate the demands upon employees with their respective functional bosses, the resulting confusion and ambiguity may lead to power struggles among managers.

Network Structure

A network structure results from linking a central group of core staff with loosely coupled partners, such as subcontractors. The core group sets a strategic direction for the organization and provides operational support to sustain the network.[31] The key operational activities, however, are subcontracted to various organizations or individuals. Figure 10-12 presents a network structure for an automotive manufacturing company.

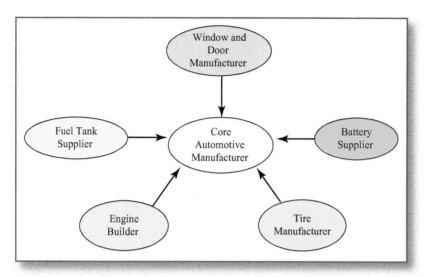

Figure 10-12
Network Structure: Automotive Manufacturer

Toyota revolutionized the automotive industry in the late 1950s and 1960s by utilizing a network structure for its vehicle design and manufacturing. The Japanese car maker relied upon a network of suppliers to design and manufacture the best components to meet each vehicle's needs. By *out-sourcing* component parts manufacturing (i.e., not building the components in house), Toyota had the ability to choose from the best suppliers in Japan at the time. Toyota believed in dealing with a small group of suppliers to maintain close relationships with them and to ensure the best designed and highest quality automotive innovations for its vehicles.[32] This network structure laid the foundation for Toyota for the next 60 years, as efficiency and productivity became the hallmark of the Japanese car company. Toyota's network structure created sustainable competitive advantages of product quality, volume flexibility, and manufacturing speed. Because of its structure, Toyota utilizes a just in time (JIT) manufacturing system, which requires suppliers to carry inventory instead of Toyota. The Toyota Production System (TPS) employs a unique production control method called the "kanban system," also referred to as the "supermarket method." In this system, manufacturing parts are assigned kanban signs, similar to barcodes on supermarket merchandise, that carry vital information such as product name, code and storage location. This system has eliminated waste, inconsistencies, and unreasonable requirements, and resulted in improved productivity for Toyota.[33]

Pandora is another example of a company that utilizes a network structure. The Internet based music radio service does not produce and broadcast its own music, unlike Spotify which produced and marketed such musical acts as Major Lazer and Justin Bieber.[34] Instead, it sources different genres of music from major record labels. The Federal Government's Compulsory Licensing System allows Pandora to pay rates determined by federal copyright judges in exchange for access to the music as long as their users do not pick the songs themselves. Pandora maintains a network of suppliers of music that the company then provides to its listeners.[35]

Structure, Diversification, and Expansion

As the strategy and priorities of an organization change over time, so should the structure, as illustrated in Figure 10-13. The two axes in Figure 10-13 represent the *degree of diversification*, which is defined as the number of different industries that a company competes in, and the number of business units a company has. As mentioned before, GM has several business units and brands, including domestic brands like Buick, Cadillac, GMC, and Chevrolet, and international brands, such as Holden, HSV, Opel, Vauxhall, Wuling, Baojun, Jie Fang, and UzDaewoo. As illustrated in the figure below, a simple structure is best suited for a company that has a very low degree of diversification and operates a single business unit. As the company diversifies into various industries and adds new business units, the structure changes to support the strategy. In other words, the complexity of the structure matches the increased complexity of the strategy, as shown in Figure 10-13.

Structure Follows Strategy: An Example
Proctor & Gamble (P&G) is a global company that manufactures and distributes products in four core categories: (1) beauty, hair & personal care, (2) baby, feminine, & family care, (3) health & grooming, and (4) fabric & home care. These products are sold in over 180 countries. P&G's Selling & Market Operations (SMOs) are divided into six geographic regions (Asia Pacific, Europe, Greater China, India, the Middle East & Africa (IMEA), Latin America, and North America) to focus on selling and

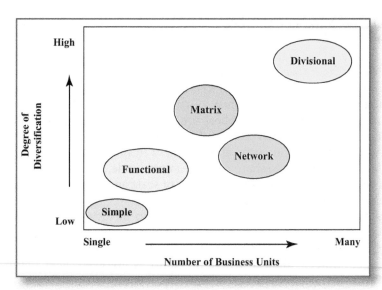

Figure 10-13
Diversification Strategy and Organizational Structure Relationship

distribution. These SMOs are responsible for developing and executing local plans that serve distinct consumers wherever, whenever and however they shop for P&G products. At the core of P&G's structure are its global business services and corporate functions that aid all global operations, such as the finance, human resources, communications, legal and IT departments.[36]

Organizations pursuing a low cost strategy strive to maintain stability and efficiency that can be achieved through task standardization, job specialization and formalization. A functional structure that puts specialists together minimizes duplication of personnel and equipment and results in economies of scale. Thus, a functional structure is normally best suited to pursue a low cost strategy. On the other hand, organizations pursuing a differentiation strategy need to maintain their uniqueness. Matrix and network structures are well suited to pursue a differentiation strategy as these structures can be easily molded to handle changes in the task and environment. The inherent advantages of these structures include flexibility and adaptability.

A simple structure is also suitable for pursuing a differentiation strategy, but is appropriate for smaller businesses. The best form of organization structure for an entrepreneurial firm is often a simple structure.

Organizations pursuing a focused differentiation or focused low cost strategy may want to create autonomous divisions to cater to the needs of a particular market segment. Such needs are met by creating divisions on the basis of products, geographic markets, or customer focus. A divisional structure can accommodate a focus strategy.

INTERNATIONAL ASPECTS OF STRATEGY IMPLEMENTATION

In Chapter 6, we identified several reasons why firms seek global expansion of their operations. Overseas business is central to the continued existence of manufacturing companies. In today's competitive world, companies must search out resources on a global scale, having products designed from a source that offers the best competitive advantage, obtaining technology from the best source, and manufacturing in those countries that offer best access to markets or a favorable cost structure.[37] Declining transportation and communication costs, and advances in information technology have made it easier for companies to share resources worldwide. Furthermore, international mergers also afford partners the economies of scale and international reach that they need in order to compete globally.

Different strategies to achieve international expansion include: licensing, joint ventures, mergers & acquisitions, and greenfields. From Chapter 3, we know that strategic alliances are cooperative agreements between two or more organizations. *Licensing* is a form of strategic alliance where no equity is involved. *Joint ventures* were identified as another kind of strategic alliance with equity contributions from partners. *Mergers & acquisitions* result in one legal entity that emerges when (a) two organizations merge into one, or (b) one acquires another. *Greenfields* are created by the parent company through complete internal development (i.e., without a strategic partner). A greenfield operation is a wholly owned subsidiary of the parent company.

Each of the four strategies for international expansion has different implementation requirements regarding financial, technical and managerial resources. The *financial factors* include capital requirement, financial risk, and profit potential to the investor. The *technical or industrial factors* encompass access to customer feedback, risk of know-how proliferation, and the ability to exploit economies of scale and other cost advantages. The *managerial factors* include the speed of entry and the need for and level of parent company involvement in management affairs. These requirements are compared across the four international expansion strategies in Table 10-5.[38]

As seen in Table 10-5, financial requirements—the need for capital, profit potential, and the financial risk—are lowest for a licensing strategy, and highest for a greenfield, with joint ventures and mergers & acquisitions falling in between. Two of the three technical or industrial factors—access to customer feedback and the ability to exploit economies of scale—also follow the same pattern—least for licensing and the highest for a greenfield. The risk of know-how proliferation, however, runs in the opposite direction, with the greatest risk being associated with a licensing strategy, and the least risk with a greenfield operation.

Table 10-5 Implementation Requirements for Different International Strategies

	INTERNATIONAL STRATEGIES			
IMPLEMENTATION REQUIREMENTS	LICENSING	JOINT VENTURE	MERGER & ACQUISITION	GREENFIELD
Financial				
• Need for capital	None	Medium	High	Very High
• Profit potential	Low	Medium	High	Very High
• Financial risk	Low	Medium	Medium	High
Technical or Industrial				
• Access to customer feedback	Low	Medium	High	Very High
• Risk of know-how proliferation	High	Medium	Low	Very Low
• Ability to exploit the economies of scale	Low	Medium	Medium	High
Managerial				
• Speed of entry	High	High	Medium	Low
• Need for and level of parent company's involvement in management affairs	Low	Medium	High	Very High

With regards to managerial factors, licensing affords the greatest speed of entry into a foreign market, with the least requirement for the parent company's involvement in managing the foreign operations. On the other extreme, a greenfield strategy requires greater involvement of the parent company and takes a long time to set up, delaying access to the foreign market.

STRATEGY IMPLEMENTATION: AN EXAMPLE

To illustrate many of the organizational issues of strategy implementation discussed in this chapter, let's look at Southwest as an example of successful implementation. How does Southwest Airlines create value for customers, employees and owners? It does so through strategy-systems alignment, and by creating a strong culture that abhors waste, rewards efficiency and communicates the message of "Low fares. Nothing to Hide."[39] Southwest has successfully positioned itself as a low-cost/low-fare airline by carefully designing and configuring its organizational systems and structure to support its strategy. Southwest maintains its advantage by keeping costs down, and offering on-time arrivals, convenient schedules, and a fun flying experience. These objectives are consistently communicated and supported throughout the organization.

For example, Southwest's operations function helps drive down costs by increasing the utilization of its planes, and reducing docking or gate time. Specifically, Southwest aims to take only 25 minutes to load and unload planes as compared to the industry average of about 45 minutes.[40] For quick loading of planes and to keep costs low, Southwest allows passengers to print their boarding pass online up to 24 hours before their flight or at a self-service kiosk at the airport. Passengers who print their tickets prior to arrival can skip the ticket counter and take advantage of Southwest's Express Bag Drop kiosk. Southwest also launched a mobile device app for passengers to check in to their flights and manage their travel. This added convenience resulted in 67% of all 2015 passengers checking in via their mobile devices.[41] Southwest does not assign seats, so passengers can take any available seat within their assigned zones when they get onboard. To keep training, maintenance, and inventory costs low, Southwest flies a standardized fleet of aircraft (the Boeing 737). Flight scheduling supports the low cost strategy through point-to-point routes, which also save time for passengers.

In 2016 Southwest began running a marketing campaign promoting honest pricing titled "Transfarency." This campaign emphasizes no baggage check fees and actively communicating with and listening to customers. In 2015, Southwest communicated with 694,719 customers through social media.[42] Southwest was the first major airline to use the Internet for booking and selling tickets. The cost per booking to Southwest via the Internet is about $1, compared to about $10 per booking through a travel agent. Southwest has steadily increased its proportion of revenues generated from online bookings via southwest.com and its mobile application. In 2015, online booking reached 79% of total bookings.[43]

The human resources function helps in creating value for customers by hiring people who have a sense of humor, and "who know how to have fun." By using its frequent flyers on the recruiting committee, it not only keeps the recruitment costs down but also takes into account customer expectations. Further, it helps create a strong company culture by creating a sense of responsibility and ownership through profit-sharing plans.

Southwest has adopted a functional organization structure[44] as presented in Figure 10-14. It is, however, interesting to note that the company did not have an

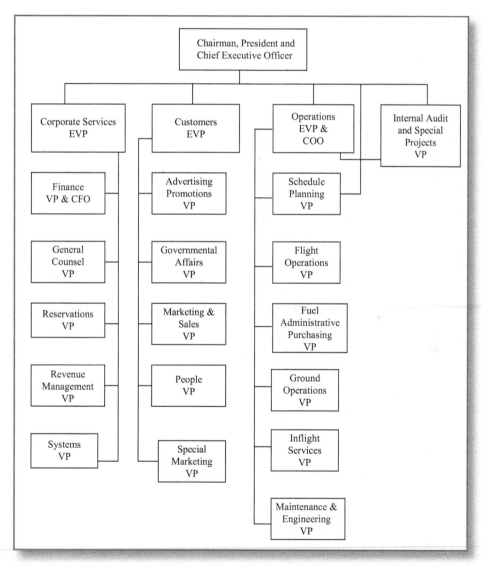

Figure 10-14
Southwest Airlines Organization Structure

organizational chart for years.[45] Southwest shuns organizational hierarchy—pilots have been known to assist ground crews, and employees often violate the chain of command by going above or around their supervisors to get answers. Not bound by its functional structure, Southwest promotes cross-functional accountability, which diffuses blame and encourages learning.[46] Prior to the early 1990s, Southwest followed the practice of identifying delays and attributing them to a particular crew or function, such as a flight crew or a station. That approach was difficult and expensive to administer and would lead to arguments between various groups of employees, which neither favored teamwork nor the company's strategy of cost leadership. This practice has been stopped.

Despite adding new international flight destinations to Belize, Costa Rica, and Mexico in 2015,[47] Southwest's organization is relatively simple compared to its major competitors. For example, American Airlines and United Airlines need to manage added complexity due to international operations and strategic alliances with other international carriers. Other major airlines also have to contend with their hub-and-spoke systems which increase administrative burdens due to the higher level of coordination required. Southwest's point-to-point system is a simpler configuration that facilitates quick turnaround and supports its overall strategy of low cost.

CONCLUSION

In this chapter, we discussed the role of three organizational factors in successful implementation of strategy—project management, organizational alignment, and organizational design. Blue Cross and Blue Shield of Louisiana (BCBSLA) utilizes project management as a tool for implementing various strategic initiatives. Philip Diab, a project manager of BCBSLA, stated that "project management is specifically used to implement corporate strategic initiatives deemed critical to the corporation and its competitive advantage."[48] By integrating project management techniques with strategic planning and implementation, BCBSLA has witnessed enhanced communications throughout the organization, realized productivity increases, and made better resource allocation decisions.

Two forms of organizational alignment (vertical and horizontal), and ways to achieve them, were also examined in this chapter. Vertical alignment is done to ensure coordination of goals, priorities, action plans and decisions through various hierarchical levels in the organization. Horizontal alignment refers to efforts to achieve cross-functional and intra-functional integration.

The various types of organizational structure were identified, and the relationship between strategy and structure was emphasized. We also considered the implementation requirements of four different ways to enter an international market. The international entry strategies—licensing, joint ventures, mergers & acquisitions, and greenfields—offer unique opportunities and place different demands on the parent organization in terms of financial, technical and managerial requirements.

KEY TERMS AND CONCEPTS

After reading this chapter you should understand each of the following terms.

- Horizontal Alignment
- Vertical Alignment
- Enterprise Resources Planning
- Organizational Design
- Functional Structure
- Matrix Structure
- Network Structure
- Divisional Structure
- Project Management

- Cross-functional Integration
- Intra-functional Integration
- Resource allocation
- Action plan
- Gantt chart
- Organizational Reconfiguration
- Chain of command
- Span of control
- Diversification

DISCUSSION QUESTIONS

1. How does Southwest Airlines maintain a low cost operation and high levels of employee and customer satisfaction in the context of a functional organization structure?
2. For an organization of your choice, identify its strategy and structure by visiting its website. Evaluate if the two are in alignment.
3. What is vertical alignment? Horizontal alignment? Explain the steps necessary to achieve vertical and horizontal alignment for a service organization, such as an electric company.
4. What is Project Management? How can it be used to facilitate the implementation of strategy?
5. What is Enterprise Resources Planning (ERP)? How can it help achieve horizontal alignment?
6. What are the different types of strategies available to a firm for entering an international market? Discuss the implementation requirements and organizing principles for the different types of strategies.

EXPERIENTIAL EXERCISE

Develop an *action plan* for the merger of two hotel chains. See Table 10-2 for guidance. Identify major activities for the project, determine interdependence of activities, estimate activity times, and identify the departments/ functions responsible for each activity.

ENDNOTES

1. "2015 Southwest Airlines Annual Report." *Southwest Airlines*. Accessed 25 April 2016.
2. "World's Most Admired Companies: 2016." *Fortune*. Accessed 21 April 2016.

http://fortune.com/worlds-most-admired-companies/

3. Shook, D., "Southwest's Lean, Mean Flying Machine," *Business Week*,

January 29, 2001, accessed December 5, 2001.

4. "About FedEx: Corporate Facts Sheet." *FedEx*. Accessed 22 May 2016. http://about.van.fedex.com/our-story/company-structure/corporate-fact-sheet/

5. "About FedEx: Corporate Facts Sheet." *FedEx*. Accessed 22 May 2016. http://about.van.fedex.com/our-story/company-structure/corporate-fact-sheet/

6. FedEx, Press Release, November 25, 2005, http://fedex.com/cgi-bin/content.cgi?template=gb_pr&content=about/pressreleases/emea/pr112505&cc=gb, accessed March 25, 2011.

7. Pierce, David. "iPhone Killer: The Secret History of the Apple Watch." *WIRED*. Conde Nast Publications. May 2015. Web. 23 May 2016.

8. Meredith, J. R., and S. J. Mantel Jr. *Project Management: A Managerial Approach*. 4th ed. New York: John Wiley and Sons, 2000, 195.

9. "2015 GM Annual Report." *General Motors Company*. Accessed 19 May 2016.

10. Porter, M. E. *Competitive Advantage*. New York: The Free Press, 1985.

11. Kathuria, R., and F. Y. Partovi, "Aligning Workforce Management Practices with Competitive Priorities and Process Technology: A Conceptual Examination," *The Journal of High Technology Management Research* 11, no. 2, 2000, 215–234.

12. Kathuria, R., and F. Y. Partovi, 2000, op cit

13. Schroeder, R. G., J. C. Anderson, and G. Clevelend, "The Content of Manufacturing Strategy: An Empirical Study," *Journal of Operations Management* 6, no. 4 (1986): 405–415.

14. Swamidass, P. M., "Manufacturing Strategy: Its Assessment and Practice," *Journal of Operations Management* 6, no. 4 (1986): 405–415; and Porth, S., R. Kathuria, and M. P. Joshi, "Performance Impact of the Fit Between Manufacturing Priorities of General Managers and Manufacturing Managers," *Journal of Business and Economic Studies* 4, no. 1 (Spring 1998): 13–35

15. Strahle, W. M., R. L. Spiro, and F. Acito, "Marketing and Sales: Strategic Alignment and Functional Implementation," *Journal of Personal Selling and Sales Management* 16 (1996): 1–20.

16. Kathuria, R., S. Porth, and M. P. Joshi, "Manufacturing Priorities: Do General Managers and Manufacturing Managers Agree?" *International Journal of Production Research* 37, no. 1 (1999): 2077–2092.

17. Kathuria, R., and M. Igbaria, "Aligning IT Applications with Manufacturing Strategy: An Integrated Framework," *International Journal of Operations & Production Management* 17, no. 6 (1997): 611–629.

18. Hochfelder, Barry, "Papa John's Scores a Supply Chain Touchdown," *Supply & Demand Chain Executive*, March 2011.

19. "Papa John's Announces First Quarter 2016 Results." *Papa Johns*. Accessed 23 May 2016.

20. Hayes, R. H., and S. C. Wheelwright. *Restoring Our Competitive Edge*. New York: Wiley, 1984.

21. Kathuria, R., and F. Y. Partovi, "Workforce Management Practices for Manufacturing Flexibility," *Journal of Operations Management* 18, no. 1 (1999): 21–39; and Kathuria, R., and F. Y. Partovi, 2000, op cit.

22. Kathuria, R., and F. Y. Partovi, 2000, op cit.

23. Chandler, A. D., Jr. *Strategy and Structure: Chapters in the History of the American Industrial Enterprise*. Cambridge, MA: M.I.T. Press, 1962.

24. Urwick, L. *The Elements of Administration*. New York: Harper & Row, 1944.

25. Mintzberg, H., "Organization Design: Fashion or Fit?" *Harvard Business Review* (January–February 1981): 103–116.

26. Based on the discussion in Chandler, A. D., Jr., 1962, op cit.

27. Mintzberg, H., 1981, op cit

28. Mintzberg, H., 1981, op cit

29. Galbraith, J., "Matrix Organization Designs: How to Combine Functional and Project Forms," *Business Horizons* (February 1971): 29–40.

30. Turner, S. G., D. Utley, and J. D. Westbrook, "Project Managers and Functional Managers: A Case Study of Job

Satisfaction in a Matrix Organization," *Project Management Journal* (September 1998): 11–19.

31. Morgan, G. "From Bureaucracies to Networks: The Emergence of New Organizational Forms." In *Creative Organizational Theory: A Resource Book*, Newbury Park, CA: Sage, 1989, 64–67.

32. Wolf, Bernard M., "Rev. of *The Machine that Changed the World*" Journal of International Business Studies, Third Quarter 1991. Web. 17 November 2015.

33. "Toyota: Just-In-Time—Philosophy of complete elimination of waste." *Toyota*. Accessed 24 May 2016. http://www.toyota-global.com/company/vision_philosophy/toyota_production_system/just-in-time.html

34. Karp, Hannah. "Spotify and Musicians Are Playing a New Tune." *WSJ*. 21 March 2016. Web. 15 April 2016.

35. Karp, Hannah. "Pandora Counts on Founder to Strike Deals." *WSJ*. 29 March 2016. Web. 13 April 2016.

36. "P&G Corporate Structure" *Proctor & Gamble*. Accessed 22 May 2016. http://us.pg.com/who_we_are/structure_governance/corporate_structure

37. Collins, T. M., and T. L. Doorley III. Teaming Up for the 90's: A Guide to International Joint Ventures and Strategic Alliances. Homewood, IL: Business One Irwin, 1991.

38. Based on the analysis in Kathuria, R., and M. P. Joshi. "Globalization of Services:

Do Service Characteristics Impact the Globalization Process?" Paper presented at the POMS Conference, Orlando, FL, March 2001

39. Gilbertson, Dawn. "Southwest Airlines zings competitors' fees in new ads." *USA Today*. Gannett Company. 14 October 2015. Web. 21 May 2016.

40. Leib, Jeffrey. "Southwest Airlines hustles to reduce turnaround times" *The Denver Post*. Digital First Media. 25 September 2010. Web. 12 May 2016. Southwest Airlines, 2007 Stewardship Report, accessed March 28, 2011.

41. "2015 Southwest Airlines Annual Report" *Southwest Airlines* Accessed 20 May 2016.

42. "2015 Southwest Airlines Annual Report" *Southwest Airlines* Accessed 20 May 2016.

43. "2015 Southwest Airlines Annual Report" *Southwest Airlines* Accessed 20 May 2016.

44. Based on the case analysis of Southwest Airlines by NYU Stern at www.stern.nyu.edu/MET98/structure.htm, accessed December 4, 2001.

45. Matthew, B., "In Herb's Way," *The Boston Sunday Globe*, November 5, 2000, F4

46. Gittell, J. H., "Paradox of Coordination and Control," *California Management Review*

47. "2015 Southwest Airlines Annual Report" *Southwest Airlines* Accessed 20 May 2016.

48. Diab, P. "Strategic Planning + Project Management = Competitive Advantage," *PM Network* (July 1998): 27

Chapter 11

Assessing Value Creation

CHAPTER LEARNING OBJECTIVES

After studying this chapter, you should be able to

- Understand the purpose and process of assessing value creation in the strategic management process;
- Explain and apply a framework for assessing value creation;
- Create a balanced scorecard of measures to assess value creation for the firm of your choice.

Conrad Hilton purchased his first hotel in Cisco, Texas in 1919. The first hotel to carry the Hilton name was built in Dallas in 1925. In 1943, Hilton became the first "coast-to-coast" hotel chain in the United States; and in 1949, Hilton opened its first hotel outside the U.S., in San Juan, Puerto Rico. Hilton was the first to build an airport hotel and the first hotel in the world to earn both LEED and Green Seal environmental certifications. Today, Hilton operates over 550 hotels and resorts in 78 countries across six continents.[1] The Hilton portfolio includes major hospitality brands such as Hilton Hotels & Resorts, Embassy Suites, Waldorf Astoria Hotels & Resorts, Doubletree, Hampton Inns, and Hilton Grand Vacations. To learn more about Hilton, visit www.hilton.com.

*T*he focus of the strategic management process ends where it began—value creation. Just as we set out to create value at the beginning of the process, we conclude by determining the value we were able to create. The purpose of this chapter is to discuss how this is done in the fifth and final major step of the strategic management process—*assessment of value creation*. This step and its relationship with the overall process are shown in Figure 11-1.

The strategic management process begins with a vision, mission and set of strategies that strategic managers believe will result in value for the organization's customers, employees, owners and other key stakeholders. As the firm implements these strategies it monitors and measures its success in creating value. In addition to *measuring* value creation, the firm must *manage* it by feeding back the results of the measurement process to appropriate functional managers so that corrective actions, if necessary, can be identified and taken.

Consider the example of Hilton Hotels. The Hilton name, synonymous with the word "hotel," is the most recognizable in the industry. Hilton's mission is "to be the most hospitable company in the world—by creating heartfelt experiences for Guests, meaningful opportunities for Team Members, high value for Owners and a positive impact in our Communities."[2] Hilton's research, conducted during its strategic planning process, determined that the key to delivering value was to ensure a consistent guest experience across all Hilton properties. The research showed that Hilton customers expected, among other attributes, a clean, quiet, comfortable room, but the quality of the guest experience was inconsistent among Hilton properties, especially between franchised properties and

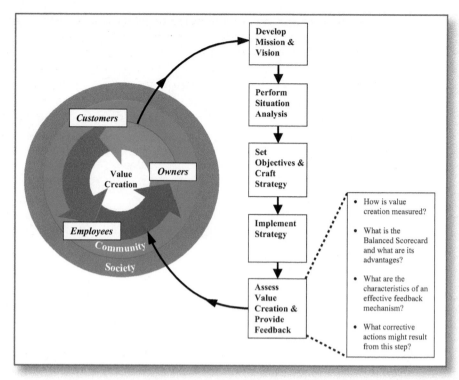

Figure 11-1
The Strategic Management Framework

company-owned hotels. This inconsistency undermined Hilton's ability to create value and resulted in less than acceptable rates of customer satisfaction.

Hilton's response is a good example of how the *assessment of value creation* step of the strategic management process should work. First, the company set targets of performance in several areas and measured its actual results versus its targets. Next, Hilton pinpointed the areas where performance was inconsistent or substandard and provided feedback to appropriate managers for their review and consideration. Using this information, corrective actions were identified and taken. In time, performance improved and Hilton began to be able to ensure a more consistently positive guest experience across all Hilton properties.

Hilton's approach—measurement, feedback, and corrective action—illustrates the three essential components of the final step of strategic management. Think of the thermostat in your home as an analogy. You set your desired room temperature on the thermostat. The system measures the actual temperature of the room and compares it to your desired temperature. When a significant deviation between actual and desired temperature occurs, that information is fed back to the heating (or air conditioning) unit which then takes corrective action by generating more hot (or cool) air.

In addition to explaining each of these activities—measurement, feedback and corrective action—we introduce and discuss approaches or tools for performing them. In particular, the balanced scorecard is emphasized. After reading this chapter you should be able to answer each of the questions about assessing value creation listed in Figure 11-1 and, as an example, be familiar with Hilton's approach to measuring and managing value creation.

MEASURING VALUE CREATION: TWO APPROACHES

Accountability is required in the strategic management process. To achieve accountability, each organization must find ways to translate its mission and strategies into daily operating activities, assign responsibilities for the activities, and measure and evaluate the progress being made. All levels of the organization and each individual employee must understand their roles in carrying out the mission and strategies (recall our discussion of vertical alignment in Chapter 9), and be held responsible for their results. Thus, accountability depends first on establishing clear goals and standards that are communicated and understood throughout the organization. Only then can appropriate measures of progress be identified. As we stated in the first chapter, "If you can't measure it, you can't manage it."[3] Thus, decisions about what will be measured and how measurements will be taken are critical. Let's examine alternative approaches for measuring value creation.

The Traditional Approach

Financial measures of value creation, such as those discussed in Chapter 4, have been the traditional tools of strategy evaluation and control. These include different measures of profitability such as Return on Equity (ROE), earnings per share, and various profit margins (e.g., net, gross and operating). In addition, analyses of cash flow, the growth rate of sales, and stock price performance are common traditional measures of value creation.

These measures continue to be important barometers of the health of the company and its ability to create value. Their strengths lie in their ability to gauge *current* organizational performance and in their focus on value for *owners and shareholders*. On the other hand, the traditional approach has limitations. First, its exclusive focus on financial indicators is overly narrow and owner-oriented. Value for customers, employees and other key stakeholders is not adequately assessed. In addition, financial measures do not necessarily reflect or suggest the *future* performance of the organization. Today's financial results are primarily the result of business conditions and management decisions made yesterday. These results may not be a reliable indicator of the overall health of the organization and its future prospects for value creation. Let's consider an example.

The Limitations of Financial Measures: An Example

What would you conclude about the strategic health of an oil and gas company that provides fuel for transportation and energy for heat and light with the following credentials? Despite the global economic crisis, the company generated a profit of $21.7 billion in 2008 and $16.8 billion in 2009. Earnings per share (EPS) in 2009 were $88.49 and return on equity (ROE) was 16.32%, as compared to 17.44% for the industry leader, Exxon Mobil.

Based on this information we would most likely conclude that this firm has done reasonably well in the midst of a recession. Its financial performance was strong. Judging from its financial statements, value was created for owners, and based on sales, it appears customer value was also being realized. And what can we conclude about the firm's future prospects for value creation? Wouldn't it be safe to assume that this firm's strategic health can be sustained if not improved as the economy recovers? Careful! This is one area where the traditional financial measures are limited.

The example above is real and the numbers are accurate. The company is BP (formerly British Petroleum), which has indeed achieved an impressive level of financial performance, as the numbers suggest. But all of this changed suddenly in April of 2010 when an explosion at BP's Deepwater Horizon drilling rig resulted in the worst offshore spill in U.S. history. Eleven employees were killed and nearly 4.9 million barrels of oil leaked into the Gulf of Mexico over a span of three months, causing one of the worst natural disasters the world has ever seen. BP incurred $41 billion in expenses related to the oil spill in 2010 alone. This resulted in a reported loss of $3.3 billion for 2010.[4] In 2015, BP agreed to pay up to $18.7 billion in penalties to the United States government and five states affected by the spill; and in 2016, BP agreed to pay $175 million to investors to settle claims that the company lied about the size of the oil spill.[5]

Following the Gulf of Mexico oil spill, BP's gross profit dropped and stock prices fell from $60 to $27 per share at one point. Since the spill, BP's share price started to recover as 2014 marked a 5-year highpoint of $53, only to drop to $33 per share in 2016 due to increased global oil production and lingering post spill litigation and settlements.[6] BP's earnings per share (EPS) fell from $88.49 in 2009 to -$19.81 in 2010. Furthermore, BP cancelled its planned first quarter 2010 dividend. No one could have predicted that BP would be in this position by looking solely at financial measures.

Chipotle is another example of a company whose financial measures did not provide a comprehensive view of the health of the company. For fiscal year 2015, Chipotle revenues increased by 27.8% to $4.11 billion, operating margin increased by 60 basis points to 27.2%, net income increased by 36.0% to $445.4 million, and diluted earnings per share increased by 35.0% to $14.13.[7] However, in the second half of 2015, the presence of E. coli and norovirus were detected and traced back to multiple Chipotle locations across the country. Since the outbreak in late 2015, Chipotle's stock price fell from $750 on October 13 to a low of $480 on December 31. Chipotle has taken measures to ensure that this does not occur again by precooking beef and delivering it to restaurants in vacuum sealed bags, but the damage has been done.[8] Again, simply looking at Chipotle's financials would not have provided any indication of such a crisis.

The implications of these examples should be apparent—financial measures of value creation are useful for evaluating current performance but financial measures alone are not enough. The financial perspective emphasizes current performance and value for owners. To be confident in our predictions about the future strategic health of this company, or any company, we need a more balanced and comprehensive set of assessments and measures.

The Balanced Scorecard

The balanced scorecard concept was developed by Robert Kaplan, an accounting professor at the Harvard Business School, and David Norton, a management consultant who is president and CEO of the Balanced Scorecard Collaborative. The purpose of the scorecard is to identify and track the key elements of a company's strategy. Organizations that use it have found that it helps them to clarify and translate their vision and strategies into specific operational tasks and activities that must be performed. It becomes the link between strategy and action.

The **balanced scorecard** has important advantages over the traditional financial approach. It is based on the premise that financial measures are necessary but not sufficient for providing a clear and comprehensive focus on all of the critical areas of business. The balanced scorecard includes financial measures that indicate the results of actions already taken but goes beyond this perspective to get a more balanced assessment of value creation. Its advantages include:

- a combination of financial and non-financial measures of value creation
- an assessment of current and future indicators of value
- a focus on value for customers, employees, and owners/shareholders
- An internal and external perspective on value creation

As shown in Figure 11-2, the balanced scorecard provides managers with information from four different perspectives. The *financial* perspective focuses on value creation for owners using the financial tools discussed in the section above. This perspective is complemented by three others. The *customer* perspective puts the spotlight on the organization's relationships with its customers and its ability to build and retain satisfied customers. The *internal* perspective focuses on employees and operations. It emphasizes the organization's success at developing and keeping qualified and motivated employees. It also examines the internal operations of the organization and seeks to achieve higher levels of efficiency and effectiveness. The *future* perspective assesses the firm's ability to innovate and learn, and questions whether it can continue to improve and create value.

The specific measures used to assess performance in the four areas will depend on the company, its strategic objectives, and the nature of its products and services. The scorecard can be adapted to suit any organization. Some of the common measures for a business organization are listed in Figure 11-3.

Most of the measures in Figure 11-3 have either been explained in a previous chapter (e.g., ROE, asset turnover) or are self-explanatory (e.g., sales to employee, market share). A few need further explanation. **MVA** (market value added) is a measure of change in the stock price of the firm (growth or decline over time). SG&A Efficiency is a measure of the firm's ability to control sales, general, and administrative

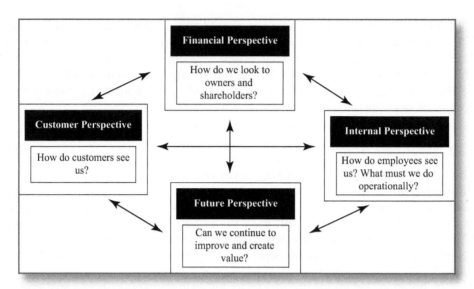

Figure 11-2
The Balanced Scorecard

Reprinted from "The Balanced Scorecard–Measures That Drive Performance," by R.S. Kaplan and D.P. Norton, *Harvard Business Review* (Jan-Feb 1992), by permission of Harvard Business Publishing.

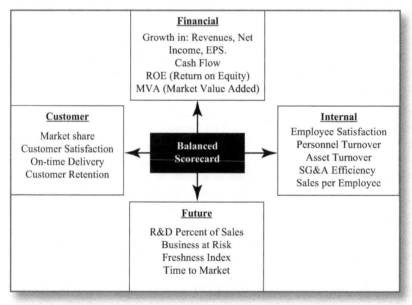

Figure 11-3
Common Measures in the Balanced Scorecard

(SG&A) costs. The increased room listings and growing popularity of Airbnb is an example of **business at risk** for Hilton, a measure of impending threats to sales. The **freshness index** measures the percentage of total sales from new products. For example, from Chapter 4 we know that 3M places a strong emphasis on innovation. This is reflected in 3M's goal of achieving a Freshness Index of 30 percent of total revenues each year from products that have been on the market for less than four years. **Time to market** is a measure of cycle time, or how long it takes a company to develop a new product concept and introduce it to the market.

This collection of metrics is not meant to be exhaustive. In fact, the possibilities for developing and customizing measures are almost unlimited. For example:

- To assess customer value, a semiconductor company asked each of its major customers to rank the company against its competitors on attributes such as quality, delivery time, and price. When results indicated that the company was ranked in the middle of the pack, managers made changes to move the company to the top of the list.[9]
- To evaluate its record on sustainability, The Walt Disney Company tracks a set of initiatives that include zero direct greenhouse gas emissions, retired carbon credits (metric tons of CO_2), zero waste to landfills, and minimized water use.[10] Similarly, Apple measures its environmental footprint by adding up its emissions from manufacturing, transportation, etc.[11]

While these examples suggest that strategic managers have many options in establishing the measures to be used in the scorecard, each company is faced with the same challenge—choosing the right measures. Research indicates that an organization's measurement system will strongly affect the behaviors of its managers and employees. What you measure is what you get.[12] In addition to choosing the right measures, managers must not be distracted by the temptation to measure too much. Information overload is counterproductive and overwhelms managers and employees. If the balanced scorecard is to truly drive value creation as it is meant to do, it must focus on a clear and manageable set of relevant factors. Let's consider an example to see how one company used the balanced scorecard to assess and manage value creation.

Hilton Hotels and the Balanced Scorecard[13]

To use the balanced scorecard, Hilton conducts an annual planning process that translates its business strategy into operational activities and corresponding goals in each of the four areas—financial, customer, internal, and future. Goals are stated in SMART format as we have discussed in Chapter 6. The strategy and operational goals are communicated and reinforced continuously throughout the year. People at all levels of the organization know what is expected of them.

Hilton uses the scorecard concept to provide information on how each individual hotel performs relative to its own historical averages, to competitors, and to other Hilton properties. Eight measures are used to provide a balanced view of the hotel's performance. Table 11-1 identifies and briefly defines each measure.

Hilton's measures are a combination of financial and non-financial metrics, and address value creation for shareholders, guests, and team members. Once goals and measures are clearly established, performance can be monitored in each of the specified areas. Hilton uses a simple but effective way to communicate performance results. Measures are reported numerically and by color code. There are three color zones—results in the green zone indicate that the hotel meets or exceeds goals for

Table 11-1 Hilton's Balanced Scorecard Measures

MEASURE	DESCRIPTION
Room RevPAR	RevPAR is a standard performance measure in the lodging industry. It measures revenue generated per available room.
RevPAR Index	RevPAR compared to competitors in the local market
EBITDA	A measure of operational effectiveness based on earnings before interest, taxes, depreciation, and amortization
Guest Satisfaction	Customers complete guest-comment cards to indicate their overall satisfaction.
Customer Satisfaction Tracking	Telephone interviews of a sample of guests are used to measure satisfaction.
Team Member Satisfaction	All hotel employees are surveyed to determine their overall satisfaction.
Mystery Shopper	Average of scores from random visits by auditors posing as guests
Standards Compliance	A measure of the hotel's compliance with brand standards such as courteous service, fresh food, clean bathrooms, quiet rooms

Adapted from: Huckestein, D. and R. Duboff, Hilton Hotels: A comprehensive approach to delivering value for all stakeholders, *Hotel and Restaurant Administration Quarterly*, August 1999, p. 31.

that measure, yellow signifies results slightly below the standard, and red identifies results where the hotel is significantly below the goal.

Results are communicated widely using graphs and charts so that hotel managers and employees can see how well they are doing. The color-coding system draws attention to each hotel's problem areas and clarifies where attention and resources need to be focused. Since results are tracked over time, managers receive feedback on their problem-solving ability as they see the outcomes of their efforts to move performance from the red to green zone.

Hilton's reward system is tied directly to results from the balanced scorecard. Hotel-specific goals are linked to bonus programs, merit-pay increases, stock options, and the performance reviews of hotel managers. One example is Hilton's Million-Dollar Team Pride Award. Hotels must score in the green zone on all eight measures to be eligible. An annual pool of up to $1 million of Hilton stock is divided equally among all full-time team members at all eligible hotels.

The end result for Hilton is a tight link between its strategy and the operating activities of individual hotels. Value creation is defined, measured and managed.

Using the Balanced Scorecard

The example of Hilton provides some helpful insights into how organizations can develop and use the balanced scorecard. These may be summarized as follows:

- Begin with a clear strategy—a lack of clarity at the top (strategy) will also muddle thinking at lower levels (operations). An effective use of the scorecard depends on a clear understanding of the drivers of value.

- Set goals that link strategy and operations—develop realistic and measurable targets and customize them to the operating unit.
- Carefully select measures—employee behavior will be strongly influenced by the measures they are held accountable to achieve. Measures should give an accurate (i.e., valid and reliable) reading of goal accomplishment and focus on outcomes that employees can control.
- Communicate upfront and provide feedback—people need to understand the strategy, goals, and measures, and receive prompt feedback on performance results.
- Take corrective action—use performance results to learn where to focus attention and develop solutions to problems.

- Follow through with the reward system—link pay and other rewards to performance. Reward employees for significant accomplishments.

A FRAMEWORK FOR ASSESSING VALUE CREATION

As the discussion above suggests, assessing value creation, the fifth step in strategic management, means more than just *measuring* value creation. In fact, three activities are needed:

- Measuring value creation
- Feeding back results
- Taking corrective action, if necessary, and striving for continuous improvement.

If a Hilton property, for example, determines that it has fallen short of its target in its mystery shopper index (*measurement*), results are communicated to managers and employees (*feedback*) so that the problem can be understood and addressed by new ideas or programs (*corrective action*). Even when there is no problem per se, we look for opportunities to learn and develop (*continuous improvement*).

Let's examine a framework that incorporates the balanced scorecard and may be used to accomplish all three of the activities in assessing value creation. The components of the model include reviewing the situation analysis to examine the underlying bases of strategy, applying the balanced scorecard, feeding back results and taking corrective actions, if needed. The relationship between the components is shown in Figure 11-4.

Figure 11-4 is a straightforward and practical tool for assessing value creation. It stresses the need to monitor the assumptions underlying our choice of strategy by first revisiting the situation analysis. Have major changes occurred in our internal or external strategic position? That is, do we have a new understanding of our strengths, weaknesses, opportunities or threats? If so, we may need to take corrective action even if our value creation continues to be strong.

For example, suppose you are a hotel manager in Miami. You just learned that your closest competitor has acquired property less than a mile from you and intends to build and open a new hotel within two years. Your current results have

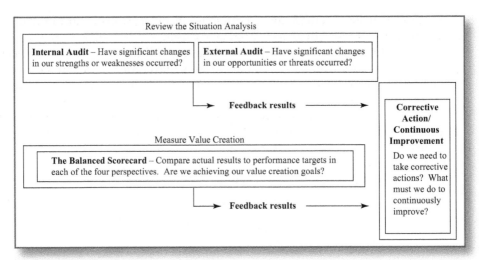

Figure 11-4
A Framework for Assessing Value Creation

not changed. You are still meeting all your value creation goals. But obviously your external opportunities and threats have changed dramatically and you need to consider your strategic response (i.e., corrective action). This example highlights the importance of not relying just on results to trigger corrective actions. If you wait to take corrective action until after you experience some loss of value creation, it may be too late. But by acting now, you may be able to either avert the threat or at least minimize it.

The next part of the framework emphasizes the balanced scorecard. Using the approach described in the previous section, we measure our results in relation to our targets in the four areas—financial, future, customer, and internal. If we have not made satisfactory progress toward stated goals, that feedback is relayed to employees and managers for their analysis and action. On the other hand, if the review of our situation analysis and balanced scorecard do not uncover any significant changes or shortfalls, corrective action may not be necessary. Under these circumstances, the model suggests that a continuation of the current strategy and supporting operational activities is expected to produce value now and into the future. No corrective action is needed.

At the same time, just because corrective action is not called for, does not mean we should sit back and be comfortable with the status quo. Successful companies look for ways to reinvent themselves through continuous improvement even when things are going well. The search never ends.

Feedback and Corrective Action/Continuous Improvement

We have focused extensively on measuring value creation but let's further examine the feedback and corrective action/improvement components of the framework. What are the characteristics of an effective feedback mechanism? Think of the Hilton example. The feedback is comprehensive but simple to understand. Hilton's green, yellow, and red color scheme communicates results on eight variables in a clear and direct way. It is supplemented with graphs and charts that track results over time. Furthermore, this information is widely communicated in report form and posted for all employees and managers to see in high-visibility locations such as employee entrances and lunchrooms.

Hilton makes feedback available on a timely basis so that team members may respond quickly to both problems and opportunities. The information helps to build a common understanding among employees and focuses attention on the goals of value creation and continuous improvement. These characteristics are summarized in Table 11-2.

The final component of the framework is corrective action and continuous improvement. What are some examples of actions to correct problems or achieve continuous improvement? The list is extensive since it could range from minor adjustments of operational procedures to a wholesale revamping of the organization's mission. The incremental changes in operations are more common and much easier to implement. At Hilton, for example, this might mean a simple change to the room service menu, having beach towels available at poolside, or changing the way front desk employees greet guests as they arrive for check-in.

At the other end of the spectrum, corrective action may entail a fundamental redirection of the mission, vision, and strategies of the organization. That is why the feedback loop in the Strategic Management Framework connects back to the first step of the process—developing the mission and vision.

We saw an example of this fundamental redirection in Chapter 3. Microsoft Corp. revised its mission statement several times in the last two decades as it searched for more effective ways to generate value in a highly competitive and volatile technology industry. Originally, Microsoft's mission and strategies were aimed at putting a PC on every desk and in every home. Microsoft did so by dissolving its software partnership with rival IBM, aggressively developing innovative features for its Windows operating systems, and strategically partnering with certain hardware firms. Since that time, Microsoft has again refocused to emphasize the seemingly endless possibilities of cloud computing. Similarly, in its search for greater value, GE sold off its white goods division to its competitor, Haier, to focus on being an industrial technology company that writes and develops software for its industrial divisions. These are all examples of corrective actions taken by firms looking for value creation.

Table 11-2 Characteristics of an Effective Feedback System

- Comprehensive but simple to understand
- Results are disseminated widely (to all team members for whom it is useful)
- Communicated in a variety of formats (e.g., reports, graphs, posters, e-mail)
- Timely
- Fosters a common understanding of issues, challenges, opportunities
- Focuses attention on shared purpose

CONCLUSION

Assessing value creation is the fifth step in the strategic management process. The three components of this step—measurement, feedback, and corrective action/continuous improvement—are explained in this chapter. It is important to emphasize that these steps are ongoing throughout the strategy process. The Strategic Management Framework (see Figure 11-1) suggests that this is the final step in the process, and logically this is true. Before we can assess our success in creating value with our strategies, we must first develop and implement those strategies. But as we know, the actual practice of strategic management is not a neat sequence of discrete, non-overlapping steps. There are lots of things happening simultaneously. While we may be working on developing a new strategy, we are also implementing existing strategies and assessing their results. Feedback is a constant process of communicating the results of ongoing efforts. We don't wait until the end of the process to evaluate results and take corrective actions, if needed. Indeed, as stated above, we continuously search for new and better ways to achieve the overriding objective of strategic management—to create value for our stakeholders, especially our customers, employees, and owners.

KEY TERMS AND CONCEPTS

After reading this chapter you should understand each of the following terms.

- The Balanced Scorecard
- Time to Market
- Feedback
- The Traditional Approach to Measuring Value
- Freshness Index
- Corrective Action
- Business at Risk
- MVA (Market Value Added)
- Continuous Improvement

DISCUSSION QUESTIONS

1. What are the three activities involved in assessing value creation?
2. What are the advantages of a balanced scorecard for measuring value creation versus the traditional approach?
3. Do you agree or disagree with the following statement: If a firm is meeting its value creation goals and a review of its situation analysis determines that no internal or external strategic changes have occurred, the organization should stay the course. No action is necessary.
4. Can the balanced scorecard be customized to meet the unique needs of any organization? Explain.
5. Check the company's website to determine Hilton's current corporate-level financial performance. Has it been consistent? Does it look like corrective action is needed? Explain.

EXPERIENTIAL EXERCISE

The Balanced Scorecard Either in teams or on your own, select a company or organization that you know well. Develop a balanced scorecard for the organization. Identify specific goals in the SMART format for each of the four areas of the scorecard. Describe the measures you would use to assess value creation and the ways you would feedback results within the organization. Be specific.

ENDNOTES

1. "Our Brands" *Hilton Hotels & Resorts*. Accessed 25 May 2016. http://hhonors3. hilton.com/en/explore/brands/index.html

2. "Vision, Mission and Values" *Hilton Worldwide*, Accessed October 18, 2016. http://hiltonworldwide.com/about/ mission/

3. Garvin, D. A., "Building A Learning Organization," *Harvard Business Review* (July–August 1993): 89

4. "BP's 2010 Performance Muddied by Gulf Oil Spill," Nasdaq.com, http://community.nasdaq.com/News/2011–03/ bps-2010-performance-muddied-by-gulf-oil-spill.aspx?storyid=62608, accessed April 5, 2011.

5. Saintvilus, Richard. "BP Stock Rises After $175M Oil Spill Settlement" *Investopedia. com*. IAC. 6 June 2016. Web. 7 June 2016.

6. Saintvilus, Richard. "BP Stock Rises After $175M Oil Spill Settlement" *Investopedia. com*. IAC. 6 June 2016. Web. 7 June 2016.

7. "Chipotle 2015 Annual Report and Proxy Statement" *Chipotle*. Accessed 20 May 2016.

8. Newman, Jesse; Jargon, Julie. "Chipotle weighs stepping back from some food safety changes." *WSJ*. Wall Street Journal. 16 March 2016. Web. 28 March 2016.

9. Kaplan, R. S., and D. P. Norton, "The Balanced Scorecard—Measures That Drive Performance," *Harvard Business Review* (January–February 1992): 74

10. "2015 Disney Citizenship Data Table." *The Walt Disney Company*. Accessed 10 May 2016.

11. Apple, "Apple and the Environment," www.apple.com, accessed April 5, 2011.

12. Kaplan, R. S., and D. P. Norton, "The Balanced Scorecard—Measures That Drive Performance," *Harvard Business Review* (January-February 1992): 71.

13. Hilton's use of the Balanced Scorecard is explained in detail in an article by Dieter Huckestein, President of Hotel Operations at Hilton, and Robert Duboff, Vice President at Mercer Management Consulting. See Huckestein, D., and R. Duboff, "Hilton Hotels: A Comprehensive Approach to Delivering Value for all Stakeholders," *Hotel and Restaurant Administration Quarterly* (August 1999): 28-38 for more information. The examples of Hilton used throughout this chapter were obtained from this article and from a review of Hilton's website

Index

barnesandnoble.com, 37
Batch process, 290
Bayer Aspirin, 78
Behavior, strategic choice and,
    184–189. *See also* Strategic choice
Benchmarks, 14, 98
Benioff, Marc, 66
Berkshire Hathaway, 163, 237
Better-off test, 163
Bezos, Jeff, 194, 257, 261
BJ's Wholesale Club, 105
Blackberry, 124, 199–200
Blockbuster, 86
Blog, 145, 146
Blue Cross and Blue Shield of
    Louisiana (BCBSLA), 308
Blue Nile, 10
Board of Directors, 9, 17
Bonobos, 10
Book value, 239
Borders, 37
Boston Consulting Group (BCG)
    Matrix, 164–165, 168
BP Horizon, 49–50, 316
Branching tree
    Minnesota Mining and
        Manufacturing Company
        (3M), 113
Branding, 33
Brin, Sergey, 171
British Petroleum (BP), 84
Budweiser, 124
Buffet, Warren, 237
*Built to Last: Successful Habits of
    Visionary Companies*, 45
Business at risk, 318
Business ethics, 186
Business level strategy, 10
Business scope, 9
Business strength, 167
Business valuation, 237–244
    methodologies, 239–243

C

Calico, 170
Camaro, John, 292

Campbell's Kitchen, 33
Campbell's Meal-mail, 33
Campbell Soup Company, 33, 228
Capital budgeting, 225
    decisions, 225
Capital structure, 223
Carfax.com, 35
Cash cow, 165
Cash flow, 249
Central Intelligence Agency, 261
Cerebus Capital Management, 136
Chain of command, 296
Championing strategic alternatives
    management role, 260
Change
    principles for implementing, 274
Change, employee resistance to,
    271–273
    four-phase response to, 272
    reasons for, 271
Changing phase, 274
Chapter 11 bankruptcy, 26
Charter Communications, 81
Chevrolet, 181
Chevron Corporation, 26, 28, 36, 44,
    81, 85
    value creation and, 28, 40
Chief Executive Officer (CEO), 16,
    17, 18
Chipotle, 34, 136, 316
Christensen, Clayton, 203
Chrysler, 136, 185
Chung Ju-Yung, 265
Citizens Bank Park, 74
Climate change, 70
Coca Cola, 10, 81, 138, 180
Code of ethics, 20
Cole Haan, 10
Collins, John, 45
Comcast, 80
Commitment phase, 272
Communities, 140
Compaq, 57
Competitive actions, 175–176
    competitor analysis and
        identification, 177–178
    types of, 176

Hamel, G., 109, 110
Hansen Natural, 141
Harley-Davidson, 11, 88
Harvard Business School, 317
Harvesting strategy, 165
Harvest strategy, 86
Healthcare, technology and, 130
H.E. Butt Grocery, 143
Hershey, 139
Hershey Foods, 10
Hierarchy of imagination, 267
High-involvement planning, 266–268
    stages of, 267
High-involvement strategic planning,
    17
High performance management
    practices, 39
High-tech industries, strategy in,
    202–206
    disruptive/incremental innovation,
        204–205
    first-mover and fast-follower
        advantages, 205
    geographic clustering of innovation,
        205–206
Hilton, Conrad, 313
Hilton Hotels Corporation, 313
    balanced scorecard and, 319–321
Hofstede, Geert, 269, 270
Home Depot, 35, 37
Honda, 110, 170
Hoover's, 134
Horizontal alignment, 291–295
    within a function, 294–295
    consequences of weak, 293–294
    cost leadership and, 291–292, 293
    cross-functional, 291
    through cross-functional
        integration, 291
    defined, 291
    differentiation and, 292, 293
    Enterprise Resource Planning (ERP)
        and, 295
    intra-functional integration, 291
    at Papa John's Restaurant, 292–293
Horizontal integration, 81
Horizontal scope, 134

Horn, Michael, 85
HP, 183
*Human Equation: Building Profits by
    Putting People First, The,* 39
Human Resource (HR) legislation, 128,
    129
Human resource (HR) practices, 39
Hurley International LLC, 9
Hyundai Group, 265

I

IBM, 57, 323
Identity, 64
Iger, Robert, 220
IKEA, 77, 84
Imitability, 115
Implementation, 12, 259–275, 281–308.
    See also Strategy implementation
Implementing deliberate strategies,
    260
Income (or DCF) method of valuation,
    239, 240–241, 242
Income statement, 245
Incremental/disruptive innovation,
    204–205
Individual Citizens, 141
Individualism, 187, 269
Industry, 131
    comparison for supermarkets and
        drugstores, 135
    growth rates, 199
    norms, 98
Industry consolidation, 81
Industry environment, 124. *See also*
    Task environment
Industry Life Cycle and Five Forces
    Models, 197, 198, 202
Industry sector sustainability metrics,
    example of, 72, 73
Information Resources, Inc., 47
Infrastructural decisions, 294
Initiative for Responsible Investment
    (IRI), 70
Innovation, 130, 131
    Minnesota Mining and

Time value of money, 227–230
Time Warner, 81
Tmall Global, 82
Tootsie Roll, 139
Top down management style, 265–268
Total cost, 30
Total S.A., 85
Toyota, 138, 302
Trade/Professional Associations, 141
Traditional approach, 17
    to value creation, 315
Traditional management role, 259
Trend analysis, 98, 100, 101, 125, 246
Triangulation, 243
Triple bottom line (TBL), 69
Tropicana, 9
Truman, Harry, 196
Tums, 78
Twitter, 68, 141
Tyco International, 19
Tylenol®, 55

U

Uber, 140, 177
Uncertainty avoidance, 269
Underwater stock options, 41
Unemployment Services Trust (UST), 215
Unfreezing phase, 274
Unrelated diversification, 80
UPS, 36, 185
Upstream activities, 106
U.S. Air Force, 213
U.S. Census Bureau, 133
U.S. Chamber of Commerce, 141
U.S. Department of Labor, 128
U.S. Justice Department, 65
U.S. Navy Special Projects Office, 284
Utility analysis, 187

V

Valdez, Arthur, 106
Valuation. *See* Business valuation

Valuation methods, 239–243
    cost, 239–240
    income, 240–241, 242
    market, 241
Value, 115
Value chain, 103–105
    analysis, 212
    internal evaluation of, 106–107
    primary activities of, 103–104
    support activities of, 104–105
Value creation, 26–48, 108, 211
    assessing, 13–14
    change adaptation and, 21
    for customers, 30–35
    defined, 3–5
    e-business and, 47
    emerging technologies and, 46–48
    employees and, 39–42
    examples of, 5
    feedback, 13–14
    financial or economic, 27
    importance of, 26–30
    measuring, 13
    owners and, 42–46
    short-term vs. long-term, 44–45
    technology and, 46–48
    value disciplines in, 35–39
Value creation assessment, 315–324
    balanced scorecard approach to, 317–321
    feedback and corrective action in, 322–323
    framework for, 321–323
    limitations of financial measures, 316–317
    traditional approach to, 315
Value disciplines, 35–39
    achieving customer, 38–39
    customer intimacy, 36–38
    operational excellence, 36
    product leadership, 38
Value for owners, 43–44
Value Line Investment Survey®, 134
Value system, 106
Vehix.com, 35
Veiga, J. F., 39, 40, 42
Vertical alignment, 288–291

X

W

Y

Z